BUSINESS BASICS

Organisational behaviour

PUBLISHING

Third edition September 2000

ISBN 0 7517 2132 8
(previous edition 0 7517 2123 9)

British Library Cataloguing-in-Publication Data

A catalogue record for this book is available from the British Library

Printed in England by DACOSTA PRINT
35/37 Queensland Road, London, N7 7AH
(0207 700 1000)

Published by
BPP Publishing Limited
Aldine House, Aldine Place
London W12 8AW

www.bpp.com

BPP Publishing would like to thank the following:

Tessa Jenkins for authorial input

Genesys Editorial for editorial and production input

We are grateful to the Chartered Institute of Management Accountant, the Association of Chartered Certified Accountants and the Institute of Chartered Secretaries and Administrators for permission to reproduce past examination questions in this text, the suggested solutions to which have been prepared by BPP Publishing.

CONTENTS

PREFACE

BUSINESS BASICS are targeted specifically at the needs of:

- Students taking business studies degrees
- Students taking business-related modules of other degrees
- Students on courses at a comparable level
- Others requiring business information at this level

This *Organisational Behaviour* text has been written with two key goals in mind.

- To present a substantial and useful body of knowledge on information technology at degree level. This is not just a set of revision notes – it explains the subject in detail and does not assume prior knowledge.

- To make learning and revision as easy as possible. Therefore each chapter:
    - Starts with an introduction and clear objectives
    - Contains numerous activities
    - Includes a chapter roundup summarising the points made
    - Ends with a quick quiz

    And at the back of the book you will find:
    - Multiple choice questions and answers
    - Exam style questions and answers

The philosophy of the series is thus to combine techniques which actively promote learning with a no-nonsense, systematic approach to the necessary factual content of the course.

BPP Publishing have for many years been the leading providers of targeted texts for students of professional qualifications. We know that our customers need to study effectively in order to pass their exams, and that they cannot afford to waste time. They expect clear, concise and highly focused study material. As university and college education becomes more market driven, students rightly demand the same high standards of efficiency in their learning material. The BUSINESS BASICS series meets those demands.

BPP Publishing
September 2000

Titles in this series:

Accounting
Law
Quantitative Methods
Information Technology
Economics
Marketing
Human Resource Management
Organisational Behaviour

> You may order other titles in the series using the form at the end of this book. If you would like to send in your comments on this book, please turn to the review form following the order form.

HOW TO USE THIS BOOK

This book can simply be read straight through from beginning to end, but you will get far more out of it if you keep a pen and paper to hand. The most effective form of learning is *active learning*, and we have therefore filled the text with exercises for you to try as you go along. We have also provided objectives, a chapter roundup and a quick quiz for each chapter. Here is a suggested approach to enable you to get the most out of this book.

(a) Select a chapter to study, and read the introduction and objectives at the start of the chapter.

(b) Next read the chapter roundup at the end of the chapter (before the quick quiz and the answers to activities). Do not expect this brief summary to mean too much at this stage, but see whether you can relate some of the points made in it to some of the objectives.

(c) Next read the chapter itself. Do attempt each activity as you come to it. You will derive the greatest benefit from the activity if you write down your answers before checking them against the answers at the end of the chapter.

(d) As you read, make use of the 'notes' column to add your own comments, references to other material and so on. Do try to formulate your own views. In economics, many things are matters of interpretation and there is often scope for alternative views. The more you engage in a dialogue with the book, the more you will get out of your study.

(e) When you reach the end of the chapter, read the chapter roundup again. Then go back to the objectives at the start of the chapter, and ask yourself whether you have achieved them.

(f) Finally, consolidate your knowledge by writing down your answers to the quick quiz. You can check your answers by going back to the text. The very act of going back and searching the text for relevant details will further improve your grasp of the subject.

(g) You can then try the multiple choice questions at the end of the book and the exam level question, to which you are referred at the end of the chapter. Alternatively, you could wait to do these until you have started your revision – it's up to you.

Further reading

While we are confident that the BUSINESS BASICS books offer excellent range and depth of subject coverage, we are aware that you will be encouraged to follow up particular points in books other than your main textbook, in order to get alternative points of view and more detail on key topics. We recommend the following books as a starting point for your further reading on Organisational Behaviour.

Armstrong, P and Dawson, C, *People in Organisations*, 1996, Elm Publications

Buchanan and Huczynski, *Organizational Behaviour*, 1997, Prentice Hall

Burns and Stalker, *The Management of Innovation*, 2nd edition 1994, OUP

Chryssides and Kaler, *An Introduction to Business Ethics*, 1993, Chapman and Hall

Cole, GA, *Management Theory and Practice*, 1996, DP Publications

Hampden-Turner, *Corporate Culture*, 2nd edition 1994, Piatkus

Holmes, *Total Quality Management*, 1992, PIRA

Hunt, *Managing People at Work*, 3rd edition 1992, McGraw-Hill

Van Maurik, *Discovering the Leader in You*, 1994, McGraw-Hill

Mintzberg, *The Structuring of Organizations*, 1979, Prentice Hall

Power In and Around Organizations, 1983, Prentice Hall

The Financial Times contains at least one page a week devoted to management issues which will give you an idea as to current and fashionable thinking on this subject.

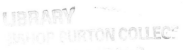

Chapter 1 :
THE IDEA OF ORGANISATION

Introduction

Chapter 1 begins this book with a descriptive and then an explanatory discussion of the idea of organisation.

- People in organisations can often behave quite differently from the way they behave as free-standing individuals.

- Organisations can develop a momentum and continuity of their own, which seems to operate independently of the individuals who (temporarily) work there.

Why is it that organisations play such a large part in our lives? This chapter addresses some of the theories which purport to explain why organisations come into existence, how they perpetuate themselves, why they die, and how they operate, both internally and as regards their relationship with the external world. Chapter 1 is an essential foundation stone for what follows in subsequent parts of the book.

In this chapter you will learn about these things

- What is meant by the term 'organisation'

- The benefits of organisations, especially when contrasted with the possible achievements of individuals acting alone

- The essential differences and similarities between business (profit-making) organisations, public sector organisations, and organisations such as charities and trade unions

- The contributions to organisation theory produced by some of the principal writers on the subject, especially Henri Fayol, Max Weber and Frederick Taylor

- The essential features of both systems theory and contingency theory as models for structural design in organisations

- The significance of increasing change and turbulence in the world of organisations, not only in general terms but also in relation to your own career.

1 WHAT IS AN ORGANISATION?

The following are examples of organisations.

(a) A multinational company making and selling cars
(b) An accountancy firm
(c) A charity
(d) A local authority
(e) A trade union
(f) An army
(g) A political party

These organisations seem, on the surface, to be very different. They do different things and draw their resources from different sources. However, according to Buchanan and Huczynski work organisation is defined as follows.

Definition

> A *work organisation* is a 'social arrangement for the controlled performance of collective goals.'

A few words of explanation are in order.

(a) *Social arrangements*. Organisations are collections of people and machines, whose relationships are structured in a particular way. This feature is not exclusive to organisations. Other social arrangements exist, such as the family or a club.

(b) *Collective goals*. Organisations exist because solitary individuals cannot achieve the goals that organisations are capable of achieving. This characteristic is not restricted to organisations: families exist, at least partly, in order to bring up children.

(c) *Controlled performance*. A family can exert quite effective control but this is hardly a point of definition. Organisations, however, have two distinct features, as identified by Buchanan and Huczynski.

    (i) A preoccupation with *performance*. The performance of the organisation as a whole determines its survival, and this performance depends on the efficient use of scarce resources. Resources are derived, ultimately, from the environment.

    (ii) Individuals and systems carry out *control functions*. In other words, they set standards, measure performance, and correct deviations to ensure that the organisation adheres to standard.

    The need for controlled performance leads to 'a deliberate and ordered allocation of functions, or division of labour, between organisation members'.

Activity 1   **(10 minutes)**

Using Buchanan and Huczynski's definition of an organisation and its three principal dimensions, how far would you describe each of the following as an organisation?

(a)   A university
(b)   A prison
(c)   A pop/rock group
(d)   The National Lottery

1.1   Why organisations exist

In general terms, organisations exist because they can achieve results which individuals cannot achieve alone.

(a)   By grouping together, individuals overcome limitations imposed by both the physical environment and also their own biological limitations.

(b)   Organisations meet an individual's need for companionship.

(c)   Organisations increase productive ability because they make three things possible.

       (i)   *Specialisation* (division of labour) as recognised by Adam Smith in The Wealth of Nations

       (ii)   *Exchange*

       (iii)   *Synergy.* This concept implies that the whole is greater than the sum of the parts. In other words, by bringing together two separate and individual units of resource, the output of the units combined will exceed the joint output of the separated units

(d)   They accumulate knowledge (for subsequent use and further learning), the continuity of organisations ensures opportunities to use such knowledge.

(e)   They save time: organisations make it possible for objectives to be reached in a shorter time than it would take for individuals to achieve them.

(f)   They reduce the cost of transactions in complex environments. For example, assume for the time being that you do not have access to a typewriter or word processor, but that you need regularly to get letters typed.

       (i)   Without the existence of the organisation in which you work, you might perhaps have to sign a contract with a typist each time you need work done.

       (ii)   However, the existence of an organisation, which employs both you and the typist, means that you can avoid the trouble of negotiating a contract each time you wish to have a letter typed: the relationship between you and the typist is formally defined; the organisation takes care of the typist's salary (as well as yours!).

       This is called the *transaction-cost economics* approach to organisations.

(g)   They also experience reduced cost through economies of scale.

We will return to some of these issues later in this chapter. Meanwhile, we shall now look at some of the different types of organisation.

NOTES

2   BUSINESS ORGANISATIONS

A *business organisation* exists to make a profit. In other words, the costs of its activities should be less than the revenues it earns from providing goods or services. Profits are not incidental to its activities but the driving factor. Business organisations can be classified according to three criteria.

    (a)   Legal constitution
    (b)   Size
    (c)   Activity

There is no necessary correlation between these three factors. A key issue is the degree to which a business is a separate legal entity from its owners.

Definitions

> A *sole tradership* is a business owned and run by one individual. Although the individual will keep separate his or her business and personal accounts, this has no significance other than for convenience. The individual's business and personal affairs are, for legal and tax purposes, identical.
>
> *Partnerships* are arrangements between individuals to carry on a business in common with a view to profit. Partnerships involve obligations to others, and so a partnership will be governed by a partnership agreement.
>
> *Limited company status*, on the other hand, means that the business's debts and the personal debts of the business's owners (shareholders) are legally separate. The shareholders cannot be sued for the debts of the business unless they have given some personal guarantee. This is called *limited liability*. Businesses with 'plc' or 'Ltd' after their names are limited companies. They are *owned* by shareholders; shares can be traded. They are run by directors. *Ownership* and *control* are legally separate.

Sole traderships and partnerships are concentrated in the small business sector. With the exception of large partnerships (which exist mainly in the professions such as accountancy and the law) most businesses of any size are limited companies. Some small businesses are limited companies, too, but often the owner is required by his or her bank to give a personal guarantee of the debts of the business.

Definition

> *Co-operatives* are businesses owned by the workers who share their profits.

The first successful co-operative was founded in 1844 by Rochdale textile workers to buy and sell foodstuffs. Examples include Co-operative Retail Society, and the Co-operative Bank. Most of the principles of co-operative trading adopted by the Rochdale pioneers are today recognised throughout the world.

    (a)   Open membership
    (b)   Democratic control
    (c)   Distribution of the surplus in proportion to purchases
    (d)   Promotion of education

2.1 Business activities

Business organisations can also be classified by what they do. Here are some examples.

(a) *Manufacturing*. The organisation acquires raw materials and by the application of labour and technology turns them into a product (eg a car).

(b) *Extractive/raw materials*. The organisation extracts and refines raw materials (eg mining).

(c) *Energy*. The organisation converts one type of resource (eg coal) into another (eg electricity).

(d) *Retailing/distribution*. These organisations deliver goods to the end consumer.

(e) *Intellectual production*. Such organisations are engaged in various types of knowledge work, such as publishing and software. They are set up to create and/or disseminate information or intellectual property.

(f) *Service industries*. Services are distinguished from products on the following grounds.

   (i) *Services are intangible*. A service cannot be seen, touched or displayed. Money transmission is a service which customers pay for and which is performed by banks, but the customer does not obviously have anything to show as a result.

   (ii) *Services are inseparable*. In general, it is impossible to separate the production and consumption of a service. For example, you buy a ticket to the theatre before the actors go on stage. After the play, you cannot carry the performance out with you.

   (iii) *Services are heterogeneous*. The quality of the service product is typically highly dependent on the quality of the person conducting the transaction.

Activity 2   **(5 minutes)**

Can you think of any organisations whose activities intermingle all five of the classification groups, or three or four of them?

2.2 National and international businesses

Some organisations have an international dimension to them.

(a) They might export goods to another country or import goods from another country.

(b) They might make goods or offer services in more than one country.

(c) They might own assets in more than one country.

(d) They might have a complicated network of plants over the world.

(e) Some companies claim to be 'global' or even 'stateless' if their activities are so diverse that they cannot call any country their 'home'. Most so-called global companies, upon close examination, do not really exist.

   (i) Senior management are generally drawn from one country or region.

(ii)   Research and development, or the most important aspects of it, are often concentrated in one country.

We discuss this issue in more detail in Chapter 5.

Activity 3   (10 minutes)

Some organisations are international in the sense that they distribute and sell their products/services in more than one country, but operate centrally from a single location, or from several locations, in one country – usually the country of the organisation's origin. Other organisations are multinational, ie they will operate virtually independent business units in different parts of the world, though control is still exercised chiefly through a system of expatriate managers and business strategies which are centrally imposed. Finally, a few organisations are genuinely global: they function worldwide, through a network of managers and executives who are appointed to positions as they become vacant, without any regard for national connections; such global organisations will have research and development units and manufacturing plants (where appropriate) scattered across their territories, and may grant considerable autonomy (in strategic terms) to the various parts of the organisation.

Given this framework, in which of the above three categories – international, multinational or global – would you place each of the following organisations?

(a)   Philips
(b)   General Motors
(c)   Sony
(d)   Coca-Cola
(e)   McDonalds
(f)   Hutchinson Telecom
(g)   News International
(h)   IBM

What do you think are the reasons for the fact that so few organisations are global in the genuine sense of the term?

International issues for UK companies are likely to become increasingly important.

(a)   For many UK companies, the main opportunities for growth will be in developing or newly industrialising countries such as China.

(b)   The single European market and the World Trade Organisation will lead to increased competition from companies based overseas, but also provide new opportunities to compete overseas. Legal impediments to trade (eg different standards) are being slowly brushed away.

(c)   For certain goods and services, international trade offers opportunities for additional economies of scale which may help to cope with competition from abroad.

(d)   Particular issues relating to international operations include the following.

(i)   Distribution systems
(ii)   Differences in language and culture
(iii)   Product standards and legal systems
(iv)   Human resource requirements

3 PUBLIC SECTOR ORGANISATIONS

Governments make laws and influence the environment for private sector activity in other ways. In addition to this indirect influence, in many economies, the state owns and controls a large variety of organisations. The state, however, is not generally a monolith, and so public control can be exercised in a variety of ways.

(a) Road transport in the UK is managed directly by central and local government.

(b) Some organisations are run by local government (eg social services, most schools, libraries).

(c) Other arrangements include bodies such as English Heritage, NHS trusts, which are publicly funded by, but organisationally separate from, central government.

The following are examples of public sector bodies.

(a) The army
(b) Most schools and universities in the UK
(c) The Bank of England
(d) Local authorities
(e) The Department of Social Security
(f) Most hospitals in the UK

Note the diversity of activities in the public sector. Public sector organisations provide a variety of goods and services. Some have a commercial objective, others do not.

(a) The Post Office exists to make a profit out of mail services, but at the same time it has a social function.

(b) The army, on the other hand, is not a profit making organisation.

The distinguishing characteristics of the non profit orientated public sector are as follows.

(a) The public sector can ultimately command resources (through raising taxes).

(b) The public sector is based on equity. Ideas of fairness (eg in correcting market deficiencies) underpin service provision (eg everybody should have the right to an education).

(c) The public sector is based on the idea of equality. Each individual should have the right of protection from invasion, and everybody should be equal under the law.

3.1 Developments in the public sector

Public sector bodies are ultimately accountable to the electorate. Four recent trends in the UK's public sector are worthy of note; each clearly demonstrates how central government policy may affect organisations

(a) More public sector activities are to be carried out autonomously, away from the *direct control* of central government. Policy is set by ministers, but is implemented by *executive agencies* which are autonomous. Executive agencies have control over their own procedures (in theory). The same is true in some respects of local government. Schools are now largely free of local government control.

(b)   Public bodies are more likely to become purchasers rather than providers of services. In other words, rather than provide certain services directly, the public sector will subcontract them to a private sector company. An obvious example is refuse collection. At one time directly managed by local authorities, this service is now performed by private sector businesses on fixed term contracts. This approach is now being adopted by central government (such as in the prison service). Certain cost and performance targets must be achieved.

(c)   Market-type structures are being introduced to public sector bodies. In the NHS internal market, hospitals have to compete for funds.

(d)   Full scale *privatisation* has been implemented in industries that were once the province of the state. Public utilities such as the electricity and water industries have been privatised. These industries, however, are still subject to state regulation (for example through Oftel, which regulates the telecommunications industry) as many of them are monopolies or near-monopolies.

Activity 4   **(10 minutes)**

Think about the public sector organisations with which you came into contact, and especially those which have been wholly or partially privatised. Among the typical effects of such change, from the customer's viewpoint, are higher prices (although not in every case) coupled with much-improved standards of service. From the perspective of people working in privatised organisations, the consequences include higher expectations about work performance and reduced job security. Why has privatisation produced these results? To the extent that the results are beneficial to the customer (ie higher levels of customer service, wider range of products and services offered, and so forth), and why did these things not happen quite so readily when such organisations were more firmly in the public sector?

---

4   OTHER NON PROFIT MAKING ORGANISATIONS

Some organisations do not exist to make a profit, but nor are they public services. They are formed for many different purposes.

Definitions

Trade unions are organised associations of working people in a trade, occupation or industry (or several trades or industries) formed for protection and promotion of their common interests, mainly the regulation and negotiation of pay and conditions. They receive subscriptions.

Employers' associations have a role similar to that of trade unions insofar as they protect and promote the interests of members, but their membership and aims are very different. They represent the employers – the 'management side' of the business – and promote and protect their business interests.

Charities are organisations which exist for a variety of purposes. *Help the Aged,* for example, exists to promote the welfare of the elderly, in particular those who are poor, sick and vulnerable. It raises money by a variety of means. Its performance can be measured by the success it has in promoting the interest of its beneficiaries, raising public awareness and raising money.

Many *clubs* are not organisations in the sense that Buchanan and Huczynski define the word, but some are. In the UK, the AA and the RAC exist to provide services for their members. They are concerned with performance – as their respective advertising campaigns demonstrate.

Professional associations, such as the main accountancy institutes, exist for people doing a similar job.

Regardless of whether or not an organisation is profit making, a clear definition of objectives is needed.

5 IMAGES AND PERCEPTIONS OF ORGANISATIONS

The world of organisations has almost as much variety as the animal kingdom. Organisations have a pervasive influence over our lives. As Henry Mintzberg states (in *Mintzberg* on Management):

'Ours has become, for better and for worse, a society of organisations. We are born in organisations and are educated in organisations so that we can later work in organisations. At the same time, organisations supply us and entertain us, they govern us and harass us (sometime concurrently). Finally, we are buried by organisations.'

The diversity of the organisations to which we belong and which influence every aspect of our lives is clear. We therefore need to adopt a certain amount of mental flexibility when discussing organisations. Focusing exclusively on one model may exclude valuable insights into how a given organisation works.

In *Images of Organisations* (1986), Gareth Morgan identifies eight metaphors for organisations. None of them claims to be an exclusive definition of an *organisation:* these metaphors are ways of looking at organisations.

(a)   *Organisations are machines*. This idea is in part related to *systems theory* discussed later in this chapter. We can look at organisations as a set of interrelated components whose combined, structured operation carries out a common task. It is often said that machines have replaced labour to carry out certain tasks, but it is also the case that machines have replaced organisations: for example, the printing press has replaced the need for groups of scribes to be organised and controlled to copy books by hand.

(b)   *Organisations are biological organisms.* Biological organisms are born, grow, mature and die, and are in a series of constant interchanges with the environment. Some of them adapt. Do organisations have a life cycle? Is organisational decline inevitable? Although many companies have been in continued existence for many years (eg British Petroleum), still more no longer exist.

(c)   *Organisations are human brains.* This metaphor leads to three insights.

(i)   Organisations are stocks of knowledge. Any organisation contains expertise accumulated from experience. This ties in with notions of synergy: knowledge exists in teams and ways of working as well as in individuals.

(ii)   Organisations can learn. New expertise can be developed.

(iii) Organisations are networks of information flows rather like, to use yet another metaphor, the telecommunications network.

(d)   *Organisations are cultures or subcultures.* Culture refers to shared assumptions, beliefs, values and ways of behaving. A religious organisation is the most obvious example.

(e)   *Organisations are political systems.* How often have you heard the phrase: 'Office politics'?

(i)   Organisations are arenas where managers compete with each other for status (empire building).

(ii)   Organisations are arenas where outsiders (eg shareholders, pressure groups) compete for power over the organisation's activities.

(iii) In the Marxist analysis, an organisation is but one of the battlegrounds on which the class struggle is conducted.

(f)   *Organisations are psychic prisons.* Arguably, this a much stronger version of the metaphor of organisations as cultures. It is arguable that living in an organisation can create a sense of psychological dependency on it: witness the problems that real prisoners encounter on leaving prison and its familiar, if unpleasant, routines. Life inside an organisation, may, quite irrationally, seem preferable to the uncertainties of living outside. On the other hand, some people reluctantly work for organisations, abhor the rat race and consider organisations as places to escape from.

(g)   *Organisations are systems of change and transformation.* A business organisation converts inputs of resources into outputs of goods and services, adding value as it does so.

(h)   *Organisations are instruments of domination.* This argument can relate to an organisation's relationship with its environment: organisations influence society. The best example is that of the ruling party in a totalitarian state, or an army imposing a military dictatorship. Some argue that in capitalist societies, organisations control people's relationships with society and their expectations of it (eg by advertising).

Activity 5   **(15 minutes)**

Let us go further with one of Morgan's metaphors, namely the reference to the organisation as a psychic prison. Referring specifically to mental hospitals, Erving Goffman (*Asylums*, 1968) mentions four ways in which newly-admitted patients are assimilated into – or adapt to – the organisation known as the hospital.

(a)   *Situational withdrawal:* 'The inmate withdraws apparent attention from everything except events immediately surrounding his body.'

(b)   *The intransigent line:* 'The inmate intentionally challenges the institution by flagrantly refusing to co-operate with staff.'

(c)   Colonisation: 'A stable, relatively contented existence is built up out of the maximum satisfactions procurable within the institution.'

(d)   Conversion: 'The inmate appears to take over the official or staff view of himself and tries to act out the role of the perfect inmate.'

How far can you see similarities between these four types of adaptation and the behaviour you have observed in yourself and in others, within the organisations of your experience? When thinking about your response, look back to your schooldays, reflect on your perceptions of university/college, or recall your own coping mechanisms developed when you've been undertaking paid employment at weekends or in vacations.

---

6 TRADITIONAL APPROACHES TO ORGANISATION AND MANAGEMENT

Organisations have existed since the growth of complex human societies. The Chinese Empire was run by a bureaucracy, whose members were selected by competitive examination and which even had its own internal auditors (the Censorate), for over two thousand years. However, it was the industrial revolution in the West, the growth of large enterprises and the associated increasingly complex inter-relationships of people and machines that saw the growth of organisation and management theory.

As you read this section it is worth remembering that there are no right or wrong ways to manage. Each theory is best considered as an alternative view which may shed light on a particular problem. This is a point that will be strongly reiterated when we consider the Contingency School later in this section.

6.1 Early ideas about organisation: Fayol

The industrial revolution led to an expansion in the number of organisations, and the range of activities undertaken by them. It is hardly surprising, then, that organisations began to be studied in their own right. Henri Fayol (1841-1925) was a French industrialist, who exemplifies the classical school of management thought which popularised the concept of the universality of management principles. The classical school was primarily concerned with the structure and activities of the formal organisation, and the rational principles by which they could be directed most effectively. Henri Fayol's ideas about organisations and management were based on his own personal experience, rather than a scientific programme of investigation.

(a)   *Division of work (ie specialisation).* The object of specialisation is to produce more and obtain better results.

BPP PUBLISHING

(b) *Authority and responsibility.* Fayol distinguished between a manager's official authority (deriving from his office) and personal authority (deriving from his experience, moral worth, intelligence and so on). 'Authority should be commensurate with responsibility', in other words the holder of an office should have enough authority to carry out all the responsibilities assigned to him. He also suggested that

'generally speaking, responsibility is feared as much as authority is sought after, and fear of responsibility paralyses much initiative and destroys many good qualities.'

A good leader should encourage those around to accept responsibility.

(c) *Discipline:* 'the state of discipline of any group of people depends essentially on the worthiness of its leaders'. A fair disciplinary system, with penalties judiciously applied by worthy superiors, can be a chief strength of an organisation.

(d) *Unity of command:* for any action, a subordinate should receive orders from one boss only. 'This rule seems fundamental to me...' Fayol saw dual command as a disease, whether it is caused by imperfect demarcation between departments, or by a superior S2 giving orders to an employee, E, without going via the intermediate superior, S1.

(e) *Unity of direction:* there should be one head and one plan for each activity. Unity of direction relates to the organisation itself, whereas unity of command relates to the personnel in the organisation.

(f) *Subordination of individual interests:* the interest of one employee or group of employees should not prevail over that of the general interest of the organisation.

(g) *Remuneration:* it should be 'fair', satisfying both employer and employee alike.

(h) *Scalar chain:* the scalar chain is the term used to describe the chain of superiors from lowest to highest rank. Formal communication is up and down the lines of authority, eg E to D to C to B to A. If, however, communication between different branches of the chain is necessary (eg D to H) the use of a gangplank of horizontal communication saves time and is likely to be more accurate. We discuss this in more detail in Chapters 6 and 7.

Scalar chains: ———   Gang planks: - - - - - -

ABCDE
ABJL
ABJM
AFGHI
AFKN
AFKOP

CG
DH

If C has a problem which affects G, instead of referring it up to B (who might then refer it to A before it could be discussed with G's boss, F) C could cross the gangplank – and communicate directly and horizontally with G. The problem might then be solved jointly by C and G.

(i) *Stability of tenure of personnel:*

'It has often been recorded that a mediocre manager who stays is infinitely preferable to outstanding managers who merely come and go.'

(j) *Esprit de corps:* personnel should not be isolated: cohesion should be encouraged. 'In union, there is strength'.

(k) *Initiative:* 'it is essential to encourage and develop this capacity to the full'.

6.2 Bureaucracy: Max Weber

The sociologist, *Max Weber* (1864-1920), developed the notion of bureaucracy. It is similar to Fayol's in its concern with hierarchy, but also develops the idea that the best way to secure efficient administration is to design procedures to reduce individual initiative.

Weber regarded an organisation as an authority structure. He was interested in why individuals obeyed commands, and he identified three grounds on which legitimate authority could exist.

(a) *Charismatic leadership:* in such an organisation, a leader is regarded as having some special power or attribute; decision-making is centralised in him and delegation strictly limited. The leader expects personal, sycophantic devotion from his staff and followers. Decisions are frequently irrational or emotional, the charismatic leader being driven by intuitive preferences producing results which are either spectacularly successful or cataclysmically disastrous.

(b) *Traditional, or patriarchal leadership:* in such organisations, authority is bestowed by virtue of hereditary entitlement, as in the family firm, the lord of the manor. Tradition is glorified. Decisions and actions are bound by precedent.

(c) *Bureaucracy:* in such organisations activities are grouped into specialist areas (production, marketing, sales and so on) each with specified duties. Authority to carry out these duties is given to the officials who are appointed on the basis of their qualifications and expertise, and rules and regulations are established in order to ensure their achievement. Leadership is therefore of a *rational-legal* nature: managers get things done because their orders are accepted as legitimate and justified.

Activity 6   (5 minutes)

Real-life organisations can often embrace all three *ideal types*, or any two of them, simultaneously. Can you think of an organisation which exemplifies each of the following categories?

(a)   A combination of charismatic leadership, traditional leadership and bureaucracy.

(b)   A combination of charismatic leadership with bureaucracy.

(c)   A combination of traditional leadership with bureaucracy.

(d)   A combination of charismatic leadership and traditional leadership.

Weber specified several general characteristics of bureaucracy, which he described as 'a continuous organisation of official functions bound by rules'.

(a) *Hierarchy:* each lower office is under the control and supervision of a higher one.

(b) *Specialisation and training:* there is a high degree of specialisation of labour. Employment is based on ability, not personal loyalty.

(c) *Impersonal nature:* employees work full time within the impersonal rules and regulations and act according to format, impersonal procedures.

(d) *Professional nature of employment:* an organisation exists before it is filled with people. Officials are full-time employees, promotion is according to seniority and achievement; pay scales are prescribed according to the position or office held in the organisation structure.

(e) *Rationality:* the 'jurisdictional areas' of the organisation are determined rationally. The hierarchy of authority and office structure is clearly defined. Duties are established and measures of performance set.

(f) *Uniformity* in the performance of tasks is expected, regardless of whoever is engaged in carrying them out.

(g) *Technical competence* in officials, which is rarely questioned within the area of their expertise.

(h) *Stability*.

Compared with other types of organisation the potential advantages of bureaucracy may seem apparent. Weber was impressed with the development and accomplishments of bureaucracy, and especially with the role of technical knowledge in bureaucratic administration which he regarded as the primary source of the superiority of bureaucracy as an organisation. He was also ready, however, to acknowledge the deadening effect of bureaucracy and deplored an organisation of 'little cogs, little men, clinging to little jobs and striving towards bigger ones.' He was less prepared to acknowledge the fact that bureaucracies do not always cope well with change.

Activity 7 (15 minutes)

Why do you think it might be difficult for bureaucracies to cope with change?

When developing your answer, it may be helpful to take account of *Michel Crozier's* view (in The Bureaucratic Phenomenon, 1964) that 'a bureaucratic system will resist change as long as it can; it will only move when serious dysfunctions develop and no other alternatives remain'. Crozier goes further: 'The essential rhythm prevalent in such organisations is... an alternation of long periods of stability with very short periods of crisis and change' – as opposed to the regular adjustment process which can accommodate change in other, more flexible organisations. Crozier concludes, in fact, that 'a bureaucratic system of organisation is not only a system that does not correct its behaviour in view of its errors' it is also 'too rigid to adjust without crisis to the transformations that the accelerated evolution of industrial society makes more and more imperative'. [Our italics]

6.3 Scientific management

Scientific management was an approach to the work process which has some similarities with the ideas of bureaucracy, in that it supports the idea that there should be procedures governing each job.

Frederick W Taylor (1856 – 1915) pioneered the scientific management movement. He argued that management should be based on 'well-recognised, clearly defined and fixed principles, instead of depending on more or less hazy ideas.' Taylor's famous four principles of scientific management were as follows.

(a) *The development of a true science of work:* all knowledge which had hitherto been kept in the heads of workmen should be gathered and recorded by management.

   '*Every single subject, large and small, becomes the question for scientific investigation, for reduction to law.*'

   Very simply, he argued that management should apply techniques to the solution of problems and should not rely on experience and 'seat-of-the-pants' judgements.

(b) *The scientific selection and progressive development of workmen:* workmen should be carefully trained and given jobs to which they are best suited. Although 'training' is an important element in his principles of management, 'nurturing' might be a more apt description of his ideas of worker development.

(c) *The bringing together of the science and the scientifically selected and trained men.* The application of techniques to decide what should be done and how, using workmen who are both properly trained and willing to maximise output, should result in maximum productivity.

(d) *The constant and intimate co-operation between management and workers:* 'the relations between employers and men form without question the most important part of this art.'

The practical application of the approach was the use of work study techniques to break each job down into its smallest and simplest component parts: these single elements became the newly-designed job. Workers were selected and trained to perform their single task in the most efficient way possible, as determined by techniques such as time and motion study to eliminate wasted motions or unnecessary physical movement. Work study also enabled the determination of 'a fair day's pay for a fair day's work'. Workers were paid incentives on the basis of acceptance of the new methods and output norms. For Taylor the most effective motivator was money.

Application of the scientific management approach

It is useful to consider an application of Taylor's principles. In testimony to the House of Representatives Committee in 1912, Taylor used as an example the application of scientific management methods to shovelling work at the Bethlehem Steel Works.

(a) Facts were first gathered by management as to the number of shovel loads handled by each man each day, with particular attention paid to the relationship between weight of the average shovel load and the total load shifted per day. From these facts, management was able to decide on the ideal shovel size for each type of material handled in order to optimise the speed of shovelling work done. Thus, scientific technique was applied to deciding how work should be organised.

(b)   By organising work a day in advance, it was possible to minimise the idle time and the moving of men from one place in the shovelling yard to another. Once again, scientific method replaces 'seat-of-the-pants' decisions by supervisors.

(c)   Workers were paid for accepting the new methods and norms and received 60% higher wages than those given to similar workers in other companies in the area.

(d)   Workers were carefully selected and trained in the art of shovelling properly; anyone falling below the required norms consistently was given special teaching to improve his performance.

(e)   'The new way is to teach and help your men as you would a brother; to try to teach him the best way and to show him the easiest way to do his work. This is the new mental attitude of the management towards the men...'

(f)   At the Bethlehem Steel Works, Taylor said, the costs of implementing this method were more than repaid by the benefits. The labour force required fell from 400-600 men to 140 men for the same work.

An appraisal of scientific management

Peter Drucker made some useful comments about scientific management, as follows.

(a)   Scientific management has contributed a philosophy of worker and work.

'As long as industrial society endures, we shall never lose again the insight that human work can be studied systematically, can be analysed, can be improved by work on its elementary parts. Like all great insights, it was simplicity itself.'

(b)   However, it is capable of providing solutions to management problems only up to a certain point, and it seems incapable of providing significant further developments in future.

'Scientific management...has been stagnant for a long time...During the last thirty years, it has given us little but pedestrian and wearisome tomes on the techniques, if not on the gadgets, of narrower and narrower specialities...'

(c)   One major weakness of scientific management is that by breaking work down into its elementary parts, and analysing a job as a series of consecutive 'motions', the solution to management problems often provided is that each separate 'motion' within the entire job should be done by a separate worker. This is profoundly un-satisfying to workers, and treats them like (poorly designed) 'machine tools': operations *should* be analysed in this way, but then *reintegrated* into a whole job.

(d)   A further criticism of scientific management is that it divorces planning work from doing the work.

'The divorce of planning from doing reflects a dubious and dangerous philosophical concept of an elite which has a monopoly on esoteric knowledge entitling it to manipulate the unwashed peasantry.'

Scientific management (satirised by Charlie Chaplin in his film *Modern Times*) was responsible for a massive increase in productivity, even though its failings are readily apparent. It can be analysed as consisting of two main ideas.

(a)   The detailed analysis of work.

(b)   The separation of planners from doers.

Scientific management as a science of work is very much alive. It prospers in factories and offices where continuous *improvement* programmes are implemented. An article in the *Harvard Business Review*, January-February, 1993 entitled 'Time and Motion regained' by *Paul S Adler* indicates the value of scientific management techniques in increasing productivity. Where scientific management has failed is in the division of 'planning' from 'doing'. Continuous improvement programmes require that people actually involved in doing the work are responsible for suggesting improvements.

7   HUMAN RELATIONS, SYSTEMS AND CONTINGENCY APPROACHES

7.1   Human relations

In the 1930s, a critical perception of scientific management emerged. Elton Mayo (1880-1949) was pioneer of a new approach, which emphasised the importance of human attitudes, values and relationships for the efficient and effective functioning of work organisations.

This was called the *human relations* approach. It was developed mainly by social scientists – rather than practising managers – and based on research into human behaviour, with the intention of describing and thereafter predicting behaviour in organisations. Like classical theory, it was essentially prescriptive in nature. The human relations approach concentrated mainly on the concept of '*Social Man*' (*Schein*): people are motivated by *social* or *belonging* needs, which are satisfied by the social relationships they form at work.

This emphasis was based on *Mayo's* interpretation of a famous set of experiments (the *Hawthorne Studies*), which were carried out at the *Western Electric Company* in the USA. The company was using a group of young women as 'guinea pigs' to assess the affect of lighting on productivity: they were astonished to find that productivity shot up whatever they did with the lighting. Their initial conclusion was that the women's sense of being a group singled out for attention raised their morale.

Mayo's ideas were followed up by various social psychologists (eg *Maslow, Herzberg, Likert* and *McGregor*), but with a change of emphasis. People were still considered to be the crucial factor in determining organisational effectiveness, but were recognised as having more than merely physical and social needs. Attention shifted towards their 'higher' psychological needs for growth, challenge, responsibility and self-fulfilment. Herzberg suggested that only these things could positively motivate employees to improved performance: work relationships and supervisory style, along with pay and conditions, merely ward off dissatisfaction (and then only temporarily). This phase was known as the *neo-Human Relations school*.

In contrast to Taylor's 'Scientific Management' approach, the human relations approach tends to emphasise the importance of work to the workers but does not really address the economic issues: there is still no proven link between job satisfaction and motivation, or either of these and productivity or the achievement of organisational goals.

EXAMPLE: WESTERN ELECTRIC COMPANY

Institutionalising the Hawthorne effect: a case study in organisational failure

The Western Electric Company was so impressed by the constantly improving output secured from the young women in Mayo's study, that they tried to replicate the

'Hawthorne effect' on an organisation-wide basis. It had been thought that the rising output was a consequence of the fact that the women felt themselves to be important and significant, certainly much more so than ever had been the case previously. Their enhanced status was associated with their participation in an experiment which entailed the frequent presence of the researchers, headed by a live professor; they had much more opportunity, moreover, to talk about themselves and their problems.

Clearly it was not feasible for Western Electric to employ Elton Mayo and his colleagues on a permanent basis, so instead they instituted a programme of employee counselling, which commenced in 1936 with a group of five counsellors covering 600 employees and grew to a peak of 55 counsellors covering 21,000 employees in 1948. Thereafter the activity declined and was finally discontinued in 1956.

The programme was expensive, not only in terms of direct cost but also in the hidden costs of employee and supervisory time. In the annual budget reviews there was little to show in the way of measurable benefits. As the original management which had introduced the plan disappeared from the scene, so enthusiasm was dissipated.

More significantly, some of the very reasons which were responsible for the successes achieved in the initial Hawthorne experiments were absent when the same approach was tried with the whole organisation. For the young women in the experiment to feel their status had been enhanced, it was necessary for the status of others to remain unchanged, or even to deteriorate: to give every employee enhanced status means, in effect, that nobody has enhanced status relative to others. They only have enhanced status compared with their status in the past – and unfortunately memories are short.

7.2 The systems approach

Systems theory

There is no universally accepted definition of a *system*. However, it can be described as 'an entity which consists of interdependent parts', so that systems theory is concerned with the attributes and relationships of these inter-acting parts.

Every system has a boundary, which defines what it is. The boundary will be expressed in terms of areas, or constraints that separate it from other departments, such as the financial accounts department. System boundaries may be natural or artificially created (an organisation's departmental structures are artificially created). Anything which is external to a system belongs to the environment and not to the system itself. The environment exerts a considerable influence on the behaviour of system; at the same time the system can rarely do much to control the behaviour of the environment.

The systems approach to organisations suggests the importance of taking the *environment* into account. There are two approaches, complementary not contradictory, which we can take to review this problem.

(a) The relative openness of the system to its environment
(b) The subsystems approach (as seen in the idea of socio-technical systems)

Open and closed systems

General systems theory makes a distinction between open, closed and semi-closed systems.

(a) A *closed system* is a system which is isolated from its environment and independent of it, so that no environmental influences affect the behaviour of the system, nor does the system exert any influence on its environment.

Shut off from
its environment

(b)   An *open system* is a system connected to and interacting with its environment. It takes in influences from its environment and also influences this environment by its behaviour. An open system is a stable system which is nevertheless continually changing or evolving.

Inputs from the
environment

Transforming the
inputs in some way

Outputs

(c)   In practice, few systems are entirely closed. Many are semi-closed, in that their relationship with the environment is in some degree restricted.

Organisations, such as businesses and government departments, are by definition open systems. Why? All social organisations consist of human beings.

(a)   Human beings participate in any number of social systems, of which the work organisation is only one, although it is important.

   (i)   The family is a social system.
   (ii)   An individual's network of friends is a social system.
   (iii)   The class system is a social system.

(b)   In most societies, human beings are exposed to a variety of influences from the social environment.

   (i)   Advertising messages
   (ii)   Family attitudes and pressures
   (iii)   Government demands (eg for tax revenue)

(c)   Organisations generally have a variety of interchanges with the environment, obtaining inputs from it, and generating outputs to it.

Inputs to the organisation include the following.

(a)   Materials, components and sub-components
(b)   Labour
(c)   Money
(d)   Information and ideas
(e)   Tangible property

Outputs from the organisation include the following.

(a)   Goods and services

(b)   Money (dividends, interest, wages)

(c)   Information

(d)   Environmental consequences of its activities (eg pollution, increased traffic noise)

(e)   Social consequences of its activities (eg in the case of newspapers, the prevalence of certain ideas; in the case of tobacco companies, tobacco related illnesses)

An organisation, or its management, might however try to limit the extent to which these external environmental influences are imported to the organisation's smooth functioning. For example, as we have discussed, organisations like to standardise work for the sake of predictability. Furthermore some social organisations (eg monasteries) limit the degree of environmental information they import, and try to cut themselves off from the wider society.

Business systems have some of the operational features of a semi-closed system. The inputs to a nuclear power station are predictable (nuclear fuel), as are its outputs (a steady supply of electricity).

Activity 8 (15 minutes)

Consider the idea of a university as an open system. What are the *inputs* to this system? What are the *outputs* (both intended and unintended)? What are the *transformation processes* which occur between the arrival of the inputs and the departure of the outputs? What does your analysis suggest about the appropriateness of the way a university is organised, when it is viewed as an open system?

Socio-technical systems

An organisation is not simply a structure: the organisation chart reflects only one subsystem of the overall organisation. A subsystem is part of a system, which itself is a coherent whole. For example, the wiring system in a house is separate from the plumbing, even though the two systems do interact sometimes (eg electric showers). *Trist* and his associates at the Tavistock Institute have suggested that an organisation is a 'structured *socio-technical* system', that is, it consists of at least three sub-systems:

(a)   a structure;

(b)   a technological system (concerning the work to be done, and the machines, tools and other facilities available to do it); and

(c)   a social system (concerning the people within the organisation, the ways they think and the ways they interact with each other).

The problem is to find a fit that will meet technical demands and human needs.

The contribution of the systems approach

General systems theory contributes to management in several ways, not least by enabling managers to learn from the experience of experts and researchers in other disciplines.

(a)   It draws attention to the *dynamic* aspects of organisation, and the factors influencing the growth and development of all its subsystems.

(b)   It creates an awareness of subsystems, each with potentially conflicting goals which must be integrated. *Sub-optimisation* (where subsystems pursue their own goals to the detriment of the system as a whole) is a feature of organisational behaviour.

(c)   It focuses attention on interrelationships between aspects of the organisation, and between the organisation and its environment, and on the needs of the system as a whole: management should not get so bogged down in detail and small political arenas that they lose sight of the overall objectives and processes.

(d) It teaches managers to reject the deterministic idea that A will always cause B to happen. *Linear causality* may occur, but only rarely, because of the unpredictability and uncontrollability of many inputs.

(e) The importance of the environment on a system is acknowledged. One product of this may be customer orientation, which Peters and Waterman note is an important cultural element of successful, adaptive companies.

The approach has appeal and offers practical insights for managers.

(a) As we have seen it is possible to draw the analogy between living systems and organisations (the organic analogy) and make some assumptions about how organisations are likely to behave on that basis. The analogy provides a framework for thinking about organisations and designing their structure.

(b) However, it is only an analogy, and as such cannot be stretched too far, or provide a basis for devising testable hypotheses. It is therefore not a 'theory' at all in scientific terms. As an *approach*, it offers a useful, accessible language for discussing organisations, but – as with many behavioural frameworks – its scientific status cannot be reckoned in the same way as theories in the natural sciences.

7.3 The contingency approach

The *contingency approach* to organisation developed as a reaction to prescriptive ideas of the classical and human relations schools, which claimed to offer a universal best way to design organisations, to motivate staff, or to introduce technology. Research by *Blain, Burns and Stalker, Joan Woodward, Lawrence and Lorsch* and others indicated that different forms of organisational structure could be equally successful, that there was no inevitable correlation between classical organisational structures and effectiveness, and that there were a number of variables to be considered in the design of organisations. Essentially, it depends on the internal factors and external environment of each organisation and the design of organisational structure is a best fit between the tasks, people and environment *in the particular situation*.

(a) *The environment. Lawrence and Lorsch* compared the structural characteristics of a high-performing container firm, which existed in a relatively stable environment, and a high-performing plastics firm which existed in a rapidly changing environment. They concluded that in a stable environment the most efficient structure was one in which the influence and authority of senior managers was high and of middle managers low: the converse was true of the dynamic environment firm.

(b) *Technology*. Joan Woodward's research with firms in Essex highlighted the importance of technology as a major factor contributing to variances in organisation structure:

'It appeared that different technologies imposed different kinds of demands on individuals and organisations and that these demands have to be met through an appropriate form of organisation.'

Burns and Stalker identified two types of organisation structure: mechanistic and organismic (or organic). The mechanistic structure was very like Weber's bureaucracy. The organismic structure was much looser in form, less bound by procedure and precedent and less governed by hierarchy. This form was more successful in dealing with the very dynamic environment of the electronics industry.

A criticism of the contingency approach was outlined by *John Child:*

'One major limitation of the contemporary contingency approach lies in the lack of conclusive evidence to demonstrate that matching organisational designs to prevailing contingencies contributes importantly to performance.'

However, awareness of the contingency approach will therefore be of value in two ways.

(a) It encourages managers to identify and define the particular circumstances of the situation they need to manage, and to devise appropriate ways of handling them. A belief in universal principles and prescriptive theories can hinder problem-solving and decision-making by obscuring some of the available alternatives. It can also dull the ability to evaluate and choose between alternatives that are clearly open, by preventing the manager from developing relevant criteria for judgement.

(b) It encourages responsiveness and flexibility to changes in environmental factors through organisational structure and culture. Task performance and individual/group satisfaction are more important design criteria than permanence and unity of design type. Within a single organisation, there may be bureaucratic units side by side with task-centred matrix units (for example in the research and development function) which can respond to particular pressures and environmental volatility.

It is important however to remember that the environment is not static – effective managers do not base ongoing decisions on a snap-shot at one point in time. Instead they are constantly aware of environmental change and adapt accordingly.

8   THE NEW ORGANISATION?

In the past, the adoption of classical management principles (exemplified by writers like Fayol and Weber) has meant that organisations developed the following characteristics.

(a) Belief in *universal laws* like the *span of control* principle (which states that no one brain can effectively control more than five or six other brains).

(b) Very *tall structures* (ie lots of different management levels) with close supervision at every level.

(c) *Hierarchical control* through adherence to a rigid chain of command.

(d) *Problem-solving* of a fragmented, directive, mechanistic kind, solely devoted to putting things right once they had gone wrong (instead of making sure they did not go wrong in the first place).

(e) *Single function specialisms* like production and sales, with departmental barriers and careers concentrated in one activity.

(f) *Individualism* reflected in incentive systems and the encouragement of competitive behaviour.

(g) *Focus on tasks and responsibilities* in job descriptions rather than the concept of adding value and using initiative.

(h) Systems which were reactive and procedure-bound.

In an environment where there was little competition, business organisations and certainly public sector organisations, could laze along, carrying superfluous employees (the people who in Japan are known as 'window-watchers'), many of them under-utilised, under-developed and psychologically amputated.

EXAMPLE: HITACHI AT HIRWAUN

In 1981, run as a joint venture between GEC and Hitachi, the Hirwaun factory (in south Wales) achieved a one-day output of 1,750 TV sets with 2,200 employees. By 1986, with Hitachi running the business on its own, Hirwaun was routinely churning out, every day, 2,400 TV sets, 500 hi-fi units and 500 video recorders, with a workforce of 1,000 employees. Many of these 1,000 employees were the same people who had worked there in 1981.

Despite our opening discussion of classical management and universal principles we have reached the conclusion that the most effective management and organisational style is contingent on the environment (defined in its broadest sense). Gradually organisations have shifted away from the traditional form. The reasons for this include the following.

(a) *Everything global:* we now live in what has been described as a global village, with a global economy, a global marketplace, battered by global forces (political, economic, social, technological and religious).

(b) *Everything new:* organisations have come to appreciate that they are unlikely to survive unless they are responsive to the expectations of their customers; for some, there is a very new perspective if they previously operated in a monopolistic (or quasi-monopolistic) environment and did not regard their clients as customers at all (BT, for instance, used to call us *subscribers*; British Rail used to call us *passengers*).

(c) *Everything faster:* with techniques of *mass customisation*, it is now possible to order a tailor-made Toyota from a Tokyo car showroom and have the car delivered 24 hours later.

(d) *Everything different:* it is no longer sufficient to keep doing the same things but progressively to do them better. The world of work has entered a major paradigm shift towards entirely different expectations about performance, challenging the conventional assumptions of old.

(e) *Everything turbulent:* there is no going back to the peace and quiet of organisational stability in a world of slow social and technological change – instead, organisations nowadays must continue to cope with messy, paradoxical, ambiguous scenarios.

The essential features for the new world of work have been eloquently discussed by *Michael Hammer and James Champy* in *Re-Engineering the Corporation: A Manifesto for Business Revolution* (1993). Hammer and Champy envisage the following trends.

(a) *Work units:* from functional departments to process teams.

(b) Jobs: from simple tasks to multi-dimensional work. The old model (represented by Taylorism) offered simple tasks for simple people, whereas the new approach reflects complex jobs for smart people.

(c) *Roles:* from *controlled* to *empowered*. In a process team environment, people have the chance to learn more about the work process as a complete entity; performing the role becomes more satisfying, with a greater sense of completion, closure and accomplishment, and more learning and growth built in. The corollary is that jobs are more challenging and difficult as the older-style routine work is eliminated or automated.

(d) *Values:* from protective to productive. People in organisations have to believe that they work for their customers, not for their bosses.

(e) *Managers:* from supervisors to coaches.

(f) *Executives:* from scorekeepers to leaders.

(g) *Structures:* from hierarchical to flat (explored in Chapter 6).

The difficulty for most organisations is the need to manage the tension between two opposing sets of forces.

(a) The *centralising* impact of professional management, designed to produce a cohesive corporate strategy and the rational, efficient allocation of resources which will support this strategy.

(b) The *centrifugal* effect of the forces important for fostering entrepreneurship, empowerment, risk-taking and innovation.

EXAMPLE: ICL

The transformation of ICL

ICL was born in 1968; in 1976 it increased its small-systems capability and geographical presence by taking over Singer Business Machines; in 1984 it merged with STC, and in 1990 became part of the Fujitsu Group. ICL today employs some 25,000 people and operates in 70 countries.

By the early 1980s, management had become convinced that urgent changes were needed if ICL was to maintain its position as a major European competitor in the information technology industry. Note that these changes were introduced while ICL was still successful – unlike many other organisations where change is the outcome of (usually) a performance/profit crisis.

The new top management at ICL quickly generated a mission statement:

'ICL is an international company dedicated to applying IT to provide profitable high-value customer solutions for improved operational and management effectiveness.'

ICL's cultural change, moreover, was achieved through a set of three inter-locking elements.

(a) *Top management vision and determination.* The publication of The ICL Way contained a set of commitments for staff and obligations for managers, representing the values, beliefs and the corporate environment needed for ICL's future.

(b) *Education and communication.* This took the form of training from top management down to first-line managers (supervisors). The middle-management programme, for example, included presentations by each director on his/her current and longer-term strategies.

(c) *Structure and process change.* Attention was concentrated on objective-setting, career structures and career management, effective employee appraisals, and ways of making 'people issues' an integral part of the business. One threshold placed on ICL managers is that unless 95% of their staff receive a quarterly appraisal, the manager receives no bonus. This tries to instil into managers the cultural value that they should be properly concerned for the performance, reward and development of their staff.

What do all these developments mean for the managerial role in organisations? Some writers have been very pessimistic, especially about the future for middle managers.

(a) *Rosabeth Moss Kanter* suggests that middle managers 'are squeezed between the demands of strategies they do not influence and the ambitions of increasingly independent-minded employees.'

(b) Peter Drucker, in a 1988 article for the Harvard Business Review, notes:

'Whole layers of management neither make decisions nor lead... instead their main, if only function, is to service as relays, human boosters for the faint, unfocused signals that pass for communication in the traditional, pre-information organisations.'

Our own conclusions are much more optimistic, having reviewed 21 research studies (produced between 1958 and 1993) covering managerial populations in the UK, continental Europe and the USA. The evidence is ambiguous, but suggests the following.

(a) Managerial roles are now more generalist, with increased responsibilities and more tasks.

(b) Managers are managing larger teams or groups of people, with a wider mix of staff.

(c) The new manager is more accountable: this greater focus on performance means attempts to measure added-value more carefully and, hence, redesigned performance review (appraisal) systems.

(d) Because of the explosion in IT, managers have better information on which to base their decisions.

(e) Moreover, because IT has taken much of the drudgery out of the manager's administrative activities, the manager has more time for the people aspects, for strategic thinking, for customer service, and for dealing with routine tasks more efficiently.

(f) Managers are learning new skills, concerned with managing change, financial know-how, marketing, strategic planning and the motivation of multi-function teams.

In these research studies, the majority of participating managers are positive about the changes and how these changes are influencing their roles. Indeed, many argue that previous frustrations have been removed.

(a) Flatter hierarchies (in *delayered structures*) mean that most managers are closer to top management in the strategic and policy-making areas. Further, most managers are more likely to have their own clear domains of responsibility, plus more control over the resources needed to achieve results.

(b) Often empowerment is generating, among managers, the opportunity to take on new challenges, to broaden their expertise, to innovate and to take risks.

(c) Managerial careers may be more problematic, but it is a mistake to assume that all managers are continually striving for advancement and are eager for what *Torrington and Weightman* call the 'halcyon realms' of senior and top management.

A very different form of 'new organisation' is described below. Here the pressures on managers are quite different, and result from taking 'empowerment' of the workforce to its logical conclusion.

EXAMPLE: SEMCO

Semco is a Brazilian company which makes pumps, dishwashers and cooking units. The company has attracted enormous media and business interest. Here's why.

(a)   All managers are rated by their subordinates every six months, on a scale of 1 to 100. Those managers who consistently under-perform are squeezed out.

(b)   Workers elect their own boss: 'in a plant where everyone has a financial stake in its success, the idea of asking subordinates to choose bosses seems an eminently sensible way to stop accidents before they are promoted.'

(c)   Workers set their own salaries – but they know that they might price themselves out of the department's budget.

(d)   The workers decide how much of the profits to share and how much to invest.

(e)   Workers are encouraged to work from home.

(f)   Everyone 'from the cleaner upwards has access to the company's books.'

Semco's boss, Ricardo Semler, believes that democracy has been introduced to the workplace: this is a radical departure from Fayol and Taylor, but, at a time when firms like IBM are being overtaken by smaller competitors, his ideas are gaining currency in the US.

Despite the interest 'so far, only one or two companies have tried direct emulation. But if the hundreds of companies beating their way to Semler's shop floor are any guide, there is a considerable appetite for civilising the Western norm of capitalism. The trouble is that the corporate world is run by people not exactly busting keen to lose their parking lots, let alone to subject themselves to monthly scrutiny by people whom, currently, they can hire and fire. Even corporate turkeys don't vote for Christmas'. (Quotation from an article by Victor Keegan in *The Guardian* 28 September 1993).

Organisational *learning* is a term used to describe the process by which knowledge is created in organisation. We shall see in a later chapter the significance of organisational learning: but the days when the workforce could be viewed simply as robots carrying out managerial instructions are numbered.

This section has to conclude with a caveat about the danger of reading too much into changes which, when one studies them carefully, apply to only a small minority of organisations (albeit a highly visible minority). Currently the corporate fashions dictate lean and mean structures, decentralisation and autonomy for separate units, rewards entrepreneurial behaviour, and a single-minded concentration on customers. It is plausible to assume (merely by looking back at the evidence from the past two decades or so) that these current fashions will not last forever. Within the decade we may see a wholesale conversion back to a justification for impressive headquarter buildings, centralised functions and many-layered hierarchies – so the whole cycle can begin again.

Chapter roundup

- Organisations are social arrangements for the controlled performance of collective goals.

- Organisations exist as they achieve results which individuals, in isolation, are unable to do. They enable:

  (i)   division and specialisation of labour;
  (ii)   synergy;
  (iii) savings in 'transactions costs'.

- There are many types of organisations

  (i)   Business organisations include private unincorporated businesses, partnerships and limited companies. These are distinguished from each other by their legal status.

  (ii)   Business organisations carry out a variety of activities (ie manufacturing, services etc).

  (iii) Business organisations exist to make a profit for their owners. Public sector organisations, on the other hand, have a service element to them: they are constrained by the resources available to them.

- Business organisations operate in an environment increasingly international in context.

- Non profit making organisations, such as charities, are independent of the government, but act to further some social benefit.

- All organisations are open social systems (arrangements of people) and are thus susceptible to environmental influences.

- The impact of organisations on the people that deal with them is wide ranging and varied. There are a variety of metaphors for thinking about organisations, all of which have some useful insights. Morgan lists eight metaphors (organisations are: machines, biological organisms, human brains, cultures, political systems, psychic prisons, systems of change or transformation, instruments of domination).

- Organisation and management theory developed in the late 19th century with writers such as Henri Fayol and social scientists such as Weber and F W Taylor. Although different in many ways, those approaches emphasise issues of:

  (i)   hierarchy and structures of authority;

  (ii)   control by managers and technical specialists, rather than workers, over the job done;

  (iii) impersonality.

- The human relations approach was a reaction against such policies.

- New theories of the organisations suggest these approaches are less relevant than before.

BPP PUBLISHING

Quick quiz

1   Define 'organisation'.

2   What is limited liability?

3   What distinguishes services from goods?

4   What three bases did Weber give for legitimate authority?

5   Who aimed to establish a true science of work?

6   What is a system?

7   How does a closed system differ from an open system?

8   What is sub-optimisation in a system?

9   What effect does delayering have on structure?

Answers to quick quiz

1   A social arrangement for the controlled performance of collective gains

2   Owners are not liable for the business's debts.

3   Intangibility, heterogeneity, inseparability of production from consumption

4   Charisma, tradition and bureaucracy

5   FW Taylor

6   An entity made up of interdependent parts

7   A closed system is shut off from its environment

8   Subsystems pursue their own goals to the detriment of the performance of the system as a whole

9   The hierarchy becomes flatter

Answers to activities

1   Arguably all four are organisations within the Buchanan and Huczynski definition. A university has social arrangements, collective goals and is concerned about performance, although the extent to which the academic staff commit themselves to the so-called 'collective goals' is often problematic – and this raises the issue of individual behaviour within organisations. The idea that an organisation is a homogeneous entity, with all its members pulling together harmoniously for the common good, is clearly unrealistic, and is especially so when applied to organisations like prisons, where some of the 'members' are there against their will. In fact, prisons are a particularly classic instance of the fact that any organisation is a complex network of 'stakeholders', each with its own purposes, power-base and position to defend.

So far as the National Lottery is concerned, we could be talking either of the Lottery institution itself, or of the organisation which runs it (Camelot), and any discussion on whether the National Lottery is an 'organisation' needs to begin with a clear account of the perspective from which the issue is being examined.

2   You may be able to produce your own examples. Many pharmaceuticals firms not only manufacture drugs but research and develop new drugs, whose formulation is protected from imitation by *patent*. Patents are a form of intellectual property.

There are plenty of business organisations whose activities embrace several of the classification groups listed, such as Hanson, Imperial Tobacco and Unilever. Some have embarked on this route as a deliberate exercise in diversification; others have done so for defensive reasons because they have foreseen the decline and eventual collapse of their existing business.

3   In our view, the classification for the organisations listed is as follows.

International:	None
Multinational:	General Motors, Sony, Coca-Cola, McDonalds, Hutchinson Telecom
Global:	Philips, News International, IBM

Relatively few organisations are genuinely global because they fear loss of control if too much discretion is devolved from the centre; they may also be sceptical about the abilities of locally-recruited managers, and cannot easily manage the culture clashes when groups of managers, from differing countries, have to operate as a team.

4   Privatisation generates greater concern about performance, coupled with reduced job security, because concerns about profitability take precedence – and some of the individuals who worked in the previously sheltered context of the public sector are unable to adapt to these new requirements, either because they are risk-averse or because their own personal value-systems are unsympathetic to the profit motive.

Concern for the customer is less evident in monopolistic public sector organisations for the simple reason that the customers have no choice. They cannot take their business elsewhere, and they may even have to pay for services whether they use them or not (eg through the Council Tax): against this background, it would scarcely be surprising if the service provider acquired a face of arrogance and complacency.

5   *Situational withdrawal* can occur in organisations among individuals who adapt themselves to their working environment by simply refusing to think about it. They come to work, do their job, and go home afterwards without displaying any sense of engagement or commitment to what they are doing – probably because their work is so repetitive and tedious that if they focused on it at all they would come to hate it. Possessing such strong negative emotions, and also aware of their inability to find alternative employment that could be more meaningful, their lives could become intolerable. The sanest thing to do, therefore, is to switch off more or less completely.

The *intransigent line* is found among individuals who become labelled as 'trouble makers' because they are constantly challenging the organisation's goals and methods of working. In mental hospitals, Goffman reports that intransigent patients were more likely to receive electro-convulsive therapy (ECT), but as a sanction and a deterrent more than as a form of treatment. In business organisations, intransigent employees may be sidelined or ousted; occasionally they can be given something useful to do, like handling a turnround scenario (ie the need to rescue part of the business which has become unprofitable); otherwise they seldom enjoy satisfactory careers.

Colonisation describes the approach of people who, unable to progress further, convince themselves that the position they occupy represents an optimum combination of job satisfaction elements and earning power. According to this view, all other possible jobs in the organisation – even

PUBLISHING

those further up the hierarchy – would necessitate a negative and counter-productive trade-off: the fact that no such jobs are actually available is conveniently forgotten. Colonisation happens, too, among employees who concentrate exclusively on their wages or salary, and who 'forget' or denigrate other possible rewards associated with work.

Conversion represents the behaviour of staff who have been totally assimilated into the organisation. They fully reflect and exemplify the organisation's credo; they conform to the expectations of their seniors; they act as positive role-models for those beneath them. In particular, they are to be found in organisations like Mars, Marks & Spencer, Nissan and IBM – in fact within all organisations where great attention is paid to the recruitment of people who will fit in with the prevailing cultural values.

6 (a) This mix could be found in large (therefore bureaucratic), family (therefore traditional) organisations where nonetheless the leader has charisma. Examples are rare, although Sainsburys does seem a relevant case in point. The same combination can occur in hereditary monarchies where, from time to time, a charismatic individual emerges at the top.

(b) Charismatic leadership plus a bureaucratic organisation were a feature of ICI in the era of John Harvey-Jones, or SmithKline Beecham under its one-time chief executive Bob Bauman. McDonalds, under Ray Croc, is a further instance: centrally-imposed systems, rigorously supervised and controlled, yet operating under a dynamic and innovative leader.

(c) Well-established family dynasties operate traditional controls against a framework of bureaucratic procedures: some merchant banks and many smaller limited companies fall into this category.

(d) Charisma linked to traditional leadership represents organisations justifying themselves through hereditary succession, yet occasionally producing an inspired leader – more by chance than by design. The inspired leader will often want to take the organisation in a completely different direction, and this is likely to promote havoc among the family members who see their long-term interests being jeopardised.

7 There are many reasons why bureaucracies find change painful. Crozier emphasises some; others arise from the fact that bureaucratic organisations are characterised by security and stability – hence they will attract employees who are motivated by security and stability, which are in turn qualities associated with rigidity and resistance to innovation. Patterns of control in bureaucracies are dependent on tight formal structures and reporting procedures. As Tom Lupton has pointed out, these help to induce the "'I-won't-do-more-than-I-have-to" attitude, the empire-building, the sub-optimisation, and the rat-racing, which characterise large-scale bureaucracy and the "resistance to change" it exhibits. This kind of organisation is likely to be anything but flexible and adaptive, because the structure places a premium on defensive play-safe untrusting people. It is not as if people are inherently defensive etc; it is the organisation that makes them so.'

8 The *inputs* to a university will include the relevant sources of financial investment, the academic staff, the administrators, the students, the presence of other universities, the expectations of the university's various stakeholders, and so forth.

The university's *outputs* must embrace: its graduates and those emerging with professional qualifications; the more subtle impact of the university's presence on its immediate neighbourhood; the flow of research results, thinking and 'knowledge', both pure and applied; and organisational improvements (in the case of those universities which specialise in management education/development/training).

The relevant *transformation processes* consist of teaching, research, preparing material for publication, the development of links with other organisations (academic, professional, civic and so on).

Most universities are structured around clusters of broadly compatible academic disciplines. Is this ideal? When viewed from an open systems perspective, might there not be a case for at least part of the university being focused on the conversion process of teaching and learning, with other parts concentrating on, say, research? In a sense, this already happens, given that some staff are called 'lecturers' and others have the word 'research' in their job titles ('research fellow') but the distinction is seldom taken to its logical conclusion.

Further question practice

Now try the following practice questions at the end of this text

Multiple choice questions: **1 to 7**

Exam style question: **1**

Chapter 2 :
MISSION, GOALS AND OBJECTIVES

Introduction

Three people were at work on a construction site. All were doing the same job, but when each was asked what his job was, the answers varied. 'Breaking rocks', replied the first. 'Earning a living', answered the second. 'Helping to build a cathedral', said the third.

This homily (from a speech by *Peter Schultz*, chief executive of *Porsche* in the USA) provides a helpful introduction to the uses and abuses of mission statements – those phrases which are meant to encapsulate the organisation's essential purpose and character. The idea of boiling down an organisation's *raison d'être* into a sentence or two, which can be instantly understood by shareholders, employees and customers, sounds eminently sensible. A mission statement, properly written, could be a powerful unifying force: it explains *why* the organisation exists, and can be supplemented by a vision statement which outlines *what* the organisation is trying to achieve, and a values statement which sets out *how* (both prescriptive and prospective). Unfortunately, as we shall see, many mission statements are masterpieces of obscurity or, even worse, obscurantism; because of this, they cannot act as a unifying force and they supply little or no guidance about the organisation's purposes, aims and methods.

Where the mission, vision and values are properly designed, they will tell us useful things about the *why*, the *what* and the *how*; goals, targets and objectives are then essential in order to translate these generalities into specific, operational actions. Terms like 'goal', 'target' and 'objective' are often used interchangeably, but in this chapter we shall endeavour to promote more rigorous definitions so that ambiguity is minimised. Further, we shall explore the merits of open and closed objectives, as well as some of the political issues surrounding the specification of organisational objectives within a framework of multiple *stakeholders*.

In this chapter you will learn about these things.

(a) The differences between an organisation's mission, its vision and its values

(b) The potential benefits to be gained from production of an explicit set of mission/vision/values statements, both for strategic planning purposes and as a motivational tool

(c) The different types of goals and objectives that organisations pursue

(d) The 'TRAMPS' formula for the specification of meaningful objectives applied to an organisation, to organisational units (like departments and divisions) or to individual employees

(f) The significance of stakeholders in the governance and management of organisations

1   MISSION

Definition

> *Mission* 'describes the organisation's basic function in society, in terms of the products and services it produces for its clients' *(Mintzberg).*

Mission describes the purpose of the organisation as a whole, the total output of the system. In practical terms it is useful to consider mission in terms of four elements.

(a)   *Purpose*. Why does the company exist, or why do its managers and employees feel it exists?

    (i)   To create wealth for shareholders, who take priority over all other stakeholders?

    (ii)   To satisfy the needs of all stakeholders, including employees and society at large, for example?

    (iii)   To reach some higher goal such as the advancement to society?

    Purpose answers this question.

(b)   *Strategy*. This provides the commercial logic and the basis for strategic planning for the company, and so defines the business the company is in, its products and its market. For example *Rolls Royce* and *Lada* are both producers of cars – but in terms of the target market they wish to serve they are markedly different; Rolls Royce catering for the luxury end of the market, Lada the price sensitive budget purchaser. This element approximates to *Mintzberg's* definition.

(c)   *Policies and standards of behaviour*. Strategy needs to be converted into everyday performance. For example, a services industry that wishes to be the best in its market must aim for standards of service, in all its operations, which are at least as good as those found in its competitors. In service businesses, this includes simple matters such as politeness to customers, speed at which phone calls are answered, and so forth.

(d)   *Values*. These relate to the organisation's culture and in order to be effective must be compatible with the beliefs of the people who work in the organisation. For example, a firm's moral principles might mean refusing an assignment if it believes the client will not benefit, even though this refusal means lost revenue. Mintzberg sometimes defines values as *ideology*, in other words a means of control through shared beliefs. As we shall see in a later chapter primary socialisation and national culture will influence the compatibility of organisational values with those of the individual.

For there to be a strong sense of mission, the elements above must be mutually reinforcing. Incompatibility between the elements, or inconsistency between formal statements of mission and actual practice will rapidly undermine the usefulness of a mission.

These values must be reflected throughout the organisation as a whole, for example in personnel practice, reward systems, recruitment etc.

A sense of mission will therefore be at its strongest where the employees' personal values and organisational values coincide. The most obvious example is a religious organisation where an individual's faith and organisational teaching and purpose are the same. Sometimes employees can have a sense of mission even where there is chaos in management. For example, a doctor's dedication to his or her patients may be strong despite poor management, say, by the health authority. In other cases incompatibility between individual and organisational values may prevent an organisation fulfilling its stated purpose. Take for example the case of an organisation which claims to be dedicated to customer service, but which is staffed by people who firmly believe that at 5 pm work stops – regardless of what remains outstanding. What happens when a customer reports a problem that will take two hours to solve at 4.50 pm on a Friday evening – will they consider waiting till Monday an example of 'excellent customer service'?

The above examples illustrate two ways in which mission impacts on organisational performance.

(a)   A shared sense of mission and values can have an important motivating effect on the behaviour of employees. It also provides an important guide to acceptable behaviour.

(b)   Marketers have demonstrated the impact of values and feelings on buying decisions. Purchasers may therefore be influenced by the extent to which an organisation's mission is compatible with their own values.

Moreover, some writers believe there is an empirical relationship between strong *corporate values* and profitability. The *Financial Times* reported (22 February 1993) the result of research by the Digital Equipment Corporation into a sample of 429 company executives.

(a)   80% of the sample said that their firm has a formal mission statement.

(b)   80% said that they believed mission contributes to profitability.

(c)   75% said that they believed they have a responsibility to implement the mission statement.

(d)   *Only* 6% admitted, openly, that corporate values make *little* difference in practice, although 30% believed that values should be subordinated to commercial gain in case of conflict.

Activity 1   **(5 minutes)**

'Whistle-blowers' are people who give information to the government or the press about those activities of their employers which they think are immoral. Whistle-blowers rarely gain in financial or career terms from so doing. What motives do you think they have?

Despite these benefits there can be situations where strong values may have a negative impact on organisational performance.

- They can result in filtering out uncomfortable environmental information.
- They can delay necessary decision making.
- They can cause resistance to necessary change.

To summarise:

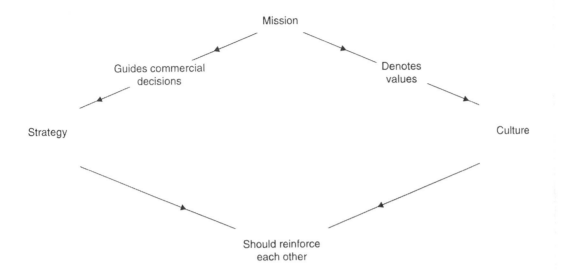

1.1 Mission statements

Mission statements are formal documents, which might be reproduced in a number of places (eg at the front of an organisation's annual report, on publicity material, in the chairman's office, in communal work areas). There is no standard format.

Most mission statements will include the following.

(a) The identity of the persons for whom the organisation exists, such as shareholders, customers, staff and other employees.

(b) The nature of the organisation's activities: that is, the product it makes or services it provides and the markets it produces for.

(c) The way the organisation goes about its business. This might include reference to such matters as reliance on quality, innovation and low prices; policy on acquisition versus organic growth; and the geographical spread of operations.

(d) The organisation's principles of business, such as commitment to suppliers and staff; policies in the environment and equal opportunities; and commitments to customers.

Many commentators are suspicious of mission statements because they may not in fact reflect the actual mission of the organisation.

(a) They are often public relations exercises rather than an accurate portrayal of the firm's mission.

(b) They can often be full of generalisations which are impossible to tie down to specific strategic implications (eg, 'best' 'quality' 'major').

(c) They may be ignored by the planners responsible for formulating strategy.

Once again the problems created by inconsistency between statement and practice apply. Consistency is therefore perhaps the most important guiding principle for the preparation of a mission statement.

More guidance on the preparation of effective mission statements is contained in *Selling the Dream* (1991). Here *Guy Kawasaki* suggests that good mission statements exhibit three qualities.

(a)   *Brevity*. Brief and simple mission statements are easy to understand and remember – they are also evidence of clear thinking. For example, the Girl Scouts' mission statement is 'To help a girl reach her highest potential'. It is short, simple, easy to understand and easy to remember.

(b)   *Flexibility*. Flexible mission statements can last a long time. For example, 'ensuring an adequate supply of water' is inflexible and confining; it may not survive the next rainy season. By contrast, the Macintosh Division's mission statement was: 'To improve the creativity and productivity of people'. It was flexible enough to accommodate a computer and peripheral products such as laser printers, software, books and training.

(c)   *Distinctiveness*. Distinctive mission statements differentiate your cause from other organisations with similar missions.

Activity 2   **(10 minutes)**

Does a mission statement mean what it says? You would certainly hope so, but here are two examples of mission statements which are either completely misleading or tell you virtually nothing about the organisation. In the second example, the company's name has been deleted.

Example 1
'We aim, by excellence of management and pre-eminence in technology, to grasp the great opportunities created by the ever-increasing worldwide demand for information, prosperity and peace.'

Example 2
'– will be the most highly focused, the most skilled and the most technologically advanced company in – worldwide. We will provide the highest quality of products and services for customers; deliver consistently good financial results for shareholders; enable employees to realise their full potential; and ensure a positive impact on the communities we serve.'

Can you guess which organisations produced these mission statements? Answers will be supplied at the end of the chapter.

EXAMPLE: NATIONAL POST

Here is an example of a proposed mission statement for a national postal organisation. How good do you think it is?

NATIONAL POST: MISSION AND VALUES

National Post Business Mission

As National Post our mission is to be recognised as the best organisation in the world distributing text and packages. We shall achieve this by:

- excelling our Collection, Processing, Distribution and Delivery arrangements

- establishing a partnership with our customers to understand, agree and meet their changing requirements

- operating profitably by efficient services which our customers consider to be value for money

- creating a work environment which recognises and rewards the commitment of all employees to customer satisfaction

- recognising our responsibilities as part of the social, industrial and commercial life of the country

- being forward looking and innovative

National Post Business Values

We care about:

- Our customers and their requirements for:

  – Reliability
  – Value for money
  – Accessibility
  – Courtesy
  – Integrity
  – Security
  – Prompt and timely response

- All our fellow employees and their needs for:

  – Respect
  – Training and development
  – Involvement
  – Recognition and reward

- The way we do our job and the way it affects our customers both inside and outside the Business

  – Our role in the life of the Community
  – We are proud to be part of National Post

> **Activity 3** (15 minutes)
>
> Evaluate the following mission statements against Kawasaki's three criteria.
>
> Glaxo 'is an integrated research-based group of companies whose corporate purpose is to create, discover, develop, manufacture and market throughout the world, safe, effective medicines of the highest quality which will bring benefit to patients through improved longevity and quality of life, and to society through economic value.'
>
> IBM (UK): 'We shall increase the pace of change. Market-driven quality is our aim. It means listening and responding more sensitively to our customers. It means eliminating defects and errors, speeding up all our processes, measuring everything we do against a common standard, and it means involving employees totally in our aims'.
>
> Matsushita: 'The duty of the manufacturer is to serve the foundation of man's happiness by making man's life affluent with an inexpensive and inexhaustible supply of life's necessities.'
>
> Komatsu: 'Encircle Caterpillar.'
>
> Apple Computer: 'Our goal has always been to create the world's friendliest, most understandable, most useable computers – computers that empower the individual ... Our mission is to transform the way people do things by focusing on their experience with our computers. We believe the innovation and creativity of a person's work depends directly on the quality of his or her total experience, not just on the speed of a microprocessor.'

1.2 Mission and planning

Although the mission statement might be seen as a set of abstract principles, it can play an important role in the planning process.

(a)   Plans should outline the fulfilment of the organisation's mission. To take the example of a religious organisation (the best example of a 'missionary organisation'), the mission of 'spreading the gospel' might be embodied in plans to send individuals as missionaries to various parts of the world, plans for fund-raising activities, even targets for the numbers of new converts.

(b)   Mission also acts as a yardstick by which plans are judged. Take the example of a financial services organisation which runs a number of *ethical investment funds*. Ethical investment funds exclude from their investment portfolios shares in firms involved in alcohol, tobacco and armaments. Therefore, if a new fund manager proposed as part of an investment strategy to invest in shares of a large company involved in a number of activities, the company would be examined to see if its activities included those which the investment fund considered unethical. The investment strategy would be assessed with reference to the investment fund's mission.

Mission can be embodied in the policies and behaviour standards of the firm.

1.3 Mission, vision and strategic intent

Mission, values, and vision are three interrelated concepts. A vision is a view of the future state of the organisation or its industry. It might be encapsulated in a vision statement: for example, the managing director of a personal computer firm might have the vision of 'A computer in every kitchen'.

(a)   Whilst this can set the overall direction of the firm, it might be too vague and too far removed from current activities to motivate successfully.

(b)   Some visions fail to take into account pragmatic realities (such as securing cash flow or making a profit.

(c)   Visions can go out of date.

A vision is more a goal than a way of thinking or behaving. The differences between mission and vision are as follows.

(a)   Mission is about the here and now, whereas vision refers to the future.

(b)   A vision which is too vague will fail to motivate, whereas a mission is designed to motivate.

(c)   A vision, when achieved, might lose its motivating power, unless it can be reinvented.

Strategic intent is similar to the strategy concept of mission as outlined earlier. A famous example is Komatsu's stated desire to 'Encircle Caterpillar' (a competitor) as the filter through which its various projects were assessed.

Definition

Strategic intent, as defined by *Hamel and Prahalad*, involves the following.

(a)   The desire to attain a particular leadership position.

(b)   Communicating the value of the target as the main motivating factor to employees.

(c)   A guide to resource allocation.

Campbell, Young and Devine consider that this concept fails because it does not take note of the fact that people are motivated by current values and activities. To use strategic intent as a means of motivating employees presupposes that the workforce is already motivated and committed to the company.

2 GOALS AND OBJECTIVES: INTRODUCTION

'Organisations are social arrangements for the controlled performance of collective goals'
(Buchanan and Huczynski).

An enduring problem for management is to try to ensure that the desires of employees and managers as *individuals* are in conformance with, or at least not opposed to, the goals of the organisation.

Definition

Mintzberg (*Power In and Around Organisations*) defines goals as '*the intentions behind decisions or actions*, the states of mind that drive individuals or collectives of individuals called organisations to do what they do.'

(a) *Operational goals* can be expressed as objectives. Mintzberg says that an objective is a goal expressed in a form by which its attainment can be measured. Here is an example.

(i) An operational goal: 'Cut costs'
(ii) The objective: 'Reduce budget by 5%'

(b) *Non-operational goals* on the other hand do not express themselves as objectives. Mintzberg quotes the example of a university, whose goal might be to 'seek truth'. This cannot really be expressed as an objective. To 'increase truth by 5% this year' does not make a great deal of sense.

Activity 4   **(5 minutes)**

Here is the text which appears before the start of the chapter on objective-setting in Igor Ansoff's classic book *Corporate Strategy* (2nd edition, 1987). The source is someone's diary, quoted by the *New Yorker* magazine.

Long-range goals

(1) Health – more leisure
(2) Money
(3) Write book (play?) – fame !!!!??
(4) Visit India

Immediate

(1) Pick up knitting pattern at Hilda's
(2) Change faucets – call plumber (who?)
(3) Try yoghurt??

Which of these can be genuinely described as 'goals' in Mintzberg's sense? How could any of them be re-worded in order to turn them into 'objectives'?

In practice, however, the words goals and objectives are often used interchangeably. Mintzberg believes that organisations have goals 'to the extent that there is some consistency in the intention behind the decisions and the actions taken by its participants'.

(a) *Ideological goals* usually focus on the organisation's mission. They are shared sets of beliefs and values.

(b) *Formal goals* are imposed by a dominant individual or group (eg shareholders). People work to attain these goals, as a means to their personal goals. (In other words, you do what your boss tells you to in order to earn a wage to support your family, and so on.)

(c) *Shared personal goals*. Individuals reach a consensus about what they want out of an organisation (eg a group of academics who decide they want to pursue research).

(d) *Individual personal goals*. Individuals may also hold personally specific goals which, although they have no direct link to the organisation and its activities, will in some way be facilitated by the individuals' involvement with the organisation, (eg pursuit of promotion, in order to get a payrise, in order to purchase a bigger house in a more upmarket area).

(e) *System goals*. These are goals which derive from the organisation's existence as an organisation, independent of mission or whatever.

3   COMMERCIAL GOALS AND OBJECTIVES

Objectives are normally quantified statements of what the organisation actually intends to achieve. Whereas mission statements describe a value system for the organisation and some indication of the business it is in, objectives are well defined. Here is an example.

Mission: deliver a quality service.

Goal (operational): enhance manufacturing quality.

Objectives: over the next twelve months, reduce the number of defects to 1 part per million.

All the organisation's objectives should be directed towards achieving the organisation's mission. In business organisations, a paramount consideration is profitability. The mission of any business, whether this is stated or not, must include carrying on its activities at a profit.

Objectives are targets or standards which orientate the activities of the organisation. Although, in *theory*, they should be directed towards the fulfilment of the organisation's mission, in practice this may not be the case: how an organisation actually behaves may be significantly different from how it ought to behave if it followed the mission: more about this in Chapter 3.

Objectives can also be used as standards by which the performance of the organisation as a *whole* can be measured.

Definition

> *Corporate objectives.* Corporate objectives are those which are concerned with the firm as a whole. Objectives should be explicit, quantifiable and capable of being achieved.

The corporate objectives outline the expectations of the firm and the strategic planning process is concerned with the means of achieving the objectives. According to *Drucker*, the range of objectives for a commercial organisation should embrace the following dimensions.

(a)   *Profitability*. Some of the corporate planning literature (eg by Argenti) argues that there can only be one legitimate objective for organisations, namely, the search for profitability, measured as return on shareholders' funds. A logical flow of decision-making routines should emanate from this central focus so as to achieve the optimum strategy, but everything hinges on the goal of maximising profitability.

(b)   *Market standing*. This factor collectively addresses not only market penetration and market share, sales and public relations, but also more recent areas for concern among organisations such as customer satisfaction and the perceived quality of the organisation's products and services.

(c)   *Productivity*. There is no clear-cut way of measuring productivity. One approach is to compare sales turnover with other factors, like manpower costs (wages and salaries), capital employed, or physical resources consumed; a more reliable measure is added value, ie the difference between the value of the goods/services produced, and the cost of resources consumed in manufacturing (or supplying) those goods and services. Thus it becomes possible to assess £ of value-added per £ of labour cost, per machine hour, per square metre of floor space, per £ of capital employed.

(d)   *Financial and physical resources*. Possible fields for objective-setting within this category include warehouse and storage facilities, changes in production capacity, synergistic acquisitions and improved systems of budgetary control.

(e)   *Innovation*. In this arena, the scope for objective-setting depends on whether the organisation is genuinely market-led (ie customer-*driven*) or marketing-led (ie customer-*focused*). Organisations driven by their customers are invariably reactive because they survive by responding to customer wants, needs and expectations; a customer focus, on the other hand, implies an urgent desire to stay ahead of customers by improving standards ahead of customer taste, and by introducing new products or services before customers (actual or potential) even know they want them. Some firms have quantified objectives for innovation. The American firm *3M*, for example, has as an objective that a set percentage of total income each year should derive from new products or new variants on existing products.

(f)   *Manager performance and development*. Manager performance is an input to the specific organisational output objectives like profitability, market standing and innovation. However, since no objectives can be achieved without deliberate managerial action, it is essential to concentrate some attention upon this aspect of organisational effectiveness. Relevant objectives within the field of manager performance and development include the actual requirement to generate meaningful corporate objectives, to produce succession plans and to ensure that the appraisal (performance review) system generates added-value. *Management by objectives* is a technique whereby corporate objectives are broken down into individual objectives for managers.

(g)   *Employee performance*. In *The Human Side of Enterprise*, *Douglas McGregor* claims that 'there are no problem children, only problem parents'. If front-line employees are not performing at their best, therefore, the responsibility must rest with the management – yet this does not invalidate the benefits to be gained from specifying some objectives targeted towards employees across the board. Appropriate themes for such objectives may include reduction in overtime costs, global involvement with 'customer care' and 'quality improvement' projects, and increased employee flexibility in an environment of constant change.

(h) *Public responsibility*. This dimension of corporate activity concerns the extent to which the organisation seeks to involve itself in community affairs, either locally (eg through sponsorship of charity events in the immediate vicinity of the organisation's premises) or nationally (eg through participation in high-profile public bodies or support of pressure groups like the CBI). There are benefits from establishing and sustaining a reputation in the world at large, in terms of corporate image and the ability to influence legislation and the direction of public policy. On the other hand, there is a price to be paid in terms of managerial time, uncertainty over the link between effort and results, and the difficulties of precise targeting.

How can such a generalised concept be expressed as an objective? After all, no organisation would claim to be irresponsible in what it does, yet such things are hard to measure.

(i) Firms can monitor pollution targets from their factory, and take efforts to reduce them. Some firms conduct an *environmental audit* of their activities, publishing measures on a year-on-year basis.

(ii) Firms can set standards for health and safety, etc, higher than the legal minimum.

Similar objectives can be developed for each strategic business unit (SBU) which is a part of the company that for all intents and purposes has its own distinct products, markets and assets.

Unit objectives. Unit objectives are objectives that are specific to individual units of an organisation, and are often objectives. Here are some examples.

(a) From the commercial world

(i) Increasing the number of customers by x% (an objective of a sales department)

(ii) Reducing the number of rejects by 50% (an objective of a production department)

(iii) Producing monthly reports more quickly, within 5 working days of the end of each month (an objective of the management accounting department)

(b) From the public sector

(i) To introduce x% more places at nursery schools (an objective of a borough education department)

(ii) Responding more quickly to calls (an objective of a local police station, fire department or hospital ambulance service)

3.1 Primary and secondary objectives

Some objectives are more important than others, and it could be argued that in the hierarchy of objectives, there is a *primary corporate objective* (restricted by certain constraints on corporate activity) and other secondary objectives which are strategic objectives which should combine to ensure the achievement of the overall corporate objective.

(a) For example, if a company sets itself an objective of growth in profits, as its primary aim, it will then have to develop *strategies* by which this primary objective can be achieved. An objective must then be set for each individual strategy, and so many secondary objectives may simply be targets by which the success of a strategy can be measured. A strategy is a course of action, specifying the resources required to achieve a given objective.

(b) Secondary objectives might then be concerned with sales growth, continual technological innovation, customer service, product quality, efficient resource management (eg labour productivity) or reducing the company's reliance on debt capital etc.

3.2 The precision of objectives

Operational goals can be expressed as objectives, which are *closed* in the sense that they can be achieved at some future time; other objectives are *open* because they can never be achieved and will always persist. If someone says his aim is to make more money, he can always make more money no matter how much money he makes, even though, for any given time period, an amount of money can always be specified.

Many writers have argued that goals and objectives are not worthwhile unless they are capable of being measured and achieved, that is unless they are closed. This is the thinking behind the development of the 'SMART' acronym which argues that an objective is only genuine if it is Specific (and Stretching), Measurable, Attainable, Realistic and Time-bounded. An alternative acronym, created by management consultant *Ted Johns*, is that an acceptable objective should satisfy the 'TRAMPS' criteria.

- *Time-bounded* – there should be a deadline.

- *Result-oriented* – objectives should be concentrated within the organisation's (or the individual's) key tasks or key performance areas, ie those responsibilities which genuinely make an added-value difference; objectives are far less productive if they deal with inputs (like personal efficiency).

- *Achievable* – an objective should be seen to be within the grasp: if it is viewed as unattainable, then nobody will make the effort.

- *Measurable* – there must be some quantifiable yardstick for attainment (though one aspect of this yardstick may well be the delivery deadline, ie the time boundary).

- *Precise* – all objectives should deal with some managcable feature of the organisation or the individual.

- *Stretching* – achieving objectives should require positive effort and willpower, so that the result evokes a conscious sense of triumph and accomplishment.

By contrast, there are three main arguments against the position that the only meaningful goals are operational goals, expressed as measurable objectives.

(a) Operational goals which remain *open objectives can be just as helpful as closed objectives*. For example, a mission statement – which is often expressed in the form of an open objective – can be a very important influence on strategy. It may concentrate a manager's perception on the needs of his customers and on the professionalism of his service; it may also set the boundaries within which the organisation may develop. When *SmithKline Beecham* produced a mission statement which focused on healthcare, it wanted to develop its core strategic strengths, rather than dissipate its efforts across a whole repertoire of unrelated products which were a legacy of the days when it was the strategic wisdom to diversify and become a conglomerate: it has therefore sold *Brylcreem*, *Yardley* perfumes, *Uhu* solvents, and so forth. By contrast, *Eastern Electricity plc* has renamed itself *Eastern Group* and produced a mission statement which talks about *energy* as the core business rather than electricity – this enables it strategically to attack energy-related activities concerned, for example, with gas and oil.

(b) *Some goals are important but difficult to quantify or express in measurable terms.* A goal may be 'to become a leader in technology': it is a relevant aim, for some organisations, but could become absurd if it had to be expressed in a measurable way. Much the same could be said about 'objectives' or goals in the field of business ethics and corporate values.

(c) *Many highly successful organisations do not have precise, explicit objectives* – or, if they do, they keep very quiet about them. In the USA, *Quinn* has found that

'successful executives 'announced' relatively few goals to their organisation. These few were frequently broad and general, and only rarely were they quantitative or measurably precise.'

Quantified objectives tend not to be generated or announced for four reasons.

(i)   Their effect could be to over-centralise the organisation.

(ii)   Declared objectives could become a focus for opposition from outside the organisation, or even from within.

(iii) Once an objective has been set, it can be very difficult to change, especially if it appears to be comprehensively quantified.

(iv)   There is a risk that competitors will get to know too much about the intentions of the organisation.

Activity 5   **(10 minutes)**

Despite the above, there are times when objectives have to be specific, irrespective of whether quantified objectives are perceived as valuable in general terms. Can you think of any organisational scenarios where the production of specific, TRAMPS-type objectives would not only be desirable, but could even be essential?

Trade-off between objectives

When there are several key objectives, some might be achieved only at the expense of others. For example, a company's objective of achieving good profits and profit growth might have adverse consequences for, say, the quality of the firm's product if the profits are achieved by cutting corners or using cheaper substandard materials. Attempts to achieve good product quality, or to improve market share (eg by cutting prices), might call for some sacrifice of profits.

There will be a trade-off between objectives when strategies are formulated, and a choice will have to be made. For example, there might be a choice between the following two options.

Option A   15% sales growth, 10% profit growth, and reduced product quality and customer satisfaction.

Option B   8% sales growth, 5% profit growth, and maintenance of high product quality/customer satisfaction.

If the firm chose option B in preference to option A, it would be trading off sales growth and profit growth for better product quality and customer satisfaction. (Note that the long-term effect of reduced quality has not been considered.)

3.3   Long-term and short-term objectives

Objectives may be long-term and short-term.

(a)   A company that is suffering from a recession in its core industries and making losses in the short term might continue to have a primary objective in the long term of achieving a steady growth in earnings or profits, but in the short term, its primary objective might switch to survival.

(b)   Secondary objectives will range from short-term to long-term. Planners will formulate secondary objectives within the guidelines set by the primary objective, after selecting strategies for achieving the primary objective.

For example, a company's primary objective might be to increase its profits from £3m to £5m in the next five years. Strategies for achieving the objective might be selected to include the following.

(a)   Increasing profitability in the next twelve months by cutting expenditure.

(b)   Increasing export sales over the next three years.

(c)   Developing a successful new product for the domestic market within five years.

Secondary objectives might then be re-assessed to include the following.

(a)   Improve manpower productivity by 10% within twelve months.

(b)   Improving customer service in export markets with the objective of doubling the number of overseas sales outlets in selected countries within the next three years.

(c)   Investing more in product-market research and development, with the objective of bringing at least three new products to the market within five years.

3.4   Conflict

As has been indicated, there are conflicts between different types of goals (eg long term vs short term), and between the goals of different interest groups within the organisation. The way in which they dealt with is by no means as rational as might appear. In addition to rational analysis, there might be four ways of dealing with goal conflict.

(a)   *Bargaining*. Managers with different goals will compete and will form alliances with other managers to achieve their goals.

(b) *Satisficing.* Organisations do not aim to maximise performance in one area if this leads to poor performance elsewhere. Rather they will accept satisfactory, if not excellent, performance in a number of areas.

(c) *Sequential attention.* Goals are dealt with one by one, as it were, in a sequence.

(d) *Priority setting.* Certain goals get priority over others. This is determined by senior managers, but there are quite complicated systems to link goals and strategies according to certain criteria.

4 Stakeholders' goals and objectives

Johnson and Scholes (Exploring Corporate Strategy) argue that although 'economic' objectives are an important influence on strategy formulation, choices are made 'within the cultural and political realities of the organisation.'

The development of objectives and the strategies can therefore be seen as the result of the following.

- The organisation's mission
- The power and influence of stakeholder groups
- Economic requirements
- Social responsibilities of the organisation
- General and environmental influences

4.1 Stakeholders and constituents

There is a variety of different groups or individuals whose interests are directly affected by the activities of a firm. These groups or individuals are referred to as *stakeholders* in the firms.

It is useful to be aware of a variety of stakeholders and their objectives. The following list is not comprehensive.

(a) *Internal stakeholders* include *management and employees;* they make a variety of demands on the organisation

  (i) Appropriate remuneration
  (ii) Job security
  (iii) Good conditions of work
  (iv) Job satisfaction
  (v) Providing medical care for employees and their families
  (vi) Providing a good pension scheme
  (vii) Training and career development

(b) *Connected stakeholders* include the following.

  (i) *Shareholders,* whose interests include profitability, return on their investment, stable and growing dividends.

  (ii) *Customers,* whose interests include products at the right quality and price.

  (iii) *Bankers and financiers* are interested in the overall profitability of the relationship with their client and the security of loans they advance (ie that the company will be able to repay principal and interest).

  (iv) *Suppliers* and other *creditors* are interested in selling goods and services and ensuring that they *get paid.*

(c)   *External stakeholder groups* – the government, local authorities, pressure groups, the community at large, professional bodies – are likely to have quite diverse objectives and have a varying ability to ensure that the company meets them.

   (i)   The *government* has many interests.

      (1)   Tax revenue (corporation tax, VAT) or other revenue (in the case of the public sector)

      (2)   Compliance with legislation (eg on health and safety)

      (3)   Statistics

      (4)   Regional development (as companies, all employers and wealth creators)

   (ii)   *Local authorities* are also interested, because companies can bring local employment and can affect the local environment (eg by increasing road traffic).

   (iii)   *Professional bodies* are interested to ensure that members who work for companies comply with professional ethics and standards.

   (iv)   The *public* generally and pressure groups in particular will be interested in such matters as safety, pollution and investment.

   (v)   *Customers and suppliers* have an interest in the continued success of the organisation, and in its business practices.

How stakeholders relate to the management of the company depends very much on what type of stakeholder they are – internal, connected or external – and on the level in the management hierarchy at which they are able to apply pressure. Clearly a company's management will respond differently to the demands of, say, its shareholders and the community at large.

The way in which the relationship between company and stakeholders is conducted is a function of the character of the relationship, the parties' relative bargaining strength and the philosophy underlying each party's objectives.

		Stakeholders' bargaining strength		
Weak				Strong

Company's conduct of relation-ship	Command/ dictated by company	Consultation and consideration of stakeholders' views	Negotiation	Participation and acceptance of stakeholders' views	Democratic voting by stakeholders	Command/ dictated by stakeholders

In the long run, managers are supposed to run a business on the behalf of *shareholders*. The most obvious example of when other shakeholders become more powerful is when *bankers* and/or other *creditors* call in an *administrator* or *receiver* if they have not been paid, and the activities of the company are directed towards repaying those debts.

NOTES

EXAMPLE: BRITISH AIRWAYS

In 1989, British Airways' publicity indicated the following corporate goals.

(a)   Safety and security
(b)   Strong and consistent financial performance
(c)   Global reach
(d)   Superior services
(e)   Good value for money
(f)   Healthy working environment
(g)   Good neighbourliness

'Overall, our aim is to be the best and most successful company in the airline industry.'

(1)   BA's success is measured according to its standing in comparison with other airlines. BA was one of the industry's few profit-makers shortly after the Gulf War: although it may not top all league tables, quality of service has improved massively. It has operated effectively over a large number of its goals, in comparison with competitors.

(2)   BA has also achieved consistent performance over a variety of its goals. Had it plunged into loss, there would be some doubts about its effectiveness.

Chapter roundup

- Mission describes an organisation's basic function in society, in terms of the products and services it produces for its clients.

- Mission can also act as a system of values, which helps bind individuals to the organisation's objectives.

- Mission may be embodied in a mission statement.

- The mission has to be translated into actual business practice. Individual goals and objectives covering the various parts of the business and the various client groups of the business.

- Although in practice people use the words goal and objective interchangeably, it is useful to keep in mind the difference between those goals which can be expressed as quantitative objectives and those which cannot.

- An organisation has many goals and objectives. A business has profitability as an overriding goal. However a number of different stakeholders groups have different expectations of the business.

Quick quiz

1   What are two views of the role of mission in organisations?

2   What might you find in a typical mission statement?

3   What is the distinction sometimes drawn between goals and objectives?

4   What aspects of corporate effort might objectives relate to?

5   What are the ways of dealing with goal conflict?

6   Draw up a list of external stakeholders.

BPP
PUBLISHING

7   What sort of expectations might employees have of a business?

8   What are the components of a 'good' objective, according to the TRAMPS acronym?

9   What are the differences between 'open' and 'closed' objectives?

10   What are the four reasons for the fact that some organisations deliberately fail to produce (or announce) quantified objectives?

Answers to quick quiz

1   Motivation for employees. Impact on purchaser's decisions.

2   Purpose; strategy; policies and standards of behaviour; values.

3   Objectives are more precise and measurable than goals; goals are overall, generalised targets.

4   Profitability; market standing; productivity; resources; innovation; human resource performance and development; public responsibility.

5   Bargaining; satisficing; sequential attention; priority setting.

6   Government; customers; suppliers; professional bodies; the public.

7   Fair treatment, including pay and conditions; job satisfaction; training and career development; a healthy and safe environment.

8   Time-bounded; result orientated; achievable; measurable; precise; stretching.

9   Closed objectives are achievable targets; open objectives are continuing aspirations.

10   Their centralising effect; their capacity to focus opposition; the difficulty of changing them; and the way they revel the organisation's intentions.

Answers to activities

1   Research has shown that whistle-blowers seldom act purely for personal and financial gain, though they may be paid for information by, say, newspapers and other media sources. More commonly, whistle-blowers may be individuals who experience conflicting missions.

   (a)   An employee's mission to his/her 'clients' or 'customers' (eg a doctor's mission so far as patients are concerned) may be stronger than loyalty to the managerial hierarchy of the organisation, especially if the whistle-blower disagrees with management decisions.

   (b)   An employee's code of professional ethics (eg for accountants or solicitors) may take precedence over commitment to the corporate culture.

2   Example 1 was the mission statement of Maxwell Communications plc, headed by the late fraudster, Robert Maxwell. As Timothy R V Foster points out (101 Great Mission Statements, 1993) you would never have expected Maxwell Communications plc to produce a mission statement like this:

      'We aim, through the consistent and creative application of double dealing, contempt, bullying, lying, subterfuge, connivance, theft and fraud, to cheat our investors, our employees, our pensioners, our suppliers and other business partners and the regulatory bodies of the countries where we choose to operate, or die in the attempt!'

Example 2 is actually the mission statement for North-West Water, but could equally well fit many other organisations, so bland and vacuous are its sentiments. As Martin Vander Weyer writes ('Mission improvable', Management Today, September 1994), 'it is hard to imagine the typical shareholder or customer leaping out of this bath shouting, "Eureka, so that's what they're up to". The managers (there and elsewhere) should go back to the whiteboard and come up with something original, memorable and inspiring, which helps them all to understand the uniqueness of their company and to agree on where it is going.'

3   Of course, readers may generate their own evaluations of the four mission statements presented as Activity 3. In our view, however, the Glaxo sentence is stylistically inelegant and almost unreadable; it is virtually impossible to imagine anyone (let alone Glaxo employees) being able to reproduce it, or even to capture its essence, from memory. IBM (UK)'s mission, which actually dates from 1990, sounds more like a set of idealistic business practices than a proposition about the nature of IBM's business – indeed, the statement says nothing about that at all.

Matsushita's mission is completely non-specific and gives no strategic guidance whatsoever: the company could do whatever it liked and still claim that it was fulfilling the precepts of its mission statement, although we are struck by the materialistic flavour of Matsushita's apparent claim that 'happiness' is associated with 'affluence'. Also questionable is the degree to which Matsushita's business activities are genuinely associated with 'life's necessities'.

'Encircle Caterpillar', from Komatsu, sounds more like a vision than a mission. In that sense it is like Fuji's 'Kill Kodak'. However, the message is simple, captivating, memorable, single-minded and provides a straightforward focus for strategic direction.

We like Apple Computer's desire to create friendly, understandable and useable computers. The company need not have wrapped it up in quite so many words, but their sentiments are admirable, the mission clear, and the words not strangulated with syntactical challenge.

4   All the diarist's 'long-range goals' could legitimately be described as pious hopes rather than specific aspirations: readers could be forgiven for thinking it unlikely that the diarist would fulfil any of these 'goals' in reality. The 'immediate' goals are reminders of current priorities but could be re-phrased as objectives if 'Pick up pattern at Hilda's' became 'Collect pattern from Hilda's by Friday evening and complete the knitted sweater by the end of January'.

'Health' and 'money' could be translated into quantifiable, time-bounded objectives, with 'health' measured by body-weight (with a suitable target for reduction), blood pressure and so forth, or 'money' reflected in precise salary levels.

5   There are times when management's attention has to be concentrated on a limited number of essential requirements, in moments of crisis or of major strategic transition (eg a turnround situation or the need to assimilate an acquired organisation). If the choice is between going out of business or survival, then there is no room for latitude through vaguely stated requirements.

For example, a company which is well established in a mature market may learn that an impending technological advance, developed elsewhere, is likely to take over this market within two to three years. The very existence of the firm is challenged – and yet the time available to do anything about it is short. In these circumstances, the sole objective for the firm will be survival.

- If overheads have to be pruned to maintain short-term viability, then so be it – even if morale has to fall in the process.

- If board members who disagree or who are unable to commit themselves to the new policy have to go, then so be it – even if skilled managers are lost.

- If reduced profit margins have to be accepted as the price for getting established in a new market, then so be it.

Further question practice

Now try the following practice questions at the end of this text

Multiple choice questions: **8 to 12**

Exam style question: **2**

Chapter 3 :
ORGANISATIONAL GROWTH

Introduction

Most of the literature about organisations is unrealistic because it explains how organisations (or the people in them) *should* behave, rather than how they actually *do* behave. Reading this literature would encourage you to believe that, for example, individual employees may collaborate selflessly, in order to translate the organisation's mission into a palpable reality. When you start work, you may observe that life does not match the ideals portrayed by these theorists. Why? Is the organisation employing you dysfunctional in some way? Should you resign and search for the organisation that matches your ideals?

In reality most organisations are made up of people who are motivated principally by self-interest. If you analyse your own motives, you will doubtless find that they too are characterised by self-interest. You want a job which will satisfy *your* needs and aspirations; joining an organisation is an accepted means for accomplishing this goal. The organisation is more likely to secure *your* loyalty and commitment (to its mission, vision and values) if you believe that the organisation will reciprocate by supplying you with benefits of some kind.

Much of this chapter is concerned with the implications of individual self-interest for the dynamics of organisational life. Curiously, such self-interest is seldom articulated openly, but is hidden behind protestations about concern for employees and customers and, indeed, for the organisation as a personalised entity. *Mintzberg* shows the extent to which self-interest can acquire respectability: thus managers favour organisational growth allegedly because it strengthens the organisation, but principally because growth favours managerial careers much more than does stagnation or (even worse) decline. *Parkinson's* more anecdotal arguments are convincing simply because they are resonant with the experiences of practising managers. The accuracy of Parkinson's insights may have itself contributed to the backlash against bureaucracy exemplified by downsizing, delayering and empowerment, but it is significant that these trends are producing their own counter-reaction.

Even if you may never have *worked* in an organisation before, as a paid employee, you are likely to have inhabited organisations like school and university/college. In your experience are the employees of such establishments continually dedicated to corporate goals? Or is their behaviour more consistent with the pursuit and defence of individual and group/team/departmental interests?

In this chapter you will learn about these things.

(a)   The importance of system goals, like survival, in activating the behaviour of people in organisations and as a (partial) explanation for conflicts between individuals and groups within organisations

(b)   Organisational life-cycle models and their application to actual corporate scenarios

(c)   The empirical relevance of the organisational life-cycle model as an analytical tool

(d)   The diseconomies of scale associated with large organisations

(e)   Typical mechanisms for overcoming the disadvantages of large organisational size while, preferably, retaining the more significant benefits

1   SUBVERTING MISSION

We have talked about mission, objectives and goals in general terms, as if objectives necessarily were devised to support an organisation's mission. In practice, however, the stakeholder view should indicate to you that it is very easy for mission to be ignored or adhered to in the letter rather than in the spirit, or to degenerate into a PR-driven gloss on the organisation's activities.

Mintzberg provides a useful analysis of the sorts of goals that organisations, and people in them, pursue. We identified these in a previous chapter.

(a)   *Ideological goals* usually focus on the organisation's mission. They are shared sets of beliefs and values. (In a sense, a job is a vocation.)

(b)   *Formal goals* are imposed by a dominant individual or group (eg shareholders). People work to attain these goals, as a means to their personal goals. (In other words, you do what your boss tells you to in order to earn a wage to support your family, for example.)

(c)   *Shared personal goals*. Individuals reach a consensus about what they want out of an organisation (eg a group of academics who decide they want to pursue research).

(d)   *Individual personal goals* – goals that are unique to the individual that holds them (for example the desire to retire at 45).

(e)   *System goals*. These are goals which derive from the organisation's existence as an organisation, independent of mission.

A mission is all very well providing it is meaningful.

(a)   The inherent danger of *mission* is that it will not be implemented. Mintzberg writes

'organisations, too, can have trouble operationalising their lofty goals, with the result that their official goals – what they claim to be their goals – often do not correspond with the end they actually seem to pursue. Sometimes, of course, the official goals are merely for public consumption, not for internal decision making'.

(b)   Remember too, Mintzberg's quotation from *Warringer* who said that the official statements of organisational purpose must be considered as

'fictions produced by an organisation to account for, explain, or rationalise its existence to particular audiences.'

Mintzberg argues that *systems goals* are those which organisations as *systems* pursue. These goals have a habit of subverting mission, by making mission subordinate to these goals. *Systems goals* include the following.

(a)   *Survival*. Individuals benefit from the organisation's existence (as their employer, for their social life), irrespective of what the organisation actually does. People invest time and effort in an organisation: consequently its demise is more than simply *economic* failure for the people that work for it.

Organisations are also places where people build careers. There is a strong incentive for an organisation to survive simply because it keeps its managers in work. Hence the purchase, say, by a tobacco company of an insurance company to safeguard the future of the organisation. Shareholders could simply have switched investments.

(b) *Efficiency*. This is the greatest benefit for a given cost. However, as *Drucker* first pointed out, an organisation can be efficient (doing things well) without being effective (doing the right things). Effectiveness means concentrating on the things that product benefits: things like customers, innovation and people. Efficiency takes precedence over effectiveness according to Mintzberg, because it is easier to measure *costs* than *benefits*, and because it is harder to measure social costs and benefits than economic costs and benefits.

(c) *Control*. This is the attempt by organisations 'to exercise some control over their own environments'. Examples of control are vertical integration to control supply, and diversification to reduce uncertainty.

(d) *Growth*. Managers benefit directly from growth, in terms of salaries and status. 'Growth is the natural goal of the manager' as it may be seen as reducing vulnerability to the environment and to other organisations, although in practice this is not always true.

Mintzberg notes that these goals are interrelated. Growth can bring efficiency, for example.

How do these relate to mission? Mission can – some argue *should* – be a *primary* goal (in Mintzberg's definition) of an organisation. This will be the case in the following circumstances.

(a) Powerful persons or groups with power within the organisation (eg the owner) can impose their idea of the mission on others.

(b) A professional organisation (eg a hospital) might pursue mission as part of the professional ethics of the organisation's members.

(c) The organisation with a strong ideology (eg a religious sect) is missionary. Perhaps *Campbell, Devine and Young* are trying to infuse organisations with this particular sense of mission.

Mintzberg believes that mission is often displaced by the systems goals identified above.

(a) Historically, *growth* has been favoured by professional managers, who have taken over the running of organisations from the owners. Managers proliferated in administration. *Growth favours careers*. Management is a skill in its own right.

(b) Technical experts (eg work study analysts) are less concerned with mission than *exercising their specialisation* for whoever is interested. They have less interest in the survival of the organisation than do line managers.

Activity 1 (10 minutes)

The Octagon company is a firm which employs about 150 managers and staff. It has recently obtained a stock market listing. Its business is the supply of unusual high quality fabrics in small quantities to fashion designers in London. There is no likely competition. The Managing Director feels that he needs a Director of Information Systems; one is appointed to the Board. About six months into his appointment, the new director of information systems produces a plan to the board, which he has largely dreamed up from scratch. 'If we are to grow,' he says, 'we'll need new systems.'

'Grow where? Why?' says the MD.

Discuss.

It is also worth noting the danger of excessive adherence to a particular goal or set of goals even when there is evidence to suggest that they are unattainable or undesirable. Goals like all other aspects of organisational behaviour should be reassessed and revised on a regular basis.

The reason why we have discussed these issues here is that the next section discusses organisation evolution: the driving forces behind it are more than just *business* imperatives.

2 MODELS OF GROWTH AND DEVELOPMENT

Organisations grow in a number of ways.

- Sales revenue (a growth in the market served)
- Profitability (in absolute terms, and as a return on capital)
- Number of goods or services sold
- Number of outlets or sites
- Number of employees
- Number of countries in which the organisation has a presence

Growth is pursued for a number of reasons.

(a) It is an organisation's system goal, as described in section 1 above. In other words, it maintains management careers.

(b) There is a genuine and increasing demand for the products and services offered at the price offered. For example, there is likely to be a growth in the number of UK hospitals specialising in geriatric illnesses, simply because the number of elderly people in the population is expected to rise.

(c) Growth is occasionally necessary for an organisation to compete effectively. For example, economies of scale can arise from producing in bulk, as high fixed costs can be spread over more units of output.

(d) Companies take over competitors, suppliers and customers in order to gain *control over resources*, or the *value added* in the production processes.

Organisational growth in size can occur by *acquisition* or *organically* (ie growth generated by an expansion of the organisation's activities). It is to organic growth that we shall now turn. Some commentators argue that organisations have a life-cycle. In other words, they are born, they grow and die. Before we discuss whether this is a valid way of looking at organisations at all, in principle or empirically, let us examine two of the models upon which this is based.

The *organisation life cycle model* was suggested by Greiner. It assumes that, as an organisation ages, it grows in size, measured, perhaps, by the number of employees and diversity of its activities. This growth is characterised by a number of discrete phases. Each phase is characterised by a distinctive factor that directs the organisation's growth and a crisis, through which the organisation must pass before achieving the next phase.

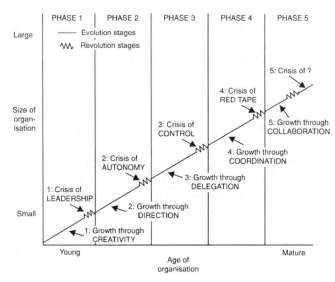

Phase 1. The organisation is small, and is managed in personal and informal ways. The founders of the business are actively involved in the operation. Apple Computers, for example, started up in a garage. However, sooner or later there comes a need for distinct management skills, relating less to products and marketing issues and more to co-ordination of the organisation's activities. This is a *crisis of leadership*.

Phase 2. Clear direction is provided by *professionalising* the management. At the same time, there are more employees. Their initial enthusiasm might be tempered by loss of autonomy and the growth of hierarchy. The problem that arises is that of delegation. The top finds it harder and harder to keep in detailed control as there are too many activities, and it is easy lose a sense of the wider picture. Employees resent the lack of initiative and their performance falters. There is a *crisis of autonomy*.

Phase 3. The response to the problems of Phase 2 is *delegation*. This has the advantage of decentralising decision-making and giving confidence to junior managers. However, this in itself leads to additional problems of co-ordination and control. Over-delegation can result in different departments acting sub-optimally. There is a *crisis of control*.

Phase 4. The addition of internal systems, procedures and so forth aims to ensure co-ordination of activities and optimal use of resources. This increased complexity results in a *crisis of red tape*.

Phase 5. The crisis of red tape is resolved by increased *informal collaboration*. Control is cultural rather than formal. People participate in teams. Greiner thinks that this growth stage may lead to a crisis of psychological saturation, in which all become exhausted by teamwork. He postulates a sixth growth phase involving a dual organisation: a *habit structure* for daily work routines and a *reflective structure* for stimulating new perspectives and personal enrichment.

Another, simpler version of the organisational life cycle approach is the Sigmoid Curve, discussed at length in *Charles Handy's The Empty Raincoat*. The Sigmoid Curve (itself a variant of the product life cycle curve) is said to reflect not only a pattern applicable to organisations, but also the birth-growth-maturity-decline phases through which individual human beings pass.

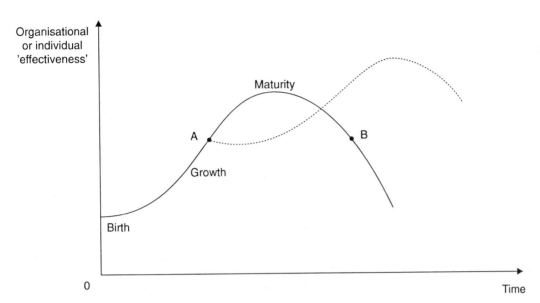

Corporate (or individual) readiness to change and adapt often only occurs at point B on the Sigmoid Curve, when the entity is already in crisis through sustained losses (if it is an organisation) or enforced redundancy and 'early retirement' (if an individual). Rare is the organisation/individual who begins to prepare for change at point A, while still on the upward growth phase in the cycle – yet that is exactly what is necessary nowadays so that, from point A, another Sigmoid Curve can begin – and survival/prosperity becomes more probable.

2.1   Applications of organisational life cycle models

Undoubtedly the general frameworks produced by Greiner and Handy do have resonance with our experience of organisations and individuals. To deal with the latter first, many people are taken by surprise when made redundant because they have not kept their skills and knowledge up to date with changing requirements.

Equally, organisations can be very resistant to any changes suggested while they are still in the growth phase of the Sigmoid Curve, their collective attitude perhaps being epitomised by the colloquial phrase, 'If it ain't broke, don't fix it'. When *Paul Chambers* was head of *ICI* in the 1970s, he proposed organisational changes which were rejected by the ICI board at a time when the company was still enjoying impressive profits; *John Harvey-Jones* was able to implement similar changes in the 1980s when ICI, in effect, was at point B in the Sigmoid Curve, having registered its first losses for many years.

2.2   Criticisms of organisation life cycle models

The models above refer to organisational growth punctuated by crisis. A different approach adopted by *Quinn* was *logical incrementalism*. This means that businesses make small adjustments, building consistently on what they have, and adapting to the environment. Change is continuous and gradual. This alternative model was based, like Greiner's, on a study of real organisations.

Another criticism is based on the fact that not all organisations are founded by a visionary controlling entrepreneur, selling a product or service.

(a)   A new organisation can be formed from the merger of two existing ones.

(b)   Two or more companies might collaborate *jointly* on a joint venture. The *Airbus* project, for example, did not start as a small business, but as a result of co-operation between governments and existing companies.

(c)   New organisations are created by existing ones and have a substantial complement of staff.

The models also combine too many issues: organisation structure, organisation culture, product/market scope, leadership and management style.

It is possible to combine an obsession with procedures and efficiency (bureaucracy) with a strong sense of mission. Hospitals depend on the devotion and professionalism of staff – but clinical procedures *have* to be adhered to.

The growth of the business can be curtailed by the growth of competition. In other words, a business can be hemmed in, but still survive.

A business can grow quickly in some aspects but not in others. The UK niche retailers of the 1980s (eg those specialising in ties or socks) expanded in terms of the number of sites, locations, employees, and growth, but the product/market scope was restricted.

Although both the Greiner model and the Sigmoid Curve may be conceptually attractive, neither is easily quantifiable nor empirically verifiable. So, even if it can be agreed that organisations (and/or individuals) pass through birth-growth-maturity-decline phases, there is little or no consensus on the precise point at which each phase begins or ends. Organisations often speak glibly about being in a mature market, but this is as likely to be a consequence of complacency, inertia and marketing myopia as it is to be a product of genuine saturation. Looked at from the viewpoint of individuals, it is self-evident that maturity (both physiological and psychological) does not begin at a fixed point and does not last for a fixed amount of time: given that the same is true for organisations, then it can be hard to see the practical benefits to be derived from an organisational life cycle approach.

Activity 2   **(10 minutes)**

Heifetz and Kyung are partners in a business that makes violins and other stringed musical instruments. They are based in a small workshop in Stoke Newington, north London. They are both experts at their craft. They believe that their future is rosy: Kyung, in particular, realises that, as western classical music becomes popular in China, Japan and other Asian countries, demand for instruments will pick up.

Although there is enough demand in the UK to keep them going, both want to expand the business. Kyung asks her brother, who lives in Hong Kong, to help them market their products to Asian orchestras and violinists. With the recent trade liberalisation involved in the GATT agreement, they assume that exporting will be easy. They also hire and train three more skilled instrument-makers. Kyung's brother has sent them a number of official forms relating to customs, import and export, and some ideas as to agents.

Required

What issues relating to Greiner's life cycle model are raised by this scenario?

---

3   LARGE ORGANISATIONS

3.1   Bureaucracy

To a layman, the word *bureaucracy* has unpleasant associations; however *Weber* was inclined to regard bureaucracy as the ideal form of organisation, *'from a purely technical point of view, capable of attaining the highest degree of efficiency and is in this sense formally the most rational means of carrying out imperative control over human beings.'*

It is wrong to equate bureaucracy with large organisations, because the features of bureaucracy can be found in some small and medium-sized organisations too. Nevertheless, many (if not all) large organisations are bureaucratic, and it will be useful to start by summarising the characteristics of bureaucracy. (For more details go back to Chapter 1.)

(a) *Hierarchy*. Each lower office is under the control and supervision of a higher one.

(b) *Specialisation and training:* there is a high degree of specialisation of labour.

(c) *Impersonal nature:* employees work full time within the impersonal rules and regulations.

(d) *Professional nature of employment:* an organisation exists before it is filled with people.

(e) *Rationality*. The 'jurisdictional areas' of the organisation are determined rationally.

(f) *Uniformity* in the performance of tasks is expected.

(g) Officials are *technically competent*.

(h) *Stability*. The reward for employees who do their jobs well is stability.

A bureaucratic organisation structure can be both efficient and effective, but there is a tendency, especially in large organisations, for inefficiencies to creep in. A major problem with bureaucracy is its limited ability to deal with changing circumstances.

3.2 The problems of large organisations

A large organisation is one which has a large amount of resources at its disposal and so, typically, employs a lot of people. The problems of large organisations stem mainly from the difficulties of getting a lot of people to work well together. How can large numbers of people share the work that has to be done, and how can their work be properly planned, co-ordinated and controlled?

These problems are discussed elsewhere in this text, but it will be useful here to draw them together.

(a) *Organisation structure*

(i) Sharing out tasks and responsibilities. Who does what?

(ii) How much specialisation/functionalisation should there be?

(iii) What span of control is suitable? And so how tall/flat will the organisation be? There is a tendency for the management hierarchy to develop too many levels. The more management levels there are, the greater the problem of communication between top and bottom, and the greater the problems of control and direction by management at the top.

(iv) To what extent should authority be delegated? How much centralisation/ decentralisation should there be? Can junior/middle managers be trusted to exercise discretion and make decisions? How should managers be trained and developed?

(b) *Planning and control*

    (i) How should the organisation identify its objectives and set targets for achievement? In the case of large diversified 'conglomerate' corporations, can the organisation have a major objective other than a financial one (eg profit maximisation)?

    (ii) Developing formal management information systems to enable managers to plan and control properly. Communication problems.

    (iii) The problem of making managers accountable, monitoring performance and setting up effective control systems.

    (iv) The difficulties of co-ordinating the efforts of managers: problems of conflict (such as interdepartmental rivalries).

    (v) Difficulties of setting up a system of rewards that is directly linked to performance appraisal and the achievement of objectives.

(c) *Adapting to change*

Large organisations might be slow to adapt to change because of a bureaucratic system of operating and decision-making that stifles ideas for innovation.

(d) *The organisational multiplier*

Hicks and Graves suggest that an addition to personnel in one part of an organisation will spark off a series of additions to personnel (or other resources) throughout the organisation. One extra manager, for example, will create extra volumes of reports and letters (which must be read and answered), attend meetings (someone else is required to meet with him) and require services from the payroll office, personnel office, and so on.

'*The organisational multiplier is that factor by which a primary change in a particular sector of the organisation is multiplied to determine the total change in the whole organisation.*'

In its extreme form, an organisation might grow and multiply by 'feeding on itself', so adding nothing to corporate objectives and creating no extra external output. Hicks and Graves cited instances of fundraising organisations which spent 90% of the money they collected on their own internal administration. They suggested that wasteful multiplication is more likely to occur in non-profit making organisations and large organisations; that it is often overlooked; and that it is rarely costed when the decision to increase personnel is taken.

The organisational multiplier is an example of a system goal.

(e) *Motivation*

    (i) It is difficult for individuals to identify themselves with the objectives of a large organisation. The organisation's objectives and their personal objectives will differ.

    (ii) Difficulties for individuals to see how their efforts contribute to achieving the organisation's objectives (due to narrow specialisation of jobs etc).

    (iii) Possible problems in getting employees to enjoy working in a large organisation, where a bureaucratic culture predominates.

(iv)   Decision-making might be slow, with managers not allowed the authority and discretion they would like.

As an organisation grows it will also often diversify its range of products and services: this may cause additional management problems. It becomes difficult, if not impossible, for management to integrate all of the organisation under a common objective and within a single 'management philosophy' and 'organisation spirit'. The different parts of the organisation will not complement each other, and might tend to pull the organisation in different directions. Drucker argued that

'this danger is particularly great in the business that originated in a common technology, such as chemistry or electrical engineering. As the technology unfolds, it creates more and more diversified products with different markets, different objectives for innovation and ultimately even with different technologies ... The point may be reached where objectives and principles that fit one business (or group of businesses) endanger another.'

The sheer size of an organisation provides both top management and more junior management with problems of co-ordination, planning, effective control and therefore the achievement of economies of scale and versatility in the range of products and services offered. For example, a junior manager might find the organisation so large that he or she has relatively little influence. Decisions which he or she regards as important must be continually referred up the line to superiors for interdepartmental consultations. At the same time, the top management might find the organisation so large and complex to understand, and changes in policy and procedures so difficult and time-consuming to implement, that they also feel unable to give direction to the organisation. The organisation is therefore a monster which operates of its own accord, with neither senior nor junior managers able to manage it effectively.

In a large organisation, many of the specialised tasks for junior functional managers, and many day-to-day tasks of junior operational management are routine and boring. Even middle management might be frustrated by the restrictions on their authority, the impersonal nature of their organisation, the inability to earn a just reward for their special efforts (owing to the standardisation of pay and promotion procedures) and the lack of information about aspects of the organisation which should influence their work. These problems are likely to result in poor motivation amongst managers; consequently, poor motivation amongst their junior staff; and a reluctance to accept responsibility.

3.3   Large organisations and the management of change

The issue of change-management in bureaucratic systems has already been discussed briefly in Chapter 1. Here the issue is amplified because of its powerful relevance to the turbulent world in which we now operate.

According to *Crozier* (*The Bureaucratic Phenomenon*), much organisational change is in practice prompted by the need to rectify faults which have come to light through the constant feedback of information from, say, suppliers, customers or environmental analysis. In some organisations this process functions efficiently (or relatively so). In large organisations – especially bureaucracies – the feedback system of error-information-correction does not function well, so there cannot be any quick readjustment of programmes of action in the light of mistakes.

On the contrary, if a bureaucratic rule seems to be inadequate in dealing with a particular case, this does not generate pressure to abandon the rule but rather initiates efforts to make the rule, in Crozier's phrase, 'more complete, more precise, and more binding'.

A principal cause for this effect is the fact that bureaucracies are, by definition, highly centralised. Change could be accomplished in a gradual but constant way if decisions about changes could be made by officials or managers located sufficiently near to the operating levels of the organisations. But a bureaucratic system does not allow for such initiative at the lower echelons; decisions must be made where power is located, at the top. This makes a *permanent adjustment* policy impracticable, if only because failures in upward communication systems prevent advance warnings from getting to the top.

Even when top managers do hear of a situation which appears to require alteration, they will have difficulty in making the necessary decisions because of the accumulated backlog of other impersonal rules which require amendment. This means that

'a bureaucratic system will resist change as long as it can; it will move only when serious dysfunctions develop and no other alternatives remain'

– in other words, when it has entered the downward (decline) slope of the Sigmoid Curve.

The position is further complicated by the fact that large organisations and bureaucracies adjust to change in a very peculiar way, by applying a universalistic solution to the whole structure, even to areas where dysfunctions are not seriously felt.

'The essential rhythm prevalent in such organisations,' says Crozier, *'is, therefore, an alternation of long periods of stability with very short periods of crisis and change.'*

In essence, then, change in large organisations is always 'a deeply felt crisis' for three principal reasons.

(a) The inevitable delays before any change can be initiated.

(b) The amplitude of the change when it does occur.

(c) The intense resistance it must overcome because of the personality types involved.

Crozier concludes that

'a bureaucratic system of organisation is not only a system that does not correct its behaviour in view of its errors; it is also too rigid to adjust without crisis to the transformations that the accelerated evolution of industrial society makes more and more imperative.'

3.4 Overcoming the problems of large size

These difficulties of large organisations can, to some extent, be overcome in the following ways.

(a) Decentralisation and delegation of authority. The aim of decentralisation should be to encourage decision-making at lower levels of management 'closer to the action'. Management motivation, but also management efficiency in target-setting, planning and control should improve.

(b) A pay policy which provides for rewards (individual or team bonuses) for outstanding efforts and achievements instead of paying employees on the basis of standardised annual increments which implicitly assume that seniority is equated with effectiveness.

(c) The introduction of comprehensive management and employee information systems which enable all managers and employees:

(i) to understand their planned contribution towards achieving organisational objectives;

(ii) to compare their actual achievements against their targets;

(d) A task structure within the organisation which, through empowerment stimulates employee motivation towards better performance.

(e) The gradual inculcation of an *added-value* culture in the organisation, which will promote two things.

 (i) *Continuous improvement* – doing jobs faster, cheaper, or better (to higher standards of quality as perceived by their customers, whether internal or external)

 (ii) *Change management* – constantly searching for new ways to operate, new services to supply, and so forth

The added-value culture replaces a narrow concern for the execution of job description accountabilities and what *Lupton* has described as 'the apathetic "I-won't-do-more-than-I-have-to" attitude, the empire-building, the sub-optimisation and the rat-racing, which characterise large-scale bureaucracy and the "resistance to change" it exhibits.'

Chapter roundup

- People in organisations pursue a variety of goals, not necessarily related to the product-market circumstances of the business. Systems goals (Mintzberg) derive from an organisation's existence as an organisation. They include survival of the organisation, whereas shareholders can switch investments, growth etc.

- There are many different types of growth. Ideas of growth can be concentrated on financial areas such as profits, market share and so on.

- When the 'business' is growing in sales volume, market presence etc, it is almost inevitable that it will employ more people. These give the organisation the opportunity to broaden the product range.

- Greiner suggests that as organisations grow in terms of the number of their employees, this growth is punctuated by crises of leadership, autonomy, control and red tape respectively, all dealing with the contradictory impulses of control and delegation, to ensure co-ordination of the efforts of individuals.

- Large organisations display a virtually inevitable tendency to become bureaucracies, to a greater or lesser degree.

- Bureaucracies can be efficient and effective, but tend to be conservative, resistant to change and relatively unresponsive to customers and other environmental pressures. Recognising this, many large organisations in recent years have implemented mechanisms to enable them to become more proactive.

Quick quiz

1 What four sorts of goals does Mintzberg suggest that organisations (or the people within them) pursue?

2 Why do managers promote growth?

3 List some types of growth.

4 Greiner suggests that organisational growth through central direction results in a 'crisis of autonomy'. Why?

5   How would you resolve the crisis of red tape?

6   What is logical incrementalism, when applied to organisation growth?

7   What other criticisms can be levelled at organisation growth models?

8   What are the four phases in Handy's Sigmoid Curve?

9   Why do large organisations find it so difficult to cope with change?

10   How can (and do) large organisations in the 1990s seek to offset the problems and disadvantages of large size?

Answers to quick quiz

1   Ideological goals, formal goals, personal goals, system goals

2   Growth favours careers.

3   Growth in profits, revenue, number employed, product range

4   The bureaucracy needed to overcome the crisis of leadership stifles initiative.

5   Increased informal collaboration

6   Growth in small adaptive increments

7   Not all organisations grow from the entrepreneurial model; there are many issues involved in organisational growth; bureaucracy can support mission; growth can be curtailed by competition; growth ca be lopsided, which brings its own problems.

8   Birth, growth, maturity, decline

9   Adherence to procedure and precedent stifles innovative responses.

10   Decentralisation; empowerment; continuous improvement; change management; management and employee information systems; and a reward system that recognises effort and achievement

Answers to activities

1   Growth would expand the Information Director's power and influence, and also the power and influence of other senior managers. The MD is quite happy with the market as it is. Growth is a system goal, in this case.

2   (a)   Although the firm is small, it will very soon need specialist assistance. Exporting *inevitably* involves red tape: and time must be spent dealing with bureaucracies, filling in forms, managing relationship with distributors. Somebody also has to look after the firm's accounts.

     (b)   The business shows characteristics of a pre-bureaucratic stage, but it needs detailed technical expertise as mentioned in (a) above. Operations will become *bureaucratic*, simply to deal with the export side of things.

     Greiner's model cannot predict how every organisation will grow as each faces its own unique problems. But it does indicate some of the issues that arise. You should treat it as a broad generalisation that admits of many exceptions, a tool to help you think about organisations rather than a scientific law.

Further question practice

Now try the following practice questions at the end of this text

Multiple choice questions: **13 to 19**

Exam style question: **3**

Chapter 4 :
INFLUENCES ON ORGANISATIONS

Introduction

No organisation is an island. Competitive organisations have to cope with the ever-present threat of competitive innovation, if not from existing competitors then from newcomers; even so-called monopolies (like public utilities) confront competition from substitute products and services. In addition to these obvious environmental influences, however, organisations operate in the real world of politics, economics, social and technological change: they need to be aware of these factors so that, when planning future strategy, they organise defensive plans to cope with projected negative developments, and equally prepare to capitalise on the opportunities presented by favourable trends.

In section 1, banks and supermarkets are offered as two examples of organisations which experience a particularly symbiotic relationship with their environment – and they happen to be examples which touch us all. There are plenty of others. No organisation can afford to remain indifferent to its context: even once-protected government departments and agencies like the Stationery Office now operate competitively, their new-found sensitivity to the environment being, ironically, a consequence of change in one feature (the political arena) of that environment.

In this chapter you will learn about these things.

(a) How all organisations must manage their relationships with their environment

(b) Undertaking a PEST analysis for an organisation, in order to generate both defensive and proactive strategic proposals

(c) The impact of technological developments on the manufacturing sector

(d) The impact of demographic, social and cultural developments for organisations

(e) How organisations seek to gain some mastery over their environments, especially in the political, economic and technological arenas

(f) The possible organisational implications of the trend towards globalisation

(g) The significance, for an organisation's various stakeholders, of its involvement with the external world, especially so far as employees, customers, suppliers and local communities are involved.

1   THE BUSINESS ENVIRONMENT: PEST FACTORS

The organisation receives inputs from the environment, or from other organisations in the environment. For example, the army is funded through general taxation. A motor manufacturer receives inputs of raw materials. A charity is given donations of cash by concerned members of the general public.

The organisation uses these inputs in some way to produce outputs. These outputs can be goods (eg a car) or services (eg an audit report to customers or clients), or, ultimately, money (eg in taxes to governments or dividend payments to shareholders, wages to employees). These might have some add-on social benefits or disadvantages to society as a whole. The process of converting inputs into outputs is often one of *adding value* in some way. (To a consumer, a manufactured car is of more value than the few tonnes of metal or plastic from which the car was made.)

There are three main aspects to the environment.

- The physical environment
- The social environment
- The competitive environment for commercial organisations

An organisation has a variety of exchanges with its environment.

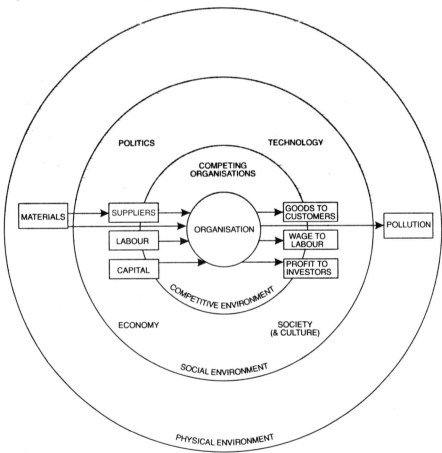

The *physical environment* is particularly important.

    (a)   It is the source of the organisation's raw materials, if it is a manufacturer or in an extractive industry like oil or mining.

    (b)   The organisation's physical distribution (eg siting of warehouses, proximity to ports) can affect its profitability.

Business Basics: Organisational Behaviour

(c)   The organisation's activities may result in the production of waste, or other pollutants, which has to be disposed of. Disposing of waste is likely to be an increasingly complex exercise, as government regulation increases. Moreover, organisations which pollute heavily might have to pay for the privilege.

The social environment includes factors conveniently contained in the acronyms, PEST, SLEPT or STEP.

Politico – legal		Sociological		Sociological
Economic		Legal		Technological
Sociological	or	Economic	or	Economic
Technological		Political		Politico – legal
				Technological

We will shortly deal briefly with each of these factors. But firstly, two examples.

Banks

The banks offer an excellent example of organisations which, with varying degrees of success, steer their strategies through environmental minefields. Because their business is money, they clearly interact with the *economic environment* at both the macro (national and international) and the micro (local branch) levels. If their lending policies are generous, they may fuel economic growth; alternatively they may be accused of unreasonable conservatism towards enthusiastic entrepreneurs. Economic policies and programmes inevitably have political repercussions, with banks and bankers portrayed by interested parties in stereotypical terms; moreover, the political philosophy of the government-in-office at any given moment will impinge upon banks' freedom to act, just as the banks, collectively or separately, will seek to moderate the actions and initiatives of politicians or governments.

Banks, too, have been significantly affected by *technological change*, and have sought to exploit technology in order to reduce their staff numbers (and hence their costs). Historically, banks have been labour intensive; they are now less so, and in the process their level of service to customers has improved. Specifically, the *competitive environment* for banks has been transformed by the arrival of telephone banking, pioneered in 1988 by Midland's First Direct. A few years ago it would have been unthinkable to contemplate a state of affairs in which bank customers would never visit 'their' branch, but it is now apparent that customers often viewed face-to-face encounters with bank staff as roughly approximate to an appointment with the dentist, so they prefer to transact business with the friendly South Yorkshire tones of First Direct's headquarters staff in Leeds. First Direct is already profitable, and expects to have one million account-holders by the year 2000, many of them moving from banks other than the Midland; indeed, because other banks have been forced to move defensively into telephone banking themselves, analysts predict that by 2000 a further five million will have transferred to an alternative telephone banking service: a total of six million in all, or about one-fifth of the market.

The absence of hierarchies and the paraphernalia of branch banking in First Direct – it has a Japanese approach to quality, for instance, with rhetorical slogans pinned to walls and noticeboards – means that it can develop an ethos and an attitude to customers which the traditional banks will struggle to copy. More significantly, there does not seem to be any reason why the closures of conventional branches, among the banks, should not continue or even accelerate, as further technological advances enable more homes to be equipped with networked PCs. It is already the case that overdrafts and loans are determined by computer program rather than by subjective bank staff

68

discretion: this paves the way for the whole relationship between banks and their customers to become much more arms-length (rather than hands-on).

Supermarkets

Another field in which the organisation's interaction with its external environment has been crucial, in the recent past, is food retailing through supermarkets. *Social change*, reflected ultimately in legislative reform, has made it acceptable for supermarkets to open on Sundays; it has also compelled supermarkets to offer a more multicultural range of products. *Political pressures* are inhibiting the continued growth of out-of-town hypermarket centres, with the result that, strategically, further profit increases have to be achieved through other mechanisms like cost-cutting. In this respect technology has much still to offer, such as the ability to read barcodes whilst the purchases still reside in each customer's trolley, thereby reducing the need to employ such large numbers of checkout personnel.

2 POLITICO-LEGAL FACTORS

> **Activity 1** **(5 minutes)**
>
> Identify at least one significant organisation or industry, other than the examples mentioned in Section 1, that has been powerfully affected, either positively or negatively, by *political* and/or *legal* changes in the UK in the recent past.

Organisations operate within a framework of laws, which is very broad in scope. Laws may affect an organisation in the following ways.

(a) How an organisation does its business (eg the law of contract, laws on unfair selling practices and the safety of goods, the law of agency and so on).

(b) How an organisation treats its employees (eg employment law, trade union law).

(c) How an organisation deals with its owners and gives information about its performance (eg the Companies Act).

(d) Criminal law.

Changes in UK and EU law are often predictable. A government will publish a green paper discussing a proposed change in the law, before issuing a white paper and passing a bill through Parliament. Whenever a change in the law is a possibility, and if it is likely to have an impact on what an organisation can do, plans should be formulated about what to do if the change takes place. For example, a law banning the use of certain particular materials or chemicals would mean that companies using these materials might have to consider developing alternative products. Good examples of this are the use of slow-burning safer foam for upholstering furniture, and the development of alternatives to CFCs in aerosols and fridges.

The legal framework is a result of government policy. Many economic forecasts ignore the implications of a change in government policy, irrespective of whether or not there is a change of government.

(a) At national level, political influence is significant and includes extensive legislation on such maters as competition, tax, employment and health and safety.

(b) Politics at *international* level also has a direct bearing on organisations. EU directives affect all countries in the EU, and so organisations will have to take note of the political trends in the wider EU environment.

(c) The *government* controls much of the economy, being the nation's largest supplier, employer, customer and investor. The slightest shift in political emphasis can decimate a particular market almost overnight. Aerospace and defence are particularly vulnerable to shifts in political decisions and in the UK, current government policy towards both the health service and the railways has serious implications for companies' order books (ie for the firms supplying those industries).

(d) *Nationalism:* for a variety of reasons, nations want to have national champions in particular industries. The shipping and airline industries have been particularly affected by the desire and insistence of many countries to have their own fleets. This has also been true of Information Technology. A problem is that national markets are often too small to support these 'national champions' and so development is impeded.

Activity 2   **(10 minutes)**

List one instance of a specific event, in each of the following categories, which has had a significant impact on organisations in the UK in the recent past. If you can also think of the organisations, specifically or by type, which have been influenced, then so much the better.

Clearly you should search for illustrations other than those given elsewhere in this text.

- Legislation on trading, pricing or tax
- Legislation on health and safety
- EU directives
- Shifts in government policy or political emphasis
- Creating a national champion

2.1 Political change

Given that organisations must operate within a political environment, political *change* also complicates the task of predicting future influences, and planning to meet them. Some political changes cannot easily be planned for. Consider the example of tour operators and holiday companies. Companies selling holidays to Yugoslavia in 1990/1991, could not predict the extent to which political disputes would degenerate into civil war. Similarly most airlines were adversely affected when the Gulf War decimated demand for business travel.

Managers ought to be aware of the following.

- Whether political change could have a significant impact on their organisation.

- What form of influence the political change might have.

- What the extent of the consequences of any such change might be.

- What is the likelihood of the change taking place.

- How the organisation can plan to cope with the change, should it occur.

2.2 State influences

The government exercises authority and provides services in three ways.

(a) Through direct action.

(b) Through delegation to other publicly funded bodies. The *public sector* refers to all publicly funded or publicly owned bodies, even though it may not form part of the obvious apparatus of government. The variety of public sector bodies was identified in Chapter 1.

(c) Through regulation of activities.

The state's economic impact, such as the determination of interest rates and tax levels, is of course considerable.

Activity 3   **(5 minutes)**

Specify at least one example of government action, against each of the above categories.

- Direct action
- Delegation to other publicly-funded bodies
- Regulation of activities

Government economic policy is conducted with a number of aims in mind, which often conflict with each other.

- Economic growth
- Full employment
- Price stability (ie no inflation)

In addition to legislation and regulations for influencing economic activity, the state uses various policy tools.

(a) *Fiscal policy* is about taxation, government borrowing and public spending.

(b) *Monetary policy*. Monetary policy deals with four things.

- Interest rates
- Exchange rates
- Control of the money supply
- Controls over bank lending and credit

Businesses are affected by a government's tax policy (eg corporation tax rates) and monetary policy (high interest rates increase the cost of investment, and depress consumer demand for credit). Similarly they are affected by fiscal policy – the raising and spending of income by central government.

What form does government spending take?

Governments, like other organisations, spend money on the following. (Note that government expenditure, in this context, includes expenditure by local government.)

- Payments of wages, salaries and pensions
- Payments for materials, supplies and services
- Purchases of capital equipment
- Payments of interest on borrowings and repayments of capital

Expenditure must be allocated between departments and functions such as health, social services, education, transport, defence and grants to industry. Expenditure decisions are of great significance to companies that are major suppliers to the government such as producers of defence equipment, medical equipment and school text books.

More indirectly, government spending decisions affect companies and other organisations.

(a)   There is a knock-on effect throughout the economy of government spending: companies supply companies which in turn supply the government.

(b)   Taxation affects consumers' purchasing power.

(c)   Taxes on company profits and tax allowances affect the after-tax return on investment that companies achieve.

Government policy towards economic regulation has undergone some changes in recent years.

(a)   Some economic decisions have been deregulated. The UK government, for example, abolished exchange controls.

(b)   In other areas there has been an *increase* in regulation, if it is felt to be in the public interest.

(i)   Regulatory bodies oversee the activities of privatised company utilities like BT, British Gas, and the electricity companies. They can influence *pricing policy*, competitive strategy (eg by restricting 'unfair' competition) and, indeed, the structure of the industry.

(ii)   The financial services industry in the City is more heavily regulated than hitherto, even though much of this regulation is carried out by the industry itself.

(iii)   There are far tighter controls on the activities of local authorities and their financial arrangements.

(c)   Some of the UK government's regulating activities have been pooled with the EU. Aspects of competition policy are managed by the EU.

Economic planning on a large scale (the minutiae of planning output, investment, fine-tuning demand to reach a growth target) is now out of favour, and has been discredited as a result of the failure of Communism in the eastern bloc and China and its unhappy history in Western Europe.

In this model, government is a *director* of economic activity.

Activity 4   **(5 minutes)**

Why do you think that large-scale economic planning, with government as a director of economic activity, has so far proved unsuccessful?

Economic planning on a lesser scale, with the government as an *enabler* of private sector activity and as a corrector of market imperfections, still has some sort of a role, however.

(a)   Governments can raise trade barriers to protect domestic industry.

(b)   Governments can subsidise exports, or promote them in other ways (eg by trade missions, export credit insurance and so forth).

Regional policy is an example of small scale economic planning, with government as an enabler rather than a director. Here are some examples.

(a) Tax incentives for investing in certain areas

(b) A relaxation in town planning restrictions, making it easier for businesses to develop

(c) Awarding contracts to companies in one region rather than another (eg dividing operations between shipyards in different parts of the country)

(d) Infrastructural developments (eg roads, rail, airports).

Activity 5 (5 minutes)

A number of US arms-manufacturing companies are diversifying into non-defence related activities. Others are winding down. What do you think is the ultimate cause of this?

To summarise, government policy affects organisations in the ways outlined in the diagram below.

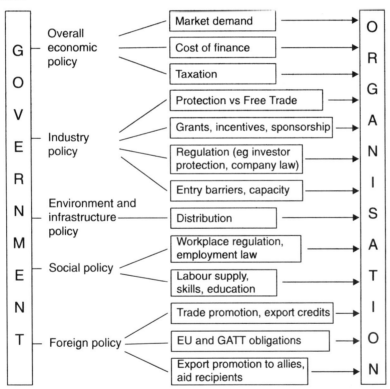

3 ECONOMIC FACTORS

We have seen how government policy influences economic activity. Governments rarely control the state of the economy, and government is only one influence, albeit a very important one, on the economic environment of organisations.

The state of the economy affects all organisations, both commercial and non-commercial. The rate of growth in the economy is a measure of the overall change in demand for goods and services. Growth is an indication of increases in demand.

There are other economic influences on an organisation.

(a) *At a regional or national level.* A company's *local* geographical environment is important. It might be located in a growth area full of modern thriving industry, such as Milton Keynes; or it may be located in an area of urban decay. The economic *future* of the area will affect amongst other things wage rates, availability of labour, disposal income of local consumers, unemployment, the provision of roads and other services.

National economic trends which can be of interest to managers are the prospects for national economic growth and growth in national income per head of population, population growth and changing demographic trends, trends in price inflation, unemployment

(b) *World* trends are obviously relevant also.

- Comparative growth rates, inflation rates, interest rates and wage rates

- The extent of protectionist measures against imports

- Freedom of capital movement between different countries

- International economic communities, such as the EU

- The levels of corporate and personal taxation in different countries

- Relative exchange rates

- Economic agreements and particularly the WTO.

Activity 6   **(10 minutes)**

From the economic influences on organisations listed above, select those which you consider might have a significant impact on a company in the consumer electronics business, producing TVs, videos, in-car entertainment and music systems for customers worldwide. Global organisations fitting this description will include Philips, Matsushita and Sony. How should such an organisation take account of these particular economic influences in determining its strategic plans and directions?

The state of the economy, or more often the forecast state of the economy, will influence the planning process for organisations which operate within it. In times of boom and increased demand and consumption, the overall planning problem will be to identify the demand. Conversely, in times of recession, the emphasis will be on cost-effectiveness, continuing profitability, survival and competition. Whether the organisation is in a buyers' market or a sellers' market will also have an important bearing on strategic plans. Economists can contribute to the strategic planning process with economic forecasts and information about economic trends.

An organisation is affected by overall economic conditions as these influence both the demand for its products and the cost of its supplies.

Conditions of high inflation also affect investment decisions, as they encourage firms to hold on to assets rather than money. Inflation erodes the value of debt.

High interest rates affect not only consumers' spending power but also the ease with which the organisation can raise money.

4 SOCIO-CULTURAL FACTORS

Societies differ in many important respects. For example, some might have a large population, others a small population. People have different beliefs. All of these factors expose the organisation to different influences.

4.1 Demography: population trends

Definition

> *Demography* is the study of human populations, using statistics relating to births, deaths and social matters such as class and ethnicity.

The adjective *demographic* is used to denote the population-related aspects of an issue.

(a) People create a demand for goods and services.

(b) Economic growth should exceed population growth for enhanced standards of living.

(c) Population is a source of labour, one of the *factors of production*.

(d) Population creates demands on the physical environment and its resources, a source of increased political concern.

(e) There is some evidence that relative differences in population structure can affect a country's economic prospects.

Activity 7 **(5 minutes)**

For what kinds of business and organisation (in both the public and private sectors) are demographic changes particularly significant?

Why is demography an important environmental factor for organisations?

(a) Over the long term, changes in society affect the demand for goods and services.

(b) Demographic changes affect the availability of labour. Falling numbers of young people entering the labour force have forced employers to change their policies regarding the recruitment of part timers, and efforts are being made to retain women in the labour force.

Changes in the rate of population growth are caused by the following factors.

(a) Changes in the *birth rate*, or fertility rate. The birth rate can fluctuate sharply in the short run, with temporary 'baby booms' and temporary falls in the rate of new births.

(b) Changes in the *death rate* or mortality rate.

(c) Emigration and/or immigration.

The *Rate of Natural Increase* in population (RNI) is the birth rate minus the death rate.

Growing populations have important effects.

• They require fast economic growth to maintain living standards.

- They result in overcrowding on land and/or cities.
- They require more resources for capital investment.
- They stimulate investment (as the market size is increasing).
- They lead to enhanced labour mobility.

Falling populations are equally important.

(a)   They require more productive techniques to maintain output.

(b)   They make some scale economies harder to achieve.

(c)   They put a greater burden on a decreasing number of young people – assuming the population fall is as a result of falling birthrates or that fewer individuals are available to support the elderly.

(d)   They exhibit changing consumption patterns.

Governments can *indirectly* influence population size by subsidising children; publicising birth control, and offering cheap provision of it; and by legislative restrictions as was done in China.

Arguably, one of the most important influences on population size is economic growth. The reasons for population growth or decline are cultural, technological and economic.

Age structure and distribution

Greater life expectancy means that a larger proportion of the population will be senior citizens (say 65 years or over) and unlikely to be working.

(a)   A country with an expanding population will have larger proportions of children and old people, and lower proportions of people of working age.

(b)   A country with a declining population will eventually have a large proportion of old people and reducing proportions of people of other ages.

The *working* population must create a country's economic wealth. With more people at retirement age, and also more young children, the proportion of the population which is at a productive (ie working) age will be lower, and the proportion which is non-working and dependent on the working population will be higher. This puts an extra burden on the working population, which must pay, through taxes, for government expenditures on old age pensions, health care and state education for the young.

Children in the population will eventually reach working age, and if they can find employment, will begin to contribute to the country's economic wealth. However, if they cannot find work, they will remain dependent on the working population until they do. A high rate of population growth is therefore potentially more serious for a country with low economic growth and mass unemployment than for a country with a high rate of economic growth and a strong demand from employers for labour.

Activity 8   **(10 minutes)**

The above comments about demography are written in general terms, without specific reference to what is happening in the UK. What do you believe to be the significant demographic trends in the UK, especially with regard to the size of the working population in relation to the proportion of the population which is below and above working age? What is likely to happen to alter these proportions in the foreseeable future?

Geographic distribution

Another important feature of demography is the location of the population. The above arguments have taken the individual country as a homogenous unit. In practice, however this is a vast oversimplification. A country may suffer the problems of overpopulation in some areas and underpopulation in others.

Demography also deals with the effect of concentration and dispersal of population in particular areas. Industrialisation has traditionally meant a shift from the countryside to the towns which is still occurring in the developing world. This is further complicated by the fact that in some other countries people are moving away from big cities to suburbs or smaller towns and are commuting elsewhere to work.

(a)   The region from which the workers have moved will suffer a distortion in the age structure of its population, with fewer people of a working age and so a much larger proportion of dependants. The region is therefore likely to sink even further into depression and relative poverty.

(b)   Eventually, the region might become virtually depopulated. This appear to be happening in parts of Scotland and, on a more localised basis, in ex-mining towns in England where coal pits have been closed down. City centres also face a fall in population.

Sex

There is often an imbalance in the population between the numbers of men and the numbers of women. The work roles played by males and females in different societies vary, even within the industrial world. In different societies, women and men have distinct purchasing and social powers.

Ethnicity

Only a few societies are homogenous, with populations of one culture and ethnic background. Japan is an example, although the population includes descendants of Koreans. Alternatively, a society like the USA has a population drawn from a variety of different areas.

Ethnicity is interesting to demographers, insofar as it acts as a marker for other social facts. An area in the UK with a population drawn from a variety of ethnic backgrounds will have to take note in its education provision, if, say, English is not widely spoken.

4.2   Culture

Culture is a much broader concept than the sense in which it is most often used by people – to refer to classical aesthetic or artistic pursuits.

Definition

> The term *culture* is used by sociologists and anthropologists to encompass 'the sum total of the beliefs, knowledge, attitudes of mind and customs to which people are exposed in their social conditioning'.

Through contact with a particular culture, individuals learn a language, acquire values and learn habits of behaviour and thought.

As suggested by our definition above, 'culture' embraces the following aspects of social life.

(a) *Beliefs and values*. *Beliefs* are what we feel to be the case on the basis of objective and subjective information (eg people can believe the world is round or flat – some beliefs are truer than others). *Values* are beliefs that are relatively enduring; relatively general and not tied to specific objects; and fairly widely accepted as a guide to culturally appropriate behaviour. They therefore provide a standard of desirable and undesirable beliefs, attitudes and behaviour. Beliefs shape attitudes and so create tendencies for individuals and societies to behave in certain ways.

(b) *Customs* are modes of behaviour which represent culturally accepted ways of behaving in response to given situations. There are various types of social behavioural norms. *Keith Williams (Behavioural Aspects of Marketing)* identifies four, on a continuum ranging from lightly to rigidly enforced patterns of behaviour, corresponding to their seriousness as a threat to social survival, if violated.

   (i) *Folkways* are appropriate patterns of behaviour, violation of which are noticeable, but not severely punished. (In the UK, friends might shake hands on greetings – where in France, say, kisses on both cheeks would be more appropriate.)

   (ii) *Conventions* are accustomed or habitual standards of behaviour. Conventional behaviour includes social etiquette (because they become habits, conventions are harder to change than folkways.)

   (iii) *Mores* are significant social norms including moral imperatives and taboos. Monogamy (one spouse) and taboos against incest, murder and theft are part of the social mores of many nations.

   (iv) *Laws* include formal recognition of the mores considered necessary in the interests of the society as a whole, with imposed sanctions for violation.

(c) *Artefacts*. Culture embraces all the physical tools designed by human beings for their physical and psychological well-being: works of art, technology, products, buildings etc are all physical manifestations of social existence. Some of these physical objects may be *symbolic* of other things: products, for example, can stand for all kinds of needs and occasions with which they become associated. A logo stands for a company.

(d) *Rituals*. A ritual is a type of activity which takes on symbolic meaning, consisting of a fixed sequence of behaviour repeated over time. *Ritualised* behaviour tends to be public, elaborate, formal and ceremonial – like religious services, marriage ceremonies, court procedures, even sporting events.

The learning and sharing of culture is made possible by *language* (both written and spoken, verbal *and* non-verbal).

Symbols are an important aspect of language and culture. A symbol is something which stands for something else. (The stars and stripes is a symbol of the USA.) Each symbol may carry a number of different meanings and associations for different people and some of these meanings are learned as part of the society's culture. The advertiser using slang words or pictorial images must take care that they are valid for the people he wants to reach.

4.3 Characteristics of culture

Having examined the areas included in the definition of culture, we can draw together some of the underlying characteristics of culture itself. Culture can be described in the following ways.

(a) Purposeful. Culture exists to satisfy the needs of people in a society.

   'It offers order, direction and guidance in all phases of human problem solving, by providing tried and true methods of satisfying physiological, personal and social needs. (Schiffman and Kanuk).'

(b) *Learned*. Cultural norms and values are taught or transferred to each new member of society, formally or informally, by socialisation. This occurs in institutions (the family, school and church) and through on-going social interaction and mass media exposure in adulthood.

(c) *Shared*. A belief or practice must be common to a significant proportion of a society or group before it can be defined as a cultural characteristic.

(d) *Cumulative*. Culture is handed down to each new generation, and while new situations teach new responses, there is a strong traditional/historical element to many aspects of culture.

(e) *Dynamic*. Culture must be adaptive, or evolutionary, in order to fulfil its need-satisfying function. Many factors may produce cultural change – slow or fast – in society: eg technological breakthrough, population shifts, exposure to other cultures, gradual changes in values. (Think about male-female roles in the West, or European influences on British lifestyles.)

Knowledge about the culture of a society is clearly of value to businesses in a number of ways.

(a) Marketers can adapt their products and appeals accordingly, and be fairly sure of a sizeable market. Marketers can also plan to participate in the teaching process that creates culture, since mass media advertising, in particular, is an important agent by which cultural meanings are attached to products, people and situations. This is particularly important in export markets.

(b) Human resource managers may need to tackle cultural differences in recruitment. Some ethnic minorities have different body languages, which may be hard for some interviewers to interpret.

Culture is deeply embedded in everyday behaviour, but it can be investigated in several ways. Here are some examples.

(a) Attitude measurement techniques

(b) Projective techniques, depth interviews and focus group sessions

(c) Content analysis (examining the content of the verbal, written and pictorial communications of a society: what kind of people are shown in advertisements? what criteria are used in design? is the society verbal or non-verbal? does it favour simplicity or complexity? what themes and images recur?)

(d) Observation of a sample of the population by trained anthropologists, in the field (eg in store), followed by inference of the underlying reasons for the observed behaviour

(e) Surveys or value inventories, measuring personal values

4.4 Acquiring culture: the socialisation process

Definition

> *Socialisation* is the process by which the individual learns the social expectations, goals, beliefs, values and attitudes that enable him or her to exist in society. In other words, socialisation is the process by which we acquire sufficient knowledge of a society and its ways to be able to function and participate in it.

Acquiring language is the most obvious example of socialisation. The learning of sex-related, consumer and occupational *roles* is also part of the socialisation process: what it means to be or behave like a girl or boy, what money is for, what buying is, what work is and what sorts of work different sorts of people do.

The *family* is the earliest contact through which socialisation to the under culture is achieved, although other socialising influences on children include formal education, reference groups (particularly peer groups, at a young age), and the mass media. Socialisation is an on-going process. Adults can be influenced towards conformity to newly-encountered roles, norms and values.

Activity 9   **(5 minutes)**

Identify two commercial situations where socialisation is relevant.

4.5 Sub-cultures in society

Culture in a society can be divided into sub-cultures reflecting social differences.

(a) *Class*. People from different social classes might have different values reflecting their position of society. These values might relate to attitudes to work, or the value of education. Different classes might dress differently.

(b) *Ethnic background*. The UK government publication *Social Trends* makes a distinction between white ethnic groups and all others (West Indian, Indian, Pakistani, Bangladeshi, Chinese, African). Within the white group, there are also many ethnic minorities (eg Irish, Italian, Greek or Turkish Cypriot). Most people from minority ethnic backgrounds were born in the UK. Some can still be considered a distinct cultural group.

(c) *Religion*. Religion and ethnicity are often related, for example most Muslims in the UK come from Pakistan, Bangladesh or Africa. Similarly many Roman Catholics have Irish ancestry or connections. Values and lifestyles are affected by religions (the prohibition on eating certain kinds of food, for example).

(d) *Geography or region*. Even in such a small country as England, there are distinct regional differences, brought about by the *past* effects of physical geography (poor communication between communities separated by rivers or mountains, say) and indeed its *present* affects (socio-economic differences created by suitability of the area for coal-mining, say, or leisure, or urbanisation). Speech accents most noticeably differ, but there are also perceived (often stereotyped) variations in personality, life style, eating and drinking habits (perhaps due to socio-economic factors) between the North and South, or the South-west and South-east – and even between West and East London! Some regions, such as Yorkshire, have a particularly strong self-image and loyalty to 'home' products.

(e)   *Age*. Age sub-cultures vary according to the period in which individuals were socialised, to an extent, because of the great shifts in social values and customs in this century. You might have heard of the 'generation gap'. Age sub-cultures also vary through each individual's life. Each individual progresses through the youth (14-24 year old) sub-culture, which includes the most strongly bonded and identifiable groups, with shared, often exaggerated, values and badges of belonging. The elderly are another distinct sub-culture. Unlike traditional stereotypes, it has been suggested that the elderly now perceive themselves to be younger than their chronological age, are self-confident about consumer decisions, are market-aware and innovative, and feel financially more secure.

(f)   *Sex*. There are some sub-cultures related to sex. Some products, for example, are targeted directly to women or to men.

(g)   *Work*. Different organisations have different corporate cultures, the shared values of one workplace may be different from another.

The exclusivity of sub-cultures should not be exaggerated, since each consumer is simultaneously a member of many sub-cultural segments. (You do not need to sell cornflakes specifically to a racial minority, when its members are also Protestants, women, young people, living in the West Midlands – and part of the mainstream UK culture, as far as cornflake consumption is concerned.)

4.6   Belief systems and attitudes to work

We have already seen that beliefs shape attitudes and therefore influence behaviour. So far as organisations are concerned, they require employees who are committed to the organisation and (preferably) capable of being motivated towards their work, their jobs and their careers. It is clear that motivation and commitment are themselves mediated by the beliefs about (and towards) work which individuals acquire as a by-product of their cultural background and socialisation.

Definition

> *Belief systems* are defined by *Rokeach* (Beliefs, Attitudes and Values, 1968) as representing 'all the beliefs, sets, expectancies, or hypotheses, conscious or unconscious, that a person at a given time accepts as true, and which in the ordinary course of events he does not question.'

Attitudes to work are shaped by the relative strengths of five major belief systems.

(a)   The *work* (or *Protestant*) ethic which holds that work is good in itself and bestows dignity on a person. Success in life is directly linked to the individual's own efforts and material wealth is a measure of personal effectiveness. At the same time, wealth should be wisely invested in order to produce still greater returns, and not foolishly or self-indulgently spent on conspicuous consumption. Thrift and frugality are positive virtues, in other words.

(b)   The organisational belief system which suggests that work is only meaningful in a group or organisational setting. Success is heavily dependent on one's ability to conform and adapt to group/corporate norms, with a high value being placed on working positively with others and achieving status through collaboration.

(c)   *Marxist-related beliefs* embrace the notion that work is basic to human fulfilment and that, therefore, individuals at work should be allowed to participate in the work process, to contribute actively to the planning and implementation of change, and to exercise autonomy within their jobs. This belief system only addresses two of the main ideas promulgated by Marx – namely, exploitation and participation – because human fulfilment from work itself is covered by the humanistic belief system.

(d)   *The humanistic belief system* claims that individual growth and development are more important than the tangible outputs from the work process, because work is the route through which people discover and fulfil themselves as human beings.

(e)   *The leisure ethic,* by contrast to the humanistic belief system, asserts that work has no particular meaning, but rather that it is a necessary prelude to the purchase of goods and services. If human beings are to fulfil themselves at all, this will not be as a result of work but rather through involvement in leisure pursuits, where individuals can become creative and exercise genuine autonomy in their lives.

Activity 10   **(15 minutes)**

(a)   Which of these belief systems coincides most closely with your own beliefs about, and attitudes towards, work?

(b)   What have been the formative influences in producing these particular attitudes and beliefs within you (in so far as you can ascertain and analyse them)?

(c)   What is occurring, do you think, to the underlying framework of belief systems about work in UK society? Bear in mind, when thinking about this issue, that the work (Protestant) ethic was the dominant belief system which inspired the Industrial Revolution. How far is the work ethic still in existence?

(d)   What are the organisational implications of any changes or trends in belief systems about work?

5   TECHNOLOGICAL FACTORS

Technology is often cited as the cause of change, but it is important to realise what we mean by the word. *Buchanan and Huczynski,* quoting *Langdon Winner,* note three uses of the word *technology.*

(a)   Apparatus (ie tools and machines)

(b)   Technique (skills and procedures governing the use of tools and machines)

(c)   Organisation (social arrangements to meet productive ends)

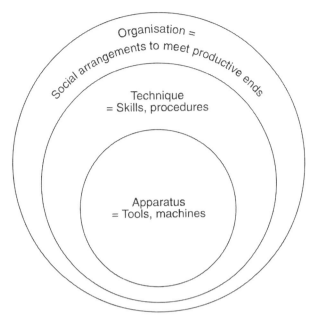

Apparatuses are used in *techniques*, and techniques are co-ordinated by *organisations*. Let us take a simple example.

(a)   The *apparatuses* in a photographer's studio include cameras, lighting equipment, a dark room, developing tanks, chemicals, enlargers, light sensitive paper for printing and so forth.

(b)   Taking a photograph of, say, a family group involves combining these machines in a particular way. A *technique* might be to shine the lights at a particular angle for a desired effect, and the use of a particular shutter speed. This is *purposive:* the photographer knows what he or she is trying to achieve and knows how to use the equipment and chemicals to get the desired result.

(c)   The *organisation* would include the whole social and technical structure. For example, it may be that there is a division of labour. One person might be responsible for arranging the lights and taking the picture, which form one set of skills. Another person might be responsible for developing the film and printing it, another set of skills.

Technological change is rapid, and organisations must adapt themselves to it. Responsiveness to the technological environment is important for two reasons.

(a)   Adopting technological change might give a firm a competitive edge.

(b)   If a firm's competitors adopt technological change, then the firm will be forced to follow suit or else be put out of business.

Examples of ways in which technological change can affect the activities of organisations are as follows.

(a)   *The type of products or services that are made and sold.* For example, consumer markets have seen the emergence of home computers, compact discs and satellite dishes for receiving satellite TV; industrial markets have seen the emergence of custom-built microchips, robots and local area networks for office information systems. Technological changes can be relatively minor, such as the introduction of tennis and squash rackets with graphite frames, fluoride toothpaste and turbo-powered car engines.

(b)   *The way in which products are made.* There is a continuing trend towards the use of modern labour-saving production equipment, such as robots. The manufacturing environment is undergoing rapid changes with the growth of advanced manufacturing technology. These are changes in both apparatus and technique.

(c) *The way in which services are provided.* We have already seen how banks and retailers have been affected by technology.

(d) *The way in which markets are identified.* Database systems make it much easier to analyse the market place.

(e) *The way in which employees are mobilised.* There is some discussion that computerisation encourages delayering of organisational hierarchies, and greater workforce skills. Using technology frequently requires changes in working methods. This is a change in organisation.

The benefits of technological change might be as follows.

(a) To cut production costs and so (probably) to reduce sales prices to the customer too.

(b) To develop better quality products and services.

(c) To develop products and services that did not exist before.

(d) To provide products or services to customers more quickly or effectively than before.

(e) To free staff from repetitive work and to tap their creativity.

In order for these benefits to be obtained technological considerations must be an integral part of the strategic planning process. Simply adopting technology without thinking strategically will not necessarily benefit the organisation – it may even cause harm.

Information technology is often used as an example of a technological development which has been widely adopted but not utilised with maximum efficiency. Often it has simply been used to automate existing processes rather than to devise new ones. This is a good example of failing to consider technology in its broadest definition embracing processes and work relationships as well as the physical technology itself.

Organisations that operate in an environment where the pace of technological change is very fast must be flexible enough to adapt to change quickly and must plan for change and innovation, perhaps by spending heavily on R & D. Technological change can be planned for by developing strategies for improved productivity and for innovation (product development).

Information technology has been widely adopted, although doubts have been raised about the efficiency with which it is used: perhaps it has been used to automate existing procedures rather than devise new ones.

Activity 11 (5 minutes)

Marinoid Papers Ltd publishes small pamphlets. Its journalists submit typed manuscript to a typesetter. The typesetter then prepares the story for printing. He selects metal letters which he assembles into a frame. The frame is inked, and the story is printed. The firm's technology is archaic. It has only one typeface, and its pamphlets look dull. Recently the managing director has purchased a desktop publishing and word processing system, with a great variety of typefaces and sizes and the chance to use graphics (charts, drawing etc) cheaply. What consequences might this have for the journalist and the typesetter?

One sector of the economy which has experienced dramatic change as a result of technological development is manufacturing. The following discussion provides evidence of change across all three aspects of technology (Apparatus, Technique and Organisation).

5.1 Developments in manufacturing

Many of the improvement processes which feature regularly in management conference nowadays have had their origin in *Japan* and in *manufacturing*.

(a) Ideas proved to work in one country like Japan have been translated and adopted in many other economies, if only for defensive reasons: faced with intensive Japanese competition, organisations have sometimes reacted by believing that the only way to survive is to become Japanese themselves, at least in terms of the way they organise themselves. On many occasions supposedly Japanese inventions – like quality circles – have been grafted on to organisations uncritically, in the expectation that they represent some competitive panacea and will, by themselves, transform performance and effectiveness. It has now been recognised that simply taking on board one feature of the Japanese way of managing, but leaving everything else unchanged, will not work: what is needed, if total quality management (TQM), or business process re-engineering (BPR) are to justify themselves, is a complete revitalisation of the organisational culture from top to bottom.

(b) Manufacturing – principally in consumer electronics and the motor industry – has been the inspiration for many continuous improvement approaches which have been applied to such unrelated fields as service companies and the public sector. Ever since the days of *Henry Ford* (and probably long before that), managements of manufacturing companies have recognised the need to keep plugging away at finding better ways to do things. There is nothing new about striving to improve product design in order to attract more sales, or working out more effective ways of using manufacturing resources in order to reduce costs, or providing a better service to customers so that they are encouraged to give you more business.

EXAMPLE: THE CAR INDUSTRY

Cars provide an excellent example. Early motor cars were individually built and expensive, so that only the rich could afford them. Henry Ford realised that if he could find a way of cutting the cost of manufacture, he could reduce the selling price of his cars to the point where many more people would be able to afford to buy them. The mass-produced Model T was the result. When Ford opened their first UK plant in Manchester in 1911, they were able to sell the Model T for £135, at a time when comparable British cars cost over £300. The number of cars on the road increased rapidly, with Ford as the market leader.

More recently, the arrival of Japanese car manufacturers *Honda*, *Toyota* and *Nissan* in the UK has stimulated indigenous car manufacturers (and also the suppliers of components to the car industry) to become much more efficient as an essential means for staying in business. This kind of stimulus in the car industry has been replicated in many other fields of commercial (and even non-commercial) endeavour, so that there are now widespread instances of organisations seeking to transform themselves through the use of fashionable management techniques like TQM and BPR, the two already mentioned. Of course, it has to be accepted that each of these new techniques has *a product life cycle*, its shape probably not unlike that of Handy's Sigmoid Curve. This means that eventually the technique will fall from favour and be superseded by something else, just as human relations in the 1930s and job enrichment in the 1960s no longer reflect organisational thinking. The existence of a product life cycle for a management technique, however, does not mean that the technique is (or was) valueless. On the contrary, many of these techniques, though to some extent ephemeral, have been responsible for significant and worthwhile changes that leave a permanent legacy of performance improvement – on which the next technique can build.

5.2 World class manufacturing

World class manufacturing (WCM) is a term much in vogue at present. It was coined in the mid 1980s to describe the fundamental changes taking place in manufacturing companies. WCM is a very broad term, but it can be taken to have four key elements.

(a) *A new approach to product quality.* Instead of a policy of trying to detect defects or poor quality in production as and when they occur, WCM sets out to identify the root causes of poor quality, eliminate them, and achieve zero effects – ie 100% quality. Eliminating waste is likely to involve building better quality into the product.

(b) *Just-in-time manufacturing (JIT).* This is a system of manufacturing that aims to eliminate waste.

Definition

> *Waste* can be described as the use of resources (including especially time) that fail to add value to the product.

Wasteful activities include the following.

- Inspection of goods
- Shopfloor queues
- Re-working of defective items
- Excessive storage
- Unnecessary movement of materials

(c) *Managing people.* The aim of WCM is to utilise the skills and abilities of the work force to the full. Employees are given training in a variety of skills, so that they can switch from one task to another. They are also given more responsibility for production scheduling and quality. A *team approach* is encouraged, with strong trust between management and workers. These are all aspects of *empowerment*.

(d) *Flexible approach to customer requirements.* The WCM policy is to develop close relationships with customers in order to achieve the following.

(i) Know what their requirements are.

(ii) Supply customers on time, with short delivery lead times.

(iii) Change the product mix quickly and develop new products or modify existing products as customer needs change.

According to *Jim Todd* (*World-Class Manufacturing*, 1995) world class means being the best in your field in the world. Best can be defined in a variety of terms.

- Product design and performance
- Quality and reliability
- Least manufacturing cost
- The ability to introduce innovative designs faster than competitors
- Shorter lead times and more reliable delivery performance
- Customer service that attracts new customers, and retains existing ones

The goals of world class manufacturing

A WCM manufacturer will have a clear manufacturing strategy aimed at issues such as the following.

- Quality and reliability
- Short lead times (the time from start to finish of production)
- Flexibility
- Customer satisfaction

World class manufacturing in the UK

In January 1993 the *Financial Times* reported the findings of a comparative study of 18 UK and Japanese companies by *Andersen Consulting* and *Cambridge University*. All of the companies were suppliers of components to the motor industry. The overall finding was that most of the UK companies lag far behind the world class productivity and quality standards set by the best Japanese companies. Specific points mentioned included the following.

(a)   UK plants had an average of 2.5 defects per 100 components, compared with 2.5 per 10,000 for the best Japanese plants.

(b)   The UK plants typically needed twice as many employees to produce the same number of parts.

(c)   The world class plants were making a more complex and rapidly changing mix of products than their rivals.

(d)   The world class plants involved more of their employees more intensively in problem-solving. In such plants team leaders were pivotal, developing the skills of team members as well as taking responsibility for quality and management issues.

(e)   The organisation of the production process in world class firms was highly significant.

   '*It starts with integrating every production step into an uninterrupted flow – so parts travel the minimum distance and hardly wait for the next operation.*'

   Thereafter,

   '*the discipline governing the flow comes from short set-up times and small lots produced just-in-time, thus eliminating waste and work in progress.*'

   Random interruptions and variability such as machine breakdowns, supplier hiccups or defective parts are eliminated.

(f)   The world class firms had a tightly integrated supply chain, marked by minimal stock, frequent deliveries of small volumes of parts, lack of disruption and stable supply volumes. The discipline of the system came from short lead times between order and delivery and building to customer order rather than to accumulate stock.

NOTES

> **Activity 12**   **(5 minutes)**
>
> Describe the importance of time in world class manufacturing.

5.3 Modern developments in manufacturing procedures

Traditionally, manufacturing industries have fallen into a few broad groups according to the nature of the production process and materials flow.

(a) *Job production:* items are produced individually, often for a specific customer order. Such a business requires versatile equipment and highly skilled workers to give it the flexibility to turn its hand to a variety of jobs. The jobbing factory is typically laid out on a *functional* basis with, say, a milling department, a cutting department, finishing, assembly and so on.

(b) *Batch production* involves the manufacture of standard goods in batches.

> '*Batch production is often carried out using functional layouts but with a greater number of more specialised machines. With a functional layout batches move by different and complex routes through various specialised departments travelling over much of the factory floor before they are completed. (Drury, Management and Cost Accounting)*'

(c) *Mass production* involves the continuous production of standard items from a sequence of continuous or repetitive operations organised on a *production line*. This is a lengthy sequence of highly specialised processes.

Cellular layout

Production lines are very expensive to set up, and in order to reduce overhead cost per item, high throughput is required. This is inappropriate for an innovative, market driven producer who will typically produce relatively small quantities of a product before replacing it with an improved version. Small groups or cells of general purposes machines are operated by multi-skilled workers. This reduces queuing of batches between functional sections without the cost of setting up a production line.

Advanced manufacturing technology

Computers have had a profound impact on manufacturing processes.

(a) *Computer aided design* (CAD) allows new products to be designed (and old ones modified) on a computer screen. 3D models can be created and rotated through any angle and there is infinite capacity for exploring the effects of changing product specifications (for example to test stress and find weaknesses or to optimise usage of materials) because these aspects of design are essentially a matter of repeated operations and calculations and are ideally suited to computerisation.

(b) *Computer aided manufacturing* (CAM) refers to the control of the physical production process by computers.

    (i) *Robots* typically comprise computer controlled arms and attachments that can perform tasks like welding, bolting parts together and moving them about.

PUBLISHING

(ii) *Computer numerically controlled* (CNC) machines are programmable machine tools for punching holes, grinding, cutting, shaping and so on.

(iii) *Automated guided vehicles* (AGVs) are used for materials handling, often in place of the traditional conveyor belt approach. They allow the movement of parts at different speeds and can go up and down as well as along, avoiding the need for bending and making the piece being worked on far more accessible. They can also be stopped at precise positions to allow robots to have access.

EXAMPLE: BOEING

The development of the Boeing 777 aircraft demonstrates some of the power of the new technology. Not only has CAD been used to speed up the design process – in itself cutting the time taken to draft design drawings by 90% – but also CAD 'makes it possible to transmit designs directly to machines that will follow them perfectly.'

(*Economist*, 5 March 1994)

Flexible manufacturing systems (FMS)

Definition

> A *flexible manufacturing system* (FMS) is a highly automated manufacturing system, which is computer-controlled and capable of producing a broad 'family' of parts in a flexible manner. It is characterised by small batch production, the ability to change quickly from one job to another and very fast response times, so that output can be produced quickly in response to specific orders that come in.

The sophistication of flexible manufacturing systems varies from one system to another. Here are some typical features.

(a) A JIT system

(b) Full computer-integrated manufacturing (CIM), or perhaps just islands of automation (IAs)

(c) Computerised materials handling systems (MHS)

(d) Automated storage and retrieval systems (ASRs) for raw materials and parts

EXAMPLE: ASEA BROWN BOVERI

Asea Brown Boveri, the Swedish-Swiss engineering business, is aiming for significant reductions in lead times in the company's activities. It has already made significant progress through the creation of what it calls 'Target Oriented High Performance' work teams made up of 10 to 15 workers. This has replaced a system whereby orders were handed down from above through different, fragmented departments with one that is organised around the flow of production through the team approach.

The traditional, highly time-consuming system involved specialised demarcation of responsibilities for sales, stocks, production and distribution and following from this a high level of bureaucratic managerial control and top-heavy administration. In place of this have been put smaller, flexible work teams with wider responsibilities, allowing the barriers between administration and production to be abolished.

Again the results are impressive. The strategy 'has cut the time for making high-voltage direct current transmission equipment from three to two years. The time for supplying customers with standard switch gear has fallen from three to five weeks to three to five days from receipt of the order to delivery. Cycle times in ABB's components division have been reduced from 86 to 35 days.' (*Financial Times*, February 1993). Meanwhile, employees have a better working environment, greater job interest, and the facility to upgrade their skills constantly.

5.4 Just-in-time

Just-in-time (JIT) has emerged from criticisms of traditional features of mass production.

- (a) Long production runs

- (b) Economic batch quantities

- (c) Few products in the product range

- (d) More overtime

- (e) Minimal time spent on preventive maintenance, in order to keep production flowing

In general terms, longer production runs and large batch sizes *should* mean less disruption, better capacity utilisation and lower unit costs.

However, Just-in-time techniques and stockless production challenge traditional views of manufacture.

- (a) Its principles include greater flexibility in production, and matching production to meet demand.

- (b) This in turn means shorter batch production runs and a greater product variety.

- (c) There will be much smaller stocks of finished goods, because output is being matched more closely to demand.

- (d) Production systems must therefore be reliable and prompt, without unforeseen delays and breakdowns. Machinery must be kept fully maintained, and so preventive maintenance is an important aspect of production.

- (e) Production management should seek to eliminate scrap and defective units during production, and to avoid the need for reworking of units. Product quality and production *quality* are important drivers in a JIT system.

- (f) The time between batch runs (closing down the old run and setting up the new one) must be managed carefully and kept short, to achieve efficiency.

- (g) Parts and raw materials should be purchased as near as possible to the time they are needed, and so for any part or material item, a special relationship might be established with a single supplier. The supplier would be offered the sole right to supply the item in return for prompt and reliable delivery.

E J Hay (*The Just-in-Time Breakthrough*) identified seven aspects which are summarised as follows in an article in *Management Accounting* in February 1992.

(a) *JIT purchasing.* The use of small, frequent deliveries against bulk contracts. This requires the close integration of suppliers with the company's manufacturing process.

(b) *Machine cells.* The grouping of machines or workers by product or component instead of by type of work performed.

(c) *Set-up time reduction.* The recognition of set-ups as non 'value-adding' activities which should be reduced or even eliminated.

(d) *Uniform loading.* The operating of all parts of the productive process at a speed which matches the rate at which the final product is demanded by the customer.

(e) *Pull system* (*Kanban*). The use of a Kanban, or signal, to ensure that products/components are only produced when needed, that is, when demanded by a customer. Nothing is produced in anticipation of need, to then remain in stock, consuming resources.

(f) *Total quality.* The design of products, processes and vendor quality assurance programmes to ensure that the correct product is made to the appropriate quality level on the first pass through production.

(g) *Employee involvement.* JIT involves major cultural change throughout an organisation. This can only be achieved successfully if employees at all levels are involved in the process of change and continuous improvement that is inherent in the JIT philosophy.

JIT should not be seen as a panacea for all the endemic problems associated with Western manufacturing. It might not even be appropriate in all circumstances.

(a) It is not always easy to predict patterns of demand. As early as 1990 *Apple Computers*, an early adopter of JIT which had significantly cut its inventory costs, was reported (*Financial Times*) as abandoning JIT methods of inventory management in favour of a more flexible system, despite higher inventory costs.

(b) JIT makes the organisation far more vulnerable to disruptions in the supply chain. An example of this is the case of Renault, the French state-owned car maker. In October 1991 the workforce at Renault's gear-box production plant at Cléon went on strike. The day afterwards a British plant had to cease production. Within two weeks Renault was losing 60% of its usual daily output a day. The weakness arose for several reasons.

  (i) Sourcing components from one plant only

  (ii) Heavy dependence on in-house components

  (iii) Low inventory

  (iv) The fact '...that Japanese-style management techniques depend on stability in labour relations, something in short supply in the French public sector'

    (*Financial Times*, 31 October 1991)

(c) JIT, originated by Toyota, was 'designed at a time when all of Toyota's manufacturing was done within a 50 km radius of its headquarters'. Wide geographical spread, however, makes this difficult.

(d)   In some industries, suppliers are rebelling. Japanese plastics suppliers have refused to send just-in-time deliveries of acrylic sheets, unless customers pay extra for two reasons.

      (i)   Delivery costs (three times a day, in some cases) are increased.

      (ii)   Severe traffic congestion makes it hard to ensure materials arrive on time.

The latter point does perhaps emphasise the adverse environmental impact in terms of vehicle pollution and congestion resulting from JIT.

Activity 13   **(15 minutes)**

(a)   Can JIT be summarised as a means of minimising stockholdings, or is there more to it than this?

(b)   What are dedicated cells dedicated to?

(c)   What do you understand by the term flexibility in a modern manufacturing environment?

---

6   THE COMPETITIVE ENVIRONMENT

Apart from PEST factors which affect all the organisations, a business organisation faces *competition*. Competition comes from other organisations. Business organisations compete for customers. Competitive failure will result in the organisation collapsing, or being taken over. *Porter* categories five competitive forces in the environment of a firm as follows.

6.1   The threat of new entrants

A new entrant will bring extra capacity into an industry and poses a threat to established firms because they may lose market share with a consequent potential loss of economies of scale. The strength of the threat from new entrants depends on the strength of the *barriers to entry* and on the likely response of existing competitors to the new entrant. If prospective new entrants think that competitive retaliation will be strong then they might think twice before deciding to enter the market.

6.2   The threat of substitute products or services

The products or services that are produced in one industry are likely to have substitutes that are produced in another industry. For example railway travel is a substitute for private motor travel.

(a)   Substitutes pose a threat because they limit the ability of a firm to charge high prices for its products and the firm is likely to find the demand for its products is relatively sensitive to price.

(b)   The strength of the threat from substitutes will depend on their price-performance characteristics. Indeed where the existing firms are unable to meet the challenge with similar offerings the market may degenerate into a price war.

6.3 The bargaining power of customers

Customers require better quality products and services at lower prices. If they have the power to get what they want they will force down the profitability of the firms in the industry.

The strength of the threat from the bargaining power of customers will depend on a number of factors including the level of differentiation amongst products in the industry (including intangible aspects such as customer service), the cost to the customer of switching from one supplier to another (for example the existence of shared research and development facilities) and whether a customer's purchases from the industry represent a large or small proportion of the customer's total purchases.

6.4 The bargaining power of suppliers

Suppliers can influence the profitability of a firm by exerting pressure for higher prices or by reducing the quality of the goods and services which they supply.

The bargaining power of the supplier depends on a number of factors including the number of suppliers in the industry, the importance of the supplier's product to the firm, the cost to the firm of switching from one supplier to another and the ease with which the supplier could integrate forwards.

6.5 The rivalry amongst current competitors

The intensity of competitive rivalry within an industry will affect the profitability of the industry as a whole. Although rivalry can be beneficial in helping the industry to expand, it might leave demand unchanged. In this case the individual firms will be incurring costs on sales promotion campaigns, advertising battles and new product development and they will be charging lower prices and so making lower profits without gaining any benefits except maintaining market share.

The intensity of competition will depend on a number of factors including the rate of growth in the industry and whether there is a large number of balanced competitors.

7 GLOBALISATION

The final environmental influence on organisations that we shall consider is the trend towards globalisation. As the following discussion illustrates, this is a process which creates both new challenges and opportunities for organisation.

EXAMPLE: SOFTWARE PRODUCTION

The *Financial Times* (17 February 1993) reported about the global market for software. Software is conventionally thought to be a high-tech product made in wealthy 'First World' countries. However, India has a flourishing software industry.

Infosys is a firm based in Bangalore in southern India: 'An engineer at Infosys.... presses a computer key in Bangalore.... and his machine connects directly with the computer centre of the Holiday Inn hotel chain 12,000 miles away in the US..... Thanks to satellite technology, engineers in Bangalore can communicate almost instantaneously with counterparts in the US, Europe and Japan... Many foreign high-tech companies believe India's engineers are hard to beat because they speak English, the language of international high-tech trade and are trained at some of the best universities in the developing world.... monthly wages for programmers in India are just $225 (£158) compared with $600 in Singapore and $2,500 in the US.'

International business conditions are having an increasingly significant impact on organisations.

(a) Some of these international issues affect the nature of the industry.

(b) Others reflect the various positions of different countries, the size and wealth of their markets and the prosperity and efficiency of their productive bases.

(c) Yet more issues reflect the management, by governments or international institutions, of the framework in which business is done.

Any discussion of the international business environment is fraught with uncertainty, simply because there is such a variety of conflicting forces. Some of these conflicting forces are shown on the diagram below.

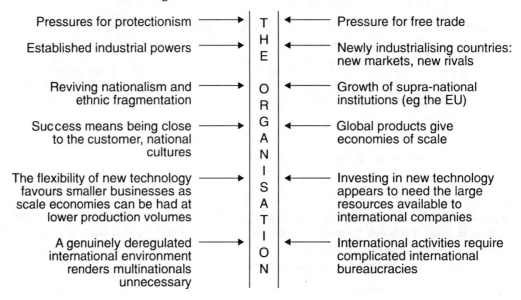

A model of how an organisation might be affected is shown below.

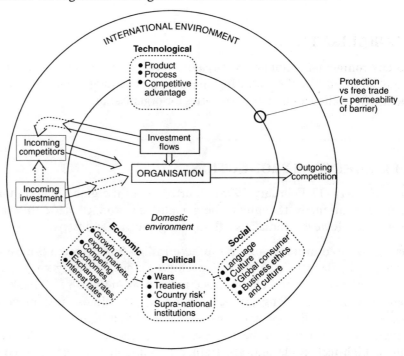

(a) In times of increasing free trade, firms (unless they have overwhelming competitive advantages in their national markets) can expect incoming competition. That said, the possibility of competing abroad is also available. Take the oil industry for example. American owned oil firms compete in the UK. UK owned firms (eg BP) compete in the US.

(b) Investment flows can also go two ways. A firm can attract investment from overseas institutions. Competing firms from overseas can receive investments from domestic institutions. For example, non-UK banks paid large sums to acquire UK stock brokers and investment firms. British firms invest in overseas companies.

(c) The permeability of barriers between the domestic environment and the international environment depends on two things.

    (i) The product (eg UK national newspapers do not compete abroad, although their owners might have overseas interests, as national newspapers are very culture-specific)

    (ii) The relative openness of the market for the product or of the economy as a whole: this influences the seriousness of threats from incoming competition and opportunities for overseas activity

(d) Political factors include the following.

    (i) Political conditions in individual overseas markets (eg package tourist firms and former Yugoslavia) or sources of supply (cg risk of nationalisation)

    (ii) Relationships between governments (eg UK exporters and investors were worried that Anglo-Chinese disputes over Hong Kong would damage their trade with China)

    (iii) Activities of supra-national institutions (eg EU regulations on product standards)

(e) Economic factors include the following.

    (i) The overall level of economic activity
    (ii) The relative levels of inflation in the domestic and overseas market
    (iii) The level and stability of the exchange rate
    (iv) The relative prosperity of individual overseas markets
    (v) Economic growth in newly industrialised countries
    (vi) A shift towards market economies

(f) Social and cultural factors include the following.

    (i) The cultures and practices of customers and consumers in individual markets

    (ii) The media and distribution systems in overseas markets

    (iii) The differences of ways of doing business (eg it is reputed that Japanese companies are concerned to avoid excessive legalism) in overseas markets

    (iv) The degree to which *national* cultural differences matter for the product concerned (a great deal for some consumer products, eg washing machines where some countries prefer front-loading machines and others prefer top-loading machines, but less so for products such as gas turbines)

    (v) The degree to which a firm can use its own 'national culture' as a selling point

NOTES

(g) Technological factors include the following.

   (i) The degree to which a firm can imitate the technology of its competitors

   (ii) A firm's access to domestic and overseas patents

   (iii) Intellectual property protection (eg copyright, patents), which varies in different countries (and was an important feature of the GATT negotiations completed in November 1993)

   (iv) Technology transfer requirements (some countries regard investments from overseas companies as learning opportunities and require the investing company to share some of its technology)

   (v) The relative cost of technology compared to labour

Activity 14   **(10 minutes)**

Tommy's Toys Ltd manufactures model cars and trucks, which are normally battery driven. The firm has not gone into exporting very much because of the trouble caused by different product standards and requirements. What are the consequences of the single European market?

Possible consequences of globalisation.

(a) Increasing competition in the 'home' market

(b) Increasing opportunities to export to overseas markets

(c) The necessity to plan activities on a global scale

(d) Opportunities to cut costs or enhance productivity by investing abroad

(e) The global market might indeed have the effect on the local market for labour. 'Low-skill' jobs might be contracted abroad, leading to greater income inequality and unemployment at home. A more recent development is the 'exporting' of high-skill jobs like software engineering. Some large software houses arrange for large quantities of their work to be undertaken by groups of Indian software engineers working from office suites in, say, Bombay or Calcutta, incurring labour costs of roughly one-tenth of those which would be involved if the same number of software engineers were to be recruited in the UK or the USA.

(f) Companies will have to consider international strategies and partnerships.

Some commentators suggest the existence of a new kind of organisation: the *global company*.

7.1 Global production and the global market

It is sometimes asserted that the 'free world as a whole can be viewed as a global market'. In other words, goods can be made and sold anywhere in the world, and competition can exist between firms from any country. In other words, trade barriers are unimportant for business decisions. There is no longer the safety of the home market.

Protectionism vs Free Trade

(a) There are good arguments to suppose that free trade, according to the principle of comparative advantage, is the most effective means of enhancing global economic welfare. The newly capitalist countries of Eastern Europe, for example, desire free trade with the EU. The United States, Canada and Mexico have made the North American Free Trade Area (NAFTA) agreement. The EU has completed the single European market programme. The World Trade Organisation enhances the prospect of free trade.

(b) At the same time there are contradictory pressures towards protectionism. That means that a country's industries are shielded from competitors or receive special treatment in some ways. Here are some examples.

    (i) Restrictions on foreign imports, usually for reasons of economic nationalism. Brazil, notoriously, prohibited companies from importing cheap US-made computers to protect its own industry.

    (ii) Restrictions on foreign ownership of key assets or industries discourages foreign investment.

    (iii) Calls for managed trade (eg President Clinton's call that 20% of the Japanese market in micro-chips be filled by American imports). Managed trade is where international trade is determined by governments, not by markets.

The existence of global trading networks is nothing new: silk was imported from China to Imperial Rome in ancient times, well before the more celebrated voyages of Marco Polo. The various European empires (eg the Portuguese, Dutch and British) were fuelled at first by competition over the lucrative global trade in spices. Even Japan, which effectively isolated itself from the world for over 200 years, allowed limited trade with the outside world through the medium of a Dutch trading post. These trading networks were effectively one way. The pattern of trade operated by the British East India Company in the first half of the 19th Century was a circular one: opium was grown in India, and exported to China: in turn, China exported tea (and silver) to Britain: Britain exported textiles and other manufactured goods to India.

Despite the doctrine of comparative advantage, the benefits of industrialisation have been sought by many nations. There have been two routes.

(a) *Import substitution*, by which a country aims to produce manufactured goods which it previously imported, by protecting local producers

(b) *Export-led growth*, by which companies, relying on cheap labour, ensured economic growth by exporting (eg Japan). The success of this particular strategy has 00depended on the existence of open markets elsewhere.

This has meant a proliferation of suppliers exporting to, or trading in, a wider variety of places. In the UK it is possible to purchase cars made in Europe, the Far East (Japan, Malaysia, Korea), the former USSR, and the US. However, the existence of global markets should not be taken for granted in terms of all products and services, or indeed in all territories.

(a) Many services are still subject to controls (eg some countries prohibit firms from other countries from selling insurance) and there are some services which by their very nature can never be exported (eg haircuts, visits to stately homes) from the home territory, although they can be provided to visitors.

(b) There is unlikely ever to be a global market for labour, given the disparity in skills between different countries, and restrictions on immigration.

NOTES

Companies can best respond by relocating, but this is perhaps not always a viable commercial option. However, certain jobs, as suggested earlier in the case of software, can be exported.

Activity 15   **(10 minutes)**

Why is it that some products or services can be marketed globally and others (so far, anyway) cannot?

In considering this issue, think about whether there is (or could be) a global market in such items as oil, luxury leather goods, McDonalds, TV sets, motor cars and financial services (banks and insurance).

7.2 Global or boundary-less corporations

The argument is as follows. Companies now produce and sell in a wide variety of countries. To serve these various markets, a company will invest in a variety of countries. Companies make decisions primarily with regard to their global ambitions, and do not take their legal nationality into account. In short, there is an increasing number of corporations, whose activities transcend national boundaries, and whose personnel come from any country. Perhaps we can summarise the differences between such global companies and multinationals by using a diagram.

(a) *Multinationals*

In this case the links between the company and countries C, B and A are likely to be severed before that with D which is the home country.

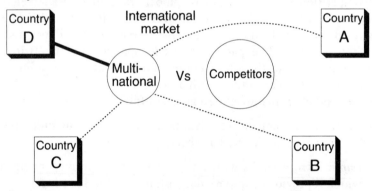

_____ = strong links (eg R&D, 'home base' head office, strategic-decision making)

·············· = weak links (subsidiaries)

(b) *Global*

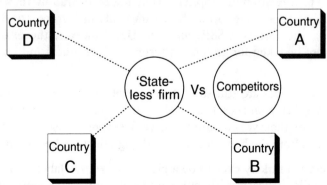

The global corporation can shift between countries.

Do these global or stateless corporations really exist? Against *Reich's* view the following objections have been raised (by *Yao-Su Hue* and, more recently, *John Cantwell* of Reading University)

(a) Most multinationals, other than those based in small nations, have less than half of their employees abroad.

(b) Ownership and control of multinationals remain restricted. This is partly because of the way in which capital markets are structured. Few so-called global companies are quoted on more than two stock markets. While capital may be mobile, different firms raise money from different sources, and investors might have different expectations of their investments.

(c) Top management is rarely as multinational as the firm's activities. This is particularly true of Japanese companies. A foreigner is rarely seen on the Tokyo-based board of a Japanese multinational. In 1991 only 2% of board members of large American companies were foreigners.

(d) National residence and status is important for tax reasons. Boundary-less corporations are not recognised as such by lawyers or tax officials.

(e) The bulk of a multinational's research and development is generally done in the home country, where strategic decisions are made. Indeed Porter says that the home market is important for product development in the information it gives about consumers.

(f) Where capital is limited, global companies stick to the home market rather than developing overseas ones.

(g) Finally, profits from a global company must be remitted somewhere. Firms like Reuters are quoted on a number of stock exchanges world wide, but they are exceptional.

It has generally been assumed that a multinational or global company must be big, no matter how decentralised. This view is increasingly being challenged.

(a) Big companies were the only ones able to surmount formidable trade barriers and the legal and tax complications of operating in more than one country. Open markets and common standards now make it easier for small firms to sell products worldwide, as these barriers are lower.

(b) When technology was expensive only big firms could afford it, so only they could benefit from the resulting scale economies. Cheap computers offer technological benefits to small firms and the scale at which economies are found is falling.

(c) Previously, international capital markets could only be accessed by large companies. More efficient capital markets are now open to smaller companies.

Chapter roundup

- It is common to analyse a business's environment into four factors, which can be given the acronym PEST (or STEP).

- Political factors relate to government activities and changes in the law. Also, they include the relationships between governments.

- Economic factors include the government's economic policy (eg rates of interest and taxation) and other issues such as the rate of economic growth, inflation and so forth.

- Socio-cultural factors include population size, structure and growth, cultural factors and practices, and changes in attitudes.

- Underlying beliefs about work are particularly significant in structuring organisational recruitment, selection and manpower utilisation practices.

- Technological factors include changes in 'apparatuses', and in the ways in which they are used (techniques) and the organisation of work processes. Technology enables new products and processes to be developed. A good illustration of this can be seen by considering the impact of technology on the manufacturing sector.

- Organisations must always be alert to competitive behaviour, competitive threats, and competitive innovation. Even public sector organisations are not immune (think about the National Health Service and its necessity to improve services, partially in response to increasing willingness among its 'customers' to take their 'business' to private hospitals).

- The international business environment is in a state of tension between pressures for liberalisation and free trade on the one hand, and pressures for the imposition of trade barriers and managed trade on the other. This tension exists to different degrees depending on the product and industry. There are few barriers to the free movement of capital.

- A result of free trade is that domestic markets are less protected than previously. This is a threat to a firm, in that the protected home market is no longer secure, but it can be an opportunity if foreign markets are available for exploitation.

- Some argue that there is now a single global market. This is true for some goods and services (eg aircraft engines) but less so for others.

- Global corporations are supposed to act independently of national considerations. Empirical research would suggest that the truly global firm is a long way off. Moreover, trade liberalisation and reduced technology costs might favour smaller businesses in the global market place.

Quick quiz

1   Give two examples of legal regulation of organisations

2   Can political change be anticipated and taken into account in management planning?

3   What is fiscal policy?

4   Give an example of regional policy.

5   List economic influences on an organisation at national level.

6   What is demography?

7   What are the major five 'belief systems' about work?

8   How can technological change affect an organisation's activities?

9   List the four key elements of WCM.

10   What is the difference between cellular manufacturing and mass production?

11   List five aspects of JIT.

12   How does a global company differ from a multinational company?

Answers to quick quiz

1   Employment law; company law; law of contract; sale of goods; health and safety.

2   Yes: governments usually publish their legislative intentions well in advance.

3   Government policy on taxation, spending and borrowing.

4   Tax incentives for regional investment; directing government contracts to development areas; special planning regimes; infrastructure investment.

5   Economic growth, inflation, unemployment, demographic change.

6   The study of human populations.

7   The work ethic; the organisational belief system, Marxism, humanism.

8   Type of products; methods of production; provision of services; identification of markets; organisation design.

9   High quality; JIT; people management; responsiveness to customers.

10   Mass production depends on high volume throughput on a production line consisting of many highly specialised processes. Cellular manufacturing can product small quantities cheaply and rapidly by having multi skilled workers carry out a sequence of operations using a *cell* of machines.

11   JIT purchasing; machine cells; set-up time reduction; uniform loading; *Kanban System*; total quality; employee involvement.

12   They make their decisions in terms of a global strategy that transcends national boundaries. They do not have identifiable primary links with any individual country, beyond legal aspects such as incorporation.

Answers to activities

1   Many instances spring to mind, especially of public-sector organisations which have been compelled to respond to the government's privatisation initiatives. Legal changes have had a significant impact on the financial services industry (with increasing regulation through controlling regulatory bodies), on health and safety practices across industry as a whole, and on the structure of the labour market through the introduction of a minimum wage. You could also consider the effects of political or legal changes originating from Brussels in the form of EU directives.

2   (a)   *Legislation on trading, pricing, dividends or tax.* This has particularly affected the former public utilities – gas, electricity, water, telecommunications – now trading as PLCs but subject to the intervention of a regulator who seeks to control pricing levels,

profitability and so forth. Tax changes in the UK are gradually eroding the financial benefits associated with company cars and with house purchase through (tax-assisted) mortgages: tax concessions in both these fields were responsible for significant distortions in the marketplace and their removal is likely to have a continuing impact.

(b) *Legislation on health and safety.* Increasingly rigorous controls affecting industrial emissions and the discharge of pollutants have created extra costs for, in particular, chemical and oil-refining industries. At the same time, it is arguable that such companies would have found it advisable to allocate more corporate funds to the prevention of environmental damage, simply because of the bad publicity arising from disasters like Bhopal.

(c) *EU Directives.* Some of these Directives have caused serious damage to businesses manufacturing cheese from unpasteurised milk.

(d) *Shifts in government policy or political emphasis.* An obvious example is the lower profile now given to defence, arising from the collapse of the Soviet empire. In welfare terms, too, a government may elect to channel funds more towards self-help projects (for example in developing countries) than towards charitable donations per se – this has an inevitable consequence for charitable organisations themselves and also for the (often small-scale) industries which design, manufacture and supply low-technology products that can easily be adapted to Third World environments.

(e) *Creating a national champion.* Malaysia's sponsorship for the *Proton* car is one illustration of this process.

3 (a) *Direct action.* The defence industry is the clearest case, with the government acting as employer for the armed forces.

(b) *Delegation to other publicly-funded bodies.* NHS hospitals and local authorities are some of the recipients of this process.

(c) *Regulation of activities* especially in financial services and the public utilities.

4 There are many reasons for the failure, so far, of large-scale economic planning. The planning organisation itself is likely to be a large organisation and will therefore endure some of the functional disadvantages of such organisations (briefly examined in the previous chapter); also it may be that economic planning pays insufficient attention to the wants, desires and needs of the individual consumers whose individual purchasing decisions collectively develop into macroeconomic activity. Centralised planning turns out to be slow, unwieldy and inadequately responsive or proactive; it is significant that countries with centralised economic planning have always been notorious for the operation of a black market.

5 A key factor in the political environment has been the end of the Cold War between the West and the Soviet bloc. This means that there is less justification for defence expenditure in the past as there are other calls on the public purse. The so-called peace dividend means that defence companies will have to adapt or go under.

6 The regional or national economic factors influencing a consumer electronics business will include all those listed since they will all have an

impact on the purchasing power of individuals and, what is more important, the willingness of such individuals to allocate their scarce disposable resources towards products in the consumer electronics field. If the rate of inflation accelerates, so does the savings ratio, thereby reducing funds available for consumer electronics acquisitions; interest rates and credit availability will have an effect on hire purchase charges; and so on.

Against a global background, again all the elements listed in will apply, to varying degrees and at different times. Protectionist measures against imports, for example, may inhibit the sales of Japanese consumer products in, say, France; exchange rates may mean that goods appear at artificially high prices (or the reverse); international trade agreements can generate restrictions on the quantity of foreign goods being allowed into a particular market. Thus there has been a voluntary ceiling on the numbers of Japanese-made cars which can enter the UK; this has been one of the factors prompting Nissan, Toyota and Honda to open factories in the UK (coupled with the need to gain privileged access to the other countries of the EU).

7 Demographic changes are particularly significant for organisations like hospitals (with maternity and geriatric units), toy manufacturers and retailers, housebuilders and undertakers. You may think of others.

8 Demographic trends in the UK suggest a continuing growth in the numbers of people below working age, not only because of the birth rate but also because more young people choose to remain within the education system, hence entering the world of work at a later stage in their lives. At the other end, life expectancy continues to grow, and this is often linked with earlier retirement ages (so far as paid employment is concerned). One implication of these developments is that no government can afford to reduce retirement ages at which individuals become eligible for a State pension, because of the enormous cost implications: indeed, governments are likely to make every effort to persuade people to make their own pension arrangements through insurance companies, in order to reduce the burden on the State.

9 (a) In marketing, children are socialised as consumers, through advertising on television, pocket money and so forth.

   (b) In human resources management, individuals joining an organisation often have to be socialised into the corporate culture. There might be various rituals on starting work.

10 (a) Clearly your answer to this question must be determined by your own personal values and beliefs.

   (b) Again, these formative influences will be very personal to you. They are likely to derive from such categories as your family and parental background, the extent to which you are an only child or whether you have siblings (your ordinal position within the family can also be significant), your ethnic and cultural circumstances, your religious affiliations, whether your parents were supportive or not, and so forth. Some research suggests that entrepreneurs are more likely to be people from certain religious backgrounds, perhaps because some religions emphasise personal responsibility rather than collective identity; also, that entrepreneurs are often individuals who have suffered unhappy childhood experiences of one kind or another (for example, bereavement, parent divorce/separation, a great deal of insecurity and geographical mobility etc).

(c)   The work (Protestant) ethic has declined in influence significantly within the past one or two decades, to be replaced initially by adherence to the humanistic belief system and then by the leisure ethic. Readers interested in knowing more would find it helpful to consult the *Dickson and Buchholz* article, 'Differences in beliefs about work between managers and blue-collar workers', *Journal of Management Studies*, 1979.

(d)   Among the organisational implications of these changes will be the impact on recruitment, selection, motivation and manpower utilisation. If the work ethic is much less powerful nowadays, then organisations can no longer rely upon sufficient employees with an internal mechanism promoting them to behave conscientiously and with commitment, so reward systems have to be consciously engineered towards the stimulation of desired behaviour. Also, if the leisure ethic is dominant among some individuals – who simply want to work between 9am and 5pm in order to earn sufficient income for a satisfactory lifestyle elsewhere – then greater efforts have to be made to turn this belief system to corporate advantage (for example, by a 'job-and-finish' system in which employees are required to accomplish an agreed level of output, but may then go home once this has been completed).

11   The journalist can type in the copy directly to the system. A good journalist, however, is not necessarily a competent graphic designer. There is a real division of labour here. The typesetter might be made redundant, or might be retrained in graphic design to exploit the opportunities afforded by the new technology.

12   You will need to pick out and pull together all the references to time in the preceding paragraphs.

13   (a)   JIT includes more than just minimising stock holdings. Read back through the section.

(b)   Dedicated cells group machines by component made rather than the type of work done.

(c)   For question (c) you will need to think through relevant parts of the whole of section 1.

14   (a)   Tommy's Toys Ltd can expect more competition.

(b)   Tommy's Toys Ltd will find it easier to compete in Europe as there should be a convergence of product standards.

15   *Kenichi Ohmae's* 1990 book *The Borderless World* contains an extensive discussion of the factors which enable some products or services to be marketed worldwide whilst others have only a narrow customer base or have to be adapted to make them acceptable in differing environments. Global products include (according to Ohmae) many battery-powered products like cameras, watches and calculators, with the reasons linked to aggressive cost reduction and economies of scale. Fashion is an additional influence and has particular resonance in the field of luxury goods like leather (think of the international designer labels like Gucci).

By contrast, some products and services have to be modified if they are translated from one country (or cultural context) to another. Causal factors include local taxation policies (so that cars marketed in the UK have to be adapted for fleet sales), religious and linguistic cues, and some specific consumer characteristics. CB radio was a success in the USA but a failure in the UK, for reasons conceivably connected to the more introverted, less communicative nature of the UK population. Even a supposedly global enterprise like McDonalds has been forced to alter the ingredients of its burgers in some countries so as not to offend Muslim or Hindu sensibilities.

TV sets are a consumer durable in many societies, but in some countries are still sold as a luxury. Financial services can be sold across national borders and indeed some British insurance companies have found a large number of customers in the newly opened countries of Eastern Europe – though of course financial products have to be tailored to the characteristics of the local economy.

One further facet of the question about global products and services concerns the extent to which an organisation will display *marketing ethnocentrism*, ie it will seek to export its indigenous activities to other societies without making any concession at all to customer expectations and characteristics. When Marks & Spencer first opened their Paris store, they implemented their well-established policy of not supplying rooms in which customers could try on the clothes, their argument being that unwanted items could always be returned without quibble. However, this was not acceptable to the French and ultimately M&S was forced to change its approach; ironically, it then implemented similar changes within its UK stores. EuroDisney in Paris was another instance of marketing ethnocentrism: initially it did not offer the possibility of wine with meals, and ignored French national days in favour of American holidays like Thanksgiving.

There are many other cases where companies have been forced to modify their products or services because of what they doubtless perceive to have been the stubborn intransigence of their potential customers.

Further question practice

Now try the following practice questions at the end of this text

Multiple choice questions: **20 to 26**

Exam style question: **4**

Chapter 5 :

ORGANISATIONAL STRUCTURE: GENERAL PRINCIPLES

Introduction

The success of two or more people in achieving an objective, depends to a large degree on whether they become *organised*, ie they determine who is going to do what and how progress is to be monitored or corrected. At the simplest level, any cohabiting arrangement between people (in marriage or flat-sharing, for example) works best when the participants practise some division of labour between shopping, housework, gardening, routine maintenance and so forth. When the purpose of the organisation is to supply a product or service on a commercial basis, or to operate in the public sector, or to undertake charitable activities, then the issue of organisation can make the difference between success and failure.

We have seen in earlier chapters competitive pressures and the influence of modern techniques like Total Quality Management or Business Process Re-engineering have focused attention on the question of organisational design. Nowadays all employees are expected to add value. This requirement and technological developments have reduced the justification for some specialised roles and departments within organisations, and, more significantly, for many of the middle layers in the managerial hierarchy.

The question of how to organise is an example of what *Tudor Rickards*, in his work on creativity, calls a *fuzzy problem*, with unclear boundaries and uncertain outcomes. However, the absence of a one-best-answer remedy still justifies the application of organisational principles, and it is these which the chapter explores in some depth. It is fashionable to denigrate bureaucratic organisations and the organisational approaches popular nowadays are built around concepts like delayering and empowerment. Ideas about structure are flexible and that there may well be a reaction against both delayering and empowerment, producing once again an argument in favour of the bureaucratic model.

In this chapter you will learn about these things.

(a) The need for an organisation to pay conscious attention to the principles of organising itself, if its objectives and purposes are to be accomplished in a cost-effective and efficient manner

(b) The need for organisational structure to be related to the contingencies within which the organisation operates

(c) Why organisations develop hierarchies, and how these hierarchies influence the motivation of employees, the communication flow (upwards and downwards), the exercise of control, and the responsiveness of the organisation to environmental turbulence

(d) The benefits and problems associated with tall and flat structures, especially when the latter take the form of delayered systems

(e) Line authority, staff authority and functional authority, and the impact of each on the organisation's technostructure

(f) The informal organisation and the achievement of the organisation's goals

(g) A contingency approach to issues of organisational design

1 CO-ORDINATION: THE REASON FOR ORGANISATION STRUCTURE

You should recall from Chapter 1 that an organisation is 'a social arrangement for the controlled performance of collective goals.' Central to the concept of organisation is the notion that the activities of the different people in the organisation – even if there are only two of them – need to be co-ordinated. So, the basic principle on which any idea of organisation is based is that of co-ordination.

At an operational level, how are the activities of disparate people co-ordinated, especially if they are doing similar tasks? *Henry Mintzberg* lists the following ways.

(a) *Mutual adjustment* co-ordinates work by informal communication. 'Work rests in the hands of the doers'. This is used for the most simple work, and the most complicated: simple, because it is an obvious mechanism for small groups (eg two canoeists); complex as in some tasks it is impossible to plan ahead if the value of the task itself is uncertain. For example, thousands of specialists may not know what needs to be done on a research project if the outcome is uncertain. They cannot predict in advance what will be discovered, and so will adjust their activities in the light of new information.

(b) *Direct supervision* achieves co-ordination by having one person responsible for the work of others. This person issues instructions and monitors performance. The division of labour is sharp.

(c) *Standardisation of work processes* occurs if the contents of work are 'specified or programmed' (eg the assembly instruction for a child's toy). This bears some relationship to *scientific management*.

(d) *Standardisation of outputs*. Outputs in this instance can mean a set level of profits (or level of performance) but the work process itself is not designed or programmed.

(e) *Standardisation by skills and knowledge* co-ordinates work by specifying the kind of training to perform the work. An example is a hospital. Doctors are trained in the necessary skills before being let loose on the patients.

Activity 1 **(10 minutes)**

Select one of the following scenarios, preferably opting for one that is familiar to you from your own experience.

(a) A conventional nuclear family of mother, father, and two children.
(b) Sharing a house or flat with others on a collective basis.
(c) Marriage or co-habitation with a member of the opposite sex.

Which of Mintzberg's methods of co-ordination are likely to be applied or to be relevant in the scenario you have selected? If you are thinking about a particular situation which you've actually experienced in the past, which methods of co-ordination were actually used? Were they sufficient? Could any others have been used as well?

BPP PUBLISHING

The importance of these co-ordinating mechanisms, Mintzberg says, is that the *relative complexity* of the work affects the chosen method of co-ordination. He suggests that the following relationships exist.

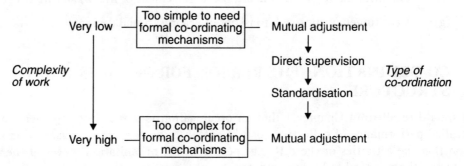

The *organisation structure* and co-ordinating methods chosen or which have emerged are responsible for the success with which a strategy is implemented, given that implementing strategy largely deals with the co-ordination and direction of individual work tasks.

As organisations grow in size, we have seen that some have a tendency to become complex. *Greiner's* model described a bureaucracy of rules and procedures. Co-ordinating the activities of people therefore implies that the organisation includes appropriate systems of communication.

2   COMPONENTS OF THE ORGANISATION

Mintzberg suggests that any organisation is based on the following principles.

(a)   Job specialisation (the number of tasks in a given job, the division of labour)

(b)   Behaviour formalisation (in other words, the standardisation of work processes)

(c)   Training (to enforce work standardisation)

(d)   Indoctrination of employees (in the organisation's culture)

(e)   Unit grouping (eg organisation by function, geographical area, or product)

(f)   Unit size (eg span of control)

(g)   Planning and control systems

(h)   Liaison and communication devices (eg task forces, networks, committees, matrix structures)

Mintzberg says that any organisation can be described in terms of five structural components, as shown on the generic diagram below.

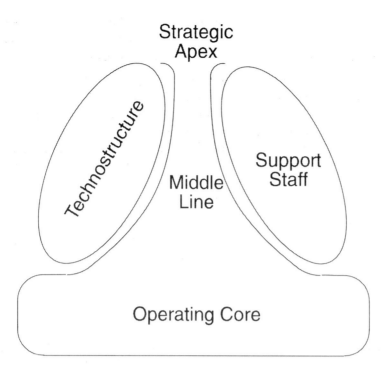

(a) The *operating core* contains those people directly involved in production (ie in securing inputs and processing them into outputs and distributing those outputs). In small organisations they are co-ordinated through mutual adjustment.

(b) The *Strategic apex* emerges with the need for supervision and control. It is the beginning of management. It ensures that the organisation follows its mission and serves the needs of its owners. Its job is supervision, boundary management and strategy.

(c) The *middle line* is the hierarchy of authority between the operating core and the strategic apex. People in this area administer the work. The chain of middle managers with formal authority runs from senior managers to front line supervisors.

(d) The *technostructure* standardises the work, although its members do not supervise it. This is a further layer of administration and planning. Work-study analysts (eg engineers) standardise work processes. Planners (eg quality staff, accountants) standardise outputs. Personnel analysts standardise skills.

(e) *Support staff* provide ancillary services such as public relations, legal counsel, the cafeteria. Support staff are different from the technostructure, as they do not plan or standardise production. They function independently of the operating core.

These elements are linked in five ways.

(a) There is an *organisation hierarchy* of formal authority. This is discussed in section 3 of this chapter.

(b) An organisation is a *flow of regulated activity*. Inputs are processed into outputs. Instructions flow down the operating hierarchy. Information passes up and down.

(c) There is a flow of *informal communication*. This denotes the real structure of communication, supplementing or bypassing the formal communication system. This is discussed in section 5 of this chapter.

(d) An organisation is a *system of work constellations*. Groups of people work on distinct tasks, each cluster deals with distinct decisions. Sometimes these are informal networks of middle managers from a number of business functions who need to co-ordinate their activities in some way. For example, in producing a set of annual financial statements, people from the finance department (for the numbers), the sales department (for detailed statistics) and public relations (for presentation) need to be involved.

(e) An organisation is a system of *ad hoc decision processes*. A decision process involves recognising a problem, diagnosing its causes, finding a solution and implementing it. For any one decision, these activities occur in a number of different places in the organisation.

3 HIERARCHY AND SPAN OF CONTROL

In Chapter 1, we quoted *Weber* who said that authority derives from charisma, tradition or reason. *Organisational authority* refers to the scope and amount of discretion given to a person to make decisions by virtue of the position he or she holds in the organisation.

The authority structure of the organisation defines two things.

(a) The part which each member is expected to perform
(b) The relationships between the members.

Delegation of authority occurs where a superior gives to a subordinate the discretion to make decisions within a certain sphere of influence.

The formal arrangement of authority is referred to as an *organisation hierarchy*. The organisation hierarchy therefore connects the strategic apex to the operating core.

3.1 Scalar chain

In Chapter 1 we introduced the *scalar chain*, the hierarchy of management within an organisation. Within this hierarchy there are line of authority or *chains of command*, running from senior management vertically downwards through the organisation connecting the various levels of managers or *links in the chain of command*.

At the head of the scalar chain and senior management, these individuals are not able to personally undertake all decision making and activity within the organisation, so they delegate. The chain of command not only represents the decision making hierarchy, it also provides a defined channel for formal communication up and down the organisation.

The number and length of chains of command varies from organisation to organisation, and tend to increase as an organisation ages. There are other influencing factors.

- The size of the organisation
- The type and complexity of the products or services produced
- The diversity of its products and services
- Its geographical spread
- The number and complexity of controls required
- The type of individuals employed.

Decisions on chains of command must also take into account the following points.

(a) *Communication effectiveness*

Most of us have played the game 'Chinese Whispers' and are well aware of the problem of distortion as information is passed from person to person; similar problems occur as additional layers are added to the chain of command. *Burns and Stalker (The Management of Innovation)* claim that upward communication tends to be filtered and neutralised as it passes from level to level; in contrast downward communications tend to be amplified. Neither scenario will benefit effective decision making or motivation.

Townsend (Up the Organisation) suggests that each additional link in the chain reduces communication effectiveness by approximately 25%.

(b) *Decision making effectiveness*

In addition to the problems of distortion, long chains of command will increase the amount of time taken for information to reach the relevant decision makers.

Similarly the longer the chain the greater the tendency towards bureaucracy, and the greater the distance of senior managers are distanced from the realities of the shopfloor.

These tendencies may limit the ability of an organisation to respond to environmental changes as quickly and effectively as its competitors.

(c) *Management development and motivation*

Long chains of command distance junior managers from thinking and decision making at the top, and limits opportunity for development into a general management role. Promotion from the bottom to the top of the chain is virtually impossible.

Staff may therefore become frustrated and de-motivated, and may leave the organisation in search of flatter organisations and greater opportunities for development and promotion.

One mechanism by which organisations can address the tendency towards lengthening chains of command is by restructuring into smaller subsidiary organisations with correspondingly shorter chains.

Encouraging the use of horizontal and informal communication channels may also promote effective communication flows.

Activity 2   **(5 minutes)**

In the paragraphs above we have argued that the chain of command should be kept as short as possible, consistent with sound management (ie efficiency and effectiveness). To what extent is this view likely to be shared by managers themselves or by people like yourself, about to embark on an organisational career?

3.2 Span of control

The *span of control* or span of management refers to the number of subordinates working for the superior official. In other words, if a manager has five subordinates, the span of control is five.

Various writers of the classical school, such as *Fayol, Graicunas* and *Urwick*, argued that the managerial span of control should be limited to between three and six. Their arguments were based on the twin beliefs that:

(a)   there should be tight managerial control from the top of the organisation; and

(b)   there are physical and mental limitations to any single manager's ability to control people and activities.

General Sir Ian Hamilton, in the classical mode of management writing, claimed that 'No one brain can effectively control more than five or six other brains'. However, the validity of this statement is conditional upon what is meant by 'control'. If it means close, day-to-day supervision, with minimal levels of delegation, then the General is probably correct; if 'control' can be exercised in other ways (eg as 'management by exception'), then his observation is flawed.

To ensure effective control, the number of subordinates and tasks over which a manager has supervisory responsibilities should therefore be restricted to what is physically and mentally possible. A narrow span of control offers certain advantages.

(a)   Tight control and close supervision; better co-ordination of subordinates' activities.

(b)   Time to think and plan; managers are not burdened with too many day-to-day problems.

(c)   Reduced delegation; managers can do more of their work themselves.

(d)   Better communication with subordinates, who are sufficiently small in number to allow this to occur.

However, a wide span of control has its positive aspects.

(a)   Greater decision-making authority for subordinates
(b)   Lower supervisory costs
(c)   Perhaps, greater motivation though job satisfaction

3.3   Tall and flat organisations

The span of control concept has implications for the *shape* of an organisation. A *tall organisation* is one which, in relation to its size, has a large number of management levels, whereas a flat organisation is one which, in relation to its size, has a smaller number of hierarchical levels. A tall organisation implies a narrow span of control, and a flat organisation implies a wide span of control.

Some theorists suggested that a tall organisation structure is inefficient, despite the advantages of a narrow span of control.

(a)   It increases overhead costs.

(b)   It creates extra communication problems, since top management is more remote from the work done at the bottom end of the organisation, and information tends to get distorted or blocked on its way up or down through the organisation hierarchy.

(c)   Management responsibilities tend to overlap and become confused as the size of the management structure gets larger.

(d)   The same work passes through too many hands.

(e)   Planning is more difficult because it must be organised at more levels in the organisation.

A flatter organisation structure would reduce these effects.

Behavioural theorists add that tall structures impose rigid supervision and control and therefore block initiative and ruin the motivation of subordinates. A wide span of control means that more authority will be delegated to subordinates. Greater discretion leads to job enrichment and motivation.

However, there are two aspects of tall organisations that may be advantageous.

(a)   It keeps span of control narrow.

(b)   A large number of career steps are provided in the hierarchical ladder. More frequent promotions are possible and this may be good for motivation.

There is a trade-off between the span of control and the tallness/flatness of an organisation.

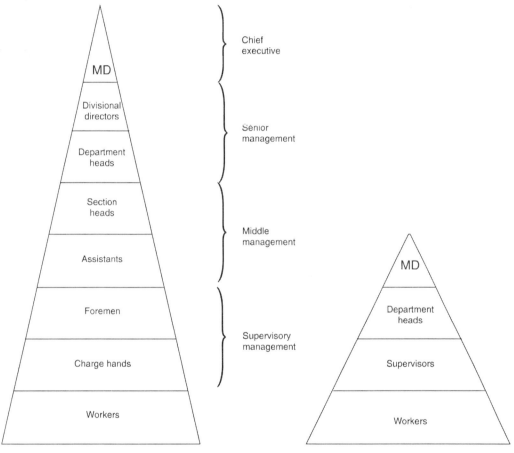

The span of control should not be too wide, but neither should an organisation be too tall.

Flat organisations have become more common as a result of the current fashion for delayering and empowerment. Moreover, some of the information analysis and processing tasks of middle management are being replaced by information technology.

EXAMPLES: BP, BT AND HARLEY DAVIDSON

The September 1992 edition of Accountancy reported a decimation of middle managers – not just penpushers but technicians also – at a number of large British companies.

(a) BP. In 1990, a new chairman announced 1,000 job losses of which 160 were head office managers – a 30% cut at head office.

(b) BT. Project Sovereign in 1990 involved a change in structure. Of a total cut in jobs of 19,000, 6,000 came from management ranks. Recently, BT has announced it also wanted to cut senior management jobs.

(c) Harley Davidson, in the US, cut the number of production controllers at one of its plants from 27 to 1.

The reasons for this trend are as follows.

(a) Information technology makes the information processing work of middle managers redundant.

(b) The trend towards team-working, whereby responsibility is devolved to groups of workers, renders redundant the directing and controlling role of middle managers.

Activity 3 (10 minutes)

Draw up an organisation chart for an organisation to which you belong.

(a) How many layers are there in the scalar chain?
(b) What is your span of control?
(c) What is your supervisor's span of control?
(d) What is the average span of control?
(e) Can you improve this design?

It is reasonable to accept the view that there is a limit to a supervisor's capabilities and that the span of control should be limited. However, the span of control is now thought to be dependent on several factors.

The nature of the manager's work load is likely to influence the span of control he or she can deal with efficiently.

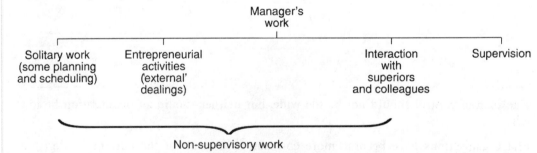

The greater the proportion of non-supervisory work in a manager's work load the narrower the span of control should be or, the greater the delegation of authority to subordinates should be.

Other factors influence the width of the span of control.

(a) The geographical dispersion of the subordinates (particularly relevant in the case of homeworking).

(b) Whether subordinates' work is all of a similar nature (wide span possible) or diversified

(c)   The nature of problems that a supervisor might have to help subordinates with

(d)   The degree of interaction between subordinates (with close interaction, a wider span of control should be possible)

(e)   The competence and abilities of both management and subordinates

(f)   Whether close group cohesion is desirable. Small groups will be more cohesive, with a better sense of team work. This would call for narrow spans of control

(g)   The amount of help that supervisors receive from staff functions (such as the personnel department)

The is no universally correct size for the span of management, and no current writer on organisations would suggest that a correct span exists, without considering the particular circumstances of any particular individual organisation or department.

4   THE TECHNOSTRUCTURE'S INFLUENCE: LINE, STAFF AND FUNCTIONAL AUTHORITY

The technostructure, as we have seen, is involved in standardising work processes or outputs. But how is this authority exercised over the middle line and the operating core? When analysing the types of authority which a manager or a department may have, the terms *line*, *staff* and *functional* authority are often used.

(a)   *Line authority* is the authority a manager has over a subordinate.

(b)   *Staff authority* is the authority one manager or department may have in giving specialist advice to another manager or department, over which there is no line authority. Staff authority does not entail the right to make or influence decisions in the department being advised.

(c)   *Functional authority* is a hybrid of line and staff authority, whereby a specialist staff manager or department has the authority, in certain circumstances, to direct activities or procedures. An example is where a finance manager has authority to require timely reports from line managers. Functional authority is the way by which the technostructure controls operations, by enforcing standards.

This means that managers must know whether their authority is line, staff or functional to avoid confusion.

Activity 4   **(2 minutes)**

What sort of authority is exercised:

(a)   by the financial controller over the chief accountant?
(b)   by the production manager over the production workforce?
(c)   by the financial controller over the production manager?

An organisation might be divided into *functions*, such as production, finance and marketing. The functions required by each business will depend on the individual situation of the business. In small companies and other such organisations, most functions of the technostructure and support staff may be provided by external agencies: for example, a computer bureau may take on many data processing applications (eg payroll work). But owing to specialisation of work, there must be both middle line and technostructure within an organisation of any size.

Activity 5 (10 minutes)

Before you read the next section, ask yourself what are likely to be the results when an organisation gives too much power and authority to the technostructure (represented by, for example, the personnel function, the accounts department, or research and development). Compare your answer with the points made in the following paragraph – and try to think of organisations which have suffered precisely because the technostructure has enjoyed excessive influence.

Too much authority to the technostructure might have the following consequences.

(a) Specialist management sometimes have divided loyalties between their organisation and their profession or speciality. Computer specialists, for example, might want to introduce up to date computer systems when these might not be the most appropriate for the organisation, nor indeed valued by the internal customers of the information technology function.

(b) Many specialist managers, such as accountants, have skills which can be marketed to other organisations, so that their career is not necessarily tied to one company. Managers in the middle line, on the other hand, might be trained exclusively for service in one company, or one type of company or organisation (eg a bank or the Civil Service). When specialist managers do not necessarily have a vested, long term interest in their organisation, it might be argued that their authority should be kept under restraint.

(c) Technostructure managers tend to introduce rules and procedures and these tend to increase the bureaucratic nature of the formal organisation, with possible adverse repercussions on its efficiency. This might restrict middle line management's freedom of choice and flexibility. For example, a formal system of job descriptions might restrict the ability of management to make frequent reviews of their organisation's job structure.

(d) When an organisation has a multi-divisional structure, with international interests, each subsidiary or division (or sub unit of a division) might have its own support functions. When there is a technostructure management at group level, divisional level and below divisional level, a further organisational problem is created because of overlapping interests, boundaries of authority and influence, and conflicting advice and opinions between the different levels.

(e) When the technostructure builds up an empire of influence and authority, it may be difficult to measure the benefits to the organisation of various aspects of its work: because the benefits of the work are indirect they cannot always be measured in money terms. The only way to restrict the growth of costly, unjustifiable technostructure work might be to appoint outside consultants from time to time to carry out a cost/benefit analysis of such a department on behalf of senior management. This is frequently the basis for an exercise in Business Process Re-engineering (BPR), which was discussed in the previous chapter. Indeed, the use of the term *empire* here helps to show why securing benefits from a BPR review can be so difficult, since individual managers naturally wish to defend their territories from what they perceive to be an unwarranted invasion.

Functional authority is a move towards *dual authority*, and carries elements of a *matrix structure* (see Chapter 7) although the line manager retains ultimate authority for the functioning of his department. For this reason, and to avoid complex political problems, functional authority is usually exercised through the establishment of systems, procedures and standards, rather than by ongoing direct intervention on the part of functional specialists.

4.1 Implications of line and staff authority for organisational design

There are drawbacks to the power of the technostructure; a knowledge of the problems should enable management to deal with them, and thus use it more effectively. These drawbacks are as follows.

(a) There is a danger that experts in the technostructure may, intentionally or not, undermine the authority of middle line managers. Subordinates might defer to the expertise of the technostructure, and show a lesser willingness to accept the judgement of their line boss.

(b) Friction may also occur when managers in the technostructure report to a higher authority in the scalar chain of command. For example, a management accountant may submit reports about the cost performance of a manager in the middle line to the production director or the managing director.

(c) Technostructure managers have no line authority and therefore no responsibility for what actually happens, other than within their own area of expertise. If they give advice which is acted on, but fails to achieve desired results, they might blame the line managers for not acting on their advice properly.

(d) The thinkers of the technostructure may have their heads in the clouds. Their ideas may be unrealistic and impracticable; middle line managers, having received poor advice from an expert, might tar all technostructure managers with the same brush and resist all future expert help.

(e) The technostructure managers may attempt to usurp line authority. Any change in the boundaries of authority should be the result of conscious planning, and not surreptitious empire-building.

The solutions to these problems are easily stated, but not easy to implement in practice.

(a) Authority must be clearly defined, and distinctions between the authority enjoyed by the middle line and technostructure clearly set out (eg in job descriptions).

(b) Senior management must encourage managers in the middle line to make positive efforts to discuss work problems with technostructure advisers, and to be prepared to accept their advice. The use of experts should become an organisational way of life.

(c) Managers in the technostructure must be fully informed about the operational aspects of the business on which they are experts. By providing them with detailed information they should be less likely to offer impractical advice.

(d) When expert advisers are used to plan and implement changes in the running of the business, they must be kept involved during the implementation, monitoring and review of the project. Specialists must be prepared to accept responsibility for their failures and this is only really possible if they advise during the implementation and monitoring stages.

There has to be a balance between line managers and technostructure managers. The problem is seen, typically, as follows.

(a)   If line managers had a superhuman ability to learn all the specialist skills necessary for management, there would be no need for staff functions.

(b)   It is only because specialist support is essential (eg accountants, computer specialists) or advisable (eg personnel specialists) – because line managers would on their own be unable to make well informed decisions – that the problem arises of finding a balance of authority or influence between middle line and technostructure.

Activity 6   **(5 minutes)**

Before you read the next section, ask yourself what are likely to be the results when an organisation gives too much power and authority to middle line managers (as opposed to the technostructure). This question has current relevance because returning power and authority to line managers has been one of the major recent structural themes. Many large-scale hierarchies have, for example, eliminated their central personnel function and required local managers to exercise largely autonomous responsibilities for personnel matters.

Too much authority to line managers might result in rapid short term business development, and high short term profits. However, it brings risks.

(a)   Legal restrictions (eg the rules of the Companies Act) will be inadvertently broken.

(b)   Personnel planning for the long term might be overlooked and staff morale lowered.

(c)   Up to date technology and management techniques might be overlooked.

(d)   Important work not directly involved with day to day operations might be neglected.

The cumulative long-term effect will be damaging to the organisation.

Activity 7   **(10 minutes)**

Ticket and Budget International is a large multinational firm of accountants. The firm provides audit, tax, and consultancy services for its many clients. The firm has a strong Technical Department which designs standardised audit procedures. The firm has just employed a marketing manager. The marketing manager regards an audit as a product, part of the entire marketing mix including price (audit fees), place (usually on the client's premises) and promotion (advertising in professional journals) The marketing manager is held in high regard by the firm's senior partner. The marketing manager and the senior partner have unveiled a new strategic plan, drawn up in conditions of secrecy, which involves a tie-up with an advertising agency. The firm will be a *one-stop shop* for business services and advice to management on any subject. Each client will have a dedicated team of auditors, consultants and advertising executives. Obviously, a member of staff will be a member of a number of different teams.

The firm has recently settled a number of expensive law suits for negligence (which it has, of course, 'contested vigorously') out of court, without admitting liability. The Technical Department is conducting a thorough review of the firm's audit procedures.

In the light of what we have covered in this section, what do you think will be the organisational influences on the proposed strategy?

---

5 THE INFORMAL ORGANISATION

The structure of an organisation is affected by the people working within it, and an *informal organisation* exists side by side the formal one. The informal organisation of a company is so important that a newcomers have to 'learn the ropes' and become accepted by his fellow workers before they can settle effectively into their job,

When people work together, they establish social relationships and customary ways of doing things.

(a)   They form social groups, or cliques (sometimes acting against one another).

(b)   They develop informal ways of getting things done: norms and rules which are different in character from the rules *imposed* by the formal organisation.

Social groups, or cliques, may act collectively for or against the interests of their company; the like-mindedness which arises in all members of the group strengthens their collective attitudes or actions. Whether these groups work for or against the interests of the company depends to some extent on the type of supervision they get. If superiors involve them in decision-making, they are more likely to be management-minded.

Given an acceptable social atmosphere, the informal organisation of a company improves communications, facilitates co-ordination and establishes unwritten methods for getting a job done. These may by-pass communication problems and lengthy procedures; and they may be more flexible and adaptable than the formal ways of doing things.

The informal structure of a company may 'take over' from the formal organisation when the formal structure is slow to adapt to change.

When employees are dissatisfied with aspects of formal organisation (if they dislike the work they do or the person they work for) they are likely to rely more and more heavily on an informal organisation at work to satisfy their personal needs in their work situation. When this happens, it has been argued (by *Argyris* and others) that the informal organisation of the individual will act against the efficiency of the formal organisation. Informal organisations always exist within a formal organisation, and if employees are properly motivated, these informal organisation should operate to the advantage of the formal organisation's efficiency and effectiveness.

Activity 8 **(10 minutes)**

Think about the role of the informal structure in any organisation with which you are familiar, either because of paid employment (perhaps on a part-time basis) or because of your voluntary membership (eg school, college, university, youth club and so forth).

(a) Was the informal organisational functional or dysfunctional, ie did it help or hinder the achievement of the organisation's goals?

(b) How influential and significant was the informal organisation?

(c) To what extent do the observations made here reflect your own thoughts about the way the informal organisation operated? In what respects, if at all, do our comments not coincide with your own recollections?

A conclusion might therefore be that management should seek to harness the informal organisation to operate to the benefit of the formal organisation. In practice, however, this will be difficult because unlike formal organisation, which does not change even when the individual employees move into and out of jobs (by promotion, transfer, appointment, resignation or retirement) most informal organisations depend on individual personalities. If one member leaves, the informal organisation is no longer the same, and new informal organisations will emerge to take its place.

EXAMPLE: A COMPUTER COMPANY

The *Harvard Business Review* in July-August 1993 reported on the significance of informal relationships.

(a) They are often reasons for high staff turnover.

(b) They indicate where people actually look for advice.

(c) They indicate those individuals who are most trusted by colleagues and subordinates.

A senior manager in a Californian-based computer company was having difficulty in getting staff to work together on a strategic plan. The co-ordinator on the task force could not get the others to work together because of his weak position on the 'trust network'. A second co-ordinator was appointed who was more trusted by a wider group of people. Thus the senior manager exploited the informal organisation.

---

6 INFLUENCES ON ORGANISATION STRUCTURE: CONTINGENCY THEORY

Are there any universally applicable rules governing organisation design? Prescriptions about organisational design and culture and so forth have been offered as some sort of elixir of success.

(a) The *human relations school (Mayo et al)* held that the key to organisational success was the individuals within it. Organisation design should remove impediments to the workforce's natural commitment to work.

(b) The *classical approach (Fayol)* was more concerned with the bureaucratic aspects identified earlier in this chapter. All organisations have similar problems which can best be solved by judicious thought and investigation.

Both these approaches rested on the assumption that a single key can be found which would unlock the door to success. The contingency approach (it is not a theory, but a number of guiding principles) holds that the success of an organisation is determined by the interaction of three main influences.

(a) Its personnel and their talents, skills, attributes and motivation
(b) The task and the activities which the organisation is involved in
(c) Its environment

This also implies that within the same organisation there will be a number of different structure types. Some areas will be bureaucratic and role-determined, others will display a less formal, organic structure. Take, for example, a theatre. Its accounts department will work in a very different way from the acting troupe. The contingency approach would hold that the type of structure must be appropriate to both *task performance* and *individual/group* satisfaction.

Buchanan and Huczynski classify the activities carried out by an organisation into four main categories.

(a) *Steady-state activities* are routine and programmable: an example would be regular account maintenance). This would imply a bureaucracy.

(b) *Policy-making activities* are concerned with the identification of goals, the allocation of scarce resources and directing people. Policy-making is the job of the strategic apex and technostructure. It is less routine.

(c) *Innovation activities* are concerned with things which change the company's goals or processes, such as new product development or new market investigation. Such activities require a flexible approach.

(d) *Breakdown activities* deal with emergencies and crises. A bureaucratic system of rules might be best here, if the emergency can be planned for (eg a fire). Otherwise an *organic* structure might be appropriate to guarantee a rapid response.

A contingency approach implies that there are different structures suitable for different activities.

NOTES

Activity 9 (5 minutes)

Imagine you are responsible for designing the organisation structure in a new general hospital. Given the comments by Buchanan and Huczynski, what kind of structures would be appropriate within each of the following.

(a)   A geriatric unit with many long-stay patients.
(b)   A maternity unit.
(c)   The strategic planning department.
(d)   The casualty/emergency unit.

Mintzberg develops some hypotheses about the influences on an organisation's structure.

(a)   The older the organisation, the more formalised its behaviour. Work is repeated, so is more easily formalised.

(b)   Organisation structure reflects the age of the *industry's* foundation.

(c)   The larger the organisation, the more *elaborate* its structure.

(d)   The larger the organisation, the larger the average size of the units within it.

(e)   The larger the organisation, the more formalised its behaviour (for consistency).

(f)   The more sophisticated the technology, the more elaborate and professional the administrative structure will be.

(g)   The automation of the operating core transforms a bureaucratic administrative structure into an organic one. This is because procedures are incorporated into equipment routines or software. It requires specialists to manage the process, and such people tend to communicate informally. An organic organisation is characterised by fluid hierarchies and communications, and is the opposite of the rigid rule-bound bureaucracy.

(h)   The more dynamic the environment, the more organic the structure. (See Chapter 7.)

(i)   The more complex the environment, the more decentralised the structure. (See Chapter 7.)

(j)   The more diversified the markets, the greater the propensity to split into market based departments.

(k)   Extreme environmental hostility is a force for centralisation, since central control permits rapid action.

(l)   Environmental disparities encourage selective decentralisation for some activities, centralisation for others.

(m)   The more an organisation is subject to external control (eg by government, holding company) the more centralised and formalised its structure.

(n)   The power needs of organisational members (to control others, or at least to control their own working conditions) lead to centralisation.

(o)   Fashion is a poor guide. For example, while bureaucracies are deeply unfashionable, they are often the best at doing certain kinds of work. Indeed, *Burns and Stalker*, who developed the concept of organic and mechanistic organisations, held after research, that *neither* type of organisation had any *intrinsic* merits, as the key variables were *product-*

PUBLISHING

markets and *technology*. A company using unchanging technology in familiar markets can work very well with a bureaucracy.

Early contingency theorists believed that certain variables – such as the environment, or technology had a *determining* influence on organisation structure. Furthermore, any one organisation could contain a variety of different structures.

Against this determinist theory of organisation structure, whether this is technological or environmental, can be set the *strategic choice* theory of organisational design, which holds that organisation structure is a management decision: organisation structure, according to *Child*, results from:

'*an essentially political process in which constraints and opportunities are functions of the power exercised by decision-makers in the light of ideological values.*'

Chapter roundup

- Organisations exist to co-ordinate the activities of different individuals. Co-ordination can be achieved by mutual adjustment, direct supervision, standardisation of work processes, outputs, and skills and knowledge.

- An organisation can be analysed into five components: strategic apex, middle line, operating core, technostructure and support staff.

- These are linked by formal hierarchies of authority, flows of regulated activity, informal communications, work groups, and decision processes.

- Formal organisation hierarchy is based on the principles of the scalar chain and span of control. There is a possible trend towards flatter organisations (fewer management levels and wider spans of control than hitherto).

- Line authority is the direct authority a superior has over a subordinate. Staff authority derives from the giving of specialist advice. Functional authority is the exercise of specialist advice. Functional authority is the exercise of staff authority through procedures, or the right by staff departments to require certain actions by line managers.

- The informal organisation describes the system of personal and political relationships in an organisation, outside the normal hierarchy.

- The contingency theory suggests that there is no one best way of designing an organisation. It holds that one or more factors will have a determining influence on organisation structure. The strategic choice theory suggests that managers are free to choose the structure which suits them.

Quick quiz

1   What might be the relationship between work complexity and co-ordination mechanisms?

2   State three of Mintzberg's principles of organisation.

3   What are the five component parts of an organisation?

4   Why might a tall organisation structure be a good one?

5   What is functional authority?

6   What types of organisational activity were observed by Buchanan and Huczynski?.

7   According to Mintzberg, what effect is environmental hostility likely to have on organisational structure/

8   What is meant by the 'strategic choice' theory of organisational design?

Answers to quick quiz

1   Both very simple and very complex forms of work are probably best coordinated by mutual adjustment. Direct supervision and standardisation of some kind are suited for work between the two extremes of complexity.

2   Job specialisation; behaviour formalisation; training; indoctrination of employees; unit grouping; unit size; planning and control; and liaison and communication devices

3   Operating core; middle line; strategic apex; technostructure; support staff

4   It keeps spans of control narrow and offers plentiful opportunities for promotion and career development.

5   The authority of a specialist, non-line manager to direct activities procedures for specialist purposes

6   Steady state activities; policy making activities; innovation activities; and breakdown activities

7   It is likely to be a force for centralisation, since central control permits rapid action.

8   Management decisions determine organisation structure.

Answers to activities

1   The answers to this exercise will obviously depend on the scenario chosen. However, in a relatively unstructured and informal setting like a family, or shared accommodation, or co-habitation, it is likely that *mutual adjustment* will feature prominently, and *standardisation by skills and knowledge* (ie using the expertise of people who, for instance, are authoritative about car maintenance or housepainting). What can happen is that one or more of the members in the group setting can display what has been termed *learned helplessness*, ie they profess congenital ignorance about a necessary task (like housework or ironing) in order to ensure that it is undertaken by others.

Co-ordination by *direct supervision* can sometimes occur in families where the parents (or one of them) is sufficiently authoritative, but since Victorian times it has become progressively rarer.

2   A short chain of command has several disadvantages from the point of view of individual employees. Access to their immediate boss may be more restricted because of his/her wider span of control; promotion possibilities are reduced (though when promotion does occur, it will involve a very significant leap up the corporate ladder); there are fewer chances of acquiring status through the kind of subtle (but nonetheless significant) differentials found in large-scale bureaucracies. On the other hand, as our material explains, short chains of command imply increased levels of autonomy at each decision-making level and therefore, potentially, much more job satisfaction.

4   (a) and (b) are both examples of line authority.
(c) is staff or perhaps functional authority.

5   Your own response to activity 5 can be compared with the five ideas suggested in the following paragraph (a) to (e).

One example of an organisation which has (in the past) suffered because of excessive influence wielded by one part of the technostructure is the global electronics firm Philips, whose headquarters are located in Eindhoven, Holland. Historically, Philips has been dominated by a powerful research and development activity, which has invented products which are exciting and interesting, technologically, but which have found little favour among customers. In other words, Philips has been R&D-led rather than marketing-led, and this has been the root cause of their difficulties with, say, video-player systems.

Other instances can occur, less dramatically, when the personnel function 'tells' line managers how many staff they may employ and even who those staff will be (perhaps because the personnel department feels it has to find a place for some people who are surplus to requirements in another part of the organisation).

6   If line managers are required to operate their departments or units as largely autonomous profit centres, then they will be excessively concerned with short-term results, because these will be the principal criteria against which they are measured. Long-term planning is neglected or receives only lip service; the process of managing becomes tactical rather than strategic; potential economies of scale are dissipated because staff functions are centralised.

7   Accountants have divided loyalties – to their firm, and to their profession. The Technical Department will almost certainly resist such a change, as the proposals devalue audit to being one of only many business services to management. An audit is undertaken for the benefit of shareholders, not the company management. The Technical Department (the firm's technostructure) is also powerful as enforcement of the standards it will suggest should reduce professional negligence costs. The technostructure will thus exert a powerful influence over strategy and business practices. External influences include professional associations which have a technostructural influence on the profession as a whole. (The marketing manager may also be misled as to the degree to which customers want a one-stop shop for accounting and advertising services.)

9   (a)   A *geriatric unit* with many long-stay patients is an example of what Buchanan and Huczynski call a 'steady-state activity' which, organisationally, implies a bureaucracy.

    (b)   A *maternity unit* needs to be relatively organic in order to cope with fluctuating workloads and short-term disruptions.

    (c)   The *strategic planning department* is concerned, in Buchanan and Huczynski's terms, with 'policy-making' and 'innovation' – which suggests that it should be flexible and organic, perhaps built around a project management approach with fluctuating project teams.

    (d)   The *casualty/emergency unit* requires some rules that will be strictly adhered to in the event of, say, a predictable emergency like an aircraft accident or major motorway disaster; on the other

NOTES

hand, some flexibility is essential, as with the maternity unit, in order to guarantee a rapid response.

Further question practice

Now try the following practice questions at the end of this text

Multiple choice questions: **27 to 34**

Exam style question: **5**

Chapter 6 :
ORGANISATION DESIGN

Introduction

In the previous chapter we looked at the general principles of organisation theory and design, with a particular focus on a contingency model. Chapter 7 is more concerned with applications. Relying closely on *Mintzberg's* insights, we argue that any organisation represents a complicated network of groups and individuals, departments and functions, mainline activities and support staff, key players and periphery people, internal and external stakeholders. The structural pattern emerging from this collection of interested parties is likely to indicate which one is dominant at any given moment. For example, where the dominant power group is the strategic apex, the structural pattern will be simple/entrepreneurial. Each power group was introduced in Chapter 6; here we investigate the principal features, and the advantages and disadvantages of the structural categories linked with the power groups, using Mintzberg's terminology and conceptualisation.

Of course, most organisations do not fall directly into one of Mintzberg's categories. This may be a result of the fact that in any transition from one dominant power group to the next, the structure at any given moment will be a mixture of current requirement plus historical legacy. Moreover, the reality of many organisation structures is that they develop from an uneasy compromise between stakeholders, none of them capable of exerting sufficient influence on their own to dictate how control within the organisation should be exercised. We have already seen, too, that widely differing views about the 'ideal' structure can legitimately be held: small wonder that when these differing views are articulated, the outcome is an untidy amalgamation of some or all of them.

So in the second half of the chapter we look at multifocused hierarchies, exemplified by hybrid and matrix designs. The continuing debate on centralisation versus decentralisation is examined, and the chapter ends with an extended discussion on the 'mechanistic'/'organic' dichotomy, first developed by *Burns and Stalker* in *The Management of Innovation*, and virtually indispensable to any analysis of organisational change.

Indeed, one of the key issues you should consider is the degree to which any given structural 'type' exhibits the flexibility to accommodate change, whether imposed externally (eg through government action, competitive pressures and so forth) or internally inspired (eg by the arrival of a new chief executive). Change is so much a feature of the organisational environment that the ability to cope with change must be a key factor in assessing the functionality of organisational designs.

To conclude we examine some of the issues involved in changing the processes that take place within the structure.

In this chapter you will learn about these things.

    (a)   Mintzberg's five categories of structural design for organisations

    (b)   The circumstances in which it may be beneficial for organisations to display hybrid or matrix features, showing how such patterns can be effective

Business Basics: Organisational behaviour

(c)   The relative merits and weaknesses of centralisation and decentralisation within organisational structures

(d)   The basis of the mechanistic/organic continuum and the relevance of this approach to the successful management of change, especially in an organisational context of permanent turbulence and discontinuity

(e)   Business process engineering

1   STRUCTURAL CONFIGURATIONS: MINTZBERG

Mintzberg's theory of organisational configuration is a way of expressing the main features by which both formal structure and power relationships are expressed in organisations. We have already mentioned the five main points.

(a)   The *operating core* encompasses those members who perform work directly related to the production of goods and services.

(b)   The *strategic apex* has to ensure that the organisation serves its mission. The apex is responsible to the organisation's owners.

(c)   The *middle line* connects the strategic apex to the operating core, in a formal hierarchy.

(d)   The *technostructure* contains analysts (eg accountants, work planners) who aim to effect 'certain forms of standardisation in the organisation'.

(e)   *Support staff* provide support outside the normal workflow. They have no standardising function or control over the work of the operating core.

Mintzberg has written that there are five *ideal types* of organisation, each of which configures the five components above in a significantly different way. Why should this be so?

Mintzberg believes that each area of the organisation has its own *dynamic*, which leads to a distinct type of organisation.

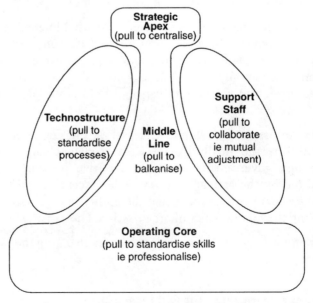

(a)   The strategic apex wishes to retain control over decision-making. An example is a manager's refusal to delegate. A more direct example is the decision-making structure in a dictatorship, where power is closely controlled at the centre. It achieves this when the co-ordinating mechanism is *direct supervision*.

(b) The technostructure's reason for existence is the design of procedures and standards. For example, the preparation of accounts has become more highly regulated. Technicians spend hours designing management information systems, when, according to Mintzberg, many managers rarely use them.

(c) The members of the operating core seek to minimise the control of administrators over what they do. They prefer to work autonomously, achieving what other co-ordination is necessary by mutual adjustment. As professionals, they rely on outside training (such as medical training) to standardise skills.

(d) The managers of the middle line seek to increase their autonomy from the strategic apex, and to increase their control over the operating core, so that they can concentrate on their own segment of the market or with their own products.

(e) Support staff only gain influence when their expertise is vital. Mutual adjustment is the co-ordinating mechanism.

1.1 The simple structure (or entrepreneurial structure)

The *strategic apex* wishes to retain control over decision-making, and so exercises what Mintzberg describes as a *pull to centralise*. Mintzberg believes that this leads to a *simple structure*, thus:

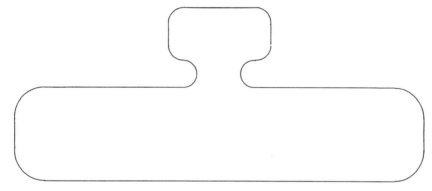

(a) Note three things.

   (i) The wide control span

   (ii) The lack of a middle line, implying minimal hierarchy

   (iii) The lack of technostructure, implying little formalisation or standardisation of behaviour

(b) Co-ordination is achieved by direct supervision with few formal devices. It is thus flexible.

(c) The environment for such a configuration should be relatively simple but fast moving, so standardisation cannot be used to co-ordinate activities.

(d) Mintzberg believes the simple structure is characteristic of small, young organisations.

(e) Centralisation is advantageous as it reflects management's full knowledge of the operating core and its processes.

(f) It is risky as it depends on the expertise of one person.

BPP PUBLISHING

Activity 1 (10 minutes)

Can you identify any examples of the simple (or entrepreneurial) structure from your knowledge of organisations, either through direct contact or through secondhand knowledge acquired by, say, reading the financial press? How far do such instances exemplify the points made by Mintzberg, especially about the riskiness associated with a structure dependent on a single person? What normally happens to such organisations as time goes on?

1.2 The machine bureaucracy

The *technostructure* exerts a pull for standardisation of procedures and processes. It thus creates a *machine bureaucracy*.

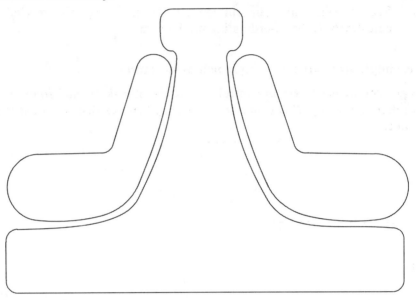

(a) This is the classic bureaucracy, working on a sophisticated and well-tuned set of rules and procedures.

(b) The operating core is highly standardised. Direct supervision by the strategic apex is limited as work standardisation ensures co-ordination.

(c) The technostructure is the key part. Power rests with analysts who standardise other people's work.

(d) Formal communication is most important. Authority is hierarchical.

(e) There is a strong emphasis on the division of labour, and in particular on control. Uncertainty has to be eliminated.

(f) Conflict is rife between different departments, between the middle line and the technostructure, and between operating core and management.

(g) The environment is simple and stable. Machine bureaucracies are associated with routine technical systems.

(h) The machine bureaucracy is the most efficient structure for integrating sets of simple and repetitive tasks.

(i) Machine bureaucracies cannot adapt: they are designed for specialised purposes. They are driven by performance, not problem solving.

Activity 2   **(10 minutes)**

Can you identify any examples of a machine bureaucracy from your direct experience or knowledge of organisations acquired through the media? How far do such instances exemplify the generalisations advanced by Mintzberg about machine bureaucracies? What is the future for such organisations?

1.3 The professional bureaucracy

The *operating core* has a pull for standardisation, not of work processes but of individual skills. The operating core seeks to minimise the influence of *all* administrators (mainly the middle line and technostructure) over work. The resulting configuration is called the *professional bureaucracy*. Examples are hospitals and accountancy firms.

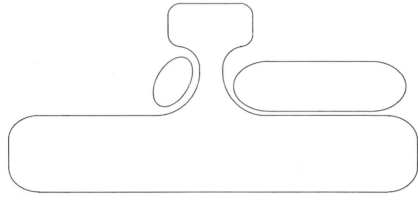

(a) It hires trained specialists who are all socialised in the skills and values of the profession. A school is an example. Teachers' work in the classroom is not directly supervised.

(b) Co-ordination is achieved by common standards, which originate outside its structure. (A hospital's procedures of doing simple operations may not be developed in-house, but imported.)

(c) Power is based on expertise, not formal position.

(d) Work processes are too complex to be standardised by a technostructure.

(e) The operating core is the key part. There is an elaborate support staff to service it. A technostructure might exist for budgeting but not for designing work processes.

(f) Work is decentralised. Professionals control their own work, and seek collective control over the administrative decisions which affect them.

(g) There might be two organisation hierarchies.

    (i)   *Bottom-up* for the operating core doing the work.
    (ii)   *Top-down* for the support staff.

    An example is a barristers' chambers. Barristers are co-ordinated by the clerk, but they retain collective authority over the clerk. The clerk, on the other hand, will exercise direct control over secretarial services.

(h) Professional administrators also manage much of the organisation's boundary.

(i) It can be democratic.

(j)   The professional bureaucracy cannot always cope with any variations of standards, as control is exercised through training.

1.4   The divisional form (or diversified form)

The middle line seeks as much autonomy for itself as possible. It exerts a *pull to balkanise* (ie to split into small self-managed units). The result is the *divisional form*, by which autonomy is given to managers lower down the line. Sometimes divisionalisation is referred to as federal decentralisation. The prime co-ordinating mechanism is standardisation of outputs.

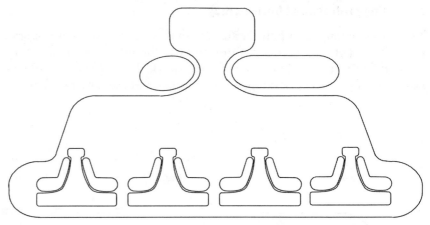

(a)   Divisionalisation is a very widely used configuration. It is the division of a business into autonomous regions or product businesses, each with its own revenues, expenditures and profits.

(b)   A machine bureaucracy is the configuration of each division. This is because each division is monitored by its objective performance towards a single integrated set of goals. In other words, divisions have to reach performance targets set by the strategic apex.

(c)   There is a division of labour between the divisions and the head office. Communication between divisions and head office is restricted, formal and related to performance standards. Influence is maintained by headquarters' power to hire and fire the managers who are supposed to run each division.

(d)   Divisionalisation is a function of organisation size, both in staff numbers and in product-market activities.

(e)   Mintzberg believes there are inherent problems in divisionalisation.

   (i)   A division's environment is restricted to products and markets. It is partly insulated by the holding company from capital markets, which ultimately reward performance.

   (ii)   It 'piggybacks on the machine bureaucracy in a simple stable environment, and may feel drawn back to that form'.

   (iii) The economic advantages it offers over independent organisations 'reflect fundamental inefficiencies in capital markets'. (In other words, different product-market divisions might function better as independent companies.)

   (iv)   The performance control system drives the divisions to be more bureaucratic than they would be as independent corporations.

   (v)   Big companies bring a threat to competitive markets.

(vi) Headquarters management have a tendency to usurp divisional profits (eg by management charges, cross-subsidies, head office bureaucracies).

(vii) In some businesses, it is impossible to identify completely independent products or markets.

(viii) Divisionalisation is only possible at a fairly senior management level, because there is a limit to how much independence in the division of work can be arranged.

(ix) It is a halfway house, relying on personal control over performance by senior managers and enforcing cross-subsidisation.

(x) Divisional performance is not directly assessed by the market.

The multi-divisional structure might be implemented in one of two forms.

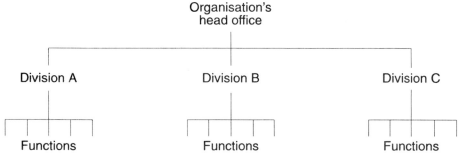

This enables concentration on particular product-market areas, overcoming problems of functional specialisation (which is discussed in Section 2 of this chapter) at a large scale. Problems arise with the power of the head office, and control of the resources. Responsibility is devolved, and some central function might be duplicated.

The holding company (group) structure is a radical form of divisionalisation. Subsidiaries are separate legal entities. The holding company can be a firm with a permanent investment or one which buys and sells businesses.

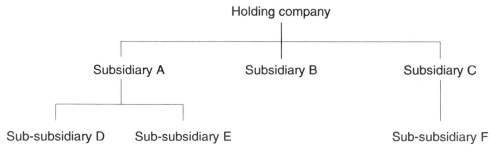

Divisionalisation has some advantages.

(a) It focuses the attention of management below top level on business performance and results.

(b) Management by objectives can be applied more easily. 'The manager of the unit knows better than anyone else how he is doing, and needs no one to tell him'.

(c) It gives more authority to junior managers, and therefore provides them with work which grooms them for more senior positions in the future.

(d) It tests junior managers in independent command early in their careers, and at a reasonably low level in the management hierarchy.

(e) It provides an organisation structure which reduces the number of levels of management. The top executives in each federal unit should be able to report direct to the chief executive of the holding company.

The rules for successful divisionalisation are as follows.

(a) It must have properly delegated authority, but strong control should be retained at the centre by head office. In other words, management of federal units are free to use their authority to do what they think is right for their part of the organisation, but they must be held properly accountable to head office (eg for profits earned).

(b) A decentralised unit must be large enough to support the quantity and quality of management it needs. It must not rely on head office for excessive management support.

(c) Each decentralised unit must have a potential for growth in its own area of operations.

(d) There should be scope and challenge in the job for the management of the decentralised unit.

(e) Federal units should exist side by side with each other. If they deal with each other, it should be as an arm's length transaction. Where they touch, it should be in competition with each other. There should be no insistence on preferential treatment to be given to a fellow unit by another unit of the overall organisation

---

Activity 3   **(10 minutes)**

Can you identify any instances of the divisional (or diversified) form of organisation, either from your direct experience or from your knowledge of organisations acquired through other sources? How far are your chosen examples successful, in your view – in other words, do they manage to achieve a productive balance between central control and divisional autonomy?

1.5 The adhocracy

The *support staff* exert a pull of their own, towards *collaboration*. The *adhocracy* does not rely on standardisation to co-ordinate its activities, yet it is much more complex than the simple structure.

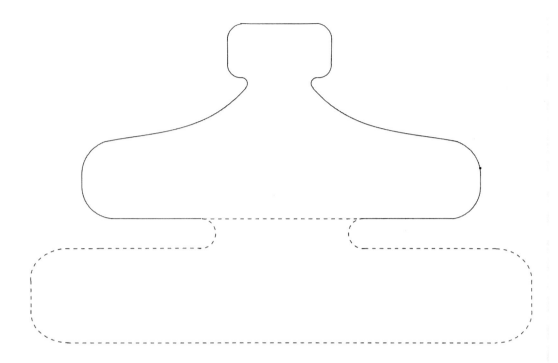

(a) The adhocracy is complex and disorderly.

  (i) There is little formalisation of behaviour.

  (ii) Specialists are deployed in market-based project teams which group together and disperse as and when a project arises and ends.

  (iii) Co-ordination is informal.

(b) The adhocracy relies on the expertise of its members, but not through *standardised* skills. Instead the mix of skills is important. For example, a film is made by a director, actors, camera people, set designers etc.

(c) A matrix structure might exist, but there are a large number of management roles eg project managers. Managers do not plan or supervise, but co-ordinate.

(d) Decision-making power depends on the type of decision and the situation in which it is made, rather than level in hierarchy. 'No-one ... monopolises the power to innovate'.

(e) The *operating adhocracy* seeks to *innovate* to serve its clients, whereas the professional bureaucracy seeks perfection. (Mintzberg uses an analogy of a theatre company. An adhocratic theatre company produces new plays. A professional bureaucratic one would seek to produce ever more perfect renditions of Shakespeare.) The operating core is retained.

(f) The *administrative adhocracy* innovates to serve its own convenience. Note that the operating core is split off, frequently subcontracted or automated, or even forms a separate organisation. The support staff are important, a central pool of expert talent from which project teams are drawn.

(g) Strategy is hard to determine in the adhocracy. It depends partly on the projects that come along (like a film studio). The strategic apex does not formulate strategies, but is engaged in battles over strategic choices (eg which films shall we make?) and liaisons with the outside parties.

(h) The adhocracy is positioned in a dynamic and complex environment.

(i)   The adhocracy is driven to bureaucratise itself as it ages. The organisation will eventually specialise in what it does best, driving it to more stable environmental conditions and predictable work processes, leading perhaps to a professional bureaucracy.

Adhocracies sometimes exist because the complexity of their technical systems require a trained support staff to operate them.

(a)   The adhocracy is an ambiguous environment for work. This elicits complex human responses, as many people dislike ambiguity.

(b)   The adhocracy is not suitable for standardised work: it is a custom producer.

(c)   It has a high cost of communication, and workloads are unbalanced.

1.6   Concluding thoughts

The usefulness of Mintzberg's theory of structural configuration is that it deals with issues beyond formal organisation structure such as the type of work the organisation does, the complexity of the tasks and the environment.

Mintzberg mentions one other co-ordinating factor: *mission*. A *missionary organisation* is one welded together by ideology or culture. There is job rotation, standardisation of values (*norms*) and little *external* control, as in a religious sect.

As a cautionary note, these 'ideal types do not exist as such. They are *simplified models* of real organisations: most contain elements of all types.'

Activity 4 **(15 minutes)**

Joan Porely has recently been appointed general manager of a prestigious eye hospital in the UK. Together with the most senior eye surgeon in the hospital, Dr Iris Glass, she is touring the world to find examples of best practice not only in surgical procedures and medical technology but also in the organisation of the hospital's work. In their travels, they visit the St Petersburg Research Institute of Eye Microsurgery. This is run by Doctor Fyodr Sviatorov, and has become a multi-million pound business. This hospital has pioneered the use of surgery to correct sight defects like short-sightedness. An operation is typically performed as follows.

1 The patient receives an anaesthetic outside the operating theatre, and lies down on a conveyor belt which takes the patient into the operating theatre.

2 A computer calculates the depth of the cuts to the cornea of the eye.

3 Surgeon A marks exactly the depth and lengths of the cuts.

4 Surgeon B makes between eight and sixteen cuts with a diamond scalpel

5 Surgeon C adjusts the cut to ensure maximum eyesight gain.

6 Surgeon D cleans and dresses all the wounds.

7 A doctor administers any necessary antibiotics.

About 200 patients per day can be processed on this conveyor belt system. Doctor Sviatorov says: 'The important thing is to make sure you know what you're doing in advance, and for the sort of standard operation that we do, that's quite easy. We employ senior surgeons, myself included, to design the operation process. They scour the medical press for any new techniques which our surgeons in the theatres can be trained to use: we try to minimise the discretion they can use so they can concentrate on accuracy. One day, I'd be happy to use robots to do all the dirty work. But still, I'm hoping to set up satellite hospitals in Minsk and Kiev. Even in the West one day!'

Doctor Glass is curious. She says: 'I think this system has some uses. But it stifles individual initiative and professional judgement, especially in more complex operations. You need professionally qualified surgeons who are able to oversee all aspects of an operation. And what if something goes wrong on this production line? And I do not doubt that we in London can be just as productive if we had proper administrative support and technical backup. I feel compelled to add that I have my doubts as to the long term safety and suitability of surgery on eyes to correct standard problems like short-sightedness. Glasses and contact lenses are cheaper and safer. I'm not sure how I could justify it in terms of medical ethics, either. After all, we want to help people, not make money out of them.'

Joan Porely is impressed with the work, especially as it makes a profit for the hospital: she has already been looking at ways to improve her hospital's financial position. Such a unit in London, she feels, could attract patients from all over Europe, the Middle East, and even North America, and this quick operation could even be sold, as Doctor Sviatorov has suggested, as part of a package holiday. ('It brings a whole new dimension to sightseeing,' he says.)

Required

Analyse the above case in the light of Mintzberg's theory of structural configurations and organisation goals.

2 Design of the formal hierarchy: departmentation

A formal hierarchy is normally adopted once an organisation reaches a certain size. The organisation might be split into different business areas. The creation of departments is known as *departmentation*. Different patterns of departmentation are possible, and the pattern selected will depend on the individual circumstances of the organisation. Various methods of departmentation are as follows.

By *geographic area* (or territory). Some authority is retained at Head Office (organised, perhaps, on a functional basis) but day to day service operations are handled on a territorial basis. Within many sales departments, the sales staff are organised territorially.

(a)   The *advantage* of geographic departmentation is better and quicker local decision making at the point of contact between the organisation (eg as represented by a salesman) and its customers. Also, it may be less costly to establish area factories/offices: For example, costs of transportation and travelling may be reduced)

(b)   The *disadvantage* of geographic departmentation is the *duplication of functions*. For example, a national organisation divided into ten regions might have a customer liaison department in each regional office. If the organisation did all customer liaison work from head office it might need fewer managerial staff.

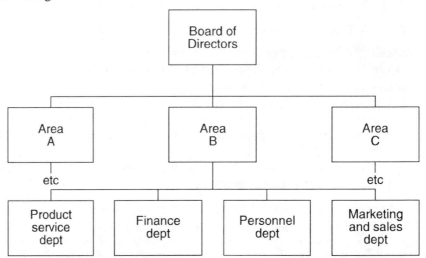

By *function*. Functional organisation is logical and traditional and accommodates the division of work into specialist areas. Primary functions in a manufacturing company might be production, sales, finance, and general administration. Sub departments of sales might be selling, marketing, distribution and warehousing. The problem is one of co-ordination. It is organisation by internal skills specialisms and individual jobs rather than by customer or product (which ultimately drive a business).

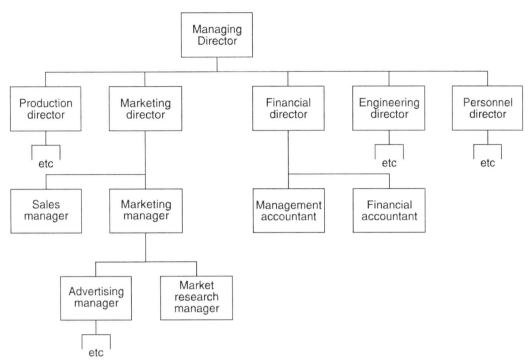

By product. Some organisations group activities on the basis of products or product lines. Some functional departmentation remains (eg manufacturing, distribution, marketing and sales) but a divisional manager is given responsibility for the product or product line, with authority over personnel of different functions.

(a) Advantages of product departmentation.

(i) Individual managers can be held accountable for the *profitability* of individual products.

(ii) Specialisation can be developed. For example, some salesmen will be trained to sell a specific product in which they may develop technical expertise and thereby offer a better sales service to customers. Service engineers who specialise in a single product should also provide a better after sales service.

(iii) The different functional activities and efforts required to make and sell each product can be co-ordinated and integrated by the divisional/product manager.

(b) The *disadvantage of product departmentation* is that it increases the overhead costs and managerial complexity of the organisation.

By brand. A brand is the name or design which identifies the products or services of a manufacturer or provider and distinguishes them from those of competitors. Large organisations may produce a number of different brands of the same basic product, such as washing powder or toothpaste. This is viable because branding brings the product to the attention of buyers and creates brand loyalty. Often the customers do not realise that two rival brands are in fact produced by the same manufacturer.

(a) Because branding is linked with unique marketing positions it becomes necessary to have brand departmentation. As with product departmentation, some functional departmentation remains (especially on the manufacturing side) but brand managers have responsibility for the brand's marketing and this can affect every function.

(b)   Brand departmentation has similar advantages and disadvantages to product departmentation. In particular, overhead costs and complexity of the management structure are increased, the relationships of a number of different brand departments with the one manufacturing department being particularly difficult.

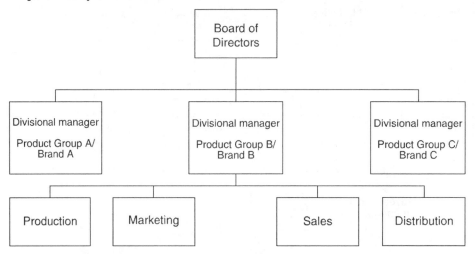

By customer or market segment. A manufacturing organisation may sell goods through wholesalers, export agents and by direct mail. It may therefore organise its sales, marketing and distribution functions on the basis of types of customer, or market segment. Departmentation by customer is commonly associated with sales departments and selling effort, but it might also be used by a jobbing or contracting firm where a team of managers may be given the responsibility of liaising with major customers, for example, discussing specifications and completion dates, quality of work and so on.

By numbers. When menial tasks are carried out by large numbers of workers, supervision can be divided by organising the workers into gangs of equal size. Departmentation by numbers alone is rare; an example might be the organisation of an army into divisions and regiments.

By shifts. With shift-working employees are organised by the clock.

By equipment specialisation. The most obvious example of departmentation based on equipment specialisation is provided by the data processing departments of large organisations. Batch processing operations are conducted for other departments at a computer centre (where it is controlled by computer specialists) because it would be uneconomical to provide each functional department with its own large mainframe computer.

Divisionalisation is the division of a business into autonomous regions or product businesses, each with its own revenues, expenditures and capital asset purchase programmes, and therefore each with its own profit and loss responsibility. Divisions of the organisation might be subsidiary companies under the holding company, or profit or investment centres within a single company.

Divisionalisation was discussed in Section 1.

EXAMPLE: BRITISH GAS

In February 1994, British Gas announced some radical changes in its organisation structure. British Gas then enjoyed a near monopoly on the supply of gas to 18m of

Britain's 24m households: this disappeared in 1996. The restructuring was perhaps a response to this.

(a) The old structure was based on twelve regions: a geographical/territorial basis. 'The regional structure was well suited to the last 25 years or so, during which British Gas expanded its share of the non-transportation energy market from 7% to 50%. But managers of the regions resisted moves which would have eroded their power bases.' (Financial Times, 25 February 1994).

(b) British Gas's monopoly had been eroded.

   (i) In 1996, about 90% of the 'small user' market (mainly residential customers) was to be open to competition: by 1998 this will be 100%.

   (ii) Of medium users, in 1991 British Gas had 100% of the market: by 1994 competitors were after up to 30% of the market.

   (iii) Of large user markets, competitors had access to 9% of the market; by the end of 1994 this was expected to rise to 78%.

(c) In response to this, British Gas announced a restructuring of the business into five business streams, based in different parts of the UK with different employees, assets etc. These were to be as follows.

   (i) Transport and storage (gas transmission to other parts of British Gas and competitors, for fee income).

   (ii) Public gas supply (domestic and low business users).

   (iii) Contract trading (for higher business users, where British Gas was already facing full competition)

   (iv) Servicing and installation (concentrating on installing and servicing gas central heating)

   (v) Retailing (sale of appliances)

Restructuring does not come cheap. The restructuring charge announced on 24 February 1994 was £1.65 billion; 5,000 jobs were expected to go.

The case emphasises the impact of environmental considerations (new competition) and business strategy on structure.

---

3 MULTIFOCUSED HIERARCHIES: HYBRID AND MATRIX DESIGNS

Many organisation hierarchies in practice combine elements of a number of these approaches. For example, a firm might have the following structure.

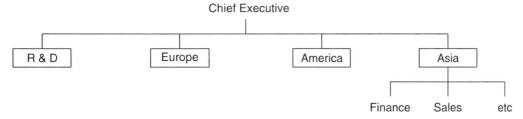

In this, research and development is centrally organised, but the operating activities of the firm are geographically arranged. This is an example of a hybrid structure.

Another example is given below. R&D, human resources and finance are centralised functions: other functions are arranged on a product basis.

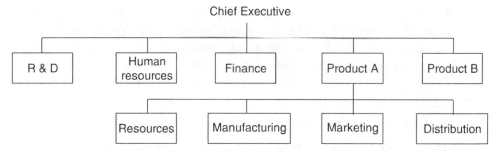

Most organisations contain features of the hybrid structure, because:

(a)   certain business activities are better arranged on a functional basis for reasons of economies of scale, pooling of knowledge and efficiency;

(b)   others are best organised on a product or territorial basis, with the particular advantages of specialisation, local knowledge, and flexibility.

Activity 5   **(5 minutes)**

The Erewhon Bank plc has branches in the UK, Eire, France, Germany and Denmark. It grew from the merger of a number of small local banks in these countries. These local banks were not large enough to compete single-handedly in their home markets. The Erewhon Bank hopes to attract both retail and corporate customers, through its use of home banking services and its heavily advertised Direct Bank service, which is a branchless bank to which customers telephone, fax or post their instructions. The bank also specialises in providing foreign currency accounts, and has set up a revolutionary service whereby participating customers can settle their own business transactions in ECUs (European Currency Units).

What sort of organisation structure do you think would be appropriate?

3.1   Matrix organisation

Matrix organisation is a structure which provides for the formalisation of management control between different functions, whilst at the same time maintaining functional departmentation. It can be a mixture of functional, product, and territorial organisation.

A golden rule of classical management theory is *unity of command:* everyone should have only one boss. Thus, staff management can only act in an advisory capacity, leaving authority in the province of line management alone. Matrix management may possibly be thought of as a reaction against the classical form of bureaucracy by establishing a structure of dual command.

Matrix management first developed in the 1950s in the USA in the aerospace industry. *Lockheed,* the aircraft manufacturer, was organised in a functional hierarchy. Customers were unable to find a manager in Lockheed to whom they could take their problems and queries about their particular orders, and Lockheed found it necessary to employ project expediters as customer liaison officials. From this developed project co-ordinators, responsible for co-ordinating line managers into solving a customer's problems. Up to this point, these new officials had no functional responsibilities.

Owing to increasingly heavy customer demands, Lockheed eventually created programme managers, with authority for project budgets and programme design and scheduling. These managers therefore had functional authority and responsibilities, thus a matrix management organisation was created. It may be shown diagrammatically as a *management grid.*

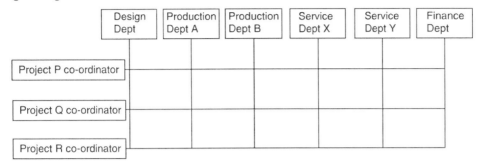

Authority would be shared between the project co-ordinators and the heads of the functional departments. Functional department heads are responsible for the organisation of the department, but project co-ordinators are responsible for all aspects of the project itself. An employee in a functional department might expect to receive directions from a project co-ordinator as well as from the departmental head.

Departmentation by product has already been described; it is also possible to have a product management structure superimposed on top of a functional departmental structure in a matrix; product or brand managers may be responsible for the sales budget, production budget, pricing, marketing, distribution, quality and costs of their product or product line, but may have to co-ordinate with the R&D, production, finance, distribution, and sales departments in order to bring the product on to the market and achieve sales targets, ie:

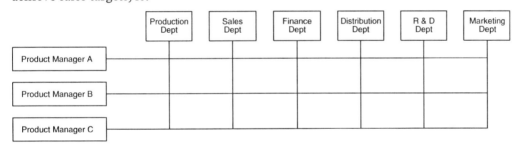

Note. The product managers may each have their own marketing team; in which case the marketing department itself would be small or non-existent.

The authority of product managers may vary from organisation to organisation. *JK Galbraith* drew up a range of alternative situations:

Business Basics: Organisational behaviour

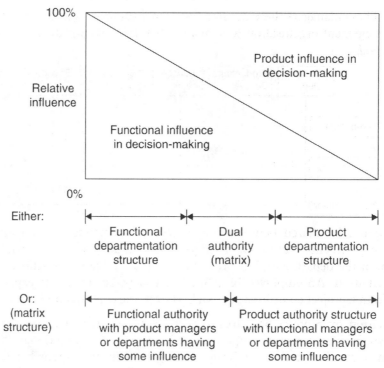

Once again, the division of authority between product managers and functional managers must be carefully defined.

Project teams are another example of a simple matrix structure. Project teams are integral to the adhocracy. A project may be interdisciplinary, and require the contributions of an engineer, a scientist, a statistician and a production expert, who would each be appointed to the team from their functional department, whilst still retaining membership and status within the department.

Level in departmental hierarchy	Department				
	A	B	C	D	E
1	X	(X)	X	X	(X)
2	(X)	X	X	X	X
3	X	X	(X)	X	X
4	X	X	X	(X)	X

Members of the project team (circled) would provide formal lateral lines of communication and authority, superimposed on the functional departmental structure. Leadership of the project team would probably go to one of the more senior members in the hierarchy, but this is not a requirement of the matrix structure.

Matrix management challenges classical ideas about organisation in two ways.

(a)   It rejects the idea that a person should only report to one superior.

(b)   It subverts the bureaucratic ethic of authority based on status in the formal hierarchy.

Matrix organisation means that subordinates have two (or more) superiors, in the sense that they must report to both a functional manager and a project manager. However, a subordinate cannot easily take *orders* from two or more bosses. There are two possible arrangements.

(a) A subordinate takes orders from the functional manager and the project manager has to ask the functional manager to give instructions to the subordinate.

(b) A subordinate takes orders from one manager about some specified matters and orders from the other about different specified matters. The authority of each would have to be carefully defined. Even so, good co-operation would still be necessary.

The advantages of a matrix structure are said to be the following.

(a) It is flexible.

    (i) Employees adapt quickly to a new challenge or new task, and develop an attitude which is geared to accepting change.

    (ii) It may be short-term, as with project teams or readily amended: a new product manager can be introduced by superimposing tasks on those of the existing functional managers.

Flexibility should facilitate efficient operations in the face of change.

(b) It should improve communication within the organisation.

(c) Dual authority gives the organisation multiple orientation. For example, a functional departmentation will often be production-oriented, whereas the superimposition of product managers will provide the organisation with some market orientation.

(d) It provides a structure for allocating responsibility to managers for end-results. A product manager is responsible for product profitability, a project leader is responsible for ensuring that the task is completed, and a study course leader has direct responsibility for the provision of a complete, efficient and effective course to students.

(e) It provides for inter-disciplinary *co-operation* and a mixing of skills and expertise.

(f) Arguably, it motivates employees to work harder and more efficiently by providing them with greater participation in planning and control decisions.

Argyris praised matrix organisations because they break down departmental monopolies and foster participative management styles based on teamwork, which he hoped would eliminate the traditional subordinate-superior relationships.

A matrix organisation is most suitable in the following situations.

(a) There is a fairly large number of different functions, each of great importance.

(b) There could be communications problems between functional management in different functions (eg marketing, production, R&D, personnel, finance).

(c) Work is supposed to flow smoothly between these functions, but the communications problems might stop or hinder the work flow.

(d) There is a need to carry out uncertain, interdependent tasks. Work can be structured so as to be task centred, with task managers appointed to look after each task, and provide the communications (and co-operation) between different functions.

(e) There is a need to achieve common functional tasks so as to achieve savings in the use of resources – ie product divisions would be too wasteful, because they would duplicate costly functional tasks.

(f) The organisation proceeds through specific assignments on behalf of its customers: as in the Lockheed case, each customer benefits from having a named individual in the organisation to whom queries and complaints can be addressed, and who can act as the link person between the organisation and the client. Thus a project type of organisation is especially appropriate to professional companies like management consultants, architects, surveyors and so forth.

(g) The organisation is seeking to concentrate attention on those aspects of its operations where *either* deficient performance needs to be corrected or continuous improvement would yield competitive advantage. A project approach enables corporate activity to be focused and spotlighted in a manner which cannot easily be accomplished through conventional control systems.

The *disadvantages* of matrix organisation are said to be as follows.

(a) Dual or triple authority threatens a conflict between functional managers, product/project managers and nation/country managers. Where matrix structure exists it is important that the authority of superiors should not overlap and areas of authority must be clearly defined. A subordinate must know to which superior he is responsible for a particular aspect of his duties.

(b) One individual with two or more bosses is more likely to suffer role stress at work.

(c) It is sometimes more costly – eg product managers are additional jobs which would not be required in a simple structure of functional departmentation.

(d) It may be difficult for the management of an organisation to accept a matrix structure. It is possible that a manager may feel threatened that another manager will usurp his authority. (Where authority is not clearly defined, this is likely to happen. The decision-making process would also be expected to slow down.)

Setting up a matrix organisation often implies the existence of a *project-based culture*, as we have seen. It is therefore worthwhile to spend a paragraph explaining the differences between a *project culture* and what *J Rodney Turner* (*The Handbook of Project-Based Management*, 1993) refers to as an 'operations environment' in which most activities are part of a regular routine. More about this in Chapter 11.

(a) The operations environment is (relatively) stable, whereas the project environment is flexible, because all projects are unique.

(b) Operations, through habitual incremental improvement or the learning/experience curve, become efficient more or less automatically over time, whereas projects, having no precedent, can be measured against genuine value-added effectiveness.

(c) In an operations environment, people fulfil roles defined by precedent, and so can lose sight of their objectives; project teams must be goal-orientated.

(d) All projects carry the risk of failure because they are breaking new boundaries; in operations, previous experience means that the level of risk is much reduced. In essence, therefore, projects are risk management; operations are *status quo* management.

4   CENTRALISATION AND DECENTRALISATION

Centralisation and decentralisation refer to the degree to which authority is delegated in an organisation – and therefore the level at which decisions are taken in the management hierarchy.

(a)   The simple structure would suggest centralisation of decision-making authority. The professional bureaucracy would suggest decentralisation.

(b)   In a machine bureaucracy, operations might be decentralised, but standards might be set centrally and distributed throughout the organisation. The same might be true of a professional bureaucracy.

Arguments in favour of centralisation and decentralisation	
Pro centralisation	*Pro decentralisation/delegation*
1 Decisions are made at one point and so easier to co-ordinate.	1 Avoids overburdening top managers, in terms of workload and stress.
2 Senior managers in an organisation can take a wider view of problems and consequences	2 Improves motivation of more junior managers who are given responsibility – since job challenge and entrepreneurial skills are highly valued in today's work environment.
3 Senior management can keep a proper balance between different departments or functions – eg by deciding on the resources to allocate to each.	3 Greater awareness of local problems by decision makers. Geographically dispersed organisations should often be decentralised on a regional/area basis.
4 Quality of decisions is (theoretically) higher due to senior managers' skills and experience.	4 Greater speed of decision making, and response to changing events, since no need to refer decisions upwards. This is particularly important in rapidly changing markets.
5 Possibly cheaper, by reducing number of managers needed and so lower costs of overheads.	5 Helps junior managers to develop and helps the process of transition from functional to general management.
6 Crisis decisions are taken more quickly at the centre, without need to refer back, get authority etc.	6 Separate spheres of responsibility can be identified: controls, performance measurement and accountability are better.
7 Policies, procedures and documentation can be standardised organisation-wide.	7 Communication technology allows decisions to be made locally, with information and input from head office if required.

Whatever system is set up, it is of paramount importance that all managers at all levels should clearly know where they fit into the organisation.

The structural trick for organisations is to balance two opposing sets of forces.

(a)   The *centralising impact* of professional management, designed to produce a cohesive corporate strategy and the rational, efficient allocation of resources which will support this strategy; and

(b)   The *centrifugal* effect of the forces important for fostering entrepreneurship, risk-taking and innovation.

The corporate nutcracker	
Professional management *(centralising forces)*	*The entrepreneurial organisation* *(centrifugal forces)*
Focused, cohesive corporate strategy	Opportunistic, unpredictable action
Centralised information, influence	Peripheral, autonomous activity(less control)
Organise for stability (bureaucracy)	Loose structure, independent business units (flexibility)
Reward administrative ability	Reward innovative ability
Preserve *status quo*	New opportunities, change
Rational, efficient allocation of resources	Unplannable, variable resource requirement
Management of risk	Taking of risk
Top-down decision making	Bottom-up decision making
Shared beliefs/common practices	Challenges to conventional wisdom

5   MECHANISTIC AND ORGANIC STRUCTURES

5.1   Bureaucracy and mechanistic structures

Bureaucracy is the term used to describe a hierarchical rule-bound organisation. *Weber* specified several general characteristics of bureaucracy, which he described as 'a continuous organisation of official functions bound by rules'. We identified these in Chapter 1. Mintzberg as we have seen, identifies two kinds of bureaucracy.

(a)   Machine bureaucracy, similar to Weber's description, based on standardisation of work processes, functional groupings, size.

(b)   Professional bureaucracy (eg hospitals) based on standardisation of skills.

Bureaucracy can be a very appropriate form of organisation when the environment is reasonably stable, since procedures can be both rational and flexible.

Criticisms of rules

The very strength of some of the characteristics of bureaucracy may in some cases be turned into a cause of weakness. *Gouldner* argued that rules are both functional and dysfunctional in a bureaucracy.

(a)   *Rules are functional:* they take away from subordinates the feeling that their superiors, in issuing orders, hold power over them. This in turn reduces the interpersonal tensions which otherwise exist between superiors and subordinates, and for this reason the 'survival of the work group as an operating unit' is made possible by the creation of rules.

(b) *Rules are dysfunctional:* employees use rules to learn what is the minimum level of behaviour expected from them, and there is a tendency for employees to work at this minimum level of behaviour. This, in turn, suggested Gouldner, creates a requirement for close supervision. Greater pressure from supervisors will make subordinates more aware of the power the supervisor holds over them, thereby increasing tension within the work group.

Activity 6   **(10 minutes)**

What do you think about working in an organisation which has a set of rules (or procedures and routines) which are meant to cover more or less any situation that you will encounter? After all, such situation is not unlike the one you will experience when you are working towards an academic or professional qualification by means of attendance at college or university, or through some form of distance learning programme. Normally, the rules governing the acquisition of your degree, diploma or professional membership will be as tightly drawn as possible.

How would you feel about operating under such similarly comprehensive rules when working as a paid employee? How could you accommodate yourself to the rules, in the sense that you (appear to) comply with them whilst nonetheless retaining some degree of individual autonomy?

Bureaucracies can be hampered by dysfunctional influences.

(a) The complexity of decision-making slows down the decision-making process.

(b) Conformity creates ritualism, formalism and 'organisation man'.

(c) Personal growth of individuals is inhibited, although bureaucracies tend to attract, select and retain individuals with a tolerance for such conditions.

(d) Innovation is discouraged; there is a school of management thinking which believes that too much bureaucracy represses creativity and initiative in moulding organisation man.

(e) Control systems are frequently out of date. According to *Michel Crozier*, the control mechanism is hampered by rigidity: bureaucracies learn only slowly from their mistakes.

(f) Bureaucracies are slow to change. Michel Crozier stated that 'a system of organisation whose main characteristic is its rigidity will not adjust easily to change and will tend to resist change as much as possible'.

(g) Decision making is over simplified (one of the criticisms of too many procedures).

Bureaucracies and change

Burns and Stalker contrasted the organic structure of management (see below), which is more suitable to conditions of change, with a *mechanistic* system of management, which is more suited to stable conditions. A mechanistic structure, which appears very much like a bureaucracy, has the following characteristics.

(a) Authority is delegated through a hierarchical, formal scalar chain, and decision-making power is based on the hierarchy.

(b)   Communication is *vertical* rather than lateral.

(c)   Individuals regard their own tasks as specialised and not directly related to the goals of the organisation as a whole.

(d)   There is a precise definition of duties in each individual job (rules, procedures, job definitions).

Mechanistic systems are *unsuitable in conditions* of change because they tend to deal with change by cumbersome methods.

(a)   The *ambiguous figure system:* in dealing with unfamiliar problems authority lines are not clear, matters are referred 'higher-up' and the top of the organisation becomes overburdened by decisions.

(b)   *Mechanistic jungle:* jobs and departments are created to deal with the new problems, creating further and greater problems.

(c)   *Committee system:* committees are set up to cope with the problems. The committees can only be a temporary problem-solving device, but the situations which create the problems are not temporary.

5.2   Organic organisations: suitability for change

In contrast to mechanistic structures, Burns and Stalker identified an *organic structure* (also called an *organismic structure*). They believed organic structures were better suited to conditions of change than mechanistic structures. The organic structure has the following characteristics.

(a)   There is a 'contributive nature' where specialised knowledge and experience are contributed to the common task of the organisation.

(b)   Each individual has a realistic task which can be understood in terms of the common task of the organisation.

(c)   There is a continual redefinition of an individual's task, through interaction between the individual and others.

(d)   There is a spread of commitment to the concern and its tasks.

(e)   There is a network structure of authority and communication.

(f)   Communication tends to be *lateral* rather than vertical (ie gangplanks, rather than up and down the scalar chain).

(g)   Communication takes the form of information and advice rather than instructions and decisions.

Burns and Stalker recognised that organic systems would only suit individuals with a high tolerance for ambiguity and personal stresses involved in being part of such an organisation but the freedom of manoeuvre is considered worth this personal cost, for individuals who prize autonomy and flexibility.

6   BUSINESS PROCESS RE-ENGINEERING

As we have discussed there are a number of important factors that managers should take into account when making decisions about how best to structure a given organisation; these factors are closely influenced by the organisation's environment. Linked to this concern with effective structure is the need to evaluate the processes that are followed within the organisation.

Definition

> Business process re-engineering (BPR), also known as process innovation and core process re-design, is the introduction of radical changes in business processes to achieve breakthrough results in terms of major gains in levels of performance plus reductions in costs.

The concept of BPR was originally formulated in 1990 by *Michael Hammer* in a seminal article for the Harvard Business Review. He contended that

'In a time of rapidly changing technologies and ever-shorter product life cycles, product development often proceeds at a glacial pace. In an age of the customer, order fulfilment has high error rates and customer enquiries go unanswered for weeks. In a period when asset utilisation is critical, inventory levels exceed many months of demand. The usual methods of boosting performance – process rationalisation and automation – haven't yielded the dramatic improvements companies need. In particular, heavy investments in information technology have delivered disappointing results – largely because companies tend to use technology to mechanise old ways of doing business. They leave the existing processes intact and use computers simply to speed them up.'

The chief BPR tool is a clean sheet of paper. Re-engineers start from the future and work backwards. They are unconstrained by existing methods, people or departments. In effect, they ask, 'If we were a new company, how would we run the place?' Hammer points out that 'At the heart of re-engineering is the notion of discontinuous thinking – of recognising and breaking away from the outdated rules and fundamental assumptions that underlie operations.'

Re-engineers ask two fundamental questions about everything that happens in organisations: 'Why?' and 'What if?'. Only when they receive satisfactory answers to these questions do they then begin to explore better ways of doing things. The critical questions they then ask are:

- What is done?
- How is it done?
- Where is it done?
- When is it done?
- Who does it?

- Why do it?
- Why do it that way?
- Why do it there?
- Why do it then?
- Why that person?

The difference between traditional approaches to efficiency improvement and BPR is that BPR breaks away from the constraints of organisational, departmental and functional boundaries. BPR is more concerned, too, with exploiting the power of information technology – not to automate existing processes, but to facilitate new ones.

Because of its strong links to overall strategic planning, BPR cannot be planned meticulously and accomplished in small and cautious steps. It tends to be an all-or-nothing proposition, often with an uncertain result. It is therefore a high risk undertaking and not worth attempting unless there is a pressing need to rethink what the organisation is doing overall or in a major area.

One application for BPR has been the case of *Barr & Stroud*, a Glasgow engineering firm that had to introduce radical changes in response to new business conditions and demands. The changes implemented through BPR included a focus on core competencies, a reduction in management layers from nine to four, and the establishment of multi-disciplinary teams with a brief to strip time and waste out of the organisation.

Many of the more celebrated BPR case histories come from the USA. Ford has re-engineered its whole accounts payable process, covering the separate functions of purchasing, material control and accounts, with the result that they have introduced a system of invoiceless processing and have reduced their accounts payable staff headcount by 75%. *Union Carbide* eliminated $400 million of fixed costs in just three years; Mutual Benefit Life reduced its turnround of customer applications from 5-25 days to 2-5 days and jettisoned 100 field office positions; *IBM Credit* cut their time for preparing quotes from 7 days to one; and *Bell Atlantic* reduced its delivery times from 15 days to just one.

It is claimed that BPR can deliver tenfold improvements in performance, but only when it works well, and that is not easy. Many organisations trying BPR do not achieve good results because they fail to think it through, do not engage hearts and minds sufficiently, act on bad advice or cannot override established departmental/functional power groups which have a vested interest in the status quo, or in incremental change rather than radical revolution.

Activity 7 (10 minutes)

Why do so many people in organisations resist processes like BPR and Total Quality Management (TQM) despite the fact that such processes are intended to improve efficiency and effectiveness, and therefore (presumably) increase the organisation's chances of long-term growth and survival?

Chapter roundup

- Each constituent part of the organisation exerts an influence on the organisation's configuration.
- The strategic apex exerts a pull to centralise, leading to the simple structure.
- The technostructure exerts a pull to standardise processes, leading to the machine bureaucracy.
- The middle line exerts a pull to balkanise, leading to the divisional form.
- The operating core exerts a pull to standardise skills, and leads to a professional bureaucracy.
- The support staff exerts a pull to collaborate, leading to adhocracy.
- An organisation's formal hierarchy can be arranged by territory, function, product, brand, customer/market, staff numbers and work patterns, and equipment specialisation.
- Hybrid structures contain elements of different kinds of departmentation.
- Matrix structures are formal mechanisms to ensure co-ordination across functional lines by the embodiment of dual authority in the organisation structure.
- Project management, contrasted with operations management, focuses on innovation and risk-taking; it is especially appropriate in organisations which specialise in undertaking large numbers of short-term 'contracts' or assignments, but also enables organisations in general to concentrate their resources on problem solving and opportunity exploiting.

- Mechanistic or bureaucratic organisations are not ideally suited to conditions of change: their strict bureaucratic hierarchies and shallow decision-making process do not encourage flexibility. Organic organisations are more flexible structures where roles are less well defined.

- BPR applies to the whole organisation and is concerned with investigating what needs to be done, how they are done, how they are done and by whom they are done – without regard for existing departmental or functional boundaries. BPR makes extensive use of information technology, not simply to automate existing processes but to facilitate new methods altogether.

Quick quiz

1   What are the characteristics of the simple structure?

2   Distinguish between machine bureaucracy and professional bureaucracy.

3   What component of the organisation leads a pull to divisionalisation?

4   What are the drawbacks to geographic departmentalisation?

5   Why do many organisations adopt a hybrid structure?

6   What leads to the development of matrix structures?

7   What are the potential benefits of a project management approach to organisational design?

8   Why are mechanistic systems unsuitable for conditions of change?

9   Give three features of organismic structures.

10   What is business process reengineering about?

Answers to quick quiz

1   Direct supervision; characteristic of young, small organisations; centralised control; dependence on the expertise of one person; wide span of control; lack of technostructure.

2   The machine bureaucracy is dominated by the technostructure which imposes procedure. The professional bureaucracy is dominated by the specialists of the operating core who contribute expertise.

3   The middle line, which seeks autonomy.

4   Geographic departmentation leads to duplication of functions and hence dissipation of management effort.

5   Some activities are best organised on a functional basis, since this brings economies of scale, pooling of knowledge and development of expertise. Other activities are best organised on a product or territorial basis, which brings specialisation, local knowledge and flexibility.

6   The need for project management responsibility to cut across functional boundaries.

7   J Rodney turner suggests that a project culture brings flexibility of thought and more rapid assessment against the criterion of adding value. However, projects are inherently riskier than routine operations.

8   They deal with change by means of cumbersome methods such as the ambiguous figure and committee systems and the mechanistic jungles.

9   Specialised knowledge and experience are willingly contributed via realistic tasks that support the organisational mission. Authority and communication flow via a network of relationships rather than hierarchically.

Communication takes the form of information and advice rather than instructions and decisions.

Tasks are continually re-defined.

10   A fundamental redesign of methods in order to support mission and strategy most effectively.

Answers to activities

1   Obviously your examples, and their implications, will be your personal choice. Some fairly well known cases, however, are those of Sir Clive Sinclair, Alan Sugar (Amstrad) and Bill Gates (Microsoft). The simple/entrepreneurial structure ultimately tends to collapse, if the originating entrepreneur introduces a product or service which fails catastrophically (the Sinclair C5), or transforms itself into a more conventional hierarchy as sheer size makes it impracticable for the entrepreneur to remain in firm control.

2   Machine bureaucracies occur typically among government departments responsible for administering social welfare systems, or the Inland Revenue, and may occur equally in other large-scale public sector organisations. Most of these organisations have sought to become more customer/client responsive in recent years, and this has inevitably implied the partial abandonment of centrally imposed, universalistic rules or procedures. Moreover, it can be increasingly difficult to recruit employees into such organisations if they are simply required to administer pre-set systems in which, very often, adherence to the rules becomes an end in itself rather than a means to an end.

The operation of a machine bureaucracy is usually capable of being transformed by technology, thereby speeding up the decision process but also eliminating large numbers of employees. We can see this happening in, say, the Inland Revenue, HM Customs and Excise, and financial sector organisations like banks and insurance firms.

3   The examples of a divisional/diversified form that you may generate could include the General Electric (the US corporation), GEC (the UK company), News International, BPP and any global car manufacturer. All these organisations (it is claimed) achieve productive synergy through combining freedom-to-act with adherence to a strategic direction imposed from the centre.

4   Although the details of this case seem far-fetched, the description of the conveyor belt approach to simple eye surgery is based on fact. Such techniques are practised by the Moscow Research Institute of Microsurgery, run by Professor Sviatoslav Fiodorov. Buchanan and Huczynski (Organizational Behaviour) note that: 'Foreigners can buy an operation package holiday, operation included, for £2,000 for a two-week stay. Professor Fiodorov is planning to replace the surgeons on his assembly line with robots'.

Mintzberg's theory of structural configurations holds that an organisation can be analysed into five components.

(a)   An *operating core* is where the work is carried out. In the case of the St Petersburg Research Institute the operating core consists of the following.

   (i)   The doctors who carry out the initial diagnosis, who conduct the eye tests to see the deficiency that needs to be corrected and to check for any other complaints that might make the treatment dangerous (this you could have inferred from the data).

   (ii)   The anaesthetist.

   (iii)   Surgeons A, B, C and D who carry out the operation.

   (iv)   The doctor who administers antibiotics at the end.

   (v)   Any ancillary nursing staff, hospital cleaners, cooks etc.

   (vi)   The computer, which calculates the cut, is a vital component of the process.

(b)   The *strategic apex*. Doctor Sviatorov set up the hospital and has plans for its expansion. He is responsible for strategic decision making.

(c)   The *middle line* is not described in the case: the work is heavily planned, but Doctor Sviatorov probably has deputies to deal with administrative matters (eg receiving bookings from the patients, purchasing supplies.)

(d)   The *technostructure* does not manage the work of the operating core, but it designs the work process. The speed of the conveyor belt, the programming of the computer, the exact sequence of cuts to be made and so forth are all determined in advance, by technicians who have designed the safest and most economical sequence of movements.

(e)   *Support staff* provide ancillary functions, such as legal advice, public relations and so forth. If Doctor Sviatorov wants to expand in the West, he will need a good support staff to win over the approval of people such as Doctor Glass, before such procedures are allowed to be exported.

With Mintzberg's categorisation, we can easily outline the differing approaches taken by Doctor Glass and Doctor Sviatorov.

(a)   Most hospitals, according to Mintzberg, are professional bureaucracies. In other words, the doctors and surgeons generally speaking decide how the work is to be done. Their professional training gives them the necessary expertise. Their work is not managed like the work, say, of a factory. In the past, hospitals in the UK were often run by committees of the medical staff. Doctor Glass's hospital, or her ideal of it, sounds like a professional bureaucracy, even though the appointment of a general manager who is not a doctor means a change.

(b)   Doctor Sviatorov's hospital appears more like a machine bureaucracy, in that for some of the work at least, the procedures are standardised to the extent that surgeons can be replaced by robots. The design of the work process is out of the hands of those who carry it out. However, professional specialists will be the designers, so they have a doctor's normal skill and training. This is quite an unusual configuration for a hospital. It could not be generally applied as most operations are more complex than the simple sequence of cuts that the eye operation needs.

5   Although some of the technical details of the products described might have appeared daunting, you should have realised that the bank basically serves two markets, the personal sector and the corporate sector. However, you would perhaps be ill advised to organise the bank *solely* on that basis. Why?

(a)   The banking needs of customers in the personal sector are likely to be quite distinct. This market is naturally segmented geographically. Users of the telephone banking service, for example, will want to speak in their own language. Also, despite the Single European Market, the competitive environment of financial services is likely to be different in each country (eg credit cards are widely used in France, but hardly used at all in Germany).

For the personal sector, a geographic organisation would be appropriate, although with the centralisation of common administrative and account processing functions and technological expertise, so that the bank gains from scale economies and avoids wasteful duplication.

(b)   For the corporate sector, different considerations apply. If the bank is providing sophisticated foreign currency accounts, these will be of most benefit to multi-nationals or companies which regularly export from, or import to, their home markets. A geographical organisation structure may not be appropriate, and arguably the bank's organisation should be centralised on a Europe-wide basis, with the country offices, of course, at a lower level.

6   Your response to these questions will depend on your own personal values and, in particular, the degree to which you are risk-seeking or risk-averse. If you like a large amount of autonomy in your life, and therefore in your work, then you will probably avoid bureaucratic organisations as a source of employment. Alternatively, if you are forced to work in a bureaucracy, you may seek to achieve a personal sense of freedom through a creative interpretation of the organisation's rules. You may even be able to stimulate compliance with the rules whilst nonetheless covertly disobeying them or subverting their purposes. Thus individuals with limited budget jurisdiction, who are not allowed to spend more than, say, £500 without authorisation from above, may deliberately break down larger expenditures into a series of smaller items, each one below the permitted maximum. The literature of corporate life is full of cases where people have become very ingenious in outwitting bureaucratic controls: indeed, such ingenuity may be the only way in which some employees can develop their creative thinking skills.

7   In theory, one might suppose that employees in an organisation would welcome any innovation which increased the organisation's chances of survival and growth, because it would thereby enhance their own job security and career prospects. The trouble with techniques like TQM and BPR is that they are often perceived to help organisational survival in a competitive world, but at the expense of job losses (eg in previously-necessary activities like quality inspection) thought to be essential to reduce costs and thus make the organisation lean and mean. If TQM and

BPR are perceived in this way, rightly or wrongly, then no wonder that employees view their introduction as threatening or potentially so.

In addition, many employees may believe that they are already conscientious in their pursuit of efficiency improvements, so they take TQM/BPR as an implied (or even an explicit) criticism of their efforts so far. And our exposition of TQM/BPR suggests that both are inclined to cut through established departmental or functional boundaries, thus undermining the value of hard-won professional expertise in, say, purchasing.

Further question practice

Now try the following practice questions at the end of this text

Multiple choice questions: **35 to 41**

Exam style question: **6**

Chapter 7 :
MANAGEMENT CONTROL AND INFORMATION SYSTEMS

Introduction

Within this chapter the topic of control is examined from various perspectives: as an organisational sub-system, as a managerial process and as the basis for information flows within the organisation. Our interpretation of the term 'control' is deliberately wide-ranging, embracing conventional forms of statistical data flow and feedback processes like performance appraisal. You will see that our material in this chapter draws extensively on the views of *Child, Ouchi, Handy* and *Humble*. Each makes a distinctive contribution to the integrating theme of control and the problem of achieving adequate levels of control without information overkill or essential data starvation. Each author offers some penetrating and analytical insights yet the merging picture is internally consistent.

The second main topic in the chapter is quantity and quality control.

In this chapter you will learn about these things.

    (a)   The need for control mechanisms within organisations, to enable progress to be monitored, corrective action to be taken and behaviour to be co-ordinated

    (b)   Control processes from a systems point of view, a management point of view and an information flow standpoint

    (c)   Child's approach to the design of management control strategies and systems in an organisation

    (d)   The difference between market control, bureaucratic control and clan control (ie the Ouchi framework)

    (e)   The value and significance of management by objectives as a control system influencing behaviour at strategic, tactical and operational levels in the hierarchy

    (f)   The basic principles behind the development and use of management information systems, decision support systems and executive information systems

    (g)   The concept of quality and the use of techniques such as Total Quality Management as control mechanisms.

1 THE SCOPE OF CONTROL

We have quoted a definition of an organisation as 'a social arrangement for the controlled performance of collective goals.' In this chapter we discuss the different types of control.

Organisations need a control mechanism for three reasons.

(a) it provides information for managers and staff to assess whether or not the organisation is on track to reach its goals;

(b) it provides a correctional mechanism to enhance individual and organisational performance;

(c) if designed in the right way, it can prevent actions, strategy or behaviour that are harmful to organisational performance.

Here are two examples of organisational control.

(a) A staff appraisal system is a type of control system: it provides feedback to staff members.

(b) A management information system, whereby managers are given *variance* information indicating differences between actual and planned results is part of a control system.

A control system can operate on two levels.

(a) It can control actual performance against planned results

(b) It can suggest changes to the plan

The question of control in organisations, however, is not as simple or as straightforward as it might seem. Why is it necessary to control? What (or who) is being controlled? What are the control mechanisms which will best enable the objectives of control to be accomplished? Why do control mechanisms sometimes break down?

Controlling processes, people and outputs can often generate dysfunctional dilemmas, with one control system contradicting another. The impression sometimes given, moreover, is that mechanical, computerised or automated control systems are somehow more objective and impartial than those monitored by human beings, but in practice any control procedure, no matter how impersonal, is only as good as its system design and the quality of the data fed into it – so all forms of control are ultimately dependent on human beings, as sources of information and interpreters of the results. People perceive what they want or expect to perceive: they have a strong drive to ignore or wilfully to misinterpret any control information which conflicts with what they believe should emerge. Even warning signals, therefore, can simply generate *cognitive dissonance* if they differ significantly from the anticipated pattern – a classic example concerns the way in which the impending arrival of the Japanese air attack on Pearl Harbour, in World War II, failed to attract attention even when the incoming planes were visible on radar screens.

Some individuals react adversely to being controlled, particularly if the control systems are conspicuous and repeatedly remind the individuals concerned that they are being controlled – a reminder which can seem like an affront to one's autonomy as a human being. Even targeted reward systems – like incentive payments to sales representatives for achievement of specific sales targets – can sometimes evoke negative reactions precisely because they implicitly encourage employees to feel manipulated. This being so, control systems based on negative outcomes – ie failure to comply leads to punishment – are capable of being resented even more powerfully. Feelings of resentment encourage creative and ingenious ways of circumventing control systems; once management becomes aware of this, new forms of control are added, or the original controls made more watertight, so that employee ingenuity is stretched to its limits – and so the process continues, indefinitely.

2   CONTROL AS AN ORGANISATIONAL SUBSYSTEM

Every system can be broken down into subsystems. In turn, each subsystem can be broken down into sub-subsystems. Separate subsystems interact with each other, and respond to each other by means of communication or observation. Any organisation contains a variety of overlapping subsystems such as technology, management hierarchies, information processing. A control system is a special type of subsystem.

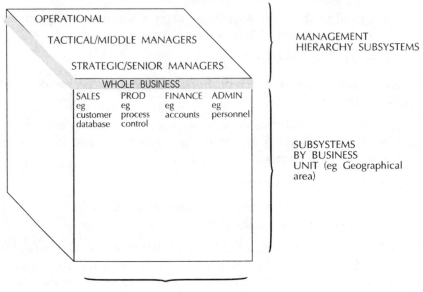

2.1   Control systems

A system must be controlled to keep it steady or enable it to change safely, in other words each system must have its control system. Control is required because unpredictable disturbances arise and enter the system, so that actual results (outputs of the system) deviate from the expected results or goals. Examples of disturbances in a business system would be the entry of a powerful new competitor into the market, an unexpected rise in labour costs, the failure of a supplier to deliver promised raw materials, or the tendency of employees to stop working in order to chatter or gossip. A control system must ensure that the business is capable of surviving these disturbances by dealing with them in an appropriate manner.

To have a control system, there has to be a *plan:* that is some sort of target or guideline towards which the system as a whole should be aiming.

Control is dependent on the receipt and processing of *information*. Information is processed for human beings by the biological senses of sight, sound, taste smell and touch. Within organisations, information may be received from a variety of sources, which include the following.

(a)   Formal sources within the organisation, designed by managers of the organisation

(b)   Informal sources within the organisation.

(c)   Formal sources outside the organisation, ie from the environment.

(d)   Informal environmental sources.

Business information is needed to plan or make rules. It is also needed to compare actual results against the plan, so as to judge what control measures, if any, are needed. The terminology, or jargon, of control systems theory may seem unusual, and it will be useful at this stage to introduce some of the more common terms.

Feedback as a means of control

Feedback is the return of part of the output of a system to the input as a means towards improved quality or correction of error. Feedback is information. In a business organisation, it is information produced from within the organisation (for example management control reports) with the purpose of helping management and other employees with control decisions.

Open and closed loop control systems

Definition

> An *open loop control system* is a system in which control is exercised regardless of the output produced by the system.

Since information from within the organisation is not used for control purposes, control must be exercised by external intervention. The output of the system is not coupled to the input for measurement. Mechanical examples of open loop systems include automatic light switches and traffic lights.

Definition

> A *closed loop control system* is a system in which part of the output is fed back, so that the output can initiate control action to change either the activities of the system or the system's input. A feedback system or a feedback loop carries output back to be compared with the input. No external control input is required or used.

A business organisation uses feedback for control, and therefore has a closed loop control system. However, external influences are not ignored. A management information system must be designed to provide proper feedback (ie information from internal sources) as well as environmental information to optimise the control system.

2.2 A control model

Control is exercised through a *control system.*

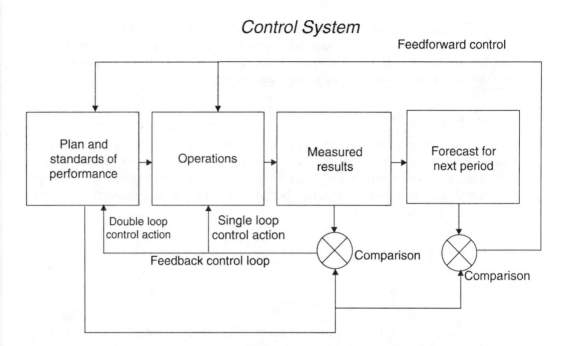

The essence of control is the measurement of *results* and comparing them with the original *plan*. Any deviation from plan indicates that *control action* is required to make the results conform more closely with plan. The control action is applied to operations via the *feedback control loop*.

Feedback occurs when the results (outputs) of a system are used to control it, by adjusting the input or behaviour of the system. Businesses use feedback information to control their performance.

Single loop feedback result is the system's behaviour being altered to meet the plan.

Double loop feedback can result in change to the plan itself.

Double loop feedback is control information transmitted to a higher level in the system. Whereas single loop feedback is concerned with 'task control' (the control loop), higher level feedback is concerned with overall control. The term 'double loop' feedback indicates that the information is reported to indicate both divergencies between the observed and expected results where control action might be required, and also the need for adjustments to the plan itself.

If a system is to react to a changing environment, which it must do to survive, then double loop feedback is essential.

The terminology of control systems has been borrowed from engineering and its usage modified to some extent. While not strictly correct in a control engineering sense, the term *negative feedback* has come to mean feedback indicating that control action is needed while *positive feedback* is commonly used to mean feedback indicating that things are going according to plan

With information technology, it has become easier and cheaper to prepare forecasts, and it is possible to have a control system based on comparisons with current forecasts.

    (a)   Comparison of original budget with current (up-to-date) forecast

    (b)   Comparison of current forecast with previous forecast

    (c)   Comparison of actual results to date with current forecast

Control based on comparing original targets or actual results with a current forecast of future results is sometimes referred to as *feedforward control*. An example of feedforward control would occur when the board of directors of a company meet each month to review profits and sales figures for the year. They might be given information not only about actual results to date compared with budget (feedback information) but also about what is now the current forecast for the remainder of the year, and how actual results to date compare with these current expectations for the year as a whole (information for feedforward control).

Activity 1   **(5 minutes)**

How *can feedforward control* be applied in an organisation such as the police?

This control model can be applied in any number of circumstances.

(a)   In a technical context, a plan would indicate the required volume of production. The sensor would detect the actual volume. This would be compared with the plan, and control action would result.

(b)   Many companies have budgets and forecasts to control expenditure and estimate the resources required over a future time period. If the forecast changes, the company takes control action. This is a form of feedforward control.

Behavioural issues

The same control model is ideal for controlling other aspects of performance which can also be measured easily. However, many control issues are not so easily reduced to quantitative data.

For example, it is widely known in service industries that the cost of attracting a new customer far exceeds the cost of keeping existing customers satisfied: repeat business, rather than new business, is the origin of success.

The factors that lead to repeat business are often intangible, such as *staff courtesy*. How do you control these factors?

(a)   Regular staff appraisal is an example, but this only occurs *after* the event.

(b)   You cannot really have a feedforward control system: you cannot *predict* when a member of staff is going to be rude. You can *train* staff in stress management, so they can control their own behaviour, perhaps.

A wider concept of control is therefore needed.

3   CONTROL STRATEGIES

Control is something that can be gained or lost in a variety or ways. John Child points to three main design choices in the structure of a management control system.

(a)   *The degree of centralisation or decentralisation of decision making.*

(b)   *The degree of formality or informality in control* (in other words, the operation of rules and procedures as opposed to managerial discretion).

(c)   *The degree of personal supervision that managers exercise over subordinates.*

Child suggests that there are four possible control strategies in an organisation.

(a)   *Personal centralised control*

(i) Centralised decision making

(ii) Personal leadership; direct supervision

(iii) Often a feature of small owner-managed companies

(b) *Bureaucratic control* (discussed in more detail later)

(i) This is based on rules and procedures, budgets and budgetary control.

(ii) Features as much programmed decision taking as possible. In other words, the amount of individual discretion is limited. For example, customers over thirty days 'Late in Payment' are always sent a letter.

(iii) Control is based on the principles of scientific management – specialisation of work, simplification of work methods, and standardisation of procedures.

(c) *Output control.* Systems of *responsibility accounting* are operated so that authority and responsibility for operational matters regarding the output are delegated to the operational managers.

(d) *Cultural control*

(i) This is achieved where all employees develop a strong personal identification with the goals of the organisation.

(ii) Examples of organisations where cultural control exists are firms of accountants and companies such as some Japanese corporations, in which a strong corporate identity is built up, and which *Ouchi and Price* have called the *industrial clan* mentality, to be discussed shortly.

The most appropriate control strategy, Child argues, will depend on *contingent factors*.

Factor	Impact	Control strategy likely to be suitable
Market demand for the	Strong	Output and/or cultural
organisation's output	Weak	Centralised and/or bureaucratic
Employee skills and education	High	Output and/or cultural
	Low	Centralised and/or bureaucratic
Change	Rapid	Output and/or cultural
	Slow	Centralised and/or bureaucratic
Size of organisation	Small	Centralised
	Not small	Any other

Similar suggestions are put forward by Ouchi who identifies three different control models, two of these are broadly similar to those mechanisms proposed by Child.

(i) *Bureaucratic control*, which is comparable to the Bureaucratic control model proposed by Child.

(ii) *Clan control* which is broadly similar Child's Cultural control strategy.

(iii) *Market control* where the price mechanism is used to control the behaviour of the organisation both internally (departments charge each other fees for services provided) and in its relationships with the outside world (performance in the market place).

Once again the contingency principles apply – different control mechanisms will be appropriate at different times and are likely even to vary across different departments in a given firm. In reality an organisation is likely to adopt a variety of approaches in an effort to ensure effective control.

Standards

It is worth stressing the point that control measurements can relate to qualitative factors as well as to quantifiable factors. However, there should be targets for qualitative performance (eg ethical standards of behaviour) because unless there is a standard or target, it will be impossible to establish whether or not actual achievements have been satisfactory.

Activity 2   **(5 minutes)**

Sally Keene works for a large department store, as a manager.

(a) At the beginning of each year she is given a yearly plan, subdivided into twelve months. This is based on the previous year's performance and some allowance is made for anticipated economic conditions. Every three months she sends her views as to the next quarter to senior management, who give her a new plan in the light of changing conditions.

(b) She monitors sales revenue per square foot, and sales per employee. Employees who do not meet the necessary sales targets are at first counselled and then if performance does not improve they are dismissed. Sally is not unreasonable. She sets what she believes are realistic targets.

(c) She believes there is a good team spirit in the sales force, however, and that employees, whose commission is partly based on the sales revenue earned by the store as a whole, discourage slackers in their ranks.

What kind of control, control system or control information can you identify in the three cases above?

EXAMPLE: MAZDA

Recruiting a compliant workforce: the Mazda plant in Flat Rock, Michigan

Applicants underwent a five-stage series of tests before being formally offered a job. The recruitment procedure consisted of an application form, written aptitude tests, personal interviews, a group problem-solving assessment and simulated work exercises over a period of many weeks. The process of weeding out 'druggies, rowdies and unionists' is typical of Japanese firms elsewhere and invariably results in a 'green' workforce to match the site of the plant.

The end result of the recruitment process at Flat Rock was a young workforce (average age 31 years old), a very inexperienced workforce (70% with no previous factory experience of any kind) and a male-dominated workforce (over 70%).

Source: J J Fucini and S Fucini, *Working for the Japanese:*
Inside Mazda's American Auto Plant, 1990

Activity 3   **(5 minutes)**

Can you think of any well-known organisations which, like Japanese firms, pay careful attention to recruiting and selecting people who will fit in with the organisation's culture and way of doing things? What are the advantages and disadvantages of this approach, as opposed to the situation for organisations which encourage diversity?

---

4   SUPERVISION AND CONTROL

Control is also exercised over individual employees. How much autonomy should they be given? Handy writes of a *trust-control dilemma* in a superior-subordinate relationship, in which the sum of trust + control is a constant amount:

$$T + C = Y$$

where $T =$ the trust the superior has in the subordinate, and the trust which the subordinate feels the superior has in him;

$C =$ the degree of control exercised by the superior over the subordinate;

$Y =$ a constant, unchanging value.

Any increase in C leads to an equal decrease in T; that is, if the superior retains more 'control' or authority, the subordinate will immediately recognise that he is being trusted less. If the superior wishes to show more trust in the subordinate, he can only do so by reducing C, that is by delegating more authority.

To overcome the reluctance of managers to delegate, the following measures are necessary.

(a)   Provide a system of selecting subordinates who will be capable of handling delegated authority in a responsible way. If subordinates are of the right quality, superiors will be prepared to trust them more.

(b)   Have a system of open communications, in which the superior and subordinates freely interchange ideas and information. If the subordinate is given all the information needed to do the job, and if the superior is aware of what the subordinate is doing:

(i)   the subordinate will make better-informed decisions;

(ii)   the superior will not panic because he or she does not know what is going on.

Although open lines of communication are important, they should not be used by the superior to command the subordinate in a matter where authority has been delegated to the subordinate; in other words, communication links must not be used by superiors as a means of reclaiming authority.

(c)   Reward effective delegation by superiors and the efficient assumption of authority by subordinates. Rewards may be given in terms of pay, promotion, status, official approval, and so on.

(d)   Ensure that a system of control is established. Superiors are reluctant to delegate authority because they retain absolute responsibility for the performance of their subordinates. If an efficient control system is in operation, responsibility and accountability will be monitored at all levels of the management hierarchy, and the dangers of relinquishing authority and control to subordinates are significantly lessened.

It is possible to identify two approaches to control in a supervisory context.

(a) *Behaviour control* deals with the behaviour of individual employees. In other words, control is exercised over the procedures. It has elements of centralised control and bureaucratic control

(b) *Output control* is where management attention is focused on results, more than the way these were achieved.

4.1 Behaviour control

Behaviour control is exercised when outcomes cannot be measured easily. Output control is exercised where they can.

An example of behaviour control in an accounting context is that exercised by audit managers over their juniors. An audit is an investigation by an auditor into a business's accounts and accounting systems so that the auditor can arrive at an opinion as to the truth and fairness of the accounts, their compliance with the law. Audit procedures have to be carried out *in the right way* for the information to be of any use. This is because audit procedures are investigative: and to ensure that the investigations are done in the right way, so that the information is reliable for the audit manager or partner to come to an opinion, control must be exercised over how the work is done. The output of the audit (whether or not to qualify the accounts) comes at the end: junior staff are not assessed as to whether they reach favourable opinions or not.

Behaviour control should not be confused with close supervision, whereby a subordinate has his or her boss hanging around in the background eager to find fault, and refusing to give the subordinate the ability to set his or her own pace, although close supervision *can* be practised with behaviour control.

Activity 4   **(10 minutes)**

What other scenarios can you identify where people undertake jobs whose outcomes cannot easily be measured?

What types of behaviour control are (or could be) used over the individuals performing such roles?

4.2 Output control

Output control is similar perhaps to management by objectives.

Business Basics: Organisational behaviour

Definition

> Management by objectives (MBO) is a comprehensive approach to managing people by setting objectives, targets and plans. MBO is a scheme of planning and control which provides co-ordination in three areas.
>
> (a) Short-term plans with longer-term plans and goals
> (b) The plans (and commitment) of junior with senior management
> (c) The efforts of different departments

The aim is the integration of organisational goals with individual goals, so that managerial self-development and the organisation's objectives are both served. The thrust is towards *results*, with the system developing individual managerial goals from corporate goals. In theory both organisational and managerial performance is enhanced.

A writer who became a leading advocate of MBO was *John Humble* (in *Improving Business Results* and *Management by Objectives*). Humble argued that against a background of long-term corporate plans, the operating and functional units of a company (branches, regions, marketing department and so on) should clarify their own objectives. The essential features of Humble's recommended approach are as follows.

(a) Clarify with each manager the *key results* and *performance standards* he should achieve. These should conform to corporate and divisional objectives, but each manager should contribute to the process of agreeing his key results and performance standards, so as to win his commitment to them.

(b) Agree, with each manager, a *job improvement plan* for himself, which will make a quantifiable and measurable contribution to achievement of the plans for the department, branch or company as a whole.

(c) Provide conditions which will help managers to achieve their key results and job improvement plans. For example:

    (i) there must be an efficient and effective management information system to provide feedback of results;

    (ii) there must be an organisation structure which provides managers with sufficient flexibility and freedom of action;

    (iii) there should be a sense of 'team spirit and corporate purpose' within the organisation.

(d) Have a systematic *performance* review of each manager's results.

(e) Hold a regular *potential review* for each manager so as to identify the individuals with potential for advancement within the company.

(f) Develop *management training plans* to improve management skills.

(g) Motivate managers by effective *salary, selection and career development plans*.

Several advantages are suggested for MBO over other management methods.

(a) The linkage of individual managerial goals (self-development, career progress) with organisation goals should serve to ensure that motivation of managers is directed in a way which is effective for the organisation as a whole.

(b) Both quantitative and qualitative assessment is possible of the performance of managers. These measures can be set as predetermined standards against which the managers can measure themselves, and as objective criteria for periodic assessment. Other methods may concentrate merely on easily quantified data – sales, costs, production figures. MBO therefore offers a wider picture.

(c) The system provides periodic feedback for the managers who are assessed. Targets and refined guidelines can thus be set which should make managerial performance the subject of an ongoing improvement.

There are a number of reasons why MBO is not as widely used as one might expect. In particular it is a very participative system, requiring a good deal of confidence and trust between senior and middle/lower management. Often this is absent, and a more authoritarian style of management is preferred. For similar reasons the system, if introduced, is often employed unenthusiastically or incompletely. If senior managers are uncommitted to the system it will not produce good results. Finally, as with many management techniques, MBO has perhaps either gone out of fashion, or its essential lessons have been absorbed in management thinking.

4.3 Choosing between output and behavioural control

Are there circumstances where either control strategy is especially appropriate? This depends on the task and the output.

(a) Can the task be programmed? In other words, can it be incorporated into a standard set of procedures, such as the production of a routine report?

(b) Can output be measured (eg number of sales orders achieved)?

We can put these on a grid.

	Low *(Task programmability)*	High *(Task programmability)*
High *(Outcome measurability)*	Output control	Either behaviour or output control
Low *(Outcome measurability)*	Clan control, cultural controls etc	Behaviour control

Task programmability

5 INFORMATION SYSTEMS

The information systems of an organisation serve two broad functions.

(a) They are used in the work process, and can be an important strategic resource.

(b) They are used to provide control information.

5.1 Management control information

Definition

> A *management information system* can be defined as a system 'which collects and presents management information to a business in order to facilitate its control'.

The aim of any management information system (MIS) is to provide managers with information, and we have to assess how well a formal MIS can do so. The diagram below illustrates, as a simplification of course, the contrast between information at the different levels.

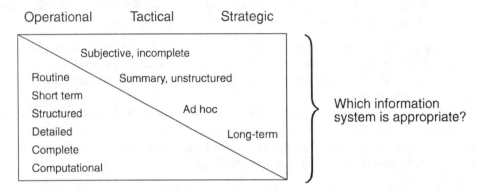

A management information system cannot realistically provide all of the information needs of management, but computer technology means that tools for decision support can be provided in the format of a computer system. IT can be used, not only in operational activities, but for those specific management functions of planning, control and decision making.

The scope of an MIS, potentially, is to satisfy all the informational needs of management. A good MIS will provide good information to those who need it. Whether this is possible will depend to some degree on the nature and type of information provided. An MIS is good at providing regular formal information gleaned from normal commercial data. For example, an MIS relating to sales could provide managers with information about these things.

(a) Gross profit margins of particular products
(b) Success in particular markets
(c) Credit control information

It may be less efficient at presenting information which is relatively unpredictable, or informal, or unstructured. So, for example, an MIS could not provide information relating to the sudden emergence of a new competitor into the market.

While an MIS may not, in principle, be able to provide all the information used by management, it should however be sufficiently flexible to enable management to incorporate unpredictable, informal or unstructured information into decision-making processes. For example, many decisions are made with the help of financial models (eg spreadsheets) so that the effect of new situations can be estimated easily.

5.2 Operational level MIS

Operational decisions are essentially small-scale and programmed, and that operational information is often highly formal and quantitative. Many operational decisions can, in fact, be incorporated into computer processing. Most MIS at operational level are essentially used for processing transactions, updating files and so forth.

5.3 Tactical level MIS

A variety of systems can be used at tactical level, and there may be a greater reliance exception reporting, informal systems, investigation and analysis of data acquired at operational level and externally generated data.

The MIS at tactical level will interact with the same systems as that at operational level, and in fact tactical information may be generated in the same processing operation as operational level information. For example, tactical level information comparing actual costs incurred to budget can be produced by a system in which those costs are recorded. Functional MIS at tactical level are typically related to other functional MIS; as a case in point, information from the sales MIS will affect the financial accounting system.

5.4 Strategic level MIS

At strategic level the information system is likely to be informal, in the sense that it is not possible always to quantify or program strategic information, and much of the information might come from environmental sources. The MIS will provide summary level data from transactions processing. Human judgement is used more often at this level, as many strategic decisions cannot be programmed.

In short, formal systems are likely to be less important at this level. However, they can be used in the gathering of information. In a finance subsystem, the operational level would deal with cash receipts and payments, bank reconciliations and so forth. The tactical level would deal with cash flow forecasts and working capital management. Strategic level financial issues are likely to be integrated with the organisation's commercial strategy, but may relate to the most appropriate source of finance (eg long-term debt, or equity).

	Inputs	Processes	Outputs
Strategic	Plans, competitor information, overall market information	Summarise Investigate Compare Forecast	Key ratios, ad hoc market analysis, strategic plans
Management/tactical	Historical and budget data	Compare Classify Summarise	Variance analyses Exception reports
Operational	Customer orders, Programmed stock control levels, cash receipts/payments	Update files Output reports	Updated files listings, invoices

5.5 Decision support systems

Definition

> The term 'decision support systems' or DSS is usually taken to mean computer systems which are designed to produce information in such a way as to help managers to make better decisions.
>
> (The term was first coined in the late 1970s by Peter Keen, a British systems specialist.) DSS can vary from fairly simple information models based on spreadsheets to expert systems.

Decision support systems (DSS) are a form of management information system. Decision support systems are used by management to aid in making decisions on issues which are unstructured. These complex problems are often very poorly defined with high levels of uncertainty about the true nature of the problem, the various responses which management would undertake or the likely impact of those actions. These highly ambiguous environments do not allow the easy application of many of the techniques or systems developed for more well defined problems or activities. Decision support systems are intended to provide a wide range of alternative information gathering and analytical tools with a major emphasis upon flexibility and user-friendliness.

Decision support systems do not make decisions. The objective is to allow the manager to consider a number of alternatives and evaluate them under a variety of potential conditions. A key element in the usefulness of these systems is their ability to function interactively. This is a feature, for example, of *spreadsheets*. Managers using these systems often develop *scenarios* using earlier results to refine their understanding of the problem and their actions.

5.6 Executive information system (EIS)

Definition

> An executive information system (EIS) is an information system which gives the executive easy access to key internal and external data.

EISs have been made possible by the increasing cheapness and sophistication of microcomputer and network technology. An EIS is likely to have the following features.

(a) Provision of summary-level data, captured from the organisation's main MIS.

(b) A facility which enables the executive to drill-down from higher levels of information to lower.

(c) Data manipulation facilities (eg comparison with budget or prior year data, trend analysis).

(d) Graphics, for user-friendly presentation of data.

(e) A template system. This will mean that the same type of data (eg sales figures) is presented in the same format, irrespective of changes in the volume of information required.

The basic design philosophy of executive information systems has four aspects.

(a) They should be easy to use as an EIS may be consulted during a meeting, for example.

(b) They should make data easy to access, so that it describes the organisation *from the executive's point of view*.

(c) They should provide tools for analysis (including ratio analysis, forecasts, spreadsheets, trends).

(d) They should provide presentational aids so that information can be conveyed 'without bothering the executive with too many trivial choices of scale, colour and layout'.

The significance of an EIS is that it is not only a tool for analysis, but also a tool for interrogating data.

When we first think about quality we probably think of it as a means of describing and comparing products or services. As the following discussion suggests, however, management theory and practice has gone beyond this narrow definition; the concept is now used by many organisations as a control mechanism.

6   QUALITY

Quality has been defined by *Ken Holmes* in *Total Quality Management*.

Definition

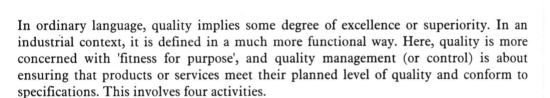

Quality is 'the totality of features and characteristics of a product or service which bears on its ability to meet stated or implied needs.'

In ordinary language, quality implies some degree of excellence or superiority. In an industrial context, it is defined in a much more functional way. Here, quality is more concerned with 'fitness for purpose', and quality management (or control) is about ensuring that products or services meet their planned level of quality and conform to specifications. This involves four activities.

(a) Establishing standards of quality for a product or service

(b) Establishing procedures or production methods which ought to ensure that these required standards of quality are met in a suitably high proportion of cases

(c) Monitoring actual quality

(d) Taking control action when actual quality falls below standard

As an example, the postal service might establish a standard that 90% of first class letters will be delivered on the day after they are posted, and 99% will be delivered within two days of posting. Procedures would have to be established for ensuring that these standards could be met (eg frequency of collections, automated letter sorting, frequency of deliveries and number of staff employed etc). Actual performance could be monitored, perhaps by taking samples from time to time of letters that are posted and delivered. If the quality standard is not being achieved, the management of the postal service could take control action (eg employ more postmen or advertise again the use of postcodes) or reduce the standard of quality of the service being provided.

6.1 Traditional approaches to quality

In the past quality control meant *inspection*. Inspection is concerned with looking at products that have been made, supplies which have been delivered and services that have been provided, to establish whether they have been up to specification. It is a technique of *identifying* when defective items are being produced at an unacceptable level. Inspection is usually carried out at three main points.

(a) Receiving inspection – for raw materials and bought out components

(b) Floor or process inspection

(c) Final inspection or testing

This approach is unsatisfactory.

(a) The inspection process itself does not add value: if it could be guaranteed that no defective items were produced, there would be no need for a separate inspection function.

(b) The production of substandard products is a waste of raw materials, machine time, human efforts, overheads (as the substandard production has to be administered).

(c) The inspection department takes up possibly expensive land and warehousing space.

(d) The production of defects is not compatible with newer production techniques such as just-in-time: there is no time for inspection.

(e) Working capital is tied up in stocks which cannot be sold.

In other words, the inspection approach allows for built-in *waste*. Where resources are scarce, this is not acceptable. Furthermore, waste reduces profitability: the resources it consumes can perhaps be put to better use.

6.2 Concepts in quality management

As we have seen, quality management implies a wide remit in ensuring quality issues are included in the planning process. Arguably, a goal for quality management should be the *prevention* of defective manufacture in the first place.

Since World War II, a number of thinkers have expanded the notion of quality. Although adopted in Japan (which suffers from a scarcity of natural resources and hence is probably more sensitive to issues of waste) many of the key concepts of quality management originated in the USA. One of the interesting insights of many thinkers is that quality is not so much determined by individuals as by the management systems.

(a) *Deming* asserted that over 90% of a company's quality problems can only be corrected by management.

(b) *Juran* held that quality problems derive from management systems and processes rather than from poor workmanship.

Juran defines quality as 'fitness for use' which in fact includes two elements.

(a) *Quality of design*, which can include the customer satisfactions built into the product. According to some commentators *design quality* (eg especially in miniaturisation), rather than conformance quality, has been responsible for much of the success of Japanese firms in some industries.

(b) *Quality of conformance*, in other words a lack of defects in the finished goods.

Activity 5 [5 minutes]

The boss of Acme Umbrellas Ltd believes that customers want robust umbrellas, so he makes one entirely out of titanium and kevlar apart from some gold decoration. 'It is a bit heavy I suppose', he says, showing an example. 'But it's perfectly made, look at the gold pins and look at the perfect, flawless finish. Why don't people want it?'

6.3 Total quality management (TQM)

Holmes defines TQM as follows.

Definition

> *TQM* is 'a culture aimed at continually improving performance in meeting the requirements in all functions of a company'.

In other words, it is a way of managing a business, not just a technique. The basic principle of TQM is that the cost of preventing mistakes is less than the cost of correcting them once they occur and the cost of loss potential for future sales. The aim should therefore be to get things right first time consistently.

BS (British Standard) 6143 gives examples of each type of quality cost and these may be summarised as follows.

(a) *Prevention costs* are the 'cost of any action taken to investigate or reduce defects and failures'.

(b) *Appraisal costs* are 'the costs of assessing quality achieved'.

(c) *Internal failure costs* are 'costs arising within the organisation of failing to achieve quality'

(d) *External failure costs*. These are 'costs arising outside the manufacturing organisation of failure to achieve specified quality (after transfer of ownership to the customer)'.

Although there are failure costs, does good quality itself cost money?

(a) High quality specification (ie design quality) costs money.
(b) High quality operating performance (ie conformance quality) saves money.

Expenditure on failure *prevention*, even if this is an investment in training, can reduce the cost of failure. It is possible that even in accounting terms, investing in failure prevention is worth it as the total savings if properly identified will have exceeded the costs. An important cost saving is the reduction in quality inspection costs. If your systems are inherently more reliable up front, then less is spent on *appraisal*.

Finally, poor quality means that too many workers, too much managerial time and too much production capacity are taken up in doing things twice.

Ideas of importance in the TQM movement include the following.

(a) *Zero defects*. No product ever made should be defective. In other words there is never an acceptable level of rejects. This might appear to violate the law of diminishing returns, but in a JIT environment zero defects takes significant operational importance: no inspection would be necessary.

(b) A corollary of this is *right first time:* no product should have to be corrected once it is built.

(c) *Continuous improvement.* We examine this in more detail below.

Continuous improvement

Quality management is not a one-off process, but is the continual examination and improvement of existing processes. The idea of continuous improvement might appear to go against the law of diminishing returns, in that it might be arguable that there is a limit beyond which there is no point in pursuing any further improvements.

Advocates of continuous improvement, however, believe that this 'law' does not always apply. Remember, that continuous improvement does not only apply to the finished product, but also to the processes which give rise to it.

(a) It is not easy to determine where diminishing returns set in.

(b) A philosophy of continuous improvement ensures that managers are not complacent, which can be a cultural disaster.

(c) Customer needs change, so a philosophy of continuous improvement enables these changes to be taken into account in the normal course of events.

(d) New technologies or materials might be developed, enabling cost savings or design improvements.

(e) Rarely do businesses know every possible fact about the production process. Continuous improvement encourages experimentation and a scientific approach to production.

(f) It is a way of tapping employees' knowledge.

(g) Improvement on a continual, step-by-step basis is more prudent in some cases than changing everything at once.

Holmes proposes an eight stage model for improving quality.

(a) *Step 1. Find out the problems* (eg from customers and employees).

(b) *Step 2. Select action targets* from the number of improvement projects identified in *Step 1*, on the basis of cost, safety, importance, feasibility (with current resources).

(c) *Step 3. Collect data* about the problem.

(d) *Step 4. Analyse data* by a variety of techniques to assess common factors behind the data, to tease out any hidden messages the data might contain.

(e) *Step 5. Identify possible causes* (eg using brainstorming sessions). No ideas are ruled out of order.

(f) *Step 6. Plan improvement action.* Significant help might be required.

(g) *Step 7. Monitor the effects of the improvement.*

(h) *Step 8. Communicate the result.*

NOTES

EXAMPLE: BOSCH

The following passage is taken from an article in *Personnel Management* in November 1992 about the TQM programme of Bosch, the German multinational company, at its car component plant in Cardiff.

'Our approach to total quality has been based on the following concepts.

Continuous improvement. This is the restless searching for continuous improvement, the little steps forward every day, that the Japanese call kaizen. This incorporates the notion that total quality is 'a race without a finish' and harnesses the innate desire to make progress that we believe is in all our employees. We have spent much time explaining to employees that everyone has a responsibility to participate in continuous improvement, and people respond enthusiastically to this approach.

Teamworking and synergy. We make extensive use of teams to work on quality issues. This is because we believe in the synergy of team working. The quality of the solution is often enhanced this way and the commitment to implementation is definitely heightened. We have a network of work groups and of problem-centred working parties, and we publicise their activities widely within the organisation.

Internal customers. Our approach stresses the customer-supplier relationship: every supplier must agree what product or service is to be delivered to the customer, then deliver it 'right first time, on time, and every time'. But this applies not only to the service to our external customers, the car makers, but to our internal customers to0o. The value of this approach is that it makes everyone aware that we all have customers.

Measurement and feedback. We have found that measurement and feedback is vital to our approach. It happens in all kinds of ways: daily feedback on progress to a production team from their team leader in their regular beginning-of-shift meetings, annual individual feedback to every employee in their performance and salary review, continuous feedback on the company's performance against all the critical indices shown on 'business report boards' in each department.'

NOTES

Activity 6 (10 minutes)

You have just overheard the following conversation. The Board of a company are in a meeting and they are having a 'full and frank exchange of views' (ie a blazing row).

Chairman: Ladies and gentlemen, please…

Marketing director: No, he's said quite enough. Customers are *our* department, and all this TQM nonsense is just *another*, yes another example of those jargon-spouting boffins and bodgers in production trying to encroach on my turf! I *do* need resources. I don't need white-coated robots criticising the angles at which I fix the paper clips on to my reports!

Chairman: Ladies and gentlemen, *please*…

Production director: No, she's said quite enough. Marketing people couldn't give one hoot, let alone two, about quality and we all know it's quality that sells the goods. Remember, when we had to abandon our solar powered torch? State of the art, state of *the art* that was, and did they try and sell it? Did they?

Chairman: Ladies and gentlemen, *please*…'

Finance director: No, they've both said quite enough. If all we get out of TQM is pointless rows like this, I might as well go back and count some more beans. At least it's *meaningful* and relaxing.

Chairman: Ladies and gentlemen! No, you've all said *quite* enough. I don't think any of you have grasped the point. I'd better get another management consultant in with a better flipchart.

What insights do each of the above characters have into TQM?

6.4 Quality assurance and standards: BS EN ISO 9000

The essentials of *quality assurance* are that the supplier guarantees the quality of goods supplied and allows the customers' inspectors access while the items are being manufactured. Usually agreed inspection procedures and quality control standards are worked out by customer and supplier between them, and checks are made to ensure that they are being adhered to.

(a) The customer can almost eliminate goods inwards inspection and items can be directed straight to production. This can give large savings in cost and time in flow production, and can facilitate JIT production.

(b) The supplier produces to the customer's requirement, thereby reducing rejects and the cost of producing substitutes.

Suppliers' quality assurance schemes are being used increasingly, particularly where extensive subcontracting work is carried out, eg the motor industries. One such scheme is BS EN ISO 9000 certification. This is a nationally promoted standard, only awarded after audit and inspection of a company's operations. In order to gain registration, a company must obtain independent verification that its quality system meets standards. The British Standards Institution is the largest of the certification bodies.

BS 5750 was first introduced in 1979. It forms the basis for the ISO 9000 standard (ISO means International Standards Organisation) and is in conformance with it. BS 5750 certification now implies conformance with ISO 9000 (and European Standard EN 29000). A company that gains BS EN ISO 9000 registration has a certificate testifying that it is operating to a structure of written policies and procedures which are designed to ensure that it can consistently deliver a product or service to meet customer requirements.

BS EN ISO 9000 falls into three parts.

(a) Part 1 covers design, manufacture and installation.
(b) Part 2 covers just manufacture and installation.
(c) Part 3 covers inspection and testing.

BS EN ISO 9000 does not dictate the quality of individual goods and services, but aims to ensure that quality management systems of a suitable standard are in place. The British Standards Institution states that BS EN ISO 9000

'sets out how you can establish, document and maintain an effective quality system which will demonstrate to your customers that you are committed to quality and are able to satisfy their quality needs.'

There have been some problems with BS EN ISO 9000.

(a) The procedure for acquiring certification is complex.

(b) It is inflexible and bureaucratic.

(c) The language and jargon make some observers suspect that quality certification is deliberately being turned into a mystique, in order to give an impression of exclusivity and also to generate fees for the management consultants who advise on quality certification.

(d) Possession of BS EN ISO 9000 does not, by itself, guarantee that the organisation is providing a *high* quality product or service, but rather that it is supplying a *consistent* standard. High quality and consistency are not necessarily the same thing.

(e) Some organisations felt compelled to seek quality certification as a necessary condition for staying in business (because their customers insist upon it) rather than because they are positively committed to it as such. In other words, their motives are purely defensive.

6.5 Organisational implications

Quality seems such a desirable objective that you might wonder why it has not been implemented before now. As ever, quality inevitably encounters a variety of organisational problems. In practice all the techniques and approaches to TQM involve a significant shake up.

(a) TQM is associated with giving employees a say in the process (eg in the *quality survey*) and in getting them to suggest improvements.

(b) TQM implies a greater discipline to the process of production and the establishment of better linkages between the business functions.

(c) TQM involves new relationships with suppliers, which requires them to improve their output quality so that less effort is spent rectifying poor input. Long-term relationships with a small number of suppliers might be preferable to choosing material and sub-components on price.

(d) It requires both work standardisation and employee commitment.

Participation is important in TQM, especially in the process of continuous improvement, where workforce views are valued. The management task is to encourage everybody to contribute. *Barriers* to participation include the following.

(a) An autocratic chief executive, who believes he or she is the sole key to the process

(b) Individualism, in which people possess ideas in order to take credit for them rather than share them for mutual benefit

(c) Ideas of managers as leaders and directors rather than facilitators and supporters

(d) Middle managers who feel their authority is threatened

There are other cultural barriers to the acceptance of TQM. Holmes quotes *Komatsu's* experience in the UK, and cites the comments of *Dr Clive Morton*:

'the team system was seen as a key factor in a total quality culture, yet the British emphasis on individual development can be very destructive of team working.'

Morton reported the hardest aspects for managers to accept.

(a) Social and status barriers are removed with the removal of office partitions.

(b) Administrative functions must now be seen as *supporting* the shop floor.

(c) The *shop floor* is the most important area.

(d) Managers are judged by their contribution to team spirit, not 'the virility of their decisions'.

(e) Meetings are used to gather information, not to take decisions.

(f) New personal skills are needed (eg the ability to listen and communicate).

(g) A manager's role is in supporting and training, not *disciplining* and *restricting*.

Holmes believes that managers most suited for a TQM culture will

'understand how people motivate themselves and direct this motivation towards good team results. They are concerned with achieving the goals of the team, supporting the individual members of the team, and keeping the team together.'

They will 'ensure time is spent setting objectives, planning, briefing, controlling, evaluating. These activities will be conducted in a participatory or controllable way'.

Chapter roundup

- Control systems are necessary to monitor current performance and to facilitate corrective action.

- Child identifies four control strategies: personal/centralised, bureaucratic, output (results are important) and cultural (whereby employees control 'themselves').

- Ouchi identifies three sorts of control. Market control is control by reference to competition and uses the price mechanism. Bureaucratic control is exercised by formal rules, policies or procedures. Clan control is partly cultural.

- A control system contains a plan or standard, a sensor, comparator, and effector. The purposes of control are target setting, measuring and monitoring, performance assessment, and feedback.

- Feedback is information generated by the system about its performance, and can be used in a control system. Positive feedback suggests that the current path should be continued. Negative feedback suggests that control action needs to be taken. Feedback sometimes suggests that the plan itself should be changed.

- Budgets are part of the organisation's control system. Their function is to authorise and plan expenditure, direct the allocation of resources, motivate and evaluate performance.

- Supervision is a managerial task: the dilemma is that of trust and control. There are two approaches to supervision: output control monitors the results of the subordinate's work; behaviour control monitors the process of the work.

- Contingency control models suggest that the types of control adopted will depend on factors such as the environment, the technology used, organisation size etc.

- An organisation's information systems are a vital part of its infrastructure. Information systems should be seen in the general context of how people communicate in organisations, and the type of communication involved in the work process: some tasks involve a variety of processes, leading to perhaps a large volume of information requirements; some tasks are easily analysed into their component parts.

- Quality is the totality of features which bears on a product's ability to meet stated needs.

- Design quality includes the degree to which customer satisfactions are built into a product.

- Conformance quality is an absence of defects in the finished goods.

- Various writes dealing with quality issues differ in the degree that they believe that changes in culture are important, in addition to the application of particular techniques.

- Quality assurance is increasingly demanded of suppliers. Quality assurance standards include BS EN ISO 9000 (formerly BS 5750). Certification is granted to companies which have an adequate system of quality assurance.

- TQM is a concept which applies quality to the whole organisation. TQM is a culture. Included concepts are statistical process control (for conformance quality) and quality function deployment (for design quality).

Quick quiz

1   What are the sources of control information?

2   What is feedback control?

3   What is feedforward control?

4   What type of control strategy does Child recommend where the organisation undergoes rapid change?

5   What is the role of market control?

6   What is clan control?

7   What are the roles of budgets in organisation control?

8   What is an executive information system?

9   What is wrong with achieving quality through inspection?

10   What are the critical features of TQM?

Answers to quick quiz

1   Informal and formal; internal and external

2   Actual results are compared with plan: any disparity is fed back as control action

3   Forecast results based on current conditions are compared with plan: any disparity is fed back as control action.

4   Output or cultural control.

5   The price mechanism is used as a control system both internally and externally.

6   There is strong personal commitment to the mission and priorities of the organisation.

7   A budget is an example of a plan against which results can be measured.

8   A computer based information system capable of providing both summary and detailed information in response to queries.

9   Inspection encourages waste by expecting a proportion of defective output. it is also a cost in itself.

10   Zero defects, right first time, continuous improvement, employee commitment, supplier commitment.

Answers to activities

1   *Feedforward control* in the police operates if police resources begin to be concentrated on a specific type of crime (drugs, car thefts, house burglaries, soccer violence) in response to a sudden increase that is not related to the forecast levels for that type of offence.

2   (a)   This shows the operation of double loop feedback. The plan has to be altered.

     (b)   This is a standard, in other words, a measure of expected performance. Counselling is control action to improve the individual's performance. Dismissal is control action too, if the employee is replaced by someone who performs better, thus raising the performance of the department as a whole.

     (c)   This is an example of cultural control, perhaps.

3   Organisations which place great value on employee conformity could include IBM, Marks & Spencer, Mars and Sainsbury's. You may not agree with these examples, or you may think of others. In a wider (European) context, EuroDisney is a further instance.

     The *advantages* of only selecting people who will fit in include the following.

     (a)   It becomes easier for the organisation to establish its corporate identity both internally and also with its suppliers.

(b) Problems of securing commitment are much reduced.

(c) For potential employees, the clarity of the organisation's culture makes it easier for them to decide whether they would want to work for it or not.

(d) For manufacturing organisations using systems like JIT (just-in-time) it is essential that groups and individuals work efficiently and without disruption – a compliant workforce is helpful in accomplishing this goal.

The *disadvantages* include the following.

(a) The organisation cannot readily develop or assimilate radical ideas and new approaches which do not harmonise with its established culture and beliefs.

(b) Perpetuation of the organisation's culture can mean that the organisation becomes progressively out of date, given that its rate of change is slower than that of the external environment.

(c) At least some employees are frustrated because their individuality is suppressed.

(d) Activities like R&D, which typically attract non-conforming individuals, find it difficult to influence the organisation's central management sufficiently.

4 There are many jobs and roles where outcomes are not easily measured. Examples include social work, research and development, some aspects of the personnel function and several tasks regularly performed in the public sector. Strenuous efforts may be made to generate some output controls in these categories – though it is notable that the relevance of such measures is regularly challenged by the employees involved, because they would prefer not to be measured at all. Indeed, even in activities where ends or outcomes can be identified – like teaching, where one might suppose that examination results could be a significant indicator of effectiveness – there is endless argument about whether the selected ends are the correct ones.

Behaviour controls often deal with such evidence as time recording and diary keeping, so that employee time allocations can be monitored – in the hope that efficient time management may be linked to output *effectiveness*. Adherence to procedures, systems and routines is also highly valued – and may even be essential for occupational categories whose work can be called to account, say, through the legal system (eg social work).

5 The *design quality* is poor, in that it does not meet customer requirements in an *appropriate* way. The umbrella is, however, perfectly made, so its *conformance quality* is *high*.

6 The chairman has got the gist. All of them miss the point as to the nature of TQM. The marketing director has a point in that TQM *does* imply a blurring of functional boundaries, but the marketing director *ought* to be pleased that, if TQM is implemented, the marketing concept will be brought into product design. The production director still has not grasped the concept. His idea of quality is 'technical excellence' not fitness for use. The finance director ought to care, as TQM has meaningful cost implications. The row is not pointless: at least the issue is being discussed, which is a beginning.

Further question practice

Now try the following practice questions at the end of this text

Multiple choice questions: **42 to 48**

Exam style question: **7**

Chapter 8 :

INDIVIDUALS AND GROUPS IN ORGANISATIONS

Introduction

This chapter examines some of the issues concerned with the performance of people in organisations, initially as individuals and subsequently as group/team members. We have already seen several times, in earlier chapters, that the impersonal structures and control systems in organisations count for little without human beings to make them work – but these same human beings, because of their foibles, perceptions, wants and idiosyncrasies, may also distort structures and control systems for their own purposes. Thus the formal hierarchy is bypassed by the informal organisation, and control systems can be circumvented by people exercising initiative (as they see it) in order to get things done. Teams and groups may work for the benefit of the organisation, or may be counter-productive: what is certain is that teams and groups will come into existence, whether management likes it or not, and will influence, therefore, the extent to which the organisation operates efficiently or achieves its goals.

In all human interactions – whether we are discussing a group or team in the conventional sense, or even a two-person interaction like a selection interview, a casual encounter in the corridor, or even the courtship ritual – there are two major ingredients. These are *content* and *process*. *Content* deals with the subject matter or the task on which the people are working; *process*, or the group dynamics, deals with such items as morale, feeling, tone, atmosphere, influence, participation, styles of behaviour, leadership, conflict, co-operation and competition. In most interactions, very little attention is paid to *process*, even when it is the major cause of ineffective group or team action. Indeed, knowledge about and sensitivity to group *process* would enable us to diagnose team problems early and deal with them: one of the major thrusts to this chapter is precisely to help encourage that knowledge and sensitivity.

In this chapter you will learn about these things.

(a) The complex interaction between the individual and the organisation, particularly so far as personality variables are concerned

(b) Typical personality changes associated with the development from immaturity to adult maturity, as outlined by *Argyris*

(c) The significance of perception and the development of self concepts for the formulation of attitudes to work

(d) Why groups come into existence in an organisational setting, the phases through which groups typically pass, and how leadership and other roles in groups are allocated

(e) The distinctions between effective and ineffective groups or teams

(f) Your own strengths and weaknesses in a group or team context

(g) Your own ability to work collaboratively with others in teams and groups

(h) The effectiveness of communication processes within an organisation, the barriers to communication, and the principal methods for ensuring that communications are improved

1 PERFORMANCE AND PRODUCTIVITY

Organisations are preoccupied with performance. Many of the control systems we discussed earlier mentioned actual performance and instituted corrective action: individuals, however, do not work in quite such a mechanical way, and it helps managers to have a fairly broad view as to the influences on individual behaviour and productivity. Many factors will influence job performance.

The diagram emphasises individual characteristics, but you should remember that these exist in an *organisation context*. People respond to the signals and controls issued by management, and management policies, both *personally* (in a manager's own personal approach to managing) and *collectively* (in control systems, reward systems, and so on) are critical influences on individual performance.

2 INDIVIDUAL BEHAVIOUR

2.1 Personality

Individuals are unique. In order to explain, describe and identify the differences between people, psychologists use the concept of personality.

Definition

Personality has been defined as 'the total pattern of characteristic ways of thinking, feeling and behaving that constitute the individual's distinctive method of relating to the environment.'

(a)   It is an *integrating, comprehensive concept.* The term usually describes properties, or features, of the individual that determine how he or she relates to his environment.

(b)   However, *it focuses on consistent or stable properties* – those that are 'characteristic' of a certain individual in different situations and at different times.

(c)   It *focuses on the distinctive behaviour patterns of individuals*, those which may be variable from individual to individual, which can be identified and used consistently in comparisons between them.

There is a 'nature-nurture' debate about whether or how far the factors of *heredity* and *environment* influence personality. Theorists disagree on the relative importance of each factor, and how (if at all) they relate to each other.

2.2   Individual development

Most accepted theories hold that the personality of any one individual is made up of various parts which combine and interact with external influences to shape the behaviour of the whole person. The general trend over time is towards increasing diversity and complexity, and usually therefore an increasing sense of selfhood, and the need to develop that personal potential.

According to Chris Argyris, psychologist and management writer, the sort of developments one might expect and observe in people as they mature are as follows.

(a)   *An increasing tendency to activity, rather than passivity* – or doing rather than being done to. This is partly because of the widening scope for action, with learning and experience, and partly to do with a growing sense of self.

(b)   *Diversification of behaviour patterns.* The personality of the individual grows more complex, and progresses from a few relatively limited forms of behaviour to a wider and more subtle range of responses.

(c)   *A tendency from dependence towards independence.* Independence is obviously relative: but generally, childish dependence on others gives way to a degree of self-sufficiency.

(d)   *Acceptance of equal or superior relationship to others.* Some people are happy to be in subordinate positions (at work or elsewhere) all their lives – but rarely in all areas of their lives. Generally, as we mature, we feel that a certain position is due to our self image, our age and experience. In the family, for example, we move naturally from the subordinate (child) to superior (parent) role.

(e)   *Lengthening perspectives.* A person's sense of time is highly subjective. To a child, 20- or 30-year-olds seem immensely aged, a year seems like a long time (to wait for Christmas to come around again, say). Increasingly, however, the pressures of responsibility, as well as experience/perception of the passage of time, lengthen the time-scales with which we are prepared to work.

(f) *Deepening and more stable interests.* Experience generally provides a wider range of potential interests; priorities are altered as personality develops; the search for new experience/knowledge has gone beyond the 'basics', which may have seemed challenging enough when the individual was younger.

(g) *Increasing self-awareness.* We behave partly in accordance with the image or concept that we have of ourselves, or 'the Self'. That self image is something we learn from interaction with other people, through their behaviour and attitudes towards us. Our self-image – and therefore our personality – is formed by experience over time, and is constantly adjusted.

These changes in personality can conflict strongly with the demands of the organisation. Many jobs require acceptance of the status quo; consistent behaviour; suppression of independent thought; acceptance of subordination and concentration on the short-term. Such jobs offer little potential for the kind increasing maturity described by Argyris.

Activity 1 (10 minutes)

Argyris's views have been criticised for being riddled with value judgements, ie the notion that being a mature person is somehow 'better' and preferable to being (by implication) immature. Yet looked at dispassionately, it is arguable that some people can be quite well-adjusted whilst nonetheless operating at what Argyris calls the 'infant' end of his development spectrum.

Think, for example, about someone who is largely passive, with limited behaviour patterns, inclined towards being dependent on others, happy to be in a subordinate position, with a relatively short time-perspective, a narrow range of interests, and restricted self-awareness. Such people evidently exist and it would be patronising to suggest that there is something wrong with them. From your reading of this book so far, what sort of organisations would be appropriate for the kind of person we have just outlined? What sort of work would they be likely to undertake?

By contrast, someone at the 'adult' end of the Argyris spectrum will be actively concerned about self-development, exhibiting a more complex range of behaviour patterns, reasonably self-sufficient and self-controlled, with longer time-perspectives, an impressive range of stable interests and substantial amounts of self-awareness. What sort of organisation would fit an individual with these characteristics? What sort of work is likely to be appropriate for them?

Development also occurs through the process of interaction with the 'external' environment. The individual learns about himself and about the 'rules' governing behaviour through taking on social roles, and through relationships with other people.

Childhood and family

The family is the earliest and one of the most important external influences on personal maturation and development: it is both a *social unit* and an extremely complex *relationship,* so it embraces a wide variety of behaviour, and affects development on many levels.

Buchanan and Huczynski

'Human beings do not behave in, and in response to, the world 'as it really is'... Human beings behave in, and in response to, the world as they perceive it.'

(a) The way an individual *perceives* people, events and the world will be highly subjective and selective, and will partly be influenced by his or her expectations, which in turn arise out of *past experience* (eg childhood).

(b) We have also noted the importance of *self awareness* in determining behaviour, and this too will be influenced in the early years. If a child is taught – by experiencing constant criticism, for example – to have a low self-image, or low expectations, his or her behaviour will tend to reflect this in later life, unless other influences intervene: the child's aspirations will be as low as his or her expectations, and his or her performance will conform to this lack of confidence. Alternatively, the person's adult behaviours may compensate for childhood privations.

Education

Learning takes place throughout an individual's life, and certainly not just in the formal education system. Research into formal education in schools, colleges and other identifiable institutions has demonstrated the way in which the socialisation of individuals is carried out. Schools recognise and reinforce mainstream social values and attitudes via three principal mechanisms.

(a) *Reward and punishment:* for example prizes for achievement, sanctions against failure or disruptive behaviour

(b) *Role definition:* the separation of boys and girls, and the areas of study and behaviour expected of them

(c) *Ethos:* definitions of success and failure, achievement, status (for example values attached to academic subjects as opposed to vocational studies) and acceptable behaviour

2.3 The organisation and the developing individual

What emerges from all this is a picture of how an individual develops into the kind of adult that his managers and colleagues later come into contact with. The main implications of this development, of (a) personality type and (b) goals, will be for *motivation:* what kind of task, environment, relationship with management and rewards will satisfy the individual, or encourage the best possible performance from him (not necessarily the same thing)? But what are the implications of the fact of development itself?

Activity 2   **(10 minutes)**

Do you think an assessment of personality should form part of an organisation's recruitment process? Does your answer apply equally whatever the job in question may be? How can an organisation assess a candidate's personality in any case?

2.4 Personality differences and work behaviour

What difference does personality make to behaviour at work, and to the management of individuals? In general terms, organisations will make certain generalised assumptions about the personalities of the individuals they employ, about the type of individuals they would wish to employ and to whom they would wish to allocate various tasks and responsibilities. You have only to look in job advertisements to see the recurrence of the desired characteristics: extrovert, steady, lively, responsible, hard-working and so on.

It has not been possible to prove frequent organisational assumptions that extrovert or stable personalities are more successful in particular occupations than any other type of individual.

(a)   The extrovert may be active, cheerful, social and not averse to risk – but may also be unreliable, easily bored, irresponsible and fickle.

(b)   Neurotics tend to be depressive, anxious, obsessive and emotional, and take too many days off sick – but they may also be conscientious, highly disciplined, and they do not fret under authority. Moreover, the ability to display and share emotion can be a healthy and desirable quality.

Nonetheless, if we assume broad consistency in traits or types of personality, we *can* make some useful observations about individual differences and work behaviour – at least enough to be going on with in the real world. Three examples are *authoritarianism*, the need for *achievement*, and *self esteem*. We will look briefly at these and other aspects of personality that might give a manager a 'handle' on individuals' work behaviour.

Authoritarianism

Control and control systems in this context may conjure up pictures of the repression or manipulation of the individual by the organisation (as represented by management), for purely economic and political ends. However, the concept of control can also be seen as necessary to create conditions of stability and predictability. People might *want* to be controlled in a work situation because control processes can do three things.

(a)   Provide feedback on the individual's performance, which may be essential for learning, satisfaction, motivation and the confirmation or adjustment of self-image among those with a need for high achievement.

(b)   Give the task itself definition and structure, standard methods and levels of performance. This is reassuring to most individuals, and essential to those with high security needs.

(c)   Encourage dependency, which is particularly welcome to a personality type known as the *authoritarian personality*.

It has been argued that such traits lead individuals to large, highly structured organisations, such as the armed services, which provide secure, ordered, controlled environments.

Need for achievement

McClelland identified the need for achievement as a prime motivator for people who have a strong desire for success (in relation to standards of excellence, and in competition with others) and a strong fear of failure. Such people tend to want work which offers four things.

(a)   Personal responsibility

(b)   Moderately difficult tasks and goals, which present a challenge and an opportunity to display their abilities – but not excessively difficult, since that might increase the possibility of failure

(c)   Acceptable, realistic levels of risk-taking – but not gambles, again because of the fear of failure

(d)   Clear, frequent feedback on performance – so that they can improve their performance, or have their success confirmed

Other personal characteristics associated with this type include:

(a)   Perfectionism, and a dislike of leaving tasks incomplete
(b)   A sense of urgency, always being in a hurry, and an inability to relax
(c)   Unsociability, if people seem to be getting in the way of performance

Low scorers on need for achievement worry more about security and status, their own ideas, feelings and self-presentation. They are not performance-orientated in the same way.

McClelland's researches suggested four things.

(a)   Entrepreneurs tend to rank high on need for achievement (see below).

(b)   Chief executives of large companies, having fulfilled their ambitions, tend to rank low on need for achievement.

(c)   Successful up and coming managers rank high on need for achievement, and

(d)   A need for achievement can be taught to managers on training courses, by getting them into the habit of thinking in achievement terms, and using achievement imagery.

The need for achievement is thought to be related to early socialisation. Children whose parents expect them to gain early independence, and impose few restrictions on them, who positively reinforce independent behaviour, and who foster an atmosphere of competitiveness, aspiration and achievement at home, are more likely to develop high achievement needs than children whose parents dominate, restrict or over-protect them.

Self esteem

Argyris, among others, has suggested that an individual continually seeks to increase his or her *self esteem*, to make his or her self-concept more gratifying, or to get closer to his or her ideal self-concept, or ego ideal. The experience of psychological success is one aspect of this, making the individual feel more competent and more secure. People who set themselves goals relating to their self concept, choose the manner of achieving them, and successfully achieve them, all experience psychological success.

The main aspects of self-esteem, as they effect behaviour at work, are these.

(a)   An individual's confidence in his or her competence, or in his or her ability to do something, contributes to the successful demonstration of that competence or ability.

(b)   A sense of competence is a secure basis for risk-taking in important personal areas.

(c)   Self-esteem is also an important factor in the success of training and appraisal schemes at work.

Activity 3   **(5 minutes)**

You have just read a short section about need for achievement as a motivator and another about the desire for self esteem. To what extent do you think that the desire for money is linked to either or both of these drives?

2.5 Perception

Perception is the psychological process by which stimuli or in-coming data are selected and organised into patterns which are meaningful to the individual. Different people see things differently: human beings behave in (and in response to) the world as *they see it*. Two major aspects of perception are relevant to organisational behaviour.

(a) Perception as the interpretation of information and events, including reasons why people misinterpret them.

(b) Social perception and social influence: ie the ways in which perception affects our attitudes to and interrelations with other people. Role theory and the influence of reference groups are two aspects of this.

The way in which we perceive other people is obviously going to be crucial to how we will relate to them and communicate with them in any context. It is the root of all attempts to motivate and manage people at work, and the basis from which individuals develop themselves (by comparison with others as they perceive them). There are two important forms of bias in the perception of other people that tend to operate in any situation.

(a) The *halo effect* is a term coined by the psychologist *Edward Thorndike*, to describe the way that our first highly selective judgements about people based on immediately obvious characteristics like dress, manner or facial expression colour our later perception of other features of those people, whether to positive or negative effect. Information subsequently gathered that does not agree with the first assessment tends to be filtered out. This happens even though the characteristics on which that first assessment was based may be largely irrelevant to the kind of judgement we may later wish to make and highly superficial. They are usually characteristics that we possess ourselves, since these are readily recognisable and generally sought after.

(b) *Stereotyping* operates through perceptual *organisation* rather than selectivity. We group together people who share certain characteristics, and then attribute traits to the group as a whole, which are (illogically) therefore assumed to belong to each individual member. The grouping may be done according to nationality, occupation, social position, age, sex or physical characteristics. The traits may be based on personal experience of particular individuals, common misconceptions or pure prejudice. Racial and sexual stereotypes are two pernicious examples.

Activity 4 **(5 minutes)**

Identify as many work situations as you can in which the halo effect or stereotyping could cause difficulties.

2.6 Social influence and self-concept development

Self-concept is partly developed through interaction with other people as we perceive them to be. There are three main sources of social influence on individual self-concept and behaviour.

(a) Role models, and self-comparison with other individuals

(b) Peer groups or reference groups;

(c)   Social experience in general, and the roles the individual is expected to play in various contexts

Selection of role models

Individuals consciously or unconsciously select and adopt *role models* for themselves, for the various roles that are relevant to their lives, and these become part of their developing self-concept. Parents and teachers can be significant role models. The selection of models may also be related to what *Festinger*, in 1951, called *social comparison theory*. People most seek to evaluate their own performance through comparison with other individuals, not by using absolute standards. Comparative performance information can be a strong motivator, as can peer reviews and even internal competition (between teams, or brands, say) in organisations. The source of an individual's attraction as a role model may come from a perception of that person's deliverable quantities.

(a)   Charisma, or personal magnetism
(b)   Expertise, or knowledge (the appeal of the parent, teacher, guru)
(c)   Demonstrated success
(d)   Moral or physical ascendancy, strength or personal domination

Reference groups

Definition

> *Reference groups* are groups with which an individual closely identifies. They have a major influence on the individual's behaviour, by offering models and norms for appropriate conduct.

The individual need not be a member of the group itself: any group to which the individual aspires is also a reference group. Reference groups influence behaviour in two ways.

(a)   By affecting *aspiration levels* – for example the junior manager who wants to get his golf up to the standard of his colleagues, who are members of the local country club

(b)   By affecting the type or direction of behaviour, by establishing conventions, norms and taboos. Styles of clothing, manner of speech, and voiced attitudes are examples of areas in which conformity may be expected.

2.7   Role theory

Role theory is concerned with the roles that individuals act out in their lives, and how the assumption of various roles affects their attitudes to other people. An example may help to explain what is meant by roles. An individual may consider himself to be a father and husband, and an active member of the local community, a supporter of his sports club, an amateur golfer, a conscientious church-goer, a man of certain political views, an academic and a research scientist. Each organisation to which he belongs provides him with one or several such roles to perform. His perceptions of other people and interactions with other people will be influenced by his varied roles, although in any particular situation one role is likely to have a stronger immediate bearing than others on what he thinks and does.

(a) A *role set* is a term to describe the individuals or group of people who relate to a focal person in one of that person's roles. For example, in the role of research scientist, an individual may be surrounded by a role set consisting of the following.

- The research director
- Research assistants
- Fellow research scientists in the department
- Other employees in the department
- Members of other scientific institutions

(b) Individuals give expression to the role they are playing at any particular time by giving role signs. An example of a role sign is clothing or uniform.

(c) *Role ambiguity* is a term which describes a situation when the individual is not sure what his or her role is, or when some members of his or her role set are not clear about this issue.

(d) *Role incompatibility* occurs when different groups have different expectations about what an individual should be doing, which may also differ from the individual's own role expectations.

(e) *Role conflict* occurs when an individual, acting in several roles at the same time, finds that the roles are incompatible. The simplest example is *whistle-blowing*. A finance officer of a company who uncovers fraud by senior management may feel a conflict between the roles of honest citizenship and that of professional confidentiality.

Activity 5   **(5 minutes)**

Try to visualise situations either at work or in your non-work life where you could experience (or have actually experienced) role ambiguity, role incompatibility or role conflict.

2.8 Attitudes

An *attitude* is the position that an individual has adopted in response to a theory or belief, an object, event or other person. Attitudes are our general standpoint on things. They are therefore linked to perception, personality, goals and so on as part of the developing package of assumptions and beliefs that each individual brings to his or her behaviour, decision-making and interactions with other individuals. They are subjective, in other words dependent on perception and personal experience, rather than wholly objective, although reasoned opinions may be part of the individual's attitudinal position.

Attitudes and work behaviour

Positive, negative or neutral attitudes to other workers, or groups of workers, to the various systems and operations of the organisation, to learning – or particular training initiatives – and to communication in the organisation will obviously influence performance at work. In particular, they may result in varying degrees of co-operation or conflict between individuals, groups, departments and different levels in the organisational hierarchy. They may also lead to varying degrees of success in communication, both interpersonal and organisation wide.

The main elements of a positive attitude to work itself might be described as a willingness to do five things.

(a) Commit oneself to the objectives of the organisation, or adopt personal objectives that are compatible with those of the organisation

(b) Accept the right of the organisation to set standards of acceptable behaviour

(c) Contribute to the development and improvement of work practices and performance

(d) *Believe* you are given a fair day's pay for a fair day's work

(e) Take advantage of opportunities for personal development

Of course, this is a positive attitude within the mainstream social culture of work: those who do not recognise the legitimacy of organisational attempts to direct and control behaviour, and to buy labour, would disagree.

Non-work factors that might influence attitudes to work include the following.

(a) *Class and class-consciousness:* attitudes about the superiority or inferiority of others, attitudes to money, as well as attitudes to work itself.

(b) *Age*. Attitudes to sexual equality, morality and education for example have varied widely from one generation to the next. Attitudes also tend to become less flexible with age.

(c) *Race, culture or religion*. Attitudes about these areas will again affect the way in which people regard each other – with tolerance, suspicion or hostility – and their willingness to co-operate in work situations. Culture and religion are also strong influences on attitudes to work.

(d) *Lifestyle and interests*. Attitudes about these areas affect interpersonal relations, and the self concept of each individual.

(e) *Sex*. Attitudes to the equality of men and women, and their various roles at work and in society, may be influential in three contexts.

    (i) Interpersonal relations at work (especially where women are in positions of authority over men: sexist attitudes may come into painful conflict with imposed power structures).

    (ii) The self-concept of the individual: women at work may be made to feel inferior, incompetent or simply unwelcome, while men working for female managers might feel their masculinity threatened.

    (iii) Attitudes to work itself. Stereotypical role profiles may be held by both men and women and may create feelings of guilt, resentment, or resignation about wanting or having to work.

Activity 6   **(15 minutes)**

Suppose you are a training manager in an organisation which has just embarked on a conscious programme to improve its customer service standards. You have been charged with the task of introducing new approaches to the treatment of customers so far as your organisation's 'front line' staff are concerned (ie the staff who normally deal direct with the customers). Given what you have read so far about behaviour and attitudes, which of the following approaches would you use, and why?

(a)   First changing the *attitudes* of your staff to customers and then altering their *behaviour;* or

(b)   first changing the *behaviour* of the staff, in the expectation that differing attitudes would ensue more or less automatically.

3   WORK GROUPS

Increasingly people in organisations are expected to work collaboratively together in groups and teams, rather than simply operate as individuals in self-contained cells. This reflected in job adverts which often emphasise teamwork skills; and at interviews where applicants are often asked to provide evidence of such skills. Once in work, you are likely to be involved in project teams and will be encouraged to regard your departmental colleagues as fellow team members; performance appraisal systems often include assessments linked to your ability for working with others; you may even find yourself participating in events designed to stimulate teambuilding.

There are a number of reasons for this focused, not least the value of commitment and identity to the team in promoting a *corporate culture* as we discussed in the previous chapter. A very real problem however is that despite the apparent emphasis on the team, reward mechanisms are often based on individual performance. Understandably this creates confusion among employees who are left to guess about the selection of priorities from their individual objectives or their group/team performance criteria.

Despite this it is widely acknowledged that properly designed and motivated groups can be effective and desirable both for organisations and the individuals who work within them. We will return to a specific discussion of these benefits in a later section.

Handy, in *Understanding Organisations* (1993). defines a *group* as follows.

Definition

A *group* is 'any collection of people who perceive themselves to be a group'.

The point of this definition is the distinction it implies between a random collection of individuals and a 'group' of individuals who share a common sense of identity and belonging. Groups have certain attributes that a random crowd does not possess.

(a)   *A sense of identity.* Whether the group is formal or informal, its existence is recognised by its members: there are acknowledged boundaries to the group which define who is 'in' and who is 'out', who is 'us' and who is 'them'.

People generally need to feel that they belong, that they share something with others and are of value to others.

(b)   *Loyalty to the group*, and acceptance within the group. This generally expresses itself as conformity or the acceptance of the norms of behaviour and attitudes that bind the group together and exclude others from it. Again, organisations try to encourage employee loyalty and commitment to the rules and objectives of the organisation, and a sense of solidarity against competition and problems.

(c)   *Purpose and leadership*. Most groups have an express purpose, whatever field they are in: most will, spontaneously or formally, choose individuals or sub-groups to lead them towards the fulfilment of those goals. Strength of personality, a high level of expertise, seniority of age or status and other factors will determine who rises to the top in any group. This hierarchy will be desirable so that the group can co-ordinate and control its members and their activities: it will of course be highly developed in formal organisations.

You should bear in mind that although an organisation as a whole may wish to project itself as a large group, with a single, united identity, loyalty and purpose, any organisation will in fact be composed of many sub-groups, with such attributes of their own. People in organisations will be drawn together into sub-groups by a variety of factors.

(a)   A preference for small groups, where closer relationships can develop

(b)   The need to belong and to make a contribution that will be noticed and appreciated

(c)   Familiarity: a shared office or canteen

(d)   Common rank, specialisms, objectives and interests

(e)   The attractiveness of a particular group activity (joining an interesting club, say)

(f)   Resources offered to groups (for example sports facilities)

(g)   Power greater than the individuals could muster alone (trade union, pressure group)

(h)   The feeling that they need to defend themselves against a real or imagined threat – from competitors, from other groups, from management, the argument being that collective defence is more powerful than unco-ordinated actions by individuals.

3.1   Formal and informal groups

Some groups will be the result of *formal* directives from the organisation: for example, specialists may be thrown together in a committee set up to investigate a particular issue or problem; a department may be split up into small work teams in order to facilitate supervision.

(a)   *Informal groups* will invariably be present in any organisation. Informal groups include workplace cliques, and networks of people who regularly get together to exchange information, groups of mates who socialise outside work and so on. They have a constantly fluctuating membership and structure, and leaders emerge usually through personal (rather than positional) power. The purposes of informal groups are usually related to group and individual member satisfaction, rather than to a task.

(b) *Formal groups* will have a formal structure; they will be consciously organised for a function allotted to them by the organisation, and for which they are held responsible – they are task oriented, and become *teams*. Leaders may be chosen within the group, but are typically given legal authority by the organisation. Permanent formal groups include standing committees, management teams (for example the board of directors) or specialist services (an information technology support). *Temporary* formal groups include task forces, designed to work on a particular project, ad hoc committees and so on.

3.2 Primary working groups

It is worth looking at *Trist's* ideas on the role of the *primary working group*. Primary groups are important in an industrial organisation for three reasons.

(a) They form the smallest units within it.

(b) They are the immediate social environment of the individual worker.

(c) The methods and team-spirit which prevail there will determine the efficiency and inter-relationships of the whole company.

The optimum size of a primary working group is important; the intimate, face-to-face relationships on which a primary group depends cannot be formed among more than, say, a dozen people. In the sense that most industrial work falls naturally into small groups of up to a dozen or so, primary groups are commonly found in industry. In the sense that these groups are provided for in the plan of organisation and given *official* leaders, primary groups have (until relatively recently) rarely been found. Too often, still, the official organisation of a company comes to an end well above the primary group level.

Whenever the formal organisation of a company fails to provide for primary groups, informal primary groups will spring up. These will usually have a self-protective purpose and will offer roles to unofficial leaders whose aims will not necessarily be in harmony with the official aims of the organisation.

There are many roles in the organisation (those of setters, overlookers and the like) which are in effect leadership roles. In many cases, however, these are recognised only for their technical content and not for their people-management content. If the people in such positions were held responsible for the whole of their leadership role – for relationships and team spirit among the group as well as for its technical working – management organisation would extend to the primary working groups.

Activity 7 **(5 minutes)**

What is the size of the primary (working) group in your current context, ie at college, university or in a conventional work environment? How far do the numbers in such groups, from your experience, support the points made in the previous paragraphs?

Who became leaders in these primary groups? Are their leadership roles 'recognised only for their technical content and not for their people-management content'?

3.3 The function of groups

From the *organisation's* standpoint, groups can be used in a variety of roles.

(a) Performing tasks which require the collective skills of more than one person

(b) Testing and ratifying decisions made outside the group

(c) Consulting or negotiating, especially to resolve disputes within the organisation

(d) Creating ideas

(e) Exchanging ideas, collecting and transmitting information

(f) Co-ordinating the work of different individuals or other groups

(g) Motivating individuals to devote more energy and effort into achieving the organisation's goals

From the *individual's* standpoint groups also perform some important functions.

(a) They satisfy social needs for friendship and belonging.

(b) They help individuals to develop images of themselves.

(c) They enable individuals to help each other in matters which are not necessarily connected with the organisation's purpose (people at work may organise a baby-sitting circle).

(d) They enable individuals to share the burdens of any responsibility they may have in their work.

Brayfield and Crockett suggested that an individual will always identify with some group or other.

(a) If the individual identifies with a social group, outside work, this will have no effect on his or her job performance.

(b) On the other hand, if the individual identifies with his or her *work-mates* and work group his or her performance will be affected. However, a congenial work group, creating high morale, can either raise or lower productivity, depending on the norm adopted by the group. The group norm will probably be based on its collective idea of a fair day's work for a fair day's pay but such an attitude is a subjective one, so what is fair may be a high or low standard of efficiency.

(c) An employee who identifies with his *company* may not be the most productive, through caring for quality rather than output level. It has been suggested that the employees who are most likely to win recognition and promotion within the company are those who are critical of its policies, and not those who identify with them.

3.4 The formation of groups

Groups are not static. They mature and develop. Four stages in this development were identified by *Tuckman:* forming, storming, norming and performing.

(a) *Forming.* During the first stage the group is just coming together, and may still be seen as a collection of individuals. Each individual wishes to impress his or her personality on the group, while its purpose, composition, and organisation are being established.

(i)   The individuals will be trying to find out about each other, and about the aims and norms of the group.

(ii)   Individuals will also be feeling out each other's attitudes and abilities: no-one will want to appear less informed or skilled than the others.

(iii) This settling down period is essential, but may be time wasting: the team as a unit will not be used to being autonomous, and will probably not be an efficient agent in the planning of its activities or the activities of others. It may resort to complex bureaucratic procedures to ensure that what it is doing is at least something which will not get its members into trouble.

(b)   The second stage is called *storming* because it frequently involves more or less open conflict between group members. There may be changes agreed in the original objectives, procedures and norms established for the group. If the group is developing successfully this may be a fruitful phase as more realistic targets are set and trust between the group members increases. The element of risk enters solutions to problems and options may be proposed which are more far-reaching than would have been possible earlier. Whilst the first stage of group development involved 'toeing the organisational line', the second stage brings out the identification of team members with causes: this may create disagreement, and there may also be political conflict over leadership.

(c)   The third or *norming* stage is a period of settling down. There will be agreements about work sharing, individual requirements and expectations of output. Group procedures and customs will be defined and adherence to them secured. The enthusiasm and brain-storming of the second stage may be less apparent, but norms and procedures may evolve which enable methodical working to be introduced and maintained. This need not mean that initiative, creativity and the expression of ideas are discouraged, but that a reasonable hearing is given to everyone and consensus sought.

(d)   Once the fourth or *performing* stage has been reached the group sets to work to execute its task. Even at earlier stages some performance will have been achieved but the fourth stage marks the point where the difficulties of growth and development no longer hinder the group's objectives.

It would be misleading to suggest that these four stages always follow in a clearly defined progression, or that the development of a group must be a slow and complicated process. Particularly where the task to be performed is urgent, or where group members are highly motivated, the fourth stage will be reached very quickly while the earlier stages will be hard to distinguish. Some groups, moreover, never progress beyond storming, because the differences are irreconcilable.

It is often the case that after a team has been performing effectively for a while it becomes complacent. In this phase, which has been called '*dorming*' (so that it sounds like the other phases in Tuckman's model), the team goes into a semi-automatic mode of operation with efforts devoted primarily to the maintenance of the team itself, even where the task has changed. We will discuss this in more detail in a coming section.

Activity 8 (5 minutes)

Can you apply the *forming-storming-norming-performing-dorming* sequence to types of human interaction other than groups and teams at work?

How far can it be applied, for example, to the process of courtship with a person of the opposite sex or to the process of developing a football or cricket team from scratch?

3.5 Group norms

A work group establishes *norms* or acceptable levels and methods of behaviour, to which all members of the group are expected to conform. This group attitude will have a negative effect on an organisation if it sets unreasonably low production norms. Groups often apply unfair treatment or discrimination against others who break their rules. Norms are partly the product of roles and role expectations of how people in certain positions behave, as conceived by people in related positions.

EXAMPLE: SHERIF'S EXPERIMENT

In a classic experiment by Sherif, participants were asked to look at a fixed point of light in a black box in a darkroom. Although the point of light is fixed, it so happens that in the darkness, it *appears* to move. Each participant was asked to say how far the light moved, and their individual estimates were recorded.

They were next put into a small group where each member of the group gave their own estimates to the others. From this interchange of opinions, individuals began to change their minds about how far the light had moved, and a group norm estimate emerged.

When the groups were broken up, each individual was again asked to re-state his estimate; significantly, they retained the group norm estimate and rejected their previous individual estimate.

The experiment showed the effect of group psychology on establishing norms for the individual; even when, as in the case of the experiment, there is no factual basis for the group norm.

The general nature of group pressure is to require the individual to share in the group's own identity, and individuals may react to group norms and customs in three ways.

- Compliance without real commitment
- Internalisation – full acceptance and identification
- Counter-conformity – rejecting the group and/or its norms

Pressure is strongest on individual when the issues are not clear-cut, when they lack support for their own attitudes or behaviour and when they are exposed to other members of the group for a length of time.

Norms may be reinforced in various ways by the group.

(a) *Identification:* the use of badges, symbols, perhaps special modes of speech, in-jokes and so on – the marks of belonging, prestige and acceptance. There may even be initiation rites which mark the boundaries of membership.

(b)   *Sanctions* of various kinds. Deviant behaviour may be dealt with by ostracising or ignoring the member concerned, by ridicule or reprimand, even by physical hostility. The threat of expulsion is the final sanction.

The group's power to induce conformity depends on the degree to which the individual values his membership of the group and the rewards it may offer, or wishes to avoid the negative sanctions at its disposal.

Groupthink

Groupthink develops when the cohesion of the group makes consensus-seeking the dominant force. A successful team or group is a very comfortable place to be. Hence it is easy for groups to move to a state where members, as a result of long adaptation to group norms, strive not to upset the group. Such behaviour can be very threatening for the survival of the group, because groups which do not change their composition, methods and aims to suit environment changes soon find themselves overtaken by events. Examples include the UK retail sector in the late 1980s and early 1990s and parts of the trade union movement during the 1980s.

The characteristics of groupthink are as follows.

- An illusion of invulnerability
- Belief in the rectitude of the group
- Negative views of competitors
- Sanctity of group consensus
- Illusion of unanimity
- Erection of a protective shield

When groupthink occurs, it is accompanied by optimism, dismissal or rationalisation of warning signs and the selective use of information to support the group's policy.

It is considered deviant within the group to express a difference of opinion that violates the warm consensus. Often, instead, individuals will express their doubts and misgivings quietly and anxiously in private; within the group itself, there will be no disagreement, no critical thinking, no testing of reality. Any individual expressing opinions contrary to those held by the group will be faced with the choice of taking the 'party line' or leaving the team.

These are the steps which may hope to counteract any tendency towards groupthink.

(a)   Encouragement of open discussion for doubts and objectives

(b)   The exercise of impartiality by the leader, including the fact that he or she avoids stating his or her own views until after the topic has been fully discussed

(c)   Formal adoption of a devil's advocate role by one of the group members

(d)   Avoidance of premature solutions

(e)   Use of sub-groups working on their own for short periods

The Hawthorne Studies

We mentioned Elton Mayo in Chapter 1. His work sheds light on the importance of groups within an organisation. His most interesting findings emerged from the Hawthorne studies, so called because they were conducted at the Hawthorne plant of the Western Electric Company.

The experiments arose from an attempt by Western Electric to find out the effects of lighting standards on worker *productivity*. As a test, it moved a group of young women into a special room with variable lighting, and moved another group into a room where the lighting was kept at normal standards. To the astonishment of the company management, productivity shot up in both rooms. When the lighting was then reduced in the first room, as a continuation of the test, not only did productivity continue to rise in the first room, but it also rose still further in the second room. Mayo was then approached to investigate further. The ideas developed from this research were later applied throughout the plant but didn't work. The conditions which made the initial experiments a success (the sense of status enjoyed by the young women in the Relay Assembly Test Room, because of their participation in the research) were no longer present when the experimental situation (the counselling service) was made available organisation-wide.

The conclusions of the studies were that individual members must be seen as part of a group, and that *informal* groups exercise a powerful influence in the workplace: supervisors and managers need to take account of social needs if they wish to secure commitment to organisational goals.

The Hawthorne studies were the first major attempt to undertake genuine social research in industry, and to redirect attention to human factors at work. They are enduringly popular with managers, not least because they have an apparent simplicity and a straightforward, enthusiastically sold message that 'happy workers are more productive'.

Buchanan and Huczynski address the question of whether a happy group is also a productive one, as the Hawthorne studies suggested.

'The Hawthorne studies signalled the birth of the Human Relations School of Management ... It was not until some time had passed that people started to question this relationship between productivity and satisfaction. Perhaps it had been a fortuitous coincidence rather than some iron law? Sociologists who reviewed the findings and compared them with other data swung to the former explanation.'

3.6 Effective and ineffective work groups

Team building is the process of diagnosing problems in the functioning of a group and then devising exercises and training activities to help improve performance. The management problem is how to create an effective, efficient work group. There are two criteria of group effectiveness.

(a) Fulfilment of task and organisational goals
(b) Satisfaction of group members

Handy takes a contingency approach to the problem of group effectiveness, which, he argues, depends on three groups of factors.

The group	
The group's task	
The group's environment	The 'givens'

Motivation of the group	
Leadership style	
Processes and procedures	The 'intervening factors'

Productivity of the group	The 'outcomes'
Satisfaction of the group members	

The givens

The personalities and characteristics of the individual members of the group, and the personal goals of these members, will help to determine the group's personality and goals. An individual is likely to be influenced more strongly by a small group than by a large group in which he or she may feel like a small fish in a large pond, and therefore unable to participate effectively in group decisions.

It has been suggested that the effectiveness of a work group depends on the blend of the individual skills and abilities of its members. *Belbin*, in a study of business-game teams at Carnegie Institute of Technology in 1981, discovered that a differentiation of influence among team members (that is, agreement that some members were more influential than others) resulted in higher morale and better performance. Belbin's picture of the most effective character-mix in a team (which many managers have found a useful guide to team working) involves eight necessary roles which should ideally be balanced and evenly 'spread' in the team:

(a) The *co-ordinator* – presides and co-ordinates; balanced, disciplined, good at working through others

(b) The *shaper* – highly strung, dominant, extrovert, passionate about the task itself, a spur to action

(c) The *plant* – introverted, but intellectually dominant and imaginative; source of ideas and proposals but with disadvantages of introversion

(d) The *monitor-evaluator* – analytically (rather than creatively) intelligent; dissects ideas, spots flaws; possibly aloof, tactless – but necessary

(e) The *resource-investigator* – popular, sociable, extrovert, relaxed; source of new contacts, but not an originator; needs to be made use of

(f) The *implementer* – practical organiser, turning ideas into tasks, scheduling, planning and so on; trustworthy and efficient, but not excited; not a leader, but an administrator

(g) The team worker – most concerned with team maintenance – supportive, understanding, diplomatic; popular but uncompetitive – contribution noticed only in absence

(h) The *finisher* – chivvies the team to meet deadlines, attend to details; urgency and follow-through important, though not always popular

Belbin has also identified a ninth team-role, the specialist, who joins the group to offer expert advice when needed. Examples are legal advisers, PR consultants, finance specialists and the like.

Activity 9 **(10 minutes)**

(a) Which of Belbin's categories do you think best describes your own character?

(b) How well does Belbin's picture describe a team of which you have been a member?

The *nature of the task*, the second of Handy's givens, must have some bearing on how a group should be managed. If a job must be done urgently, it is often necessary to dictate how things should be done, rather than to encourage a participatory style of working. Jobs which are routine, unimportant and undemanding will be insufficient to motivate either individuals or the group as a whole. If individuals in the group want authoritarian leadership, they are also likely to want clearly defined group targets.

The *group's environment* relates to factors such as the physical surroundings at work and to inter-group relations. An open-plan office, in which the members of the group are closely situated, is more conducive to group cohesion than a situation in which individuals are partitioned into separate offices, or geographically distant from each other. Group attitudes will also be affected, as described previously, by relationships with other groups, which may be friendly, neutral or hostile.

Intervening factors: processes and procedures

Of Handy's intervening factors, motivation and leadership are discussed at length in separate chapters of this text. With regard to processes and procedures, research indicates that a group which tackles its work systematically will be more effective than a group which lives from hand to mouth, and muddles through – but this is often true of individuals as well. In an ideal functioning group a number of things will happen.

(a) Each individual gets the support of the group, a sense of identity and belonging which encourages loyalty and hard work on the group's behalf.

(b) Skills, information and ideas are shared, so that the group's capabilities are greater than those of the individuals.

(c) New ideas can be tested, reactions taken into account and persuasive skills brought into play in group discussion for decision making and problem solving.

(d) Each individual is encouraged to participate and contribute and thus becomes personally involved in and committed to the group's activities.

(e) Goodwill, trust and respect can be built up between individuals, so that communication is encouraged and potential problems more easily overcome.

Unfortunately, group working is rarely such an undiluted success. There are certain constraints involved in working with others.

(a) Awareness of one's role and group norms for behaviour may restrict individual personality and flair.

(b) Conflicting roles and relationships where an individual is a member of more than one group can cause difficulties in communicating effectively, especially if sub-groups or cliques are formed in conflict with other groupings.

(c) The effective functioning of the group is dependent upon each of its members, and will suffer if members dislike or distrust each other, or if one member is so dominant that others cannot participate, or so timid that the value of his or her ideas is lost, or so negative in attitude that constructive communication is rendered impossible.

(d) Rigid leadership and procedures may strangle initiative and creativity in individuals. On the other hand, differences of opinion and political conflicts of interest are always likely and if all policies and decisions are to be determined by consultation and agreement within the group, decisions may never be reached and action never taken.

The outcomes

High productivity may be achieved if work is so arranged that satisfaction of individuals' needs coincides with high output. Where teams are, for example, allowed to set their own improvement goals and methods and to measure their own progress towards those goals, it has been observed (by *Peters and Waterman* among others) that they regularly exceed their targets.

Individuals may bring to the group their own hidden agendas for satisfaction: these are goals which may have nothing to do with the declared aims of the group such as protection of a sub-group, impressing the boss, inter-personal rivalry and so on. The danger is that the more cohesive the group, the more its own maintenance and satisfactions may take precedence over its task objectives, and the more collective power it has – even to sabotage organisational goals.

Like organisations, therefore, groups have cultures which will contribute importantly to the effectiveness or otherwise of the group's operation and member satisfaction. Peters and Waterman (*In Search of Excellence*) outline the cultural attributes of successful *task force* teams.

(a)   They should be small, which requires the trust of those who are not involved

(b)   They should be of limited duration and working under the 'busy member theorem', in other words 'get off the damned task force and back to work'

(c)   They should be voluntary.

(d)   They should have an informal structure and documentation, no bulky paperwork, and open communication.

(e)   They should have swift follow-up, and be action oriented.

The characteristics of effective and ineffective work groups

If a manager is to try to improve the effectiveness of his work group he must be able to identify the different characteristics of an effective group and an ineffective group. Some pointers to group efficiency are quantifiable measures; others are more qualitative factors and are difficult to measure. A number of different factors should be considered, because a favourable showing in some aspects of work does not necessarily mean that a group is operating effectively. No one factor on its own is significant, but taken collectively the factors will present a picture of how well or badly the group is operating.

Quantifiable factors	
Effective work group	*Ineffective work group*
(1) Low rate of labour turnover	(1) High rate of labour turnover
(2) Low accident rate	(2) High accident rate
(3) Low absenteeism	(3) High absenteeism
(4) High output and productivity	(4) Low output and productivity
(5) Good quality of output	(5) Poor quality of output
(6) Individual targets are achieved	(6) Individual targets are not achieved
(7) There are few stoppages and interruptions to work	(7) Much time is wasted owing to disruption of work flow
	(8) Time is lost owing to disagreements between superior and subordinates

Qualitative factors	
Effective work group	*Ineffective work group*
(1) There is a high commitment to the organisational goals achievement of targets and	(1) There is no understanding of organisational goals or the role of the group
(2) There is a clear understanding of the group's work	(2) There is a low commitment to targets
(3) There is a clear understanding of the role of each person within the group	(3) There is confusion and uncertainty about the role of each person within the group
(4) There is trust between members and free and open communication	(4) There is mistrust between group members and suspicion of the group's leaders
(5) There is idea sharing	(5) There is little idea sharing
(6) The group is good at generating new ideas	(6) The group does not generate any good new ideas
(7) Group members try to help each other	(7) Group members make negative and hostile criticisms about each other's work
(8) There is group problem solving which gets to the root causes of the work problem	(8) Work problems are dealt with superficially, with attention paid to the symptoms but not the cause
(9) There is an active interest in work decisions	(9) Decisions about work are accepted passively
(10) Group members seek a united consensus of opinion	(10) Group members hold strongly opposed views
(11) The members of the group want to develop their abilities in their work	(11) Group members find work boring and do it reluctantly
(12) The group is sufficiently motivated to be able to carry on working in the absence of its leader	(12) The group needs its leader there to get work done

4 COMMUNICATION

In any organisation, the communication of information is necessary to achieve co-ordination, whichever type of co-ordination is used.

(a) *Management.* Management need communication to make the necessary decisions for planning, co-ordination and control; managers should be aware of what their departments are achieving, what they are not achieving and what they should be achieving.

(b) *Departments.* All the interdependent systems for purchasing, production, marketing and administration can be synchronised to perform the right actions at the right times to co-operate in accomplishing the organisation's aims.

(c) *Individuals.* Employees should know what is expected from them. Effective communication gives an employee's job meaning, makes personal development possible, and acts as a motivator, as well as oiling the wheels of labour relations.

Communication in the organisation may take many forms.

(a) Giving instructions;

(b) Giving or receiving information

(c) Exchanging ideas

(d) Announcing plans or strategies

(e) Comparing actual results against a plan

(f) Laying down rules or procedures

(g) Job descriptions, organisation charts or manuals (communication about the structure of the organisation and individual roles)

Communication within the formal organisation structure may be of the following types.

(a) *Vertical,* up and down the scalar chain:

(b) *Horizontal or lateral* (between people of the same rank, in the same section or department, or in different sections or departments). Communication is perhaps most routine between people at the same or similar level in the organisation, that is horizontal communication. It is necessary for two reasons.

(i) *Formally:* to co-ordinate the work of several people, and perhaps departments, who have to co-operate to carry out a certain operation.

(ii) *Informally:* to furnish emotional and social support to an individual.

Horizontal communication within peer groups is usually easier and more direct than vertical communication, being less inhibited by considerations of rank.

(c) *Diagonal.* This is interdepartmental communication by people of different ranks. Departments in the technostructure which serve the organisation in general, such as Personnel or Information Systems, have no clear line of authority linking them to managers in other departments who need their involvement.

Communication media include the following.

(a) Oral methods, such as committees, team briefings, interviews, quality circles, and telephone.

(b) Written methods such as memos, procedures manuals, reports, letters, staff magazines, notice boards.

(c) Electronic methods such as e-mail, video, computer conferencing and bulletin boards.

4.1 The communication process

The diagram below demonstrates in outline the process that is involved in communication.

The communication process

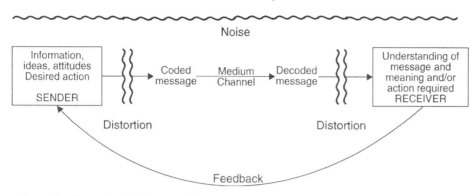

A number of points should be noted.

(a) *Coding of a message:* the code or language of a message may be verbal (spoken or written) or it may be non-verbal, in pictures, diagrams, numbers or body language.

(b) *Medium for the message:* there are a number of channels for communication, such as a conversation, a letter, a notice board or via computer. The choice of medium used in communication depends on a number of factors such as urgency, permanency, complexity, sensitivity and cost.

(c) *Feedback:* it is of vital importance that the sender of a message gets feedback on the receiver's reaction. This is partly to test the receiver's understanding of it and partly to gauge the receiver's reaction.

(d) *Distortion* refers to the way in which the meaning of a message is lost in 'handling', that is at the coding and decoding stages. Usually the problem is one of language and the medium used; most of us have found, for instance, that it is far easier to get the wrong end of the stick in a telephone call than from a letter, since non-verbal language is missing and the message is transient.

(e) *Noise* refers to distractions and interference in the environment in which communication is taking place. It may be physical noise (passing traffic), technical noise (a bad telephone line), social noise (differences in the personalities of the parties) or psychological noise (anger, frustration, tiredness). In multinational, or global corporations, it might be caused by differences in culture.

4.2 Barriers to communication

Good communication is essential to getting any job done: co-operation is impossible without it. Difficulties occur because of general faults in the communication process.

(a) Distortion or omission of information by the sender.

(b) Misunderstanding due to lack of clarity or technical jargon.

(c) Non-verbal signs (gesture, posture, facial expression) contradicting the verbal message, so that its meaning is in doubt.

(d) Overload – a person being given too much information to digest in the time available.

(e) Differences in social, racial or educational background, compounded by age and personality differences, creating barriers to understanding and co-operation.

NOTES

(f)   People hearing *only what they want to hear* in a message.

Activity 10   **(10 minutes)**

Before reading the next section, look at the six barriers to communication
listed above and identify some *specific applications* of these barriers likely to
be relevant in a work situation.

There may also be particular difficulties in a work situation.

(a)   A general tendency to distrust a message in its re-telling from one person to
another.

(b)   A subordinate mistrusting his or her superior and looking for hidden
meanings in a message.

(c)   The relative status in the hierarchy of the sender and receiver of
information. A senior manager's words are listened to more closely and a
colleague's perhaps discounted.

(d)   People from different job or specialist backgrounds (eg accountants,
personnel managers, IT experts) having difficulty in talking on a non-
specialist's wavelength.

(e)   People discounting information from those not recognised as having expert
power.

(f)   People or departments having different priorities or perspectives so that one
person places more or less emphasis on a situation than another.

(g)   Subordinates giving superiors incorrect or incomplete information (eg to
protect a colleague, to avoid 'bothering' the superior); also a senior manager
may only be able to handle edited information because he does not have
time to sift through details.

(h)   Subordinates not wishing to give information which displeases a manager
or which conflicts with the manager's assumptions or expectations. *O'Reilly
and Roberts* developed this argument in a laboratory study from which they
concluded about the upward flow of communication that:

*'If the information is important but unfavourable to the sender it is likely to
be blocked. This has implications for top-level decision-making and policy
formulation because it may mean that organisational resources are often
committed in a vacuum of relevant (particularly non-favourable)
information.'*

(i)   Managers who are prepared to make decisions on a hunch without proper
regard to the communications they may or may not have received.

(j)   Information which has no immediate use tending to be forgotten.

(k)   Lack of opportunity, formal or informal, for subordinates to say what they
think or feel.

(l)   Conflict in the organisation. Where there is conflict between individuals or
departments, communications will be withdrawn and information withheld.

The barriers to good communication arising from differences in social, racial or
educational backgrounds, compounded by age differences and personality differences,
can be particularly severe.

(a)   Different social or educational backgrounds may cause some people to feel superior to other people.

(b)   A young person might be resented by an older person of the same grade or status in the organisation. The young person might look down on the older one as someone who has failed to advance in the management hierarchy, and is therefore second-rate. Difficulties in seeing each other's point of view might be compounded by different methods of expression.

(c)   Personality differences might occur where one person appears fairly happy-go-lucky, and another is more serious in his application to work and his outlook on life. Frustration may occur in communication between the two because their different values give them conflicting views about what is important, or how to tackle particular work tasks on which they are both involved. Differences in background or personality might result in the following.

    (i)   Failure to understand the other's point of view and sense of values and priorities.

    (ii)   Failure to listen to the information the other person is giving (the information is judged according to the person who gives it).

    (iii) A tendency to give the other person ready-formulated opinions (which the other does not accept) instead of factual information which will enable the other person to formulate his own opinions.

    (iv)   Lack of shared vocabulary – whether linguistic, symbolic or body language – which might lead to lack of understanding of the message.

    (v)   Emotions (anger, fear, frustration) will creep into communications and further hinder the transmission of clear information.

    (vi)   Recipients of information will tend to hear what they want to hear; ignore anything they do not want to accept; and blame it on the other person if problems arise later on.

(d)   The culture of the organisation. Some organisations prefer secrecy, especially bureaucracies.

    (i)   Information might be given on a need-to-know basis, rather than be considered as a potential resource for everyone to use.

    (ii)   The culture of some organisations may prevent the communication of certain messages. Organisations with a can-do philosophy may not want to hear that certain tasks are impossible.

    (iii) Participative management styles inevitably encourage communication between members.

One of the problems of communication is that the recipient is able to filter out what he or she does not want to hear, and concentrates on some facts rather than others. *Active listening* is a technique to ensure that the speaker's entire message is communicated. The recipient identifies key words and phrases, and interrupts with comments testing understanding like 'So, what you are saying is ....' to ensure the message is understood.

NOTES

Chapter roundup

- Personality is the totality of an individual's thoughts, feelings and behaviours, which:

  (i)   integrate the person;
  (ii) are consistent;
  (iii) distinguish the person from someone else.

- Personality is shaped by a variety of factors, both inherited and environmental.

- In the work environment, people can assume different roles according to personality. In judging individuals:

  (i)   perceptual selectivity leads to the halo effect whereby some characteristics, in the perceiver's viewpoint, dominate others;

  (ii) stereotyping organises perceptions and assumes that people who share one characteristic share a set of others.

  People develop views of themselves through interaction with others. Social information includes:

  (i)   role models;
  (ii) peer groups;
  (iii) the variety of roles the individual is expected to play.

- Individuals have attitudes. These affect an individual's response to situations. Behaviour at work is formed by attitudes at work and attitudes to work. Attitudes to work can be set by the wider social and cultural influences on the individual, and how that individual is motivated.

- A group has certain attributes that a crowd does not possess; groups have many important functions in organisations. You should be able to describe how groups form, and a variety of features of group behaviour.

  (i)   Group norms may work to lower the standard rate of unit production.

  (ii) Groups have been shown to produce fewer – though better evaluated – ideas than the individuals of the group working separately.

- The characteristics of effective and ineffective groups are well known and concern themselves with both processes (the group dynamics, participation, leadership, communication, performance of roles and so forth) and also outcomes (the quality of decisions made, responsiveness to changing environmental demands etc).

- Groupthink is a particularly dangerous phenomenon found in so-called 'mature' groups, taking the form of complacency, introspectiveness, isolation from the external world and collective feelings of superiority.

- Communication between individuals can be impeded by individual differences and organisational culture, which can introduce distortion and noise to the communication process.

Quick quiz

1   What are the main categories of variables that affect job performance?

2   How would you expect people's sense of time to develop as they mature?

3   Why are there some contradictions between the way certain organisations operate and the psychological needs of people?

4   In what circumstances do people want to be controlled in a work situation?

5   What is meant by the halo effect?

6   What are reference groups and how do they influence behaviour?

7   What are the non-work factors that can influence attitudes to work?

8   How does a group differ from a crowd of strangers?

9   Outline Tuckman's sequence of group formation.

10   Why is it that the Hawthorne Studies are not particularly helpful to modern managers?

Answers to quick quiz

1   Individual; physical and job; situational; and organisational and social.

2   Time scales lengthen.

3   Organisational requirements for controlled, predictable performance clash with the increasing need for autonomy and fulfilment typical of the mature person as described by Argyris.

4   Control provides feedback on performance, which is generally welcomed; defines role and responsibility, which is required by those with a need for security; and encourage dependency, which is needed by the authoritarian personality.

5   First impressions colour later perceptions.

6   A group to which an individual looks for role models and normal of behaviour.

7   Class, age, race, religion, culture, lifestyle, sex.

8   A group has a purpose and leadership; its members feel loyalty to the group and are supported by it; and it has a sense of identity.

9   Forming, storming, norming and performing.

10   The group dynamics explored at Hawthorne are a basic aspect of management education, but the studies do not really offer any guidance on how group behaviour can be managed to improve performance.

Answers to activities

1   You will find some material about these issues later in this section under subheading 2.3 'The organisation and the developing individual'.

In essence, individuals with what Argyris terms an infant or immature set of expectations are more likely to be at home within a highly-regulated, paternalistic and authoritarian bureaucracy, where the exercise of initiative could be construed as dysfunctional. Employees have few

213

opportunities for taking control and work routines are fragmented, molecularised (ie with very short job cycles) and repetitive.

People at the adult end of the Argyris spectrum will seek challenging, enlarged and empowered roles, with control and autonomy over their existence. They will probably gravitate towards more organic structures, where change is a permanent feature both within and outside the organisation.

Infant expectations are reflected in the so-called *affluent worker* studies by *Goldthorpe* and his colleagues. These concluded that many employees at the *Vauxhall* car plant in Luton were motivated by what Goldthorpe describes as *instrumental* considerations, that is to say, they had made a conscious decision to tolerate unsatisfying work in order to achieve certain materialistic goals. These workers had weighed extrinsic benefits against intrinsic deprivations and had made the (perfectly rational) decision to opt for extrinsic factors, at least in the short term. According to Argyris, such behaviour is immature but, to put it mildly, there is room for debate on the merits of his argument. In fact it is plausible to imagine that Argyris is so wedded, intellectually, to a neo-human relations view of work that he cannot conceive of the possibility that any rational human being would consciously elect to sacrifice job satisfaction in favour of some alternative purpose.

2   There is room for you to have your own opinions on this topic. In practice of course job advertisements frequently do specify that they are looking for an 'outgoing personality', 'the ability to work in teams', 'a sense of humour' and so on. Sometimes, especially if certain skills are in short supply, the organisation has to accommodate the personality of the person who is otherwise best qualified for the job. Where social interaction is incidental to, rather than an actual part of, the job in question a variety of different personalities might fit the bill equally well. Techniques for assessing personality include interviews, personality tests, psychometric tests, role-playing and even graphology (hand writing analysis).

3   The motivating impact of money is discussed at greater length in the next chapter. However, money is valuable not only for what it can buy, but also as a source of other needs like security, status, self esteem and sense of achievement. In a sense, money is a universalistic measure, albeit crude: individuals can evaluate their achievements in terms of monetary success, though that is probably because the goals they have set out to achieve are monetary in character (for example, 'I want to be a millionaire by the time I am 30 years old'). Achievement objectives of a less obviously financial nature – like winning a place in the England cricket team or publishing a novel – will be evaluated in other ways.

4   Both the halo effect and stereotyping can be very significant in recruitment and selection, in the deployment of people into specific roles or geographical locations, in promotion, in evaluating ideas and in judging employee performance.

At the recruitment stage, decisions may be made to impose a narrow age band of eligibility for certain posts on the argument that older people are less adaptable or younger people insufficiently experienced: both of these statements reflect stereotyping about the categories in question.

Within the selection process itself, candidates may be viewed favourably if their dress style and appearance are similar to those favoured by the selector. The halo effect can also operate if the candidate expresses views which coincide with the interviewer's.

Because of stereotypes about women, they may be discouraged from taking up positions as, say, engineers in a manufacturing plant or financial sales representatives. People who assume that coloured people cannot succeed if working as sales people in predominantly white localities are basing this opinion on two racial stereotyes, one about coloured people, and the other about white people's attitudes. Disabled individuals are frequently the victims of stereotyping, with mistaken judgements being made about their intellectual capabilities simply because they have to operate from a wheelchair.

Managers are occasionally guilty of pre-judging ideas presented by particular members of staff simply because the latter have low status or because, in the past, their ideas have genuinely been impractical. The opposite can also happen: some ideas are given a particularly uncritical welcome because of the high status of the originator.

Finally, in the appraisal process, poor employee performance may be excused, at least in part, because the appraiser likes the individual; conversely, good performance may be dismissed (on the grounds that people are paid to perform well, so when they do they cannot expect to be praised for it) because of personal animosity.

5   Clearly the range of possible scenarios is very wide.

Role ambiguity can occur at work among jobholders described as team leaders or supervisors, who are not certain whether they are genuinely managers with the opportunity to exercise managerial authority.

Role incompatibility happens, for example, when an individual is a professional accountant. He or she is under pressure within the organisation to engage in data manipulation in order to make the financial results look better (or worse) than the reality, yet his or her own role expectations are closely linked to the demands of his or her professional body and its ethical code.

Role conflict, part from the instance given in the notes, happens frequently among women seeking to pursue a career and also operate effectively as mothers for their children.

6   The approach which is likely to prove more effective is to change the *behaviour* of the staff first – by requiring them to articulate certain words, phrases and sentences when speaking to customers face-to-face or over the telephone – in the belief that, when they have found such behaviour rewarding, their *attitudes* to customers will change. This is the method used by some companies well known for their customer service, like McDonalds. The danger is that staff who are using the correct behaviours but whose attitudes are quite different will simply mouth the words without conveying any sincere concern for customers.

On the other hand, trying to alter *attitudes* before *behaviour* may simply mean that customer-service staff feel differently about the customers but continue to behave as before.

What this discussion suggests is that, in an ideal world, the training manager will seek to modify *attitudes* and *behaviour* simultaneously.

7   The solution to this exercise depends entirely on the perceptions generated by the student attempting it. If there are any instances, however, where the primary group numbers are large than those

suggested, the student should ask whether the group is really as effective as it could be or whether, in fact, sub-groups have come into existence whose numbers are within the preferred range.

8 Supplying a solution to this exercise is dangerous because our interpretation of, say, the courtship process may not coincide with the experiences of our readers! However, many will recognise the sequence summarised below.

In the *forming* phase, the two individuals seek to impress each other and, in a sense, will behave artificially in order to (as they see it) create the 'right' impression. Their real views and attitudes are suppressed in favour of views and attitudes which each party hopes the other will find acceptable and interesting.

Storming is the phase when the two individuals begin to express their true feelings about issues. At this point, differences emerge and these may open up a gulf so wide as to be unbridgeable, in which case the courtship ritual is ended.

Norming is the settling-down phase, where the two individuals come to terms with each other and negotiate compromises – which may be about lifestyles, leisure pursuits or simply the apportionment of domestic routines.

As the notes suggest, *performing* is reached when the couple have adapted to each other and can move forward through mutual development and growth – perhaps involving marriage and children.

What may then happen is that the couple moves into *dorming*. They begin to take each other for granted (no longer is the purchase of flowers a regular weekly event!); there is no more growth and development for them; the durability of the partnership is in jeopardy unless they recognise the need to take positive remedial action.

9 Perhaps you should get a friend to answer this for you.

10 The answers to this exercise are supplied in the subsequent paragraph of the text.

Further question practice

Now try the following practice questions at the end of this text

Multiple choice questions: **49 to 56**

Exam style question: **8**

Chapter 9 :
MOTIVATION: THE KEY TO MAXIMISING PERFORMANCE

Introduction

A great deal has been written about motivation. Much of it is theoretical and speculative; some of it takes us further forward, in our knowledge and understanding, by reporting on well-conducted research; a bit of it is practical, describing how individuals have managed to motivate themselves and their teams to achieve results that nobody would have thought possible. Motivation is often seen, quite rightly, as the key to organisational effectiveness since, without enthusiastic and committed people, nothing much will happen.

In this chapter you will learn about these things.

(a) The differences between 'needs', 'wants' and 'motives'

(b) The likely relationships between needs and wants on the one hand, motivation and incentives on the other, and the resultant behaviour patterns displayed by individuals at work

(c) The relevance and practical utility of some of the major theories of motivation developed by writers like Maslow, McGregor, Herzberg, and Vroom

(d) The concept of a psychological contract between the individual and the organisation

(e) The degree to which 'alienation' is a concept which continues to have the resonance for the 1990s

1   MOTIVATION

It is in an organisation's interests to know the reasons or motives behind people's behaviour. In particular, if the organisation finds reasons why people might perform well at work, it can utilise that knowledge to maximise their effectiveness. The words motives and motivation are commonly used in different contexts to at least three different things.

(a)   *Goals, or outcomes* that have become desirable for a particular individual. These are more properly *motivating factors* – since they give people a reason for behaving in a certain way.

(b)   The *mental process* of choosing goals or outcomes.

(c)   The *social process* by which an individual's behaviour is influenced by others.

1.1   The motivation problem

For the practising manager the importance of an understanding of motivation is clear; as *John Van Maurik* puts it, in *Discovering the Leader in You* (1994),

'Healthy people have energy, they also have the ability to think creative thoughts, solve problems, and to work hard in doing so. However, for much of the time this energy remains locked up, the individual chooses not to give it to an employer'.

Managers will often complain at length about employees not being motivated, but appear reluctant to actively address the problem and are often reliant on overly simplistic solutions such as money. Interestingly when financial inducements are offered, they tend to produce disappointing results – and it may well be that the costs exceed the benefits. More interesting issues such as job design are often ignored, with many organisations still dominated by Taylorism and scientific management, so jobs are molecularised into small, repetitive, low-skill activities whose only challenge, for the employees concerned, is the threat of tedium.

Any meaningful discussion of motivation will be complex. People's motivation towards their work will be influenced by both direct and indirect factors. Some are *external to the organisation* altogether, such as the level of unemployment in the immediate locality, which may ensure that a boring job is tolerated simply because it is preferable to the alternative. Others relate to the *work* actually being undertaken: its complexity, its variety, its scope for challenge. A third set of factors are internal to the *organisation* but external to the work itself, like pay, working conditions, management and leadership style, or security of tenure. On top of these *objective* phenomena have to be fitted the *subjective* expectations, hopes and fears of the employees themselves. For example, the amount of variety in a job is one thing; quite another is whether the employees perceive that variety as an opportunity or as a threat.

Trying to use the concept of motivation in a meaningful way is a complex challenge for managers, particularly as the exact combination of influencing factors will be unique to every individual. Take the idea of job satisfaction. Satisfaction *with* a job – that is, with monetary rewards, security and so forth – may be a powerful element in job choice, particularly for manual workers; satisfaction *in a job* – in carrying it out, in performing the tasks, and in deriving a sense of achievement – can be critical in encouraging employees to stay with an organisation rather than simply go elsewhere. So both organisations and managers have to juggle both types of satisfaction.

1.2   Needs and rewards

In the most basic terms, individuals have needs which they wish to satisfy. The means of satisfying needs are 'wants'. For example, an individual might feel the need for power, and to fulfil this need, might want money and a position of authority. Depending on the strength of their needs, individuals may take action to achieve the wanted outcomes.

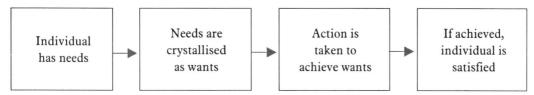

The wants of the individual thus identify the specific outcomes that can be offered as motivators to act in a certain way.

Not all motivators are directly controllable by management; for example, an individual might want to be accepted by his work-mates, to satisfy his need for friendship and affiliation with others. By and large, however, it is assumed that management can identify and offer a range of wanted rewards: money is most obviously a want which may satisfy any number of individual needs and which the organisation is in a position to supply.

Motivation is then the urge or drive to take action to achieve wants. For example, an individual might want to be promoted, but might not be sufficiently motivated to work harder or more efficiently in order to win the promotion: he or she might also want leisure, or he or she may not believe that the company will really offer the promotion if he or she does work harder. Management has the problem of creating or manipulating motivators which will actually motivate employees to perform in a desired way.

Motives are personal and internal; incentives are external inducements directed at individuals and designed to stimulate their behaviour in a particular direction. Simply put, 'incentives' can be classified into four groups.

(a) *Punishment (extrinsic):* a kick up the backside – loosely translated by *Frederick Herzberg* as 'KITA'.

(b) *Punishment (intrinsic):* the creation of a climate of fear in the organisation.

(c) *Reward (extrinsic),* money, status symbols.

(d) *Reward (intrinsic):* a sense of achievement and job satisfaction.

Herzberg makes the telling point that, in most of the above scenarios, it is not the employee who is motivated, but rather the person who devises and then applies the incentives, whether in the form of sticks or carrots. Let us examine this point further.

Many managers (according to Herzberg) think that motivation consists of saying 'Do this for me or the company, and in return I will give you a reward, an incentive, more status, some promotion and so forth'. Herzberg argues that treating people in this way in effect reduces them to the level of dogs being trained to jump for dog biscuits. In his seminal article for the *Harvard Business Review* in 1968, Herzberg develops the analogy of dog training at length.

'When it was a small puppy and I wanted it to move, I kicked it in the rear and it moved. Now that I have finished its obedience training, I hold up a dog biscuit when I want [the dog] to move. In this instance, who is motivated – I or the dog? The dog wants the biscuit, but it is I who want it to move. Again, I am the one who is motivated, and the dog is the one who moves ... Industry has available an incredible number and variety of dog biscuits ... to wave in front of the employee to get him to jump.'

You may succeed in persuading your dog to move from A to B by kicking him or offering him a reward, but when you want him to move again, says Herzberg, what do you do? You have to kick him again or offer him another reward – and your kicks or rewards may have to be stronger because of the law of diminishing returns. 'Similarly,' says Herzberg,

'I can charge a man's battery, and then recharge it, and then recharge it again. But it is only when he has his own generator that we can talk about motivation. He then needs no outside stimulation. He wants to do it.'

In other words, the individual's rewards have become primarily internal and psychological: these are potentially the most effective rewards of all.

Activity 1   **(10 minutes)**

According to the Herzberg model, punishment (intrinsic or extrinsic) and extrinsic rewards in effect treat the employee like a dog being trained to move from point A to point B, ie to change his behaviour so that performance, efficiency and effectiveness are enhanced. The person designing the incentive is motivated; the responding employee moves. Only when category (d) applies – the experience of intrinsic rewards like a sense of achievement – can we genuinely claim that the individual is motivated, ie doing things because of an internally generated desire to do them.

What do you think of this framework? How far does it apply to your own motivational patterns? To what extent do you sometimes find yourself forced into specific behaviours not because of your own inclinations but rather because you are responding to incentives administered by others?

1.3 Needs, drives and motives

Some of our behaviour is directed or influenced by human biology, which dictates the basic essentials of continuing life: self-preservation, oxygen, warmth, food, water, sleep and so on. When the body is deprived of these essentials, innate biological forces called *needs* or *drives* are activated, and determine the behaviour necessary to end the deprivation, such as to eat, to drink, or to flee. We never learn to have these drives, we cannot make them go away, and many are overpowering. However, our behaviour is not entirely a slave to our biology.

(a) Apart from the need for oxygen (and food and water, after a period of time), the mind is able to override our physical drives if they are displaced by other goals (eg people give up much needed sleep for all sorts of reasons).

(b) We retain freedom of choice about how we satisfy our drives: they do not dictate specific or highly predictable behaviour.

(c) We also behave in ways that make no direct contribution to our physical survival and health.

Apart from biogenic needs or drives, that is biological determinants of behaviour, activated by deprivation, there are *psychogenic needs* – emotional or psychological needs. The American psychologist *Abraham Maslow* argued that people have seven innate needs – of which only the first two include primary needs such as we have described. Maslow's categories are:

(a) Physiological needs   – food, drink, sleep

(b) Safety needs   – freedom from threat, but also security, order, predictability

(c)	Love needs (or social needs)	–	for relationships, affection, sense of belonging
(d)	Esteem needs	–	for competence, achievement, independence, confidence and their reflection in the perception of others, (recognition, appreciation, status, respect)
(e)	Self-actualisation needs	–	for the fulfilment of personal potential: 'the desire to become more and more what one is, to become everything that one is capable of becoming'
(f)	Freedom of inquiry and expression needs	–	for social conditions permitting free speech and encouraging justice, fairness and honesty
(g)	Knowledge and understanding needs	–	to gain and order knowledge of the environment, to explore, learn, experiment

1.4 Motivation theories

The kind of theory that we subscribe to, about what motivation is and what can be done with it, will influence all our attitudes to management and individuals in organisations. There are various ways of looking at motivation. *Handy* groups early motivation theories under three headings.

(a) *Satisfaction theories*. These theories are based on the assumption that a satisfied worker will work harder, although there is little evidence to support the assumption.

(b) *Incentive theories*. These theories are based on the assumption that individuals will work harder in order to obtain a desired reward; although most studies concentrate on money as a motivator. Handy notes that incentive theories can work, if four conditions apply.

   (i) The individual perceives the increased reward to be worth the extra effort.

   (ii) The performance can be measured and clearly attributed to that individual.

   (iii) The individual wants that particular kind of reward.

   (iv) The increased performance will not become the new minimum standard.

(c) *Intrinsic theories*. These theories are based on the belief that higher-order needs are more prevalent in modern people than we give them credit for. People will work hard in response to factors in the work itself such as participation, responsibility. Effective performance is its own reward.

Another analysis divides the major theories of motivation into two groups.

(a) *Content theories* assume that human beings have a package of motives which they pursue: they have a set of needs or desired outcomes. Maslow's need hierarchy theory and Herzberg's two-factor theory are two of the most important approaches of this type.

(b) *Process theories* explore the process through which outcomes become desirable and are pursued by individuals. This approach assumes that man is able to select his goals and choose the paths towards them, by a conscious or unconscious process of calculation. Expectancy theory is a good example of this type.

Maslow's hierarchy of needs

We have already mentioned Abraham Maslow's classification of a person's innate needs. In his motivation theory, Maslow put forward certain propositions about the motivating power of these needs.

(a) Man's needs can be arranged in a 'hierarchy of relative pre-potency'.

(b) Each level of need is dominant until satisfied; only then does the next level of need become a motivating factor.

(c) A need which has been satisfied no longer motivates an individual's behaviour. The need for self-actualisation can never be satisfied.

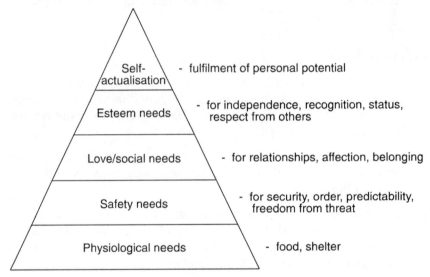

The remaining two needs do not form part of the hierarchy but are fundamental to the satisfaction of its needs.

There is a certain intuitive appeal to Maslow's theory. After all, you are unlikely to be concerned with status or recognition while you are hungry or thirsty because primary survival needs will take precedence. Likewise, once your hunger is assuaged, the need for food is unlikely to be a motivating factor.

It is also worth noting that Maslow did *not* intend his views to be applied to the specific context of behaviour at work: needs can be satisfied by aspects of a person's life outside work. However, since work provides a livelihood and takes up such a large part of a person's life, it is obviously going to play an important part in the satisfaction of that person's needs.

There are various problems associated with Maslow's theory.

(a) Empirical verification for the hierarchy is hard to come by. Physiological and safety needs are not always uppermost in the determination of human behaviour.

(b) Research does not bear out the proposition that needs become less powerful as they are satisfied, except at the very primitive level of 'primary' needs like, hunger and thirst.

(c)   It is difficult to predict behaviour using the hierarchy: the theory is too vague.

(d)   Application of the theory in work contexts presents various difficulties. For example, the role of money or pay is problematic, since it arguably acts as a representative for other rewards like status, recognition or independence.

(e)   The ethnocentricity of Maslow's hierarchy has also been noted – it does seem broadly applicable to Western English-speaking cultures, but it is less relevant elsewhere.

A major cross-cultural survey of 3,500 managers from 14 countries by *Haire, Ghiselli and Porter* established that

'The theoretical classification of the five types of needs according to their priority or prepotency exactly fits the pattern of results for the United States and England, but not for any other group of countries.'

Yet the discrepancies were not great, and only affected the rearrangement of the security, belongingness and status needs, ie the three middle levels in the Maslow hierarchy. Particularly striking in the Haire-Ghiselli-Porter investigation was

'the relative similarity of thinking from country to country with regard to a particular need. That is, for example, those types of needs which are considered most important in one country tend also to be regarded as most important in other countries.'

In fact these findings support *Alderfer's* view that people experience three different (but not mutually exclusive) orientations reflecting their perceived needs and wants, but that these orientations are *not* organised into any predetermined hierarchy.

(a)   *Instrumental orientation:* a desire for economic and material goals.

(b)   *Relational orientation:* social needs and interpersonal affiliation.

(c)   *Personal growth:* the desire for self-development and self-actualisation (or the desire to grow and become all that the person is capable of becoming – in other words, self-fulfilment).

These categories are sometimes referred to as existence, relatedness and growth, and the concept as ERG theory.

Activity 2   **(5 minutes)**

It is an essential feature of the Maslow hierarchy that people may move up or down its levels quite rapidly as their circumstances change. One of the most dramatic examples of individuals being forced rapidly through Maslow's needs can be seen in the case of the Andes survivors some years ago. A group of wealthy young Uruguayans were involved in a drastic air disaster in the middle of the Andes range of mountains; many of the passengers were killed but some were unscathed, including members of a rugby team and their friends.

The conditions were freezing and food supplies virtually non-existent. Within days the survivors were reduced to cannibalism and this kept them alive for several weeks until some eventually were able to summon help.

What does this situation tell us about the operation of Maslow's hierarchy of needs?

A two-factor content theory: Herzberg

In the 1950s, the American psychologist Frederick Herzberg interviewed 203 Pittsburgh engineers and accountants and asked two critical incident questions. The subjects were asked to recall events which had made them feel good about their work, and others which made them feel bad about it. Analysis revealed that the factors which created *dissatisfaction* were different from those which created satisfaction, these he termed *hygiene* factors and *motivator* factors.

Hygiene factors are essentially preventative. They prevent or minimise dissatisfaction but do not give satisfaction, in the same way that sanitation minimises threats to health, but does not guarantee good health. They are called maintenance factors because they have to be continually renewed. Satisfaction with these factors is not lasting. In time dissatisfaction will occur. Here are some examples of hygiene factors.

- Company policy and administration
- Salary
- The quality of supervision
- Interpersonal relations
- Working conditions
- Job security

Motivator factors create job satisfaction and are effective in motivating an individual to superior performance and effort. These factors give the individual a sense of self-fulfilment or personal growth.

- Status (although this may be a hygiene factor as well as a motivator factor)
- Advancement
- Gaining recognition
- Being given responsibility
- Challenging work
- Achievement
- Growth in the job

Herzberg suggested means by which motivator satisfactions could be supplied. Stemming from his fundamental division of motivator and hygiene factors, he encouraged managers to study the job itself (the type of work done, the nature of tasks, levels of responsibility) rather than conditions of work. If there is sufficient challenge, scope and interest in the job, there will be a lasting increase in satisfaction and the employee will work well; productivity will be above normal levels. The extent to which a job must be challenging or creative to a motivator-seeker will depend on each individual ability and his tolerance for delayed success.

EXAMPLE: 'GOOD MORNING, TEETH'

In case you are now in a state of confusion, consider the two meanings of the word satisfaction. If I say that 'I am satisfied with the amount of money I earn', I could mean either of two things.

(a) I am consciously elated by my income, continuously aware of how well-off I am.

(b) I don't think about my income very much at all, so my satisfaction is really another way of describing my indifference.

So satisfaction may refer to a strong sense of well-being or to a taken-for-granted emotional state.

Your feelings about your teeth illustrate the point very well. Should you be satisfied with your teeth, that probably means you don't think about them at all – and you would only start to do so if they began to malfunction or become painful. In other words, as with others of Herzberg's *hygiene* factors, you only become conscious of your teeth when you are *dissatisfied* with them, ie they have begun to hurt.

Of course, it is not always so simple as that. Sometimes you can feel elation (ie satisfaction in the positive sense) about the fact that your teeth are working properly, but this is generally prompted by an awareness of someone else's toothache. Your feeling of elation, what's more, is typically short-lived: soon you return to your customary state of indifference, consciousness of your teeth having receded once more into the psychic background.

> **Activity 3**   **(10 minutes)**
>
> Herzberg says that money is a hygiene factor in the motivation process. If this is true, it means that lack of money can demotivate, but the presence of money will not in itself be a motivator.
>
> How far do you agree with this proposition? Can individuals be motivated by a pay rise? What are the arguments against trying to motivate people purely by means of monetary incentives?

There are other ways of applying the Herzberg approach.

(a) *Decentralisation of decision-making and control* in the process currently known as *delayering*.

(b) *Delegation* of authority and responsibility, so that decisions are made at the lowest possible levels.

(c) *Job enrichment:* adding vertical responsibilities to the tasks normally performed by employees, so that, for example, they can quality-test their own work.

(d) *Participative and consultative management* so that employees have some voice in the decisions which affect them and in the implementation of job-design change.

Empowerment is the term more often used in the 1990s, but in practical terms it means much the same as job enrichment. A specific instance of empowerment in action concerns the front-line customer-service staff for Rank-Xerox, who are empowered to give customer refunds of up to £200 without having first to seek authorisation from higher levels of management. This not only gives these staff a significantly improved level of personal autonomy at their work, it also leads to much higher levels of satisfaction among customers whose problems are now solved instantly.

1.5 Expectancy theory: a process theory

The expectancy theory of motivation is a process theory, based on the assumptions that human beings are purposive and rational, aware of their goals and behaviour. Essentially, the theory states that the strength of individuals' motivation to do something will depend on the extent to which they expect the results of their efforts, if successfully achieved, to contribute towards their personal needs or goals.

Vroom suggested that the strength of an individual's motivation is the product of two factors.

(a) The strength of their preference for a certain outcome. Vroom called this valence. It may be represented as a positive or negative number, or zero – since outcomes may be desired, avoided or considered with indifference.

(b) The individual's expectation that the outcome will result from a certain behaviour. Vroom called this *subjective probability:* it is only the individual's 'expectation', and depends on their perception of the probable relationship between behaviour and outcome. As a probability, it may be represented by any number between 0 (no chance) and 1 (certainty). It is also called *expectancy*.

Vroom expressed his theory in the following equation:

Force or strength of motivation to do something	=	Valence ie strength of his preference for a certain outcome	×	Expectation that behaviour will result in desired outcome

If either valence or expectancy are equal to zero then there will be no motivation.

(a) If an employee has a high expectation that productivity will result in a certain outcome (say, promotion), but he is indifferent to that outcome (doesn't want the responsibility), V = 0, and he will not be motivated to productive behaviour.

(b) If the employee has a great desire for promotion, but does not believe that productive behaviour will secure it for him, E = 0, and he will still not be highly motivated.

(c) If V = –1, (perhaps because the employee fears responsibility and does not want to leave his work group), the value for motivation will be negative, and the employee may deliberately under-produce.

Expectancy theory attempts to measure the strength of an individual's motivation to act in a particular way. It is then possible to compare F values for a range of different behaviours, to discover which behaviour the individual is most likely to adopt. It is also possible to compare F values for different individuals, to see who is most highly motivated to behave in the desired (or undesirable) way.

Are human beings really so predictable, however? Are we as *rational* as expectancy theory implies? Do we carry out such an analysis and calculation before behaving in a given way, whether consciously or unconsciously? The expectancy theory has been useful in organisational practice (and also in further research) because it does make room for the subjectivity of human perceptions. In its most complex form, where a number of alternative expected outcomes are taken into account, the expectancy equation can be a fair reflection of the various influences on behaviour. We do not, after all, tend to take *all* eventualities into account in our decision making, and we are able to draw on substantial past experience for most routine responses.

Another advantage of the theory is that, in comparison with Herzberg's ideas, *a better distinction is made between an individual's goals* and the organisation's goals. An individual may not seek self-realisation through his job; his goals might be unrelated to his job. V and E add an additional insight to that offered by the content theories of motivation – they help us to better understand why some individuals pursue a particular outcome more strongly than others.

These are the psychological assumptions upon which expectancy theory is constructed.

(a) *People will behave rationally*, choosing behaviour which, in the individual's judgement, will maximise the attractiveness of the sum of outcomes likely to result.

(b) *People have preferences for different outcomes*, with 'valance' being the measure of attractiveness.

(c) *People have expectancies* about the likelihood that an action will lead to the outcome they seek.

(d) *People do not behave at random.*

Activity 4 **(5 minutes)**

In what ways can any or all of the above psychological assumptions be challenged? How far does your own behaviour exemplify these assumptions all the time? What stops it from doing so?

The major problem with expectancy theory, apart from the fact that the assumptions on which it is constructed are themselves debatable, is that measurement tests are not sufficiently advanced to enable the theory to be tested properly. Moreover, as the boxed insert suggests, it is difficult to handle the progressive multiplicative relationships: to try to do so merely increases the potential for error in the calculations.

Nonetheless, expectancy theory does have some practical applications and relevance.

(a) It enables the various relationships, elements and implications in an individual's motivational patterns to be separated out more clearly than is the case with any other theory of motivation.

(b) Expectancy theory tells us that there is no advantage to be gained from changing the relationship between performance and outcome, if the change is not perceived by the employee. Thus a bonus scheme will not increase productivity if people believe (rightly or wrongly) that the more they work, the less they will earn.

(c) If management is to supply outcomes desired by employees, it must ensure that such outcomes are only obtainable as a result of performance.

(d) Expectancy theory focuses on valance for individuals: there is no evidence that a given outcome has a particular valance for an entire population. Pay increases will not improve everyone's motivation to work; giving everyone increased responsibility (eg through empowerment) may generate negative reactions from those who have learned that responsibility is dangerous.

EXAMPLE: EXPECTANCY THEORY IN ACTION

This example illustrates the complexity of expectancy theory when applied to, say, the case of an insurance company sales representative who is male and in his 50s. For a given level of effort (E), he may perceive the possible outcomes as follows.

(a) A 75% chance of selling 17 policies in a week
(b) A 15% chance of selling 13 policies in a week
(c) A 10% chance of selling 20 policies in a week

There is 100% probability that this given level of effort (E) will produce the following effects.

- (a) Exhaustion
- (b) Sarcastic comments from his colleagues
- (c) Aggravation to his sciatica

If he succeeds in selling 17 policies a week, the perceived outcomes will be as follows.

- (a) Praise from his manager
- (b) Accusations from colleagues about setting impossibly high standards
- (c) Sufficient earnings (from commission) to buy a present for his wife

If he only sells 13 policies in the week, the perceived outcomes will be as follows.

- (a) Criticism from his manager

- (b) Tacit approval from colleagues

- (c) A poor level of commission earnings and income, leading to disapproval from his wife

Selling 20 policies in a week will generate these perceived outcomes:

- (a) Loud praise from his manager
- (b) Extreme hostility from his colleagues
- (c) Family expectations that income on this level will be sustained

The sales representative must assign a probability to each of these outcomes, eg a 75% probability that selling 17 policies will produce accusations from colleagues, and a 60% probability that selling 17 policies will produce praise from his manager.

Finally, the sales representative must attach a *valence* to each of the expected outcomes. Earning enough money to buy a present for his wife may have *high valence* for him; attracting the disapproval of colleagues may have *low valance*.

It can be seen from this (much simplified) example that trying to predict which choice will be made, in any given situation, becomes impossibly arduous.

1.6 Psychological contracts

A *psychological contract* exists between individuals in an organisation and the organisation itself. An individual belongs to many organisations, perhaps including a work organisation, a trade union, a club, a church or a political party. The individual has a different psychological contract with each. A psychological contract might be thought of as a *set of expectations*.

- (a) The individual expects to derive certain benefits from membership of the organisation and is prepared to expend a certain amount of effort in return.

- (b) The organisation expects the individual to fulfil certain requirements and is prepared to offer certain rewards in return.

Three types of psychological contract can be identified.

- (a) *Coercive contract*. This is a contract in which the individual considers that he or she is being forced to contribute his efforts and energies involuntarily, and that the rewards he receives in return are inadequate compensation. For example, if an individual believes that he does not receive enough pay for the work he does, or if he is forcibly transferred to another job he does not like, there would be a coercive psychological contract between the individual and the organisation especially if the individual cannot find employment elsewhere. Motivation to work would be low, non-existent, or even negative.

(b) *Calculative contract*. This is a contract, accepted *voluntarily* by the individual, who expects to do the job in exchange for a readily identifiable set of rewards (for example pay, status, or simply having a job of work to keep him occupied). This form of contract is the most frequent in industrial and commercial organisations. With such psychological contracts, motivation can only be increased if the rewards to the individual are improved (by extra pay or further promotion). If the organisation attempts to demand greater efforts without increasing the rewards, the psychological contract will revert to a coercive one, and motivation may become negative.

(c) *Co-operative contract*. This is a contract in which the individual becomes personally identified with the organisation and its goals, and actively seeks to contribute further to the achievement of those goals. Motivation comes out of success at work, a sense of achievement, and self-fulfilment. A co-operative psychological contract must be voluntarily entered into. The individual will probably want to share in planning and control decisions and co-operative contracts are therefore likely to occur where employees *participate* in decision-making. Since these contracts are likely to result in high motivation and high achievement, the lesson for management would be that employee participation in decision-making is the most desirable way to structure manager-subordinate relations at work – but only if subordinates want participation.

Motivation happens when the psychological contract, within which the individual's motivation calculus operates for new decisions, is viewed in the same way by the organisation and by the individual, and when both parties are able to fulfil their side of the bargain – the individual agrees to work, or work well, in return for whatever rewards or satisfactions are understood as the terms of the contract.

2 ALIENATION: WHAT IS IT AND DOES IT EXIST?

During the 1970s cheap, reliable electronic control technology was built into machine tools. Computers can initiate action according to variables in the environment, and can respond to signals (for error detection, for example) or can select from a range of programmed options (changing speed or position according to measurement data, or segregating/rejecting units according to size, or even identifying and initiating appropriate sequences of action). Computers are now even capable of *adaptive control* – responding to working conditions as they arise (over-heating, dulling of tools) and modifying their behaviour over a wide range of variables – correcting after, during, or even before the event. Human intervention is reduced even further, to loading and removing workpieces, and replacing dulled tools although robotics is beginning to encroach on these areas also.

The work of several machines may be scheduled and controlled from a single central computer, which tells the operator, via a VDU (visual display unit), which workpieces to fit on which machines.

The important question is who really benefits from these changes? One argument suggests that the systematic reduction of human intervention and control in work has made work less tiring and safer for the worker, and more efficient and less prone to human failings such as carelessness, idleness or hostility from the point of view of the organisation.

However, the American Marxist sociologist *Harry Braverman* has suggested that *'the remarkable development of machinery becomes, for most of the working population, the source not of freedom but of enslavement, not of mastery but of helplessness, and not of the broadening of the horizon of labour, but of the confinement of the worker within a blind round of servile duties.'*

Robert Blauner carried out a study in America of working conditions in various industries. He suggested that the workers' experience of technology was largely determined by the type of technology involved.

(a) Printing – dominated by *craft work* – allows workers to set their own pace, choose their own methods, practice high-status skills and have strong social relationships at work.

(b) Cotton spinning – dominated by *machine minding* – offers textile workers simple, repetitive, non-discretionary work. However, they live in close rural communities, whose culture overcomes the alienation experienced to a degree at work (see below).

(c) Car manufacture – dominated by *mass production* – gives assembly workers little control over their work, little perceived significance in their tasks, social isolation in the work place, and no opportunity to develop skills. Alienation is very high.

(d) Chemicals manufacture – dominated by *process production* – gives the process workers an advanced work environment, where manual work is automated. The workers have team work and social contact, and control over their work pace and movements. They have opportunities to learn about the processes they monitor, and also derive satisfaction from a sense of responsibility, achievement and belonging.

The Blauner study suggests that the level of alienation differs between various kinds of technology. Machine minding and mass production technologies generate alienation on a very significant scale, largely because, in the words of *Lukes*, they reflect

'a growing division of labour under capitalism where men are forced to confine themselves to performing specialised functions within a system they neither understand nor control.'

Unfortunately, the term 'alienation' has no precise meaning. Lukes has noted that

'alienation can mean anything from bureaucratic rules which stifle initiative and deprive individuals of all communication among themselves and of all information about the institutions in which they are situated, to a mode of experience in which the person experiences himself as an alien.'

Blauner identified four different aspects of alienation.

(a) *Powerlessness.* The worker feels he is an object dominated and controlled by other people or by a technological system of production which he cannot influence.

(b) *Meaninglessness.* Individual roles are perceived as lacking integration into the total system of goals for an organisation.

(c) *Normlessness.* A lack of socially-approved means to achieve culturally-prescribed goals.

(d) *Self-estrangement.* Adherence to an instrumental work orientation, namely, the degree to which work is valued as a means to an end rather than as an end in itself.

The empirical evidence to justify the presence of alienation in employees is ambiguous at best.

2.1 Conclusion

All the research and writing on motivation demonstrates that attempts to apply a standardised, across-the-board system of incentives, based on a single theory of motivation (or even on a single, idiosyncratic set of assumptions on motivation without any theoretical base) are likely to be about as effective as a blunderbuss. Although the evidence indicates there is some homogeneity of values among people at work, the similarities do not justify identical treatment for all.

In practice, a workable arrangement of rewards and motivators is likely to comprise a collection of organisation-wide incentives (such as job security, payment systems, working conditions) complemented by the more personal techniques used by individual managers on their staff, like face-to-face recognition, periodic re-arrangement of responsibilities, positive performance feedback and coaching.

It is certainly inappropriate to argue that empowerment and job satisfaction is a kind of panacea which represents a valid answer to all the problems of motivating people at work. To think in this way would be to fall into the same trap as those who, in the past, over-subscribed to the human relations package.

However well or badly the work is designed, organisations must still sell their products or services in order to survive. Becoming an excellent organisation, with a highly-motivated and committed workforce, is no substitute for effective marketing.

There is, clearly, a measure of upward (and downward) mobility – both in socio-economic and cultural terms. An individual *may* be elevated socially by intelligence or learned skill but this presupposes such variables as self-confidence, ambition and educational opportunities that may not be present precisely because of the individual's economic and cultural background. Managerial and labour classes do tend to reproduce themselves, because of varying access to scarce resources, educational opportunity, parental career models.

Goldthorpe's investigation of affluent workers in the Luton car industry served to discredit the notion of *embourgeoisement*: despite changes in surface characteristics, associated with increased income, there was no evidence of radical reshaping of the class structure. In terms of patterns of recruitment, therefore, the concept of social class is highly relevant, despite the possibility of social mobility as applied to career choice and success.

Chapter roundup

- Motivation directs individual behaviour. It is in the interests of an employer to know how to motivate employees' behaviour for the employer's benefit. Motivation theories can be classified in two ways.

  (i) Satisfaction, incentive or intrinsic theories

  (ii) Content theories and Process theories.

- Maslow's hierarchy of needs is a content theory, as is Herzberg's theory. These assume that individuals have a set of needs.

  (i) Maslow suggested seven innate needs, five of which are satisfied in a sequence.

  (ii) Herzberg suggested that needs could be divided into two groups. The first is hygiene factors; meeting these needs is not motivating but the failure to do so results in dissatisfaction (demotivation).

The second group is motivators; these are the factors that have the potential to motivate. Hygiene factors only cause dissatisfaction, and cannot motivate in a positive way.

- Process theories, such as expectancy theory assume that motivation is an individual experience based on the strength of desire for a particular outcome and an evaluation of the likelihood of achieving it.

- Individuals have both legal and psychological contracts with their employers: these can be coercive, calculative or co-operative.

- Alienation represents employee feelings of dissociation from the world of work, and is particularly linked to certain forms of technology like machine-minding and mass production. However, as a concept it is hard to pin down.

Quick quiz

1   What is meant by motivation?

2   What are the five stages of need in Maslow's hierarchy?

3   What are the differences between content and process theories of motivation?

4   How did Alderfer group needs?

5   Is status a hygiene factor or a motivator?

6   What is the main significance of the Herzberg model within organisations?

7   Expectancy theory, in its simplest form, is represented by the equation 'F = V x E'. What does this equation mean?

8   What are the three types of psychological contract?

9   Which types of technology are particularly associated with high levels of alienation?

10   What are the four constituents of alienation according to Blauner?

Answers to quick quiz

1   Variously: goals or outcomes; the mental process of choosing goals; the social processes by which individuals' actions are influenced by others.

2   Physiological; safety; love/social; esteem; self actualisation.

3   Content theories are based on the pursuit of innate needs while process theories describe motivation as subject to calculative analysis of expected efforts and benefits.

4   Instrumental orientation: material goals; relational orientation: social needs; personal growth orientation: the need for self-fulfilment. Alternatively, existence, relatedness and growth.

5   It can be either.

6   The work itself is more important for motivation than the working conditions.

7   Motivation force depends on a combination of valence, which is the strength of the preference for a desired outcome; and expectation that certain behaviour will result in the desired outcome.

8   Coercive, calculative and co-operative

9   Machine minding and mass production.

10   Powerlessness, meaninglessness, normlessness, self-estrangement.

Answers to activities

1   Your answer to this question will be based on your personal experiences and feelings about your levels of motivation in different circumstances. Try to identify and discuss a range of experiences which demonstrate the four incentives (extrinsic punishment, intrinsic punishment, extrinsic reward, intrinsic reward).

The following paragraphs offer you some ideas on which to base your answer, remember that it is always important to link theory to practice.

You may for example have worked in organisations where the 'motivation strategy' was little more than a series of material bribes, free holidays or gifts, but was that really motivational both for those who were given the incentives and those who were not?

Further it is possible that employees can be manipulated by skilful job design, on the part of an organisation's management, into wanting job satisfaction and therefore expecting it to be built into the hierarchical structure. In this sense, therefore, even employees activated by the desire for self-actualisation or a sense of achievement may simply be responding (like dogs) to incentives generated by others. What is then likely to happen, however, is that people who experience genuine job satisfaction for the first time will find the experience so rewarding that they will want to repeat it indefinitely, thereby creating some challenging scenarios for the organisation.

The ingredients of authentic job satisfaction, according to Hackman and Lawler, are as follows.

(a)   *Autonomy*. Some freedom and discretion over the specification of results and the methods to be used. Without these (ie if autonomy is low), then success or failure can more easily be attributed to others.

(b)   *Task identity*. This comprises what Hackman and Lawler call a 'clear cycle of perceived closure' (ie each task has a distinct beginning and end), high visibility of the transformation process (so that the worker can readily see what contribution he has made), and a transformation of considerable magnitude.

(c)   *Variety*. The use of several skills and abilities, implying a long job-cycle rather than one measurable in seconds.

(d)   *Performance feedback*. From the work itself or from others (like colleagues, superiors or customers). Without feedback of one sort or another, there is no opportunity for a sense of achievement.

Most people respond favourably when placed in a position where they can secure these four rewards from their work: in fact they often achieve similar rewards from the tasks they undertake in their own leisure time, like gardening, do-it-yourself and so forth.

At other times individuals have to make sacrifices: to renounce their desire for job satisfaction in favour of alternative goals. Students may feel compelled to act in this way when seeking vacation employment, at a time when the desire for money overrules other personal objectives.

Later in life, too, some people may consciously seek higher-paid employment or jobs involving opportunities for overtime and shiftwork, because their financial obligations are particularly demanding as their families grow.

2   The survival story shows that people can move up or down the Maslow hierarchy quite quickly. From Level 5 (self-actualisation) the group were rapidly reduced to Level 1. Even after their rescue, it took them a long time to return to the upper reaches of the hierarchy owing to extreme feelings of shame and some public censure. It is one thing to act in desperation and quite another thing to believe that your actions are condoned when you are back in a normal situation again.

3   Money *can* be a motivator for individuals with an *instrumental* orientation to work and who measure their success in materialistic terms. Further, money can be a relatively neutral index for evaluating achievement, responsibility and growth, ie for assessing accomplishment of some of the Herzberg motivators.

Individuals can also be motivated by a pay rise, but usually this happens only when the pay rise is larger than the person expected to receive. This excess of achievement over reality will generate a temporary feeling of elation. Unfortunately the evidence suggests that such elation is very short-lived: *Woodward's* research at the *John Lewis Partnership*, where there is a six-monthly share-out of part of the organisation's profits, supports the view that the share-out actually motivates the staff for about two weeks beforehand and two weeks thereafter. Other studies have suggested similar results, ie that after about three weeks the individual has largely forgotten the pay rise; after a further six months he is beginning to look forward to the *next* pay rise which, in order to motivate, has to be *larger* than the one received before.

This is why it is so dangerous for organisations to rely exclusively on motivating people with money. Ultimately the cost proves prohibitive, because each pay rise has to be significantly larger than its predecessor if it is to have any motivational significance at all. Indeed, a pay rise which is the same as the one given a year ago is likely to be de-motivating and therefore completely counterproductive.

4   All of the psychological assumptions can be challenged. People may think they are behaving rationally, but they often have imperfect knowledge about the range of behavioural options available and the probable consequences of each. Moreover, most human beings are driven by emotions as well as by reason, so their behavioural choices are influenced by what they feel comfortable about and what they will avoid (eg because some actions will conflict with their ethical beliefs).

Perhaps the one assumption which is much less challengeable is the statement that 'People do not behave at random'. For most individuals, their behaviour makes up a fairly predictable and consistent pattern. It is this uniformity which enables us to describes personalities as aggressive, docile and so forth.

Further question practice

Now try the following practice questions at the end of this text

Multiple choice questions: **57 to 64**

Exam style question: **9**

Chapter 10 :
CULTURE AND LEADERSHIP

Introduction

Organisational culture and leadership have become subjects for serious study only in the present century. The reasons for this are clearly connected with the growth of complex industrial societies and associated problems both in terms of production and human relations. These issues have stimulated research and speculation into ways of making production more effective, and at the same time of learning more about the principles of human involvement in the process. Increasing interest in human behaviour at work – both individually in terms of leadership and collectively in terms of corporate culture – could be ascribed, somewhat callously perhaps, to a concern for people at work simply as one of the factors of production, or alternatively to genuine humanitarian motives to make work more interesting, rewarding or pleasant.

This chapter first deals with the more amorphous concept of organisational culture, which can be defined as 'the way we do things around here'. All organisations are different in this respect: when you get to know an organisation definite differences in approach and in atmosphere become apparent. Sometimes these differences are noticeable at once, even from the exterior of the buildings and the design of the carpark; other aspects are more obscure and take longer to appreciate. The culture of the organisation is a product of its history and most of all its people – especially the norms and values set by its leaders.

In this chapter you will learn about these things.

    (a)   The nature of organisational culture

    (b)   Approaches to classifying organisational cultures

    (c)   International aspects of organisational culture

    (d)   The nature of leadership and how it relates to management

    (e)   Major theories of leadership and leadership style

    (f)   The nature of visionary leadership

1 WHAT IS CULTURE?

Culture is both internal to an organisation and external to it. There are certain patterns of behaviour, assumptions and beliefs which members of the organisation have in common, because of factors external to the organisation.

(a) Their *citizenship* of the same society or country

(b) Their status or class position within that society

(c) Their profession (eg as accountants, marketers)

The influence of the organisation overlies these factors.

Peters and Waterman, in their book *In Search of Excellence*, found that the 'dominance and coherence of culture' was an essential feature of the 'excellent' companies they observed. A 'handful of guiding values' was more powerful than manuals, rule books, norms and controls formally imposed (and resisted). They commented:

'If companies do not have strong notions of themselves, as reflected in their values, stories, myths and legends, people's only security comes from where they live on the organisation chart.'

All organisations will generate their own cultures, whether spontaneously or under the guidance of positive managerial strategy. The culture will have three basic aspects.

(a) *Basic, underlying assumptions* that guide the behaviour of the individuals and groups in the organisation, such as customer orientation, or belief in quality, trust in the organisation to provide rewards, freedom to make decisions, freedom to make mistakes, the value of innovation and initiative at all levels and so on.

(b) *Overt beliefs* expressed by the organisation and its members, which can be used to condition (a) above.

(i) These beliefs and values may emerge as sayings, slogans, mottoes. IBM's motto was 'think'.

(ii) They may emerge in a rich mythology – in jokes and stories about past successes and heroic failures or breakthroughs. Organisations with strong cultures often centre themselves around almost legendary figures in their history.

(iii) Management can encourage this by selling a sense of the corporate mission, or by promoting the corporate image. It can reward the right attitudes and punish (or simply not employ) those who are not prepared to commit themselves to the culture.

(c) *Visible artefacts:* the style of the offices or other premises, dress rules, display of trophies, the degree of informality between superiors and subordinates and so on.

Activity 1   **[10 minutes]**

All organisations have their own distinctive and unique culture. Take your own immediate and extended family, for example, and write down its cultural features against each of these headings.

(1) Its basic, underlying assumptions which guide the behaviour of the individuals in your family, for example the degree to which individual family members can exercise complete freedom of decision-making and so forth.

(2) The sayings, slogans or mottoes often used in your family.

(3) Your family's mythology: jokes and stories about the past, legends about other family members.

(4) The degree to which your family consciously or unconsciously promotes certain behaviour patterns and discourages others. What are the behaviour patterns involved? What rewards and punishments are used to encourage compliance?

Now think about other families you know and visualise how their 'cultures' differ from yours. What are the possible reasons for these differences?

Charles Hampden-Turner (in *Corporate Culture*) lists a number of characteristics of an organisation culture.

(a) Culture lies in the *potential* of an organisation's individual members, who use the culture:

      (i) to reinforce ideas, feelings and information consistent with their beliefs;

      (ii) to discourage or repress information and sentiments inconsistent with their beliefs.

A culture then, is partly *exclusive*. It gives a bias to information.

(b) Cultures embody the needs and aspirations of a group's members, thus setting the criteria by which people are judged, and defining prestige for particular achievements.

(c) Culture is strong where people need reassurance and certainty.

(d) Cultures have consequences (sometimes in the manner of self-fulfilling prophecies).

(e) A corporate culture is coherent, and its actions follow on from the *beliefs* and *assumptions* underlying it. *Deal and Kennedy* (*Corporate Cultures*) consider cultures to be a function of the willingness of employees to take risks, and how quickly they get feedback on whether they got it right or wrong.

(f) Cultures provide their members with some sense of continuity and identity, especially as things change over time.

(g) A culture is in a state of balance between different values. It is not a division of labour, but a re-integration of labour into a coherent whole.

(h) A culture is partly self-correcting. Feedback from customers, for example, might help reinforce an organisation's attempts to conform to its culture. (Is it living up to its standards?)

(i)   Cultures are patterns. Hampden-Turner argues that the way a member of staff treats a customer will be similar to the way in which the member of staff is treated by his or her supervisor.

(j)   Cultures communicate support, in that they facilitate the sharing of information and experiences. They make members supportive of each other (to the point of reinforcing wishful thinking).

(k)   Cultures deal with synergies, which in this case means that the values of management and staff must work together harmoniously.

(l)   Cultures and organisations can learn. The concept of the *learning organisation* implies that knowledge and innovation is not simply the result of a creative individual, but resides in cultures and relationships. (Hampden-Turner argues that the stereotype of the 'creative individual' gains its force from the fact that so many UK corporate cultures are resistant to innovation.)

(m)   Cultures mediate dilemmas (eg minimise cost vs maximise quality) and provide ways of solving them.

A culture then can be defined as follows.

Definition

The beliefs, knowledge, attitudes of mind and customs to which people are exposed in their social conditioning.

An organisation's culture is influenced by many factors.

(a)   The organisation's *founder*. A strong set of values and assumptions is set up by the organisation's founder, and even after he or she has retired, these values have their own momentum. Or, to put it another way, an organisation might find it hard to shake off its original culture. Peters and Waterman believed that 'excellent' companies began with strong leaders.

(b)   The organisation's *history*.

(i)   *Johnson and Scholes*, quoting *Stinchcombe*, state that the way an organisation works reflects the era when it was founded. Farming, for example, sometimes has a craft element to it.

(ii)   The effect of history can be determined by stories, rituals and symbolic behaviour. They legitimise behaviour and promote priorities. (In some organisations certain positions are regarded as intrinsically more 'heroic' than others.)

(c)   *Leadership and management style*. An organisation with a strong culture recruits managers who naturally conform to it.

(d)   *Structure and systems* affect culture as well as strategy. *Handy's* description of an Apollonian role culture (bureaucracy) is an example (among others) where organisational forms have cultural consequences. We shall discuss this in more detail shortly.

2 CULTURE AND STRUCTURE

Writing in 1972, *Roger Harrison* suggested that organisations could be classified into four types. His work was later popularised by *Charles Handy* in his book 'Gods of Management'. The four types are differentiated by their structures, processes and management methods. The differences are so significant as to create distinctive cultures, to each of which Handy gives the name of a Greek god.

Zeus is the god representing the *power culture* or *club culture*. Zeus is a dynamic entrepreneur who rules with snap decisions. Power and influence stem from a central source, perhaps the owner-directors or the founder of the business. The degree of formalisation is limited, and there are few rules and procedures. Such a firm is likely to be organised on a functional basis. Important decisions are made by key people. In Mintzberg's terms it is perhaps a *simple structure*, but with some co-ordination by mutual adjustment.

(a) The organisation, since it is not rigidly structured, is capable of adapting quickly to meet change. However, success in adapting will depend on the luck or judgement of the key individuals who make the rapid decision.

(b) Personal influence decreases as the size of an organisation gets bigger. *The power culture is therefore best suited to smaller entrepreneurial organisations, where the leaders have direct communication with all employees.*

(c) Personnel have to get on well with each other for this culture to work. Staff have to empathise with each other. These organisations are clubs of 'like-minded people introduced by the like-minded people, working on empathetic initiative with personal contact rather than formal liaison.'

Apollo is the god of the *role culture* or *bureaucracy*. *Everything and everybody are in their proper place. There is a presumption of logic and rationality.*

(a) These organisations have a formal structure, and operate by well-established rules and procedures. Job descriptions establish definite tasks for each person's job and procedures are established for many work routines, communication between individuals and departments, and the settlement of disputes and appeals. Individuals are required to perform their job to the full, but not to overstep the boundaries of their authority. Individuals who work for such organisations tend to learn an expertise without experiencing risk; many do their job adequately, but are not over-ambitious. Psychological sensitivity is a feature of this culture.

(b) *The bureaucratic style can be very efficient* in a stable environment, when the organisation is large and when the work is predictable.

(c) The Civil Service, insurance companies and many large well established companies with relatively unchanging products have been associated with bureaucratic organisations and the role culture. Unfortunately, bureaucracies are very slow to adapt to change and when severe change occurs (eg an economic depression) many run into financial difficulties or even bankruptcy (eg British Leyland and the British Steel Corporation in the late 70s). Otherwise they respond to change by doing more of the same (eg by generating cross functional liaison teams and a bureaucracy to support them).

Athena is the goddess of the *task culture. Management is seen as completing a succession of projects or solving problems.*

(a) The task culture is reflected in a *matrix organisation* or else in project teams and task forces. In such organisations, *there is no dominant or clear leader. The*

principal concern in a task culture is to get the job done. Therefore the individuals who are important are the *experts* with the ability to accomplish a particular aspect of the task. Each individual in the team considers he or she has more influence than he or she would have if the work were organised on a formal 'role culture' basis. Expertise and talent are more important than length of service.

(b) Performance is judged by results. Such organisations are flexible and constantly changing; for example, project teams are disbanded as soon as their task has been completed.

(c) Task cultures are expensive, as experts demand a market price.

(d) Task cultures also depend on variety, and to tap creativity requires a tolerance of perhaps costly mistakes. They are ideal when funds are available, in expanding industries or new situations. Where cost is a worry, controls are necessary.

(e) Since job satisfaction tends to be high owing to the degree of individual participation and group identity, 'behavioural' management theorists might recommend this type of organisation structure as being the most efficient available.

Dionysus is the god of the *existential culture*. In the three other cultures, the individual is subordinate to the organisation or task. *An existential culture is found in an organisation whose purpose is to serve the interests of the individuals within it.* These organisations are rare, although an example might be a partnership of a few individuals who do all the work of the organisation themselves (with perhaps a little secretarial or clerical assistance).

(a) Doctors come together to form a practice.

(b) Barristers (in the UK) work through chambers. The clerk co-ordinates their work and hands out briefs, but does not control them.

(c) Management in these organisations are often lower in status than the professionals and are labelled secretaries, administrators, bursars, registrars and chief clerk.

(d) The organisation depends on the **talent of the individuals;** management is derived from the consent of the managed, rather than the delegated authority of the owners.

The descriptions above interrelate four different strands.

(a) The individual
(b) The type of the work the organisation does
(c) The culture of the organisation
(d) The environment

Organisational effectiveness depends on an appropriate fit of all of them.

Activity 2 (10 minutes)

Which of Harrison's four cultures is found in your organisations (or in any other organisations with which you are sufficiently familiar)?

How far does the organisation's culture 'fit' the organisation's requirements and therefore help the organisation to be fully effective?

In what ways, if at all, does the organisation's culture get in the way?

The 'best fit' approach is like the notion that leadership is a best fit between a number of factors. As corporate culture is almost the air you breathe in your working life – so much so that its assumptions and prejudices are barely noticed – it can vitally affect an organisation's effectiveness.

EXAMPLE: TWO CULTURES

Handy cites a pharmaceutical company which at one time had all its manufacturing subcontracted, until turnover and cost considerations justified a factory of its own. The company hired nine talented individuals to design and run the factory. Result:

(a)   The *design team* ran on a task culture, with a democratic/consultative leadership style, using project teams for certain problems. This was successful while the factory was being built.

(b)   After its opening, the factory, staffed by 400, was run on similar lines. There were numerous problems. Every problem was treated as a project, and the workforce resented being asked to help sort out 'management' problems. In the end, the factory was run in a slightly more autocratic way. Handy states that this is a classic case of an *Athenian* culture to create a factory being superseded by an *Apollonian* culture to run it. Different cultures suit different businesses.

Handy says that Western organisations now face certain dilemmas, in particular 'the dilemma of Apollo'. Organisations, he says, have a trend towards Apollonian cultures and comparability and consistency of products.

(a)   Large size gives organisations – or rather their senior management – greater control over their own destinies. Large size can reduce the organisation's short term vulnerability.

(b)   Consistency enables better planning and more cost-effective operations.

(c)   Comparability is necessary so that effort can be directed at the most needy areas. Operational efficiency in different locations can be compared.

(d)   Comparability is also necessary for non-arbitrary control.

Activity 3   **(5 minutes)**

Review the following statements. Ascribe each of them to one of Harrison's four corporate cultures.

People are controlled and influenced by:

(a)   the personal exercise of rewards, punishments or charisma;

(b)   the impersonal exercise of economic and political power to enforce procedures and standards of performance;

(c)   communication and discussion of task requirements leading to appropriate action, motivated by personal commitment, to achieve the goal;

(d)   intrinsic interest and enjoyment in the activities to be done, and/or concern and caring for the needs of the other people involved.

Large size and consistency are desirable from the control standpoint. However,

'Size ... brings formality, impersonality and rules and procedures in its train... Similarly, consistency implies budgets, norms, standardised methods, fixed reporting periods, common documents and the whole barrage of bureaucracy.'

This has drawbacks. Handy believes that there are three 'strands of resistance' to Apollo.

(a)   As an organisation gets larger, it is exposed to more sources of environmental uncertainty. It becomes internally more complex and unmanageable. This imported uncertainty largely falls on to middle managers.

(b)   Apollonian cultures put the role above the individual. Individuals resent it. Apollonian organisations tolerate low individual discretion.

(c)   Finally, Handy mentions the third strand to be changes in the wider culture.

'There is in other words a growing clash in Western Society between organisation logic and the feelings of the individual'

encouraged he says, by an education system that values self-expression and team work as opposed to rote learning.

3   CULTURE, THE ENVIRONMENT AND STRATEGY

Different types of culture will be more or less appropriate in different strategic and environmental circumstances; in fact a synergy between culture and strategy would seem to be crucial to organisational success. An alternative model of culture is provided by *Denison*, who mapped the strategic orientation of organisation culture on a grid, to assess the relationship of culture with strategy.

(a)   How orientated is the firm to the environment rather than its internal workings?

(b)   To what extent does the environment offer stability or change?

Cultural types are recommended as follows.

| | | Organisations strategic orientation | |
		Internal	External
Environmental forces	Stability	Consistency	Mission
	Change/flexibility	Involvement	Adaptability

(a)   *Consistency culture*. This exists in a stable environment, and its structure is well integrated. Management are preoccupied with efficiency. Such cultures are characterised by formal ways of behaviour. Predictability and reliability are valued. This bears some similarity with the Apollonian culture.

(b)   *Mission culture*. The environment is relatively stable, but the organisation is orientated towards it. A mission culture, whereby members' work activities are given meaning and value, is appropriate. For example, hospitals are preoccupied with the sick: inevitably their values are 'customer' orientated. A church is concerned with saving souls.

(c) *Involvement culture*. This is similar to clan control identified in an earlier chapter. The basic premise behind it is that the satisfaction of employees' needs is necessary for them to provide optimum performance. An example might be an orchestra, whose performance depends on each individual. Involvement and participation, as discussed in an earlier chapter, are supposed to create a greater sense of commitment and hence performance. For example, if you train people well enough, it is assumed that they will perform. An involvement culture might take a human relations approach to management.

(d) *Adaptability culture*. The company's strategic focus is on the external environment, which is in a state of change. Corporate values encourage inquisitiveness and interest in the external environment. Fashion companies are an example: ideas come from a variety of sources.

Activity 4   **(5 minutes)**

(a)   What do you think is the most significant contrast between Denison's models and Harrison's model?

(b)   Which is better?

Because culture is a collection of shared beliefs and practices, it is thus an important filter of information and an interpreter of it. Culture is a way of looking at the world and interpreting information based on *management's* shared collective experience. After all, although the environment poses a few strategic questions, it is people who make sense of it and devise strategies. While the culture provides coherence it can impede strategic renewal. If the corporate strategy is failing, a company will try three expedients.

(a)   First it will place tighter controls over implementation (eg give tougher performance targets to sales staff)

(b)   If the controls fail, a new strategy will be developed, for example, to sell in a new market.

(c)   Only if the new strategy fails will basic assumptions be challenged.

Culture filters and reconfigures environmental information. (A recent and tragic example is the events in Waco, where members of the Branch Davidian cult interpreted environmental information about the FBI as presaging the end of the world.)

(a)   *Ignoring culture*

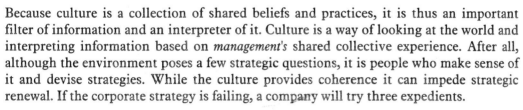

(b)   *Including culture*

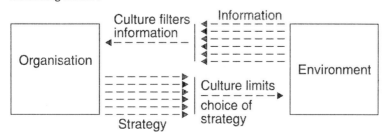

At the same time culture filters out a number of strategic choices. For example, a firm might have a cultural predisposition against embarking on risky ventures. Another culture might have an ingrained 'Buy British' approach. Finally, if culture is embodied in behaviour, existing *behaviour* may make a strategy incompatible with the culture and so impossible to implement.

Miles and Snow analyse three strategic cultures, and a fourth 'non-strategic' culture.

(a) *Defenders*. Firms with this culture like low risks, secure markets, and tried and trusted solutions. These companies have cultures whose stories and rituals reflect historical continuity and consensus. Decision-taking is relatively formalised. (There is a stress on 'doing things right' ie efficiency.)

(b) *Prospectors* are organisations where the dominant beliefs are more to do with results (doing the right things ie effectiveness). They might be less fearful of risk.

(c) *Analysers* try to balance risk and profits. They use a core of stable products and markets as a source of earnings to move into innovative prospector areas. Analysers follow change, but do not initiate it.

(d) *Reactors*, unlike the three above, do not have viable strategies. Arguably, they do not have a strategy, unless it is simply to carry on living from hand to mouth, muddling through.

Activity 5 (10 minutes)

Jarvis Tools Ltd makes machine tools for a variety of industries. Until now, it has had a captive market, but it is now facing competition from a Korean machine tool company. The threat is growing but at the moment Jarvis is in a good position. The tools are customised. They require a high degree of accuracy, so customers have to wait a fairly long time for the product, although Jarvis is recognised as being a leader in both innovation and quality. The firm historically has made all of its subcomponents in house. The company was founded by Fred Jarvis, an engineer. Every year an award is given to a favoured 'excellent' worker. Management consultants have suggested three alternatives for dealing with the competition.

(a) Speed up product design and development, perhaps by subcontracting some components to outside firms.

(b) Engage in a joint venture or marketing agreement with the Korean company, so that the Korean company will be directed to market segments that Jarvis does not serve.

(c) Achieve a BS EN ISO 9000 certification as soon as possible.

Which of the strategies do you think Jarvis Tools Ltd would adopt, if corporate culture were the determining factor?

Activity 6 **(10 minutes)**

Read the following passage (slightly adapted) from Tom Peters' book *Liberation Management: Necessary Disorganisation for the Nanosecond Nineties* (1992).

'IBM decentralises. Then decentralises again. Then decentralises one more time. And joins in alliances with this company, then that company. But it's still too sluggish by a mile. (And can't gather the nerve to deconstruct its monster Sales organisation). The long 80-year-old shadow cast by even a diminished corporate headquarters thwarts initiative after initiative. Like nearly every other clever product from IBM the innovative database language SQL had been developed in secret. The development group lied about it, then finally showed it to the big shots who were too impressed to turn the product down. The *Wall Street Journal* filed an eerily similar report on IBM's 1990 Nobel prize-winners for superconductivity, J Georg Bednorz and K Alex Mueller: "The two scientists hunted quietly, telling a supervisor a half-truth, and steering a curious visitor off track ... The issue is a sore point now for IBM brass."'

Now diagnose what was going wrong at IBM using as many as possible of the new terms and concepts you have encountered in this text so far.

---

4 MANAGEMENT CULTURES IN A GLOBAL SETTING

A factor which has an impact on the culture of transnational organisations, or organisations competing in global markets, is the *management culture*. This is the views about managing held by managers, their shared educational experiences, and the 'way business is done'. Obviously, this reflects wider cultural differences between countries, but conversely national cultures can sometimes be subordinated to the corporate culture of the organisation (eg the efforts to ensure that staff of EuroDisney are as enthusiastic as their American counterparts). The way in which business practice can be affected by management culture can be indicated by an example.

(a) The Harvard Business Review reported (July-August 1991) that

'the successful development of executives in French organisations depends on creating a distinctive shared identity, a sense of belonging to the French managerial class.'

Further quotations are illuminating:

'French managers see their work as an intellectual challenge, requiring the remorseless application of individual brainpower. They do not share the Anglo-Saxon view of management as an interpersonally demanding exercise, where plans have to be constantly 'sold' upward and downward using personal skills. The bias is for intellect rather than for action. People who run big enterprises must above all else be clever – that is, they must be able to grasp complex issues, analyse problems, manipulate ideas and evaluate solutions. The possible dangers of this approach if taken to the extreme are shown in the following joke, supposedly a comment from one senior French civil servant to another: 'That's fine in practice, but it will never work in theory'.

'The emphasis on cleverness shows up even in executive recruiting advertisements. They hardly mention the drive or initiative looked for in Anglo-Saxon recruits, rather they call for more cerebral qualities – an

analytical mind, independence, intellectual rigor, an ability to synthesise information. Communication or interpersonal skills are tacked on at the end, if they appear at all.'

'Recent French industrial achievements have occurred largely in fields requiring a co-ordinated, technologically and scientifically creative, and research-driven approach – rather than, say, marketing dash, financial wizardry, or manufacturing organisation.'

(b)   The world leadership survey conducted by the *Harvard Business Review* asked a variety of questions to managers in different countries. Although the response to the survey (which appeared in business magazines) was self-selected, it could be concluded that managers in different countries do not have the same priorities when it came to business issues. When asked what they thought of as the three most important factors in organisation success, these were listed as follows, in order of priority.

- Japan: product development, management, product quality
- Germany: workforce skills, problem solving, management
- USA: customer service, product quality, technology

The existence of these different systems of priorities and ways of doing business affects the competitive environment, international marketing and the success of joint ventures (eg which can be damaged by communication problems). UK managers, who were described by the survey as among the least cosmopolitan, may have some adapting to do.

The Hofstede model

The Hofstede model was developed in 1980 by Professor *Geert Hofstede* in order to explain national differences by identifying 'key dimensions' which represent the essential 'programmes' forming a common culture in the value systems of all countries. Each country is represented on a scale for each dimension so as to explain and understand values, attitudes and behaviour. In particular, Hofstede pointed out that countries differ on the following dimensions.

(a)   *Power distance.* This dimension measures how far superiors are expected to exercise power. In a high power-distance culture, the boss decides and people do not question.

(b)   *Uncertainty avoidance.* Some cultures prefer clarity and order, whereas others are prepared to accept ambiguity. This affects the willingness of people to change rules, rather than simply obey them.

(c)   *Individualism-collectivism.* In some countries individual achievement is what matters. A collectivist culture (eg people are supported – and controlled – by extended families) puts the interests of the group first.

(d)   *Masculinity.* In 'masculine' cultures, male and female roles are clearly differentiated. In 'feminine' ones they are not. 'Masculine' cultures place greater emphasis on possessions, status and display as opposed to quality of life or the environment.

Hofstede grouped countries into eight clusters based on these dimensions. Here are three examples.

(a)   Countries in the Anglo group

- Low to medium power-distance
- Low to medium uncertainty avoidance
- High individualism
- High 'masculinity'

(b) Countries in the Nordic group

- low power distance
- low to medium uncertainty avoidance
- medium individualism
- low 'masculinity'

(c) Countries in the more developed Asian group

- Medium power distance
- High uncertainty avoidance
- Medium individualism
- High 'masculinity'

These cultures are not immutable; they change, as society changes. But consider the following.

(a) Certain aspects of TQM are hard to introduce in the UK as people like to shine: it takes time to get used to team working. Treasured management approaches, like *individual* bonuses, performance related pay for *individuals*, are not really compatible with 'team-work' in which everybody is supposed to pull together.

(b) There have been reports of problems in cross border mergers, eg between French and German companies, simply because of the way they are run. One contributory factor might be cultural 'differences'.

5 SUBCULTURES

Despite the official organisational culture that has been fostered or actively imposed by the organisation in the person of its managers, all organisations will also contain a number of sub-units which may have their own cultures which may or may not be compatible with the attitudes and values the organisation wishes to promote. If managers wish to integrate divisionalised structures or geographically dispersed branches, for example, by promoting a strong 'central' culture, they may encounter resistance among the sub-units. However, a strong central culture is important in organisations which seek to replace personal centralised control with cultural control.

'Sub-cultures' are cultures which exist in a context dominated by the decisions, values and attitudes of others. AK Cohen, among other sociologists, defines sub-cultures as 'cultures which exist within cultures', with three major characteristics.

(a) The group shares a distinctive way of life, knowledge, beliefs, codes, tastes and prejudices.

(b) These are learned from others in the group who already exhibit these characteristics.

(c) Their way of life has 'somehow become traditional' among those who inherit and share the social conditions to which the subcultural characteristics are a response.

Definition

'*Counter cultures*' are groups of people within society whose values and norms are hostile to those held in the wider society.

'The power to create and manipulate culture as a means of controlling others is well entrenched in the social, economic and political institutions of a society but it is also continually resisted by opposing cultural forms.'

Bryn Jones (*The Politics of Popular Culture*)

Some sociologists have researched 'counter school' youth cultures, and how they are naturally carried over onto the shopfloor. In collective opposition to the dominant culture of the school, 'the lads' (as Willis calls them) are conventionally regarded as violent, undisciplined trouble makers. In fact, school is an institution which has little meaning for 'the lads': it has merely to be got through as enjoyably as possible – by 'having a laugh' and rehearsing the loyalties and possibilities for defiance and resistance which will be carried over into work. Wage labour, like school, is essentially meaningless – as is the work ethic designed to perpetuate it.

That said, management has spent much time trying to change culture. Furthermore, the decline of manufacturing employment and the legal curbs on workers' rights have meant that 'laddish' attitudes are no longer tenable; perhaps gratitude for work has replaced it. Some companies also try hard to break down the demarcations involving subcultures. Shared canteen facilities for example are symbolic of managerial efforts to break down the factory subculture.

6 THE MANAGER AS LEADER

Definition

> *Direction* or *leadership* is the process of influencing others to work willingly towards an organisation's goals, and to the best of their capabilities.

Leadership is clearly one of the activities of management.

Activity 7 [5 minutes]

Before you read on, think about the definition of leadership advanced above. In particular, do you agree with these two propositions?

(1) Leadership is the process of influencing others to work willingly towards an organisation's goals.

(2) It is the willingness of people to follow that makes a person a leader.

Historically leadership was seen as innate in individuals and based on status in society or personal charisma. The growth of industrial society has prompted a broader examination of the concept.

The study of leadership involves the influence of one person's behaviour on other members of a group and their reactions to this behaviour. It applies to a wide range of situations including the home, the classroom, the workplace and recreational and social situations. Leadership cannot be studied without considering the behaviour of groups, their pursuit of goals and the satisfaction of their needs.

Two kinds of leadership can be distinguished. One is *emergent* and spontaneously accorded; the other is *delegated* from an authority outside the group. The latter kind is often described as *headship* and is typified by royalty, military officers, ships' captains, factory managers and so forth. An important difference between the two types of leader is likely to be their sensitivity to group interaction. The distinction is important in studying and understanding the different types of leadership found in complex organisations. In factories and offices both kinds of leadership can be found, with managers acting as delegated leaders and employee representatives acting as emergent leaders.

Subordinates of a manager with poor leadership qualities may still do their job, but they are more likely to do it ineffectually or perhaps in a confused manner. By providing leadership, a manager should be able to use the capabilities of subordinates to better effect, in other words good leadership adds value. Leadership is the

'influential increment over and above mechanical compliance with the routine directives of the organisation'   **(Katz and Kahn, The Social Psychology of Organisations).**

An important distinction is between management and leadership. *John Kotter* (*The Leadership Factor, 1988*) makes an informative distinction. Management involves the following activities.

(a) *Planning and budgeting* – target-setting, establishing procedures for reaching the targets, and allocating the resources necessary to meet the plans.

(b) *Organising and staffing* – designing the organisation structure, hiring the right people and establishing incentives.

(c) *Controlling and problem-solving* – monitoring results against the plan, identifying problems, producing solutions and implementing them.

Everything here is concerned with logic, structure, analysis and control. If done well, it produces predictable results on time. *Leadership*, however, requires a different set of actions and a completely different mind set.

(a) *Creating a sense of direction* – usually the result of dissatisfaction with the status quo. Out of this challenge a vision for something different is created.

(b) *Communicating the vision* – which must meet the realised or unconscious needs of other people and the leader must work to give it credibility.

(c) *Energising, inspiring and motivating* – in order to stimulate others to translate the vision into achievement.

All of these activities involve dealing with people rather than things.

Activity 8   **[2 minutes]**

Having now read a little about leadership and how it is different from management, do you think that leaders are born or made?

In considering your response, you may find it helpful to ponder the views of Field Marshal Lord Slim, when Governor-General of Australia:

'There is a difference between leadership and management. Leadership is of the spirit, compounded of personality and vision; its practice is an art. Management is one of the mind, a matter of accurate calculation ... its practice is a science. Managers are necessary; leaders are essential.

7 TRAIT THEORIES OF LEADERSHIP

Early theories suggested that there are certain qualities, or personality characteristics that make a good leader. These might be aggressiveness, self-assurance, intelligence, initiative, a drive for achievement or power, appearance, interpersonal skills, administrative ability, imagination, a certain upbringing and education or the 'helicopter factor' (ie the ability to rise above a situation and analyse it objectively), for example.

This list is not exhaustive, and various writers attempted to show that their selected list of traits were the ones that provided the key to leadership. The full list of traits is so long that it appears to call for a person of extraordinary, even superhuman, gifts to be a leader. In a comprehensive article on the subject, *Ghiselli* listed a large number different traits of leadership cited by various authors, and pointed out that most of the traits reflected nothing more than the prejudices of the author in question. Bishops praise moral virtue; businessmen seek entrepreneurial flair; generals write about leading from the front.

There are several difficulties with the idea of viewing leadership as a bundle of traits.

(a)   No two writers on the subject can agree on a manageable list of traits appropriate to effective leaders.

(b)   Virtually all the traits listed in books about leadership are positive or desirable characteristics for human beings; seldom is there any recognition of the possibility that leaders could still be flawed or that their flaws may be the very behavioural and personality features which enable them to succeed as leaders.

(c)   Even if a list of desirable traits could be agreed and established, there is the question of measuring their presence or absence in any given individual.

(d)   Nor can it be assumed that if a specific trait is desirable in a would-be leader, then the leader should have as much of it as possible. Should courage be required, for example, then an excess of courage is as dangerous as an insufficiency.

(e)   In identifying actual leaders who possess the traits of leadership, there is an element of wish-fulfilling prophecy. If a leader takes risks and succeeds, then he is labelled as 'courageous' and 'visionary'; if he takes risks and fails, he is described as 'foolhardy'. Yet few leaders succeed all the time.

Alternative approaches to leadership theory have been developed over the years; we will examine some of them under three headings.

- Style theories, mainly of the behaviouralist school of thought
- Systems theory and leadership
- Contingency theories of leadership

8 STYLE THEORIES OF LEADERSHIP

Leaders should not play down their roles by being friendly and informal with subordinates, or by consulting them before making any decision. *Douglas McGregor* (*Leadership and Motivation*) wrote about his own experiences as a college president.

> 'It took a couple of years, but I finally began to realise that a leader cannot avoid the exercise of authority any more than he can avoid responsibility for what happens in the organisation.'

A leader can try to avoid acting dictatorially, but must accept all the consequences of being a leader. McGregor wrote that 'since no important decision ever pleases everyone in the organisation, he must also absorb the displeasures, and sometimes severe hostility, of those who would have taken a different course. '

However, whilst a leader must exercise authority, the way in which this is done (the style of leadership) might vary. It is generally accepted that a leader's style of leading can affect the motivation, efficiency and effectiveness of his subordinates.

8.1 Tells/sells/consults/joins style

The Research Unit at Ashridge Management College, based on studies in several industries in the UK (reported 1966), distinguished four different management styles.

(a) The autocratic or *tells* style. This is characterised by one-way communication between the manager and the subordinate, with the manager telling the subordinate what to do. The leader makes all the decisions and issues instructions, expecting them to be obeyed without question.

(b) The persuasive or *sells* style. The manager still makes all the decisions, but explains and justifies them to subordinates, who will then be motivated to do what is required of them.

(c) The *consults* style. This involves discussion between the manager and the subordinates involved in carrying out a decision, but the manager retains the right to make the decision personally. By conferring with subordinates before making any decision, the manager will take account of their advice and feelings. Consultation is a form of limited participation in decision making for subordinates, but there might be a tendency for a manager to appear to consult subordinates when really he or she has made up his mind beforehand. Consultation will then be false and a facade for a sells style of leadership whereby the manager hopes to win the acceptance of his or her decisions by subordinates by pretending to listen to their advice.

(d) The democratic or *joins* style. This is an approach whereby the leader joins a group of subordinates to make a decision on the basis of consensus or agreement. It is the most democratic style of leadership identified by the research study. Subordinates with the greatest knowledge of a problem will have greater influence over the decision. The joins style is therefore most effective where all subordinates in the group have equal knowledge and can therefore contribute in equal measure to decisions.

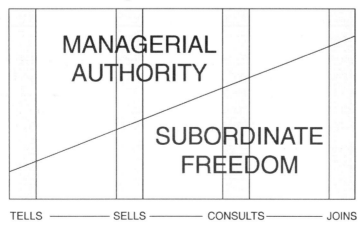

The Ashridge studies made some interesting findings with regard to leadership style and employee motivation. Compare them with the views of other writers described in this chapter.

(a)   There was a clear preference amongst the subordinates for the *consults* style of leadership but managers were most commonly thought to be exercising the 'tells' or 'sells' style.

(b)   The attitudes of subordinates towards their work varied according to the style of leadership they thought their boss exercised. The most favourable attitudes were found amongst those subordinates who perceived their boss to be exercising the *consults style*.

(c)   The least favourable attitudes were found amongst subordinates who were unable to perceive a *consistent* style of leadership in their boss. In other words, subordinates are unsettled by a boss who chops and changes between autocracy, persuasion, consultation and democracy.

The strengths and weaknesses of each style are outlined in the table overleaf.

Activity 9   **(15 minutes)**

Using the tell-sell-consult-join framework, indicate which style of leadership you would adopt if you had to manage each of the following situations. Think carefully about your reasons for choosing one style rather than another, in terms of the results you are trying to achieve and the possible need to secure *commitment* from those affected.

(a)   Due to outside factors, the personnel budget has been reduced for your department and one-quarter of your staff must be made redundant. Appraisal records are available for each person involved.

(b)   There is a recurring administrative problem which is minor, but irritating to everyone in your department. Several solutions have been tried in the past, but without success. You think you have a remedy which will work, but unknown problems may arise, depending on the decision made.

(c)   A decision must be made about the starting and finish times for work. The organisation wishes to stagger the times in order to relieve traffic congestion and each department can make its own decisions. It doesn't really matter what the times are, so long as everyone in your department conforms to the decision.

(d)   You have told your boss and others about a new idea that you want to try out in your department to reduce costs. They have all been enthusiastic and urged you to try it.

       You have worked out the plans in detail, but the decision to proceed has not yet been made.

(e)   Even though they are experienced, members in your department don't seem to want to take on responsibility for decisions. Their attitude seems to be, 'You are paid to manage, we are paid to do the work, so you make the decisions.' Now an issue has come up for a decision which will personally affect every person in your department.

Style	Characteristics	Strengths	Weaknesses
Tells *(autocratic)*	The manager makes all the decisions, and issues instructions which must be obeyed without question	(1) Quick decisions can be made when speed is required. (2) It is the most efficient type of leadership for highly-programmed routine work.	(1) It does not encourage the subordinates to give their opinions when these might be useful. (2) Communications between the manager and subordinate will be one-way and the manager will not know until afterwards whether the orders have been properly understood. (3) It dos not encourage initiative and commitment from subordinates
Sells *(Persuasive)*	The manager still makes all the decisions, but believes that subordinates have to be motivated to accept them in order to carry them out properly	(1) Employees are made aware of the reasons for decisions. (2) Selling decisions to staff might make them more committed. (3) Staff will have a better idea of what to do when unforeseen events arise in their work because the manager will have explained his intentions.	(1) Communications are still largely one-way. Subordinates might not accept the decisions. (2) It does not encourage initiative and commitment from subordinates.
Consults	The manager confers with subordinates and takes their views into account, but has the final say.	(1) Employees are involved in decisions before they are made. This encourages motivation through greater interest and involvement. (2) An agreed consensus of opinion can be reached and for some decisions consensus can be an advantage rather than a weak compromise. (3) Employees can contribute their knowledge and experience to help i solving more complex problems.	(1) It might take much longer to reach decisions. (2) Subordinate might be too inexperienced to formulate mature opinions and give practical advice. (3) Consultation can too easily turn into a façade concealing, basically, a sells style.
Joins *(democratic)*	Leader and followers make the decision on the basis of consensus	(1) It can provide high motivation and commitment from employees. (2) It shares the other advantages of the consultative style (especially where subordinates have expert power).	(1) the authority of the manager might be undermined. (2) Decision-making might become a very long process and clear decisions might be difficult to reach. (3) Subordinates might lack enough experience.

8.2 Task management

When discussing leadership it is all to easy to overlook the 'task' element of a manager's responsibilities; however a manager is primarily responsible for ensuring that results are achieved efficiently and effectively.

The managerial grid

Robert R Blake and Jane S Mouton designed the management grid. It is based on two fundamental ingredients of managerial behaviour.

- Concern for production
- Concern for people

The results of their work were originally published as 'Ohio State Leadership Studies'.

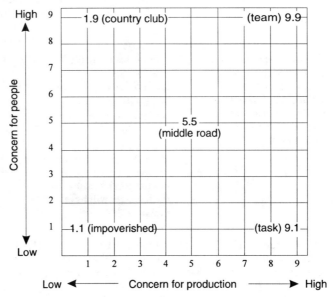

The extreme cases shown on the grid are defined below.

(a) *1.1 impoverished:* manager is lazy, showing little effort or concern for staff or work targets.

(b) *1.9 country club:* manager is attentive to staff needs and has developed satisfying relationships. However, there is little attention paid to achieving results.

(c) *9.1 task management:* almost total concentration on achieving results. People's needs are virtually ignored and conditions of work are so arranged that people cannot interfere to any significant extent.

(d) *5.5 middle of the road or the dampened pendulum:* adequate performance through balancing the necessity to get out work while maintaining morale of people at a satisfactory level.

(e) *9.9 team:* high performance manager who achieves high work accomplishment through leading committed people who identify themselves with the organisational aims.

There is also the style described as the *statistical* 5.5, where the manager veers indiscriminately around the other styles within the grid system, never being consistent from one day to the next. The conclusion is that the most efficient managers combine concern for the task with concern for people. It is worth being clear in your own mind about the possible usefulness of the grid. Its primary value is obtained from the appraisal of a manager's performance, either by the manager personally or by the manager's superiors. The ideal manager is '9.9' with high concern for both production and people. An individual manager can be placed on the grid, and his or her position on the grid should help him to see how his or her performance as a leader and a manager can be improved. For example, a manager rated 3.8 has further to go in showing concern for the task itself than for developing the work of his or her subordinates.

Reddin's 3-D Management Style Theory builds a third dimension, effectiveness, on the framework of the grid. Reddin's argument is that even a 9.9 manager, with a high concern for both production and people, may be ineffective if he is trying to operate in an organisational culture which is predominantly, say, 9.1 (is task-centred). Such a manager will be a misfit and would either have to change to a more 9.1 approach, in order to become more congruent with his cultural environment, or would have to move elsewhere.

Reddin's model shows, conversely, that managers normally viewed as ineffective on the managerial grid, may nonetheless be effective in specific organisational contexts. Even a 1.1 (*impoverished*) manager could be viewed as 'effective' within an organisation which displayed little or no concern for people or results. Hopefully such organisations are very rare.

Activity 10   **(10 minutes)**

Try to summarise for yourself the different descriptions of leadership style put forward by the style theorists. Can you think of any situations where you or your boss display more than one type of style? Why is this so?

---

9 A SYSTEMS APPROACH TO LEADERSHIP

Systems theory is concerned with the complex inter-relationships between the many different parts of a system (organisation), and the effect of the environment on the system (and vice versa). *Katz and Kahn* have developed ideas on how leadership can contribute to the better functioning of a system.

Early research by Katz and Kahn (reported in 1951) into the effect of leadership style on productivity suggested that there were three aspects of leader behaviour which affected productivity.

- Assumption of the leadership role
- Closeness of supervision
- Degree of employee-orientation

Comparisons were made between high-production and low-production groups and the following was found.

(a) In the most efficient groups the supervisor assumed the leadership role and used his supervisory talents to get the best out of his group. The leader has special functions and cannot therefore behave as an ordinary group member (ie be 'one of the boys'). In large organisations the assumption of the supervisory role is often made easier by transferring staff on promotion so that they can make a fresh start among strangers.

(b) Supervision was closer in low-production than in high-production groups. Workers expect to have some control over the means by which they perform a set task, and they resent having means specified in too much detail.

> Supervisory behaviour was found to reflect management leadership styles, ie the organisational context affects leadership.

(c) Studies of the attitudes held by supervisors towards their subordinates revealed that the men in charge of high-production groups were more employee-oriented (ie intent on promoting their welfare). In the research experiment, the attitudes of a manager were gauged by asking subordinates to rate bosses; results showed that the efficient bosses were seen by their subordinates to be more *considerate*.

Katz and Kahn later developed their ideas and suggested that the reason why the most effective managers show consideration and understanding towards their subordinates is because they supplement their formal position in the organisation and appreciate essential facts about their people.

(a) They have interests and roles outside their job.

(b) They are subject to pressures and influences from their external environment.

(c) They need information to do their job with greater understanding.

(d) They need to be guided in the dynamic, changing organisation, and to understand the significance of change.

Good leaders show a true awareness that organisations are open systems, reacting to and changing with their environment, of which their subordinates are also a part. Leaders influence those aspects of their subordinates' interests, energies and drive which cannot be harnessed by simple organisation structure, job definitions, or more formal management techniques.

The *situation* is the key to deciding how effective a leadership style can be.

'If we wish to increase organisational and group effectiveness we must learn not only how to train leaders more effectively, but also how to build an organisational environment in which the leader can perform well.'

CONTINGENCY THEORY OF LEADERSHIP

9.1 Handy's best fit approach

Handy has also suggested a contingency approach to leadership. He suggests four factors that contribute to a leader's effectiveness.

(a) *The leader* (his or her personality, character and preferred style of operating)

(b) *The subordinates* (their individual and collective personalities, and their preference for a style of leadership)

(c) *The task* (the objectives of the job, the technology of the job, methods of working etc)

(d) *The environment* (which is discussed separately)

Essentially, Handy argues that the most effective style of leadership in any particular situation is one which brings the first three factors – a leader, subordinates and task – into a best fit. For each of the three factors, a spectrum can be drawn ranging from tight to flexible.

	The leader	The subordinates	The task
Tight ↑ **The spectrum**	Preference for autocratic style; high estimation of his own capabilities and a low estimation of his subordinates., Dislikes uncertainty	Low opinion of own abilities, do not like uncertainty in their work and like to be ordered. They regard their work ad trivial; pt experience in work leads to acceptance of orders, cultural factors lean them towards autocratic/dictatorial leaders.	Job requires no initiative, is routine and repetitive, or ahas a certain outcome, short time scale for completion. Trivial task.
↓ *Flexible*	Preference of democratic style, confidence in his subordinate, dislikes stress , accepts reasonable risk and uncertainty.	High opinion of own abilities; like challenging important work; prepared to accept uncertainty and longer time scales for results; cultural factors favour independence.	Important tasks with a longer time scale; problem solving or decision-making involved, complex work.

A best fit occurs when all three factors are on the same level in the spectrum. In practice, there is likely to be a misfit. Confronted with a lack of fit, the leader must decide which factor(s) should be changed to bring all three into line. The factor over which a leader has most influence is himself and his style; hence, Handy argues, the great emphasis on leaderships in management literature.

'However, although the leader's style is theoretically the easiest to alter in the short term, there are often long-term benefits to be achieved from re-defining the task (eg job enlargement) or from developing the work group.'

The fourth factor identified by Handy in the situational jig-saw is the environment.

(a) *The position of power held by the leader in the organisation and the relationship of the leader and his group.* Power might be a position of authority but it might also be the expertise or the charisma of the leader. A person with great power has a bigger capacity to set his own style of leadership, select his own subordinates and redefine the task of his work group.

(b) *Organisational norms and the structure and technology of the organisation.* No manager can flout convention and act in a manner which is contrary to the customs and standards of the organisation. If the organisation has a history of autocratic leadership, it will be difficult to introduce a new style. If the formal organisation is highly centralised, there will be limits to how far a task can be restructured by an individual manager. In mass-production industries, where routine, repetitive work is in-built into the production technology, challenging tasks will be difficult to create, and leadership will tend, perforce, to be autocratic.

(c) *The variety of tasks and the variety of subordinates.* If the tasks of a work group are simple, few in number and repetitive, the best style of leadership will be different from a situation in which tasks are varied and difficult. In many groups, however, tasks vary from routine and simple, to complex 'one-off' problem-solving. Managing such work is complicated by this variety.

Similarly, the individuals in a work group might be widely different. One member of the group might seek participation and greater responsibility, whereas another might want to be told what to do. Furthermore, labour turnover may be frequent, and the individual persons who act as leaders or subordinates are constantly changing; such change is unsettling because the leadership style will have to be altered to suit the new situation, each time a personnel change occurs.

The environment can be improved for leaders within an organisation if top management provide the right conditions.

- Leaders are given a clear role and power.
- Organisational norms can be broken.
- The organisational structure is not rigid and inflexible.
- Subordinates in a work group are all of the same quality or type.
- Managers are kept in their job for a reasonably lengthy period of time.

9.2 Power and influence

Influence is the process by which one person in an organisation, A, directs or modifies the behaviour or attitudes of another person, B. Influence can only be exerted by A on B if A has some kind of power from which the influence emanates. Power is therefore the ability to influence, whereas influence is an active process. Note that *power* is not the same as *authority*. A manager may have the right to expect his subordinates to carry out his instructions, but may lack the ability to make them do it. On the other hand, an individual may have the ability to make others act in a certain way, without having the organisational authority to do so: informal 'leaders' are frequently in this position.

Power and influence are clearly important factors in the structure and operations of an organisation. They help to explain how work gets done. In addition, it has also been suggested that an individual who believes he or she exerts some influence is likely to show greater interest in his or her work. The research of writers, such as Likert, who support the principle of management by participation, suggests that employees may be more productive when they consider that they have some influence over planning decisions which affect their work. Also, some individuals are motivated by the need for power, and show great concern for exercising influence and control, and for being leaders.

Charles Handy (*Understanding Organisations*) identified six types of power from different sources.

(a) *Physical power* is the power of superior force. Physical power is absent from most organisations (except the prison service and the armed forces), but it is sometimes evident in poor industrial relations (for example shop floor intimidation, or the use of riot police against workers).

(b) *Resource power* is the control over resources which are valued by the individual or group to be influenced. Senior managers may have the resource power to grant promotion or pay increases to subordinates; trade unions possess the resource power to take their members out on strike. The amount of power a person has then depends on how far he or she controls the resource, how much the resource is valued by others, and how scarce it is.

(c)   *Position power* is the power which is associated with a particular job in an organisation. Handy noted that position power has certain hidden benefits.

    (i)   Access to information

    (ii)   The right of access: for example entitlement to membership of committees and contact with other powerful individuals in the organisation.

    (iii)   The right to organise conditions of working and methods of decision-making

(d)   *Expert power* is the power which belongs to an individual because of his or her expertise, although it only works if others acknowledge him to be an expert. Many jobs in an organisation's technostructure (computer systems analysts, organisation and methods analysts, accountants, lawyers or personnel department managers) rely on expert power to influence line management. An expert who is seen to be incompetent (if an accountant, say, does not seem to provide sensible information) or whose area of expertise is not widely acknowledged (which is often the case with personnel department staff), will have little or no expert power.

(e)   *Personal power*, or *charisma* is innate within the individual. Personal power is capable of influencing the behaviour of others, and helps to explain the strength of informal organisations.

(f)   *Negative power* is the use of disruptive attitudes and behaviour to stop things from happening. It is associated with low morale, latent conflict or frustration at work. Subordinates might refuse to communicate openly with their superiors, and might provide false information; a typist might refuse to type an urgent letter owing to pressure of work; a worker might deliberately cause his or her machine to break down; a manager might refuse to co-operate with colleagues, if an agreed policy adversely affects his or her position. Negative power is destructive and potentially very damaging to organisational efficiency.

Influence, the act of directing or modifying the behaviour of others, may then be achieved in a variety of ways.

(a)   The application of force, eg physical or economic power

(b)   The establishment of rules and procedures enforced through position or resource power

(c)   Bargaining and negotiation, depending on the relative strengths of each party's expert, resource or personal power

(d)   Persuasion

Handy identified two further, unseen methods of influence.

(a)   *Ecology*, or the environment in which behaviour takes place. The physical environment can be altered by a manager, who may be able to regulate noise levels at work, comfort and security of working conditions, seating arrangements, the use of open-plan offices or segregation into many small offices, the physical proximity of departments as well as individuals.

    'The design of work, the work, the structure of reward and control systems, the structure of the organisation, the management of groups and the control of conflict are all ways of managing the environment in order to influence behaviour. Let us never forget that although the environment is all around

us, it is not unalterable, that to change it is to influence people, that ecology is potent, the more so because it is often unnoticed.' (Handy)

(b) *Magnetism*, ie the unseen application of personal power or charisma.

'*Trust, respect, charm, infectious enthusiasm, these attributes all allow us to influence people without apparently imposing on them.*'

Charisma has been attributed to such leaders as Jesus Christ, Gandhi, Hitler and Lady Thatcher. Although charisma seems to be a mystical and elusive phenomenon, *Robert House* has shown that, in fact, supposedly charismatic leaders actually display five fairly straightforward behaviour patterns, summarised below.

(a) *Role modelling:* they behave in the way they want their followers to behave, they lead by example.

(b) *Image creation:* they create an impression of competence and success, through their appearance and demeanour.

(c) *Confidence building:* they communicate high performance expectations about others.

(d) *Goal articulation:* they arouse emotional commitment through morally loaded goals (eg with a vision or mission statement in order to emphasise the higher-order purposes in the organisation).

(e) *Motive arousal:* they behave in a manner designed to inspire others.

10 THE USEFULNESS OF LEADERSHIP THEORIES

Few of the concepts discussed above attempt to distinguish leadership behaviour from management behaviour, other than peripherally in the form of motivation or setting an example. It is arguable, therefore, that although they may encourage better management – through their application in management assessment and development – they are incapable of making better *leaders*, other than by adding insight into management functions for those who are leaders already.

It is also doubtful to what extent study of a concept, even where it is built into a training scheme, can in fact change a given individual's behaviour. Individual managers/leaders will not change their values in response to a theory, especially where it is one of many – often conflicting – frameworks. Even if willingness to change management values and style exists, conditions in the organisation may not allow it.

The trouble with theories is that many of them do not take relevant organisational conditions into account, and for a manager to model his own behaviour on a formula which is successful in theory or in a completely different situation will not necessarily be helpful. In addition, the following may apply.

(a) The manager's personality is rarely flexible enough to utilise leadership theories by attempting to change styles to suit a situation. A manager may not be able to be participative in some circumstances and authoritative in others where his or her personality and personal goals are incompatible with that style.

(b) The demands of the task, technology, organisation culture and other managers constrains the manager in the range of styles and leadership behaviours available. If the manager's own boss believes in and practises an authoritarian style, and the group members are incompetent and require close supervision, no amount of theorising on the desirability of participative management will be effective.

(c) Consistency is important to subordinates. If a manager practises a contingency approach to leadership, subordinates may simply perceive the manager to be fickle, or may suffer insecurity and distrust the changeful manager.

> *'There is therefore no simple recipe which the individual manager can use to decide which style to adopt to be most effective. Management style probably can be changed, but only if management values can be changed ... It is not enough to present managers with research findings and try to convince them with logical argument that change is necessary.'*
>
> *(Buchanan and Huczynski, Organizational Behaviour)*

11 THE VISIONARY LEADER

Despite some scepticism about the degree to which it is possible for individuals to take on some of the attributes of leadership, increasing attention is being paid to the notion of the visionary leader, who is capable of transforming the organisation by taking it on to even greater success or by turning it round from imminent collapse.

Analysis of books about visionary leadership suggests that much the same general motivational and skills qualities apply. Successful leadership is more likely to occur when the person in charge of an organisation possesses some generic leadership characteristics (ie suitable traits) and is then able to customise them to the particular context where leadership prowess is needed. The following profile for the visionary leader draws heavily on an article by *Bill Richardson* in the September 1993 issue of *The Administrator*.

First, the visionary leader is both *imaginative and experienced, intuitive and analytical*. The visionary takes mental leaps from what is into what could or should be. However, this imagining is not done in a void: it draws on a deep understanding of what already is and how it could be modified or revolutionised. The visionary is often a maverick: someone who sees and does things differently – possibly an outsider recruited into a failing organisation or an unconventional insider (someone from within the organisation but clearly holding different views from the mainstream about how the organisation should operate).

In reaching decisions the visionary draws from both left- and right-sided brain functions: holistic assessments of the strategy being formulated are intertwined with a detailed analysis of the situation. The visionary is relatively comfortable in situations of ambiguity, and can live without 'hard and fast' answers.

Surprisingly, perhaps, the visionary's visions are seldom very original, but take the form of linking connections between what is happening somewhere else and how this might be applied in some differing context.

EXAMPLES: RETAILING

Marks & Spencer

'The American farmer had little time or opportunity to go shopping. So the farmer received a catalogue and was given the novel guarantee of 'your money back and no questions asked'. Providing the service meant also creating new human skills, for example, by organising suppliers to achieve new standards of efficiency. After Simon Marks came back from America in 1924 he remodelled Marks & Spencer to provide high-quality goods at low prices, together with a money back guarantee.'

Habitat

'The inspiration to change things came from asking myself what I had seen on my travels that worked well. For me the markets of France and the ironmongers' shops of France had all the sorts of qualities I found fascinating and exciting. Bringing these ideas together with the market needs in Britain led me to open the first Habitat shops.' (Terence Conran).

Source: John Adair, *The Art of Creative Thinking*, 1990

The successful visionary is someone who seeks a reputation for *excellence*. A key visionary insight is often one which sees *mismatches* between how things are done currently and how things might be done more effectively; often the market-winning formula is based simply on redefining the mundane.

Visionaries are *orientated towards action:* they prefer doing rather than planning, talk rather than writing. Their common management style is one of MBWA (management by wandering about), talking, listening, observing: as Richardson says, 'The classical, planner/manager view of the leader does not reflect the reality' of visionary leadership.

Effective visionaries are usually brilliant *communicators*, and this enables deeply thought-out visions to quickly become shared meanings. They operate as role models, leading by example and their actions can be summarised in just six words: 'Do anything you see me doing'. With this in mind, the visionary is consistent in rewarding activity which fits into the visionary values and also in punishing violations of them.

The visionary leader practices *empowerment* by allowing managers to lead their departments and feel some ownership for the effectiveness of the organisation as a whole. *Mintzberg* makes the point that visionary leaders become part of an 'empowerment loop': as well as empowering, the leader is empowered by his/her own followers within the organisation, whose trust, support and applause help further to strengthen the leader's position and thus the vision.

The visionary is a *calculated risk-taker*, checking out the acceptability of the vision before becoming publicly committed to it. In this way the leader ensures that he or she is never too far adrift for the wishes and inclinations of those who will act as followers.

Successful visionaries tend to be independent individuals, capable of making up their own minds. This autocratic side to their characters is necessary for the single-minded commitment required to instil vision and to get things done.

The visionary is *passionate about achievement*, with a capacity for hard work which is greater than that of most other people. This is matched by a dogged determination to overcome setbacks and to find ways round obstacles.

Finally, visionary leaders want to *make things happen*. They have a strong need to be in charge of their destinies and to be at the top of the organisation; further, they are optimistic, believing that the world is full of opportunities and that most things are possible.

A major paradox associated with visionary leadership is that some visionaries eventually sow the seeds of their own downfall because the positive features of leadership can produce very dangerous and ultimately disastrous side-effects.

12   THE INGREDIENTS OF LEADERSHIP DECLINE

The causes for leadership decline are varied, and may take the form of an extreme fear of success in others, or the inertia of the leader who simply runs out of energy, interest and enthusiasm. According to *John Van Maurik* (*Discovering the Leader in You*, 1994), there are six key ingredients in leadership decline.

The first resides in the *pressures of power*. This can happen when people who achieve promotion become isolated from former peers or create a climate in which reality is filtered before information reaches them.

Second is an *ability to continue learning* because of the apparent belief that leadership is associated with omniscience.

Loss of touch with reality is the third danger signal, in which the leader becomes obsessed with issues which are not central to the survival and growth of the organisation. If the leader loses touch with reality, then people below the leader may find themselves doing the same, in a phenomenon described by *Manfred Kites de Vries* as a *folie à deux*. Put bluntly, a *folie à deux* occurs when a leader drives his or her followers mad: the strong and largely unopposed influence of the leader breeds a contagious instability of behaviour and culture within the organisation. The symptoms of a *folie à deux* are as follows.

(a) *'Toe the party line or else'*, in other words, the need to conform to the correct ways of thinking and behaving within the organisation, so that self-expression and, ultimately, truth are suppressed.

(b) *Lack of creativity* which is a by-product of toeing the line.

(c) A *high level of secrecy* with information released strictly on a narrow 'need to know' basis.

(d) *People problems* because independent thinkers cannot operate in a folie à deux culture, whereas conforming sycophants are promoted.

(e) *Eccentricities of strategy and planning* which reflect the overriding preoccupation of the leader.

Fourth in the list is the *misuse and over-use of strengths*, significant because a once-successful leader may mistakenly attribute success to the display of a particular personal characteristic which, if practised even more single-mindedly, will guarantee continued success on an even more impressive scale. Thus Hitler, who won some famous victories by overruling his generals, may have concluded that it was appropriate to contradict his generals all the time – which was a mistake.

Insensitivity to the organisation's culture and people's expectations is fifth: it is easy for the culture and values to regress to something less successful as the leadership comes under pressure or starts to decline.

Finally, *fair wear and tear* may eventually take their toll as the leader loses energy and enthusiasm, although the decline of the leader is not inevitably associated with age. As Van Maurik comments,

'There is a difference between out-growing one's role and declining as a leader'.

Chapter roundup

- Culture in an organisation is the sum total of the beliefs, knowledge, attitudes of mind and customs to which people are exposed. It contains the basic, underlying assumptions of the organisation's members.

- Culture is influenced by the organisation's founder, its history, management style, structure and systems.

- Harrison identifies four cultures, which he relates to organisation structure: power, task, role and existential. Individuals are suited to one of the cultures, although all organisations contain elements of each of them.

- An alternative model of culture pays less attention to organisation structure than to the degree to which it is influenced by the environment. Four types are suggested: consistency, involvement, mission, adaptability.

- Culture is a strategic issue: it affects decision-making by filtering information and limiting choice.

- The strength of corporate culture is supposedly a feature of excellent companies. However, strong cultures can be resistant to change.

- Leadership involves a concern for the task itself and also a concern for people.

- Concern for people requires an understanding of what will motivate individuals to work harder and more effectively, and also an understanding of what can make a work group as a whole improve its motivation and norms of working.

- Leadership style is a factor influencing the motivation of individual subordinates and the attitudes of work groups.

- The most appropriate style of management for raising the level of employee efficiency and effectiveness will vary according to circumstances. This means that either:

  (i)   a manager might have to change his leadership style as the circumstances of his or her job change (eg when he is moved to a new job); however, it is difficult to turn an autocrat into a democrat, or vice versa – ie a leopard cannot change its spots; or

  (ii) it might be necessary instead to appoint managers who have a particular style of leadership to jobs where that style will be the most productive in the circumstances. However, at senior levels, a consultative or democratic style of leadership will almost certainly be the most productive.

Quick quiz

1 What are three basic aspects of culture?

2 What four types of organisation culture did Harrison identify?

3 On what two axes did Denison analyse organisation culture?

4 Miles and Snow described four cultures in terms of strategy. What are they?

5 What were the key dimensions Hofstede used to analyse differences in national cultures?

6 Is leadership the same thing as management?

7 What four styles of leadership were identified by the Ashridge studies?

8 What are the axes used on the Ohio State grid?

9 What is position power?

10 What behavioural patterns do charismatic leaders display?

Answers to quick quiz

1 Underlying assumptions; overt beliefs; visible artefacts.

2 Power, task, role, existential.

3 The nature of the environment and the extent of the organisation's orientation to it.

4 Defenders, prospectors, analysers and reactors.

5 Power distance; uncertainty avoidance; individualism- collectivism and masculinity.

6 No.

7 Tells, sells, consults, joins.

8 Concern for people and concern for production.

9 Power derived from position in the organisation.

10 Role modelling; image creation; confidence building; goal articulation; motive arousal.

Answers to activities

1 Obviously the answers to the questions contained within this activity will vary according to the culture of your particular family. What you should find, however, is that your family's 'way of doing things' will have its roots in the kinds of influences listed.

   (a) Your family's *founder* – or, more correctly, the influence of key figures in your family's background

   (b) Your family's *history*

   (c) Your family's *leadership and management style.* Many of the socialisation processes for new recruits to the family – children or individuals marrying into the family – will be aimed at producing commitment to this same style.

   (d) Your family's *structure and systems.* How are decisions made, for example, about where to go on holiday?

A common source of cultural dispute in families, especially as the children become mature and acquire partners, concerns adherence to prescribed rituals at Christmas or other holiday festivals. Where is Christmas Day spent? At what time of the day are presents opened? Is Christmas dinner a traditional feast of turkey, or would it be permissible to eat something different?

2   No solution can be advanced for this activity as it depends exclusively on the organisation selected for analysis. What is particularly interesting, however, is the possibility of a lack-of-fit between the organisation's culture and its requirements, or scenarios where the organisation is characterised by a mix of cultural types, each competing for dominance.

3   (a)   Zeus
     (b)   Apollo
     (c)   Athena
     (d)   Dionysus

4   (a)   Harrison's model places much more emphasis on organisation structure and systems, which both determine and are determined by culture. Harrison's model describes actual cultures. Denison's model describes *ideal* cultures, and is more concerned with the environment and a firm's external orientation than its structure. Denison suggests that if the environment is stable and the business is most effective with an internal orientation, *then* a consistency culture will be best etc.

     (b)   It depends on what you wish to use each model for.

5   Strategy (c), the gaining of BS EN ISO 9000 certification, is the likeliest strategic option, though perhaps not the best. The company's traditions of *craftsmanship* (eg the annual award) would appear to highlight quality issues as ones in which managers already have an interest. Subcontracting would be unthinkable, if it is an assumption of the corporate culture that outsiders cannot be trusted. The culture would predispose the company to doing 'more of the same'. The company would not realise that its production delays could be a competitive weakness: timeliness is not high on its list of priorities.

6   Here are some suggestions.

     IBM seems to have attempted to decentralise without obtaining any of the benefits of decentralisation. There appears to be something of a cultural mess because the organisation cannot let go of its past: bureaucracy smothers initiative; a task culture seems to be what is called for (and what seems to exist, to some extent, informally) but the organisation is unable to adapt to change.

     There are a number of other points you could make. For example, what parts of the organisation seems to have the greatest power and influence? How effective are the communication channels? Are the supervisors' spans of control too narrow?

7   So far as the first proposition is concerned, leadership is here being defined in organisational terms, as a contribution towards the achievement of an *organisation's* goals. However, if leadership is defined more generally, as the ability to influence others to work willingly towards goals which both the leader and his/her followers perceive to be worthwhile, then it becomes possible to see anti-organisational revolutionaries as leaders. Indeed, it is arguable that such individuals are more likely to be genuine leaders because their ability to influence is not

reinforced by any position power or legitimised status in and organisational hierarchy.

As far as the second proposition is concerned, J A C Brown in his book, *The Social Psychology of Industry*, held that if you are in a cinema, detect smoke or a smell of burning, shout 'Fire!' and run towards the exit, you will be a leader – but only if other people in the cinema, seeing you escape, decide to do the same and run towards the exit themselves. If you run towards the exit but nobody else leaves their seat, then you are definitely not a leader.

In some respects Brown's example is a bad one because the individual fleeing towards the exit and shouting 'Fire!' is not deliberately encouraging similar actions from others, and therefore, if there is a panic, the process should be accurately be described as *behavioural contagion*. 'Leadership', therefore, implies a conscious effort to influence others: if you yawn, and others feel an uncontrollable urge to do the same, then this can hardly be defined as leadership.

8   People who spend their lives trying to train leaders are obviously committed to the view that leaders *can* be made, even if some are born into it. On the other hand, there is an underlying assumption, in the views of Lord Slim, that leaders are born, and that if you have not exhibited the clear signs of leadership ability by an early age then you might as well give up.

The lives of unquestionable leaders like Churchill suggest that leadership is very *situational*, ie it derives from a mix between some personal attributes and circumstances in which those personal attributes suddenly become very productive, appropriate and relevant. On the other hand, some research indicates that successful leaders do tend to have certain background features in common, such as the experience of an unhappy childhood for one reason or another. Undoubtedly this applied, for instance, to such disparate leadership figures as Churchill himself, Adolf Hitler, Montgomery and Lady Thatcher.

9   (a)   The appropriate leadership style here would be *tell*, since you have an opportunity to see the departure of some less-than-competent staff. You could possibly modify your style into *sell*, if you can persuade these staff that their disposal is actually beneficial for them.

(b)   The *consult* style could work here: you explain your remedy to the staff and seek their views on the possibility that unknown problems will impede its effectiveness. Your staff may well be able to propose solutions to these problems as well – after all, they are as irritated as you about the situation, so it will be in their interests to find a way forward.

(c)   We prefer the *join* style. So long as your department's work is covered, it does not matter to you what the start and finish times are, so your staff may as well determine the issue themselves.

(d)   The *sell* or the *consult* styles could be appropriate, the latter being especially relevant if there are parts of your proposal which you would be prepared to modify in the light of contributions from the group.

(e)   We would use the *consult* method despite the apparent reluctance of staff to take responsibility for decisions. If indeed they do believe that you are paid to manage and therefore to take decisions, this will not stop them from being resentful if you select options they find unpalatable – so it would be as well to seek their views in the first place. Also, the persistent use of a *consult* approach may ultimately help to encourage greater levels of involvement within your team, with obvious benefits for productivity and the quality of decisions.

Further question practice

Now try the following practice questions at the end of this text

Multiple choice questions: **65 to 72**

Exam style question: **10**

Chapter 11 :
CONFLICT AND STRESS

Introduction

Conflict of some kind, and to some degree, is inevitable whenever two or more people are working (or living) together. In general, conflict is healthy in organisations and groups. It certainly cannot be argued that what *Janis* calls 'groupthink' – the kind of false unanimity which breeds complacency and self-righteous confidence – generates better decision making at any level of management. The issue is not the suppression of conflict, but the opportunity to achieve the potential benefits resulting from *constructive* conflict.

If conflict is *destructive*, however, it may produce some very harmful consequences for the group as a whole and its members.

This chapter investigates not only conflict *between* individuals, but also conflict *within* individuals – the kind of scenario typically associated with stress. It is widely assumed that levels of stress in organisations today are much higher than in the past, though we believe that the evidence for this is ambiguous at best. What seems to have happened is that the causes of stress are now different.

At one time stress was a product of *role underload*, when people were under-utilised and suffered 'rust-out' as their abilities and aptitudes withered through lack of use; in the 1990s stress is linked to *role overload*, with people being asked to take on wider responsibilities and simultaneously to achieve higher standards of performance. These expectations are likely to cause stress, especially within employees who have never been trained (for example) to manage their time or select priorities effectively.

Like any other problem, the causes of stress need to be understood before solutions can be found. Meanwhile, many individuals cope as best they can, often with the aid of palliatives (alcohol, tobacco, painkillers) and temporary absences from work coupled, ironically, with the perceived need to work longer hours. Even if there has been no increase in *objective* levels of stress, there are undoubted increases in the subjective awareness of stress and its symptoms, as the topic receives enormous publicity in the media.

In this chapter you will learn about these things.

(a)   The principal theories of conflict in organisations and within groups

(b)   The effectiveness of conflict-management and conflict-resolution processes

(c)   The causes and symptoms of stress within individuals as employees of organisations

(d)   The reasons for stress within modern organisations

(e)   Personal mechanisms for preventing and controlling stress

1 WHY STUDY CONFLICT?

'Conflict' is not as clear a concept as one might think. In this chapter we will look at conflict as a social process between individuals and groups, departments, levels in the hierarchy and *perceived* groups in the organisation. We also discuss sources of conflict within the individual.

You should be clear in your mind, however, that there is no clear-cut definition of, or approach to, conflict: there is much controversy in conflict research, as to what should be studied, and how, and how meaningful the results are. Various interest groups are likely to have different perspectives on the nature of the situation itself, as well as on the particular issues that create it.

For some parties for example management conflict will be a problem to be solved. From the point of view of the behavioural scientist, however, conflict may seem to be part of the steady state of organisations, so that co-operation, order and stability are more interesting phenomena to study.

2 THEORIES OF CONFLICT IN ORGANISATIONS

Since the 1960s, there has been a shift in the management perspective on conflict, from theories which stated that conflict is avoidable, caused by disruptive elements and detrimental to organisational effectiveness, to the view that conflict is inevitable, part of change, caused by structural factors such as the class system, and is useful (in small doses) if constructively handled.

2.1 The happy family view

The happy family view presents organisations as co-operative structures, designed to achieve agreed common objectives, with no systematic conflict of interest. They are harmonious environments, where conflicts are exceptional: when they occur they are caused by dysfunctional elements such as misunderstandings, personality factors, the expectations of inflexible employees or factors outside the organisation and its control.

Drucker writes in *The Practice of Management* that:

'Any business must mould a true team and weld individual efforts into a common effort. Each member of the enterprise contributes something different, but they must all contribute towards a common goal. Their efforts must all pull in the same direction, without friction, without unnecessary duplication of effort.'

This kind of view is reasonably common in managerial literature, which attempts to come up with training and motivational techniques for dealing with conflict in what are seen as potentially conflict-free organisations. Conflict is thus blamed on bad management, lack of leadership, poor communication, or bloody-mindedness on the part of individuals or interest groups. The theory is that a strong culture, good two-way communication, co-operation and motivational leadership will eliminate conflict.

The happy family view starts from a belief in social order or industrial peace: conflict is a threat to stability, and must be avoided or eradicated.

Activity 1   **(5 minutes)**

How accurate is the happy family perspective when applied to your own organisation, or to any organisation with which you are sufficiently familiar?

To what extent would you subscribe to the claim that the happy family view is publicised by managers within their own organisations, not so much as an accurate description of reality, but rather because adoption of the happy family perspective itself helps to reduce the level of articulated conflict?

2.2 The conflict view

In contrast, there is the view of organisations as arenas for conflict on individual and group levels. Members battle for limited resources, status, rewards and professional values. Organisational politics involve constant struggles for control, and choices of structure, technology and organisational goals are part of this process. Individual and organisational interests will not always coincide.

2.3 The evolutionary view

This view regards conflict as a useful basis for evolutionary rather than revolutionary change. Conflict keeps the organisation sensitive to the need to change while reinforcing its essential framework of control. The legitimate pursuit of competing interests can balance and preserve social and organisational arrangements. A flexible society benefits from conflict because such behaviour, by helping to create and modify norms, assumes its continuance under changed conditions.

This *constructive conflict* view may perhaps be the most useful for managers and administrators of organisations. It neither attempts to dodge the issues of conflict, which is an observable fact of life in most organisations nor does it seek to pull down existing organisational structures altogether.

Ideology apart, managers have to get on with the job of managing, maintaining society as a going concern, and upholding organisational goals with the co-operation of other members.

2.4 Ideologies of conflict

Ideologies are clusters of specific beliefs that individuals or groups hold. Clashes of ideology may be a cause of conflict in organisations, whether related to work and the organisation itself (for example, ideologies of the relationship between manager and worker or about the value of work) or to non-work factors (for example political, religious or cultural ideologies which may bring an individual into conflict with others). Political and social ideologies, in particular, are carried into the workplace.

Alan Fox (in *Industrial Relations and a Wider Society: Aspects of Interaction*) identifies three broad ideologies which are involved in industrial relations.

   (a)   *Unitary ideology.* All members of the organisation, despite their different roles, have common objectives and values which unite their efforts. Workers are loyal, and the prerogative of management is accepted as paternal, and in everyone's best interests. Unions are a useful channel of communication, but are no longer necessary, and can offer unhelpful encouragement to disruptive elements.

(b) *Pluralist ideology*. Organisations are political coalitions of individuals and groups which have their own interests. Management has to create a workable structure for collaboration, taking into account the objectives of all the various interest groups or stakeholders in the organisation. A mutual survival strategy, involving the control of conflict through compromise, can be made acceptable in varying degrees to all concerned.

(c) *Radical ideology*. This primarily Marxist ideology argues that there is an inequality of power between the controllers of economic resources (shareholders, managers) and those who depend on access to those resources (wage earners). Those in power exploit the others by indoctrinating them to accept the legitimacy of their rights to power, and thus perpetuate the system. Conflict between these strata of society – the proletariat and bourgeoisie – does not aim for mutual survival, but revolutionary change.

2.5 Interest groups

Conflicts of interest may exist throughout the organisation or even within a single individual. There may be conflicts of interest between local management of a branch or subsidiary and the organisation as a whole; or between sales and production departments in a manufacturing firm (over scheduling, product variation); or between trade unions and management. These are three common examples: you can no doubt identify many others.

Activity 2 (5 minutes)

What other examples of conflicts of interest can you identify within an organisation?

Having selected some instances, can you detect any common patterns in such conflicts?

There are also formal *interest groups*, that is, groups which are perceived to represent the interests of their members. Such groups tend to wield greater power in conflict situations than their members, and indeed the very existence of the groups may be seen to anticipate and perpetuate conflict, to harden and formalise a set of attitudes and values that their individual members may not themselves have recognised or expressed.

Trade unions

Trade unions are organisations whose purpose it is to promote their members' interests. Situations occur where trade union negotiators set targets for achievement of these goals which appear to be at odds with the targets set by management for the organisation (and its employees).

Disputes between management and unions may therefore be seen in the context of inter-organisational conflict, and individual members of both organisations may then feel a tug of loyalties in opposing directions. However, the officials of both organisations might succeed in reconciling their apparently conflicting goals.

Trade unions have a vested interest in the success of the commercial or government organisation to which their members belong because unless this organisation prospers, the security and rewards of their members will be restricted. For this reason, trade unions might be active in co-operative efforts with management to achieve growth through greater efficiency. They also share with management responsibility for good industrial relations.

It is important to be aware that trade unions are organisations in their own right, and we must not assume too hastily or too readily that the goals of a trade union organisation are the same as those of its members or full-time officials. The potential divergence between individual goals and an organisation's system goals exists for a union as well as for a company.

Occupational groups

Like trade unions, occupations and professions are interest groups, in that they represent the interests of their members and of their clients. Professional bodies and other occupational associations have their own objectives.

(a) To preserve standards of skill and knowledge by requiring training, experience or some qualification for membership, and by fostering the exchange of knowledge between members

(b) To preserve appropriate financial rewards, theoretically commensurate with their skills and knowledge

(c) To create a measure of independence, for example in the regulation of conduct and ethics and the right to control their own concerns. This may be considered a kind of deal made with society and other organisations, in which self-determination is allowed in return for high standards of service.

Other interest groups include other organisations (for example suppliers or customers), shareholders, consumer associations, government and regulatory bodies, all of whom are in positions to bring a certain amount of pressure to bear on organisations to have their interests preserved.

3 THE MANAGEMENT OF CONFLICT

3.1 Constructive and destructive conflict

Given that conflict is inevitable, and assuming that organisational goals are broadly desirable, there are two aspects of conflict which are relevant in practice to the manager.

(a) Conflict can be highly desirable. It can energise relationships, clarify issues and lead to a variety of benefits.

  (i) The generation of new and different solutions to problems, because of the synergy arising from creative tensions within the group

  (ii) More clearly defined power relationships within the group, thus reducing uncertainties and role ambiguity

  (iii) Encouragement of innovative activity and brainstorming

  (iv) A focus on individual contributions rather than a mistaken sense of group consensus where dissent is inhibited or even suppressed completely

  (v) The open discussion of emotive arguments

  (vi) The cathartic expression of emotions (for example, in the expression of interdepartmental or inter-personal rivalries)

(b) Conflict can also be destructive, or negative and injurious to social systems. It can lead to a variety of undesirable outcomes.

(i)   Dislocation of the entire group, with polarised relationships

(ii) The displacement of the group's proper objectives by dysfunctional behaviour (for example, it becomes more important to denigrate ideas produced by others than to examine their merits dispassionately)

(iii) Defensive and blocking behaviour within the group

(iv) The emergence of win-lose arguments, where reason is secondary to emotion

Ultimately, destructive conflict may result in disintegration of the entire group or organisation.

When analysing a particular case, it is difficult to know whether a given conflict is constructive or destructive, because sometimes what appears to be a very heated and negative argument can have very positive outcomes. For example, although a strike may normally be seen by both managers and trade union members as destructive and hostile, in fact it can provide a subsequent focus for attention and an opportunity for catharsis. Too much co-operation and agreement may conversely produce a 'love-in', where completing the task (or achieving the group/organisational objective) becomes secondary to enjoyment of the interpersonal processes.

EXAMPLE: EXPERIMENTAL FINDINGS

Tjosvold and Deerner researched conflict in different contexts. They allocated to 66 student volunteers the roles of foremen and workers at an assembly plant, with a scenario of conflict over job rotation schemes. Foremen were against, workers for.

One group was told that the organisational norm was to 'avoid controversy'; another was told that the norm was 'co-operative controversy', trying to agree; a third was told that groups were out to win any arguments that arose, 'competitive controversy'. The students were offered rewards for complying with their given norms. Their decisions, and attitudes to the discussions, were then monitored.

(a) Where controversy was avoided, the foremen's views dominated.

(b) Competitive controversy brought no agreement – but brought out feelings of hostility and suspicion.

(c) Co-operative controversy brought out differences in an atmosphere of curiosity, trust and openness: the decisions reached seemed to integrate the views of both parties.

Charles Handy redefined the term 'conflict' to offer a useful way of thinking about destructive and constructive conflict and how it might be managed.

(a) Organisations are political systems within which there is *competition* for scarce resources and unequal influence.

(b) *Differences* between people are natural and inevitable. Differences emerge in three ways.

- Argument
- Competition
- Conflict: this alone is considered wholly harmful.

Argument and competition are potentially beneficial and fruitful; both may degenerate into conflict if badly managed.

Argument means resolving differences by discussion; this can encourage integration of a number of viewpoints into a better solution. Handy suggests that in order for argument to be effective the arguing group must have shared leadership, mutual trust, and a challenging task and the logic of the argument must be preserved: the issues under discussion must be classified, the discussion must concentrate on available information, and the values of the individuals must be expressed openly and taken into account.

Otherwise, argument will be frustrated. If this is so, or if the argument itself is merely the symptom of an underlying, unexpressed conflict, then conflict will be the result.

Competition can set standards, by establishing best performance through comparison and motivate individuals to better efforts. It can also be used to identify high performers.

In order to be fruitful, competition must be *open*, rather than *closed*; or, rather, must be *perceived* by the participants to be open, rather than closed. Closed competition is a zero-sum game, where one party's gain will be another party's loss in competition for resources, recognition and so on. Open competition exists where all participants can increase their gains, as for example, in productivity bargaining.

If competition is perceived to be open, the rules are seen to be fair, and the determinants of success are within the competitors' control, competition can be extremely fruitful. The observations of *Peters and Waterman* on the motivational effect of comparative performance information supports this view. If these preconditions are not met, competition may degenerate into conflict.

3.2   Causes, symptoms and tactics of conflict

Conflict may be caused by differences in the *objectives* of different groups or individuals. Managers have two responsibilities.

(a)   To create a system of planning whereby individual or group objectives are formulated within the framework of a strategic plan. A poor planning structure leaves the door open for conflict to enter where formal objectives, roles and authority relationships overlap or are unclear.

(b)   To provide leadership, and to encourage individuals to accept the goals of the organisation as being compatible with their personal goals. Poor leadership might also lead to conflict, with the goals of individuals or groups diverging and at odds with each other.

Conflict may also be caused by disputes about the *boundaries of authority*.

(a)   Managers from the technostructure may attempt to encroach on the roles or territory of line managers and usurp some of their authority.

(b)   One department might start empire building and try to take over the work previously done by another department.

Personal differences, as regards goals, attitudes and feelings, are also bound to crop up.

According to Handy, there will be five observable *symptoms* of conflict in an organisation.

(a)   Poor communications

(b)   Interpersonal friction

(c)   Inter-group rivalry and jealousy

(d)   Low morale and frustration

(e)   Proliferation of rules, norms and myths; especially widespread use of arbitration, appeals to higher authority, and inflexible attitudes towards change.

There are numerous *tactics* of conflict.

(a) One manager will withhold information from another. A manager who lacks some important information will be in a weak position for making decisions or urging his or her own views. Keeping information away from a rival manager is a very effective tactic for increasing influence and extending the boundaries of one's own authority and influence.

(b) Information might be presented in a distorted manner. This will enable the group or manager presenting the information to get their own way more easily. For example, if the engineering department wants to introduce a new item of equipment into service, they might give biased information about likely teething troubles with the equipment's technology or the expected costs of maintenance, or breakdown times.

(c) A group (especially a specialist group such as the finance department) which considers its influence to be neglected might seek to impose rules, procedures, restrictions or official requirements on other groups, in order to bolster up their own importance.

(d) A manager might seek to by-pass formal channels of communication and decision-making by establishing informal contacts and friendships with people in a position of importance. A departmental manager might establish informal contacts with the managing director's personal assistant, and so gain an advantage over other departmental managers, by having a friend close to the managing director's ear.

(e) Line managers might refuse to accept a member of the technostructure to fill a vacancy in their department. Similarly, line managers might refuse to accept the recommendations of staff department experts. This attitude of conflict by line managers towards staff management is more likely to occur where staff departments use tactics of their own to obtain more influence over line department operations.

(f) Conflict might also take the form of fault-finding in the work of other departments: Department X might duplicate the work of department Y – hoping to prove department Y wrong – and then report the fact to senior management.

3.3 Managerial response to conflict

Hunt identifies five different management responses to the handling of conflict – not all of which are effective.

(a) *Denial/withdrawal:* 'sweeping it under the carpet'. If the conflict is very trivial, it may indeed blow over without an issue being made of it, but if the causes are not identified, the conflict may grow to unmanageable proportions.

(b) *Suppression:* 'smoothing over', to preserve working relationships despite minor conflicts. As Hunt remarks, however: 'Some cracks cannot be papered over'.

(c) *Dominance:* the application of power or influence to settle the conflict. The disadvantage of this is that it creates lingering resentment and hostility.

(d) *Compromise:* bargaining, negotiating, conciliating. To some extent, this will be inevitable in any organisation made up of different individuals. However, individuals tend to exaggerate their positions to allow for compromise, and compromise itself is seen to weaken the value of the decision, perhaps reducing commitment.

(e) *Integration/collaboration*. Emphasis must be put on the task, individuals must accept the need to modify their views for its sake, and group effort must be seen to be superior to individual effort. Not easy.

Handy suggests two types of strategy which may be used to turn conflict into competition or argument, or to manage it in some other acceptable way.

(a) *Environmental ('ecological') strategies* involve creating conditions in which individuals may be better able to interact co-operatively with each other: they are wide-ranging, time-consuming, and unpredictable, because of the sheer range of human differences. Such strategies involve five activities.

- Agreement of common objectives
- Cultural reinforcement of team work ethics
- Providing feedback information on progress
- Providing adequate co-ordination and communication mechanisms
- Sorting out territorial and role conflicts in the organisational structure

(b) *Regulation strategies* are intended to control conflict, though in fact they make it so much a part of the formal structure of the organisation that they tend to legitimise and even perpetuate it.

(i) The provision of arbitration to settle disputes

(ii) The establishment of detailed rules and procedures for conduct by employees

(iii) Appointing a person to manage the area of conflict: a liaison or co-ordination officer

(iv) Using confrontation, or inter-group meetings, to hammer out differences, especially where territorial conflicts occur

(v) Separating the conflicting individuals

Activity 3 **(15 minutes)**

In the light of the above consider how conflict could arise, what form it would take and how it might be resolved in the following situations.

(a) Two managers who share a secretary have documents to be typed.

(b) One worker finds out that another worker who does the same job as he does is paid a higher wage.

(c) A company's electricians find out that a group of engineers have been receiving training in electrical work.

(d) Department A stops for lunch at 12.30 while Department B stops at 1 o'clock. Occasionally the canteen runs out of puddings for Department B workers.

(e) The Northern Region and Southern Region sales teams are continually trying to better each other's results, and the capacity of production to cope with the increase in sales is becoming overstretched.

4   GROUP COHESION, COMPETITION AND CONFLICT

4.1   Conflict within groups

In an experiment reported by *Deutsch* (1949), psychology students were given puzzles and human relations problems to work at in discussion groups. Some groups ('co-operative' ones) were told that the grade each individual got at the end of the course would depend on the performance of his group. Other groups ('competitive' ones) were told that each student would receive a grade according to his own contributions.

No significant differences were found between the two kinds of group in the amount of interest and involvement in the tasks, or in the amount of learning. But the co-operative groups, compared with the competitive ones, had greater productivity per unit time, better quality of product and discussion, greater co-ordination of effort and sub-division of activity, more diversity in amount of contribution per member, more attentiveness to fellow members and more friendliness during discussion.

4.2   Conflict between groups

Another experiment, conducted in 1949 by *Sherif and Sherif*, set out to investigate how groups are formed, and how relationships between groups are created. 24 boys of about 12 years old were taken to a summer camp. After a few days, natural affinities were discounted by breaking up friendships which had formed, and dividing the boys into two formal groups, the Bulldogs and the Red Devils.

It was found that when the groups were formed there was a noticeable switch of friendships. Boys whose previous best friends were moved into the other group began to switch to someone else who belonged to their group. The group identity thus had a significant effect on the attitudes of individual members.

The experimenters also tried to create friction between the groups; these efforts were so successful that by the end of the experiment there was such intense inter-group rivalry that subsequent attempts to re-unite the entire camp were insufficient to restore common goodwill. From this, and other research, it is argued that new members of a group quickly learn the norms and attitudes of the others, no matter whether these are positive or negative, friendly or hostile. It is also suggested that inter-group competition may have a positive effect on group cohesion and performance.

Sherif's later research in 1965 provided more data.

Each competing group shows similar behaviour

(a)   Members close ranks and submerge their differences; loyalty and conformity are demanded.

(b)   The climate changes from informal and sociable to work and task-oriented: individual needs are subordinated to achievement.

(c)   Leadership moves from democratic to autocratic, with the group's acceptance.

(d)   The group tends to become more structured and organised.

Three things happen when groups compete.

(a)   The opposing group begins to be perceived as the enemy.

(b)   Perception is distorted, presenting an idealised picture of 'us' and a negative stereotype of 'them'.

(c)   Inter-group communication decreases, facilitating the perceptual distortion.

Where competition is not perceived to result in benefits for both sides, the *winning group* will retain its cohesion but relax into a complacent, playful state. It will return to group maintenance and concern for members' needs and will be confirmed in its group self-concept with little re-evaluation.

The losing group will behave differently.

(a)   It will deny defeat if possible, or place the blame on the arbitrator, or the system.

(b)   It will lose its cohesion and splinter into conflict, as 'blame' is apportioned.

(c)   It will be keyed-up, fighting mad.

(d)   It will turn towards work-orientation to regroup, rather than members' needs or group maintenance

(e)   It will tend to learn by re-evaluating its perceptions of itself and the other group. It is more likely to become a cohesive and effective unit once the defeat has been accepted.

Members of a group will act in unison if the group's existence or patterns of behaviour are threatened from outside. Cohesion is naturally assumed to be the result of positive factors such as communication, agreement and mutual trust – but in the face of a common enemy (competition, crisis or emergency) cohesion and productivity benefit. *Lippitt and White* indicated that the degree of aggression displayed by a group can also be related to leadership style. Groups led in an authoritarian way tended to be aggressive.

Activity 4   **(15 minutes)**

How applicable are Sherif's 1965 research findings to the causes, symptoms and treatment of conflict in a modern organisation? In what ways, if at all, could Sherif's findings be used as a means of improving employee performance within an organisation?

4.3   Cohesion and groupthink

It is possible for groups to be *too* cohesive, too all-absorbing. Handy notes that

'ultra-cohesive groups can be dangerous because in the organisational context the group must serve the organisation, not itself.'

If a group is completely absorbed with its own maintenance, members and priorities, it can become dangerously blinkered to what is going on around it, and may confidently forge ahead in a completely wrong direction. I L Janis describes this as *groupthink:* 'the psychological drive for consensus at any cost, that suppresses dissent and appraisal of alternatives in cohesive decision-making groups.'

Highly political organisations and areas of the organisation structure – for example the top and centre – also tend to put pressure on individuals to avoid rocking the boat, whether this be expressed as cultural control through tradition and shared values or as more overt rules and sanctions.

Since by definition a group suffering from groupthink is highly resistant to criticism, recognition of failure and unpalatable information, it is not easy to break such a group out of its vicious circle. It must be encouraged to become actively self-critical; to welcome outside ideas and evaluation and to respond positively to conflicting evidence.

Conflict can thus be a valuable stimulus to thought.

The risky shift phenomenon

Risky shift is a phenomenon suggested by the discussion of groupthink above. It is the term given to the tendency of individuals in groups to take greater risks than their individual, pre-discussion preferences. *Stoner* illustrated the phenomenon in experiments with groups of management students in 1961.

Explanations for the phenomenon include the sharing and therefore diffusion of any *sense of responsibility* for the outcome of the decision and the reinforcement during discussion of *cultural values* associated with risk, like courage, boldness, strength. In some cultures – especially those fostered in the mid 1980s by contemporary ideas on excellence, innovation, entrepreneurship and so on – such values may be put forward as desirable, and risk aversion derided.

There are, however, problems of validity with the risky shift research. The experiments are conducted on artificial, short-lived, leaderless groups in artificial situations. The decisions they are called on to make are purely hypothetical, and have no practical effect: it is easy to take risks if there is no real downside involved. The research cannot be used to formulate predictions about group decision-making in real-life contexts. In addition, results have varied; the size of the shift (and even its direction) are by no means consistent, from hypothetical situation to situation, from individual to individual, or from study to study.

5 STRESS

Stress is a term which is often loosely used to describe feelings of tension or exhaustion – usually associated nowadays with too much, or overly demanding, work. In fact, stress is the product of demands made on an individual's physical and mental energies: psychological dissonance and psychological failure are sources of stress, as much as the conventionally considered factors of pressure or overwork.

It is worth remembering, too, that demands on an individual's energies may be stimulating (some people work well under pressure) as well as harmful (causing strain). Many people require some form of stress to bring out their best performance: excessive stress, however, can be damaging. This is why we talk about stress management, not stress elimination: it is a question of keeping stress to helpful proportions and avenues.

A lot of nonsense is talked and written about so-called 'executive stress' as if executives suffer from stress rather more than other occupational groups. The evidence almost universally indicates the opposite. Certainly life expectancy increases as one goes further up the occupational ladder, with white-collar groups living noticeably longer than blue-collar workers. Moreover, blue-collar workers score higher in job dissatisfaction, boredom, depression, anxiety, frustration and anger; for manual workers there is often a poor fit between job requirements and capabilities, with little change of participation in significant decision making, coupled with unclear work roles.

(a) *Hinckle et al*, in their study of 270,000 employees in a large US corporation, found that skilled manual workers are 2.5 times more prone than executives to disabling coronary heart disease.

(b) *Pell and D'Alonzo* found similar results among 1,356 cases of myocardial infarction among 10,000 employees in industrial corporations.

(c) *Finlay-Jones and Burrel* conclude that minor psychiatric morbidity is more common among blue-collar workers.

Activity 5   **(5 minutes)**

If there is indeed something of a myth about executive stress, why is this myth so widespread?

5.1   Symptoms of stress (strain) and methods of coping

Harmful stress can be identified by its effects on individuals and their performance.

(a)   *General features of stress:* stress produces persistent negative changes in psychological functioning

(b)   *Mood changes:* irritability, resentment, panic feelings, anxiety, guilt or depression

(c)   *Cognitive changes:* trouble in concentrating and difficulty in making decisions

(d)   *Behavioural changes:* making errors, double-checking everything, increasing use of palliatives such as coffee, painkillers, sleeping tablets and tranquillisers.

(e)   *Secondary physical symptoms:* disturbed sleep, headaches, chest pains, indigestion and dizziness.

Individuals have various methods of coping with stress:

(a)   Withdrawal

(b)   Repression or refusal to admit the existence of the problem. Forced cheerfulness, playfulness or excessive drinking may indicate that this is occurring, as may exhibitions of irritability outside work, if the problem has been transferred elsewhere.

(c)   Rationalisation, that is, deciding simply to endure, or come to terms with, the situation, if it is inevitable. Stress can be contained, so that its harmful effects may be alleviated. Nervous tension can be reduced by the creation of opportunities for rest, recreation and generally getting things into perspective, areas of stability and non-work stimulation. The organisation may be able to help by offering time, facilities or counselling.

In the remainder of this section we will look at the causes and control of stress under four headings.

- Role theory
- Insecurity
- Personality variables
- Management style

5.2   Role stress

The kinds of role problems discussed in the earlier chapter on perception and social influence – role ambiguity, role incompatibility and role conflict – all lead to stress. There are two other problems we might also include here.

(a)   *Role overload* occurs when an individual has too many roles to cope with, and feels out of his depth, for example on moving from an operational to a management position.

(b)   *Role underload* occurs when an individual moves into a role or set of roles which he perceives as being below his capacity and out of line with his self-concept.

Role overload leads to the kind of stress associated with *burn-out; role underload* is linked to *rust-out*, where the individual's brain atrophies because of insufficient exercise. Because of the changes typical in modern organisations, *rust-out* has been replaced by *burn-out* as a manifestation of stress: it is very doubtful whether the actual incidence of stress has altered.

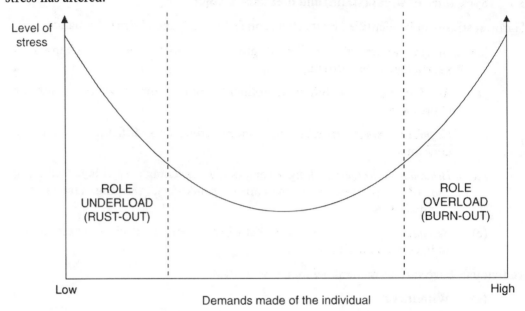

The stress in such situations can be resolved in the following ways.

(a)   The individual can take unilateral action to redefine his or her role, the scope of the job, the roles which are most personally important and those which can be downgraded. He or she will then have to force his or her expectations on the others involved – which may aggravate stress in inter-personal relations.

(b)   The individual can co-operate with other members of the role set, to try and classify or resolve his or her role(s) relative to other demands. This may be a matter of redrafting job-descriptions, boundaries of authority or timetables to make room for conflicting demands.

Only role underload offers no possibility of a co-operative solution, such as those in (b) above. It can only be alleviated by the exercise of nuisance power – which increases the individual's perceived importance, if only in a negative sense – or by encroaching on someone else's role.

5.3   Insecurity

Other situations in which stress may be particularly acute involve uncertainty, and therefore insecurity, together with a sense of responsibility for their outcome.

(a)   A manager may have to initiate change or growth: attempts at innovation may be highly stressful, especially if there is an element of risk. *Burns and Stalker* suggested that organic structures and cultures are required by conditions of rapid change in an organisation's technological or market environment, but are only suited to people with a high tolerance of ambiguity, uncertainty and change. People with high security needs suffer more from the new emphasis on innovation, flexibility and adaptability in organisation cultures. In addition, changes in skill requirements arising from new markets and technologies may threaten the individual's sense of competence and even job security.

(b) Career change, end or uncertainty. Worrying about burn-out or redundancy or retirement, or even about ability to cope with promotion can be a source of stress. The pace of change in technology and markets adds to the uncertainties which now attach to the work environment in this respect. Manufacturing industries have been declining in job terms for some years, but the same pressures are now being felt in service sectors as well.

Managers will have to ensure that uncertainty is reduced as far as possible by the availability of relevant information. Management style will be important in offering accessibility in the event of problems, offering positive reinforcement, establishing trust and arranging for counselling and training where necessary.

5.4 Personality

Most people experience stress of some kind, at some time: there are simply some individuals who handle it better than others, and it is important for organisations to identify those individuals. *Pincherle* did a study of 2,000 UK managers at a medical centre, and found that physical symptoms of stress were related to age, and to the level of responsibility, especially responsibility for other people. But are there types of people who are more prone to stress than others?

In a 1968 study of heart disease, *Drs Rosenman and Friedman* advanced the hypothesis that there are two categories of people, 'type A' and 'type B'.

(a) Characteristics of type A.

    (i) Intense drive and aggression

    (ii) Ambition and a competitive personality

    (iii) Constant pressure to get things done

    (iv) Sense of urgency

    (v) Decisiveness

    (vi) Rapid speed (but few words)

    (vii) Tendency to arrive on time or early

    (viii) 'Polyphasic thinking' (ie the capacity to juggle several balls in the air at once)

    (ix) A preference to scheduling more in less time

(b) Type B people have the opposite set of features: they are not competitive, seldom become agitated about the passage of time, are sequential thinkers, and speak slowly.

Type A people are the get up and go people in an organisation, the self-starters and the innovators – but they tend to develop some unhealthy symptoms like high blood pressure, dangerous levels of cholesterol, coupled with smoking and drinking. Thus (according to Rosenman and Friedman), type A managers are twice as prone to the onset of clinical heart disease, five times more prone to a second heart attack and twice as prone to fatal heart attacks – when compared with average members of the population. Again according to Rosenman and Friedman, type A managers are not very likely to make it to the top of corporate hierarchies, partly because of a Darwinian 'natural selection' system which (in effect) weeds them out, and partly because although type A qualities are desirable for middle managers, they are much less relevant for top management positions, where strategic wisdom is preferable to rapid response.

Some people seem to *feel* less stress than others. Others, like type A managers, may feel it acutely, but try to *overcome* it – with consequent risk to health. Personality traits which might affect one's ability to cope with stress, in either fashion, include the following.

(a)   *Sensitivity*. Emotionally sensitive individuals are pressured more by conflict and doubt, which insensitive people are more able to shrug off (although in extreme cases, insensitivity may prove such a barrier to satisfactory relationships with others, that another source of stress may be created).

(b)   *Flexibility*. Individuals who are seen to give in to pressure tend to invite further pressure from those who seek to influence them: intractable, stubborn individuals may suffer less from this. However when they are subjected to pressure, they tend to snap rather than bend, as there is more dissonance involved in their giving way.

(c)   *Inter-personal competence*. The effects of stress may be handled better from a basis of strong, supportive relationships with others, and indeed many role problems may be solved by maintaining and fostering relationships and reaching co-operative solutions. The individual who turns his back on others in times of stress, like a wounded animal, is unlikely to find a satisfactory resolution.

(d)   *Sense of responsibility*. Some individuals have a casual outlook – where their own affairs are concerned, as well as those of others that are affected by their actions. Others have a more acute sense of owing other people something, or of their accountability to others for the consequences of their decisions and actions. The burden of perceived guilt can be a very painful source of stress.

5.5   Management style

In an article in the *Administrator* (January 1987), *Sarah Rookledge* describes the findings of an American report entitled: 'Working Well: Managing for Health and High Performance'. The report pointed out particular management traits that were held responsible by workshop interviewees for causing stress and health problems (high blood pressure, insomnia, coronary heart disease and alcoholism).

- *Unpredictability:* (staff work under constant threat of an outburst).
- *Destruction of workers' self esteem* makes them feel helpless and insecure.
- *Setting up win/lose situations* turns work relationships into a battle for control.
- *Providing too much – or too little – stimulation.*

In British research, according to the same article, managers are criticised for other failings.

- Not giving credit where it is due
- Failing to communicate policy or involve staff in decisions
- Supervising too closely
- Not defining duties clearly enough

The most harmful style of management is said to be *leave alone and zap* – where the employee is given a task, left without guidance, and then zapped with a reprimand or punishment when mistakes are discovered. This simply creates a vicious circle of anxiety and guilt.

Greater *awareness* of the nature and control of stress is also a feature of the modern work environment, through the work of writers such as *Dr Cary Cooper*, and through educational programmes in the work place. *Stress management techniques* are increasingly taught and promoted by organisations.

- Time off or regular rest breaks
- Relaxation techniques like breathing exercises and meditation
- Biofeedback
- Physical exercise and self-expression as a safety valve for tension
- Delegation and planning to avoid work-load related stress
- Assertiveness to control stress related to insecurity in personal relations

In addition, *job training* can increase the individual's sense of competence and security.

Ecological control is also being brought to bear on the problem of stress, by creating conditions in which stress is less likely to be a problem. This may be achieved through job enrichment; organisation culture built on meaningful work; mutual support, communication and teamwork; and social activities and leisure facilities.

There is some good news for those who believe themselves to be in the type A mould, because according to some recent studies, type A individuals are not invariably doomed to an early death through heart disease. Instead, some type A people live and thrive, whereas some type B managers die young.

The significant discriminator here seems to be not just the presence of type A or type B characteristics, but also the degree to which individuals believe they are in control of their lives. 'Control' here is defined by *Taylor and Cooper*, in a 1989 article, as

'A generalised expectancy concerning the extent to which an individual believes that reinforcements, rewards or success are either internally or externally controlled.'

(a)   An *internal locus of control* suggests a belief in one's personal power, control and ability to influence the outcome of events.

(b)   An *external locus of control* refers to the notion that personal power has only a minimal impact on the outcome of events; more important elements are fate, chance and 'powerful others'.

Combining the type A and type B continuum on the one hand, with the control continuum on the other, produces a four-category classification of individuals.

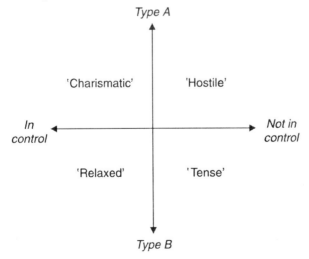

(a)   *Charismatics*, according to Friedman, are 'healthy, expressive, dominant, fast-moving, in control, coping well and sociable'. They have a high life expectancy.

(b) *Hostiles* are also competitive, expressive and dominant, but in a threatened, negative sense. They are often victims of the AHA syndrome (anger, hostility and aggression).

(c) The *relaxed* group are 'quiet, unexpressive, somewhat submissive [and] content'.

(d) *Tense* people appear to be controlled and are seemingly unexpressive and inhibited, but in fact are liable to 'explode under sufficient challenge'.

The numbers in the hostile quadrant are increasing because of the pressures placed on people nowadays, creating demands for both breadth and depth of achievement which many managers, in particular, find threatening. As a result, they may feel themselves to be running faster and faster in order to keep abreast of the pace of change, worried constantly by their inability to cope and eternally anxious about what will come next. Small wonder that such managers react violently when subordinates bring them more problems, or their bosses give them something more to be completed against a very tight deadline.

Similarly, tense people give every impression of being in charge of themselves and their lives, whilst in practice they are simply bottling up their stress and frustration.

Clearly there are personal benefits associated with being in control. Some of the remedies are listed above, but in general terms it is essential to become aware of the extent to which lives are dominated by others, so that we can attempt to be more selective in choosing priorities and more assertive in coping with avoidable interruptions.

Activity 6 (15 minutes)

There must have been times when you have felt frustrated at work and probably when you have suffered from stress (unless you are very lucky). Think of two specific occasions and see if you can identify the causes and recognise the symptoms (as described above). How did you resolve the situation in each case and what help did you have?

Do others around you suffer from stress or frustration? Are you a help or a hindrance to them?

---

6   CO-OPERATION

We have discussed co-operation by implication in our study of conflict and earlier in groups, but we will summarise its nature briefly here.

(a) Co-operation is a common cultural habit, and one that is basic to any economic system. In work organisations it is universally believed that co-operation is a Good Thing, and achieves greater productivity than lack of co-operation. For most tasks, this is proven by experience.

(b) Co-operation requires a set of shared values and the subordination of individual needs and differences to the needs of the 'team'.

(c) Co-operation has a rational appeal. It is demonstrable that a suitable number of people co-operating on a task will achieve a better result than one person doing the same task. *Synergy* may enable 2 + 2 to equal 5.

(d) Co-operation has an emotional appeal. It incorporates values about unity, teamwork, comradeship and insiders versus outsiders.

(e) Some cultures encourage this value-cluster more than others. In the UK, individualism is a major aspect of the national culture – despite stated views on the virtues of co-operation. *Hofstede's* observations of West German, Japanese and Swedish cultures, however, demonstrate an emphasis on co-operation and inter-dependence, rather than individuality.

(f) Methods of encouraging co-operation have already been discussed in connection with reinforcing cultures, communication, team cohesiveness and the control of conflict. Remember, however, that co-operation itself may even involve a certain amount of argument or competition.

Chapter roundup

- Conflict can be viewed as: inevitable owing to the class system; a continuation of organisation politics by other means; something to be welcomed as it avoids complacency; something resulting from poor management, or something which should be avoided at all costs.

- Conflict is possible owing to the different degrees of power, influence and authority that different groups have. Negative power, for example, is the power to disrupt.

- Conflict can be constructive, if it introduces new information into a problem, if it defines a problem, or if it encourages creativity. It can be destructive if it distracts attention from the task or inhibits communication.

- Managers can respond to conflict either by 'ecological' strategies which reduce the conditions for conflict, or regulation strategies which institutionalise it.

- Some conflicts at work arise out of stress, frustration and alienation endured by the individual for a number of reasons. Such behaviour might be a response to management style.

- Stress is associated with role underload (leading to rust out) and role overload (leading to burn out). The latter is more common nowadays, as a result of increasing pressures for performance throughout organisations.

- Stress can be linked to differing personality profiles with notable differences between type A and type B.

Quick quiz

1 What is the happy family view of conflict?

2 What is the pluralist ideology in industrial relations?

3 Why do trades unions have an interest in the success of the organisations their members work for?

4 What is the difference between open and closed competition?

5 What symptoms of conflict does Handy identify?

6 What conclusions may be drawn from Sherif and Sherif's 1949 experiment?

7   What is groupthink?

8   Are executives more affected by stress than manual workers?

9   How does role stress arise?

10   Which personality traits affect ability to cope with stress?

Answers to quick quiz

1   Conflict is dysfunctional, unnatural and avoidable by good management.

2   Organisations are political coalitions of interest groups and management must work towards collaboration and compromise.

3   Their members long term prosperity depends on their employers' success.

4   Open competition allows all participants to benefit; closed competition is a zero-sum game.

5   Poor communication; interpersonal friction; inter-group rivalry and jealousy; low morale and frustration; proliferation of rules, arbitration, appeals to higher authority and inflexible attitudes.

6   New group members quickly learn group norms and attitudes; intergroup competition can promote group cohesion and performance.

7   'The psychological drive for consensus at any cost that suppresses dissent and appraisal of alternatives.'

8   Probably not.

9   Role ambiguity, incompatibility, conflict, overload and underload.

10   Sensitivity, flexibility, interpersonal competence and sense of responsibility.

Answers to activities

1   The happy family perspective rarely fits most organisations, even those pursuing a common ideological goal, like a political party. Such organisations regularly face conflict (eg the Labour party's divisions over welfare policy), if only about *how* to attain their goals. Cynics argue that managers promote the happy family view to suppress conflict.

2   Conflicts occur anywhere in an organisation. Individuals, groups, departments or subsidiaries compete for scarce financial, human and physical resources.

3   (a) Both might need work done at the same time. Compromise and co-ordinated planning can help them manage their secretary's time.

      (b) Differential pay might result in conflict with management - even an accusation of discrimination. There may be good reasons for the difference, such as length of service. To prevent conflict, such information should be kept confidential. Where it is public, it should be seen to be not arbitrary.

      (c) The electricians are worried about their jobs, and may take industrial action. Yet if the engineers' training is unrelated to the electricians' work, management can allay fears by giving information. The electricians cannot be given a veto over management decisions: a win-lose situation is inevitable, but both sides can negotiate.

(d) The kitchen should plan its meals better - or people from both departments can be asked in advance whether they want puddings.

(e) Competition *between* sales regions is healthy as it increases sales. The conflict lies between sales regions and the production department. In the long-term, an increase in production capacity is the only solution. Where this is not possible, proper co-ordination methods should be instituted.

4   Sherif's work applies to conflict in organisations. To improve employee performance, win-lose conflict can be turned towards competitors, who become the enemy.

5   Some executives might like to believe that they are heroically battling for survival. So-called executive stress might even be perceived as a mark of status. Given workplace changes, it cannot be entirely written off as a myth.

6   Possible situations are: deadlines; excessive overtime; conflict with a colleague or boss; lack of confidence; boredom.

Further question practice

Now try the following practice questions at the end of this text

Multiple choice questions: **73 to 81**

Exam style question: **11**

Chapter 12 :
INNOVATION, CREATIVITY AND THE LEARNING ORGANISATION

Introduction

Much has been written in academic circles about the increasing need for innovation if organisations are to survive in a fast-moving competitive environment. In 1983, a Royal Dutch Shell survey found that one-third of the firms in the Fortune 500 in 1970 had vanished, and Shell estimated that the average lifetime of the largest industrial enterprises is less than forty years – roughly half the lifetime of a human being.

In most organisations that fail, there is abundant evidence in advance that the organisation is in trouble. This evidence goes unheeded, however, even when individual managers are aware of it. The organisation as a whole cannot recognise impending threats, understand the implications of those threats, or come up with alternatives.

Innovation, adaptability and flexibility of response are critical ingredients for organisational survival; they are equally relevant necessities for individuals. For both organisations and people, too, *continuous learning* is a precondition for prosperity, not only to keep up with change but also, preferably, to move ahead of it. Against this background, the concept of the *learning organisation* makes sense, even if the expression is confusing because, by themselves, organisations cannot learn. As we have already seen, however, in our discussion of visionary leadership, *people* can learn: in so doing, they can transform the world around them.

In his book, *The Fifth Discipline, Peter Senge* has made the distinction between adaptive and generative learning. Adaptive learning is about coping with the situation, adapting and responding positively to the changing environment. Generative learning is about being creative, about expanding one's ability and actively looking for new solutions – whether as an individual or as an organisation. Not surprisingly, this chapter links learning and innovation because of their interactive significance for the individuals and organisations of tomorrow.

In this chapter you will learn about these things.

(a) The essential roles of learning and innovation for the competitive advantage of individuals and organisations

(b) Ways in which organisations can both encourage and stifle innovation on the part of their employees

(c) The differences between entrepreneurship and intrapreneurship, and the relevance of each to organisational change

(d) The factors that encourage creativity within organisations

(e) The concept of the learning organisation and its significance for the future

(f) The techniques, processes and underlying philosophy essential to the development of a learning organisation

1   INNOVATION AND THE NEED TO LEARN

Innovation is a term that is often associated with *change*. An *innovation* is something completely new. *Change* doesn't necessarily mean doing something entirely new. Innovation creates change, but change isn't always innovative.

The rate of change might be fast or slow, depending on the organisation's circumstances, and the environment in which it operates. A rapidly changing or *turbulent* environment requires a more innovative response than a stable one. Very few organisations operate in a *static* environment. You might argue that capitalist society is geared up for change, and all organisations within such a society must innovate continually just to survive.

Tom Peters has stated that one of the keys to organisational success is constant innovation. However, constant innovation is not necessarily a terribly easy practice to achieve. After all, innovation can occur in a variety of areas. Here are some examples.

(a)   New product technology (eg Philips Digital Compact Cassette, Sony's Mini-Disk)

(b)   New features on existing technology (eg auto-focus on cameras)

(c)   Production technology (eg advanced manufacturing technology)

(d)   Storage and distribution (eg purchase of computers by mail order; increasing sales of exotic fruit)

(e)   Marketing (eg cosmetics as ecologically friendly; identifying new market segments)

(f)   Services (eg package holidays were once an innovation; credit and debit cards)

(g)   Organisational culture and structure (eg delayering and empowerment)

In short, innovation can occur anywhere in an organisation's life. All can be used for an organisation's benefit.

Peters goes further, and says that innovation is essential. Why might this be so?

(a)   One suggestion is given by a Japanese management theorist *Ikujiro Nonaka* (*Harvard Business Review* November-December 1991).

'*In an economy where the only certainty is uncertainty, the one sure source of lasting competitive advantage is knowledge. When markets shift, technologies proliferate, competitors multiply, and products become obsolete almost overnight, successful companies are those that consistently create new knowledge, disseminate it widely throughout the organisation, and quickly embody it in new technologies and products. These activities define the 'knowledge-creating' company, whose sole business is continuous innovation.*'

(b)   Another way of expressing this is to state that

'*where quality, technology and variety are all becoming widely available at relatively low cost, the only sustainable competitive advantage that a company can create may be the ability to learn faster than its rivals and to anticipate changes in the business environment.*' (*Financial Times 17 February 1992*).

However, constant innovation requires a constant flow of ideas. Where do these come from?

•   From a caste of innovators?
•   From management?

- From anyone?

As innovation can affect any aspect of an organisation's activities, so too can the ideas which drive it come from any part of the organisation, and in theory from any member of it.

1.1 The scope of innovation

The chief object of being innovative is to ensure the organisation's survival and success in a changing world. It can also have the following advantages.

(a) Improvements in quality of product and service

(b) A leaner structure, with layers of management or administration may be done away with, and the need for specialist support may be reduced

(c) Prompt and imaginative solutions to problems (through use of project teams)

(d) Less formality in structure and style leading to better communication

(e) Greater confidence inside and outside the organisation in its ability to cope with change

One of the necessary corollaries of innovation is *increased delegation*. Part of the creed is to give subordinates more authority so they can act on creative ideas. In itself delegation has great value: morale and performance are improved, top management is freed for strategic planning and decisions are made by those closest to the problems. Most importantly the organisation benefits from the imagination and thinking of its high flyers. Warning bells ring, however, when delegation is confused with lack of control.

'*The line between efficient corporate performance through delegation and anarchy resulting from a loss of total control is a very fine one.*'

Alec Reed (MD, Reed Executive)

The logical consequence of being continuously innovative and involving all personnel in initiative-taking amidst consistent change would indeed seem to be anarchy and chaos. Chaos is seen as a positive thing by Tom Peters in his 1987 book, *Thriving on Chaos*. He suggests that a company which reacts proactively with chaos will thrive; it is 'a source of market advantage, not a problem to be got round'.

The dilemma then is between the need to be innovative so as to deal with a chaotic environment and the need to retain control over employees so as to *prevent anarchy*. This can be done simply by giving employees and managers parameters within which discretion can be exercised, and by ensuring that they know they are accountable for their actions.

It is a common mistake to view innovation and creativity as special mental processes carried out by rather special people (like painters and inventors) to produce important new products, services, delivery mechanisms or manufacturing technologies. In thinking like this, we may fall into the definition trap: once we define creativity and innovation as something which special people do then we won't find examples of it in everyday life.

Another mistake is to produce only narrow definitions of the kinds of situations for which innovation and creative thinking are appropriate. As *Tudor Rickards* says, there are very few 'one right answer problems' in organisations, simply because any problem situation will always have some features which differentiate it from similar scenarios encountered in the past. Instead, most so-called problems (or one of the opportunities) for individuals and organisations fall into categories below.

(a)   *Insight ('Aha') problems* which turn out to have unexpected answers which may be discovered by a 'Eureka' experience. Insight puzzles do not usually have one demonstrably correct response, though one solution (often called the elegant solution) may have a particularly strong appeal – in that sense, insight thinking is reminiscent of De Bono's lateral approach to problem-solving.

(b)   *Wicked problems* are those where the supposed solution cannot be proved until it has actually been implemented. This applied, for instance, to organisational restructuring or business acquisitions and mergers. Decision-takers dealing with wicked problems require courage, intuition and follow-up creativity to solve the unexpected difficulties of implementation. People who need logical proof before acting will try to avoid wicked problems, but will never achieve significant innovation.

(c)   *Vicious problems* are like wicked problems, but involve people: when conventional remedies are applied, they turn out to create even bigger problems than were there in the first place (eg the introduction of competitive incentive schemes in organisations in order to improve performance may have the unexpected and unwanted side-effect of reducing interpersonal and intergroup co-operation). Other examples include industrial relations dilemmas and business scenarios with scope for 'lose-lose' outcomes. Opportunities for creativity and innovation here turn principally on looking beyond the obvious for solutions with less vicious consequences.

(d)   *Fuzzy problems* are situations with unclear boundaries which make them difficult to resolve by the use of logical or analytical approaches. Wicked and vicious problems are frequently fuzzy and so are many other non-trivial difficulties that people encounter in their working and personal lives (eg personal career planning).

Activity 1   **(5 minutes)**

Try to think of current or recent situations in your life which could be classified as 'fuzzy', 'wicked' or 'vicious' problems.

If any of your examples have already been resolved, how did that resolution come about?

---

2   ENCOURAGING INNOVATION

To encourage innovation, management should create a more outward-looking organisation. People should be encouraged to use their initiative to look for new products, markets, processes, designs and ways to improve productivity. *Thomas Attwood* suggests the following steps for creating an innovative culture from one which has previously existed in a cosy, unthreatening world.

(a)   Ensure management and staff know what innovation is and how it happens.

(b)   Ensure that senior managers welcome, and are seen to welcome, changes for the better.

(c)   Stimulate and motivate management and staff to think and act innovatively.

(d)   Understand people in the organisation and their needs.

(e)   Recognise and encourage potential entrepreneurs.

Small companies appear to produce a disproportionate a number of innovations because innovation occurs in a probabilistic setting: the sheer number of attempts by small-scale entrepreneurs means that some ventures will survive. The 90 to 99 per cent that fail are distributed widely throughout society and receive little attention.

On the other hand, large companies must absorb all potential failure costs; even if an innovation is successful, the organisation may face costs that newcomers do not have to bear, like converting current operations and customer-profiles to the new solution. Such barriers to change in large organisations are real, important and legitimate.

The research suggests that the following factors are crucial to the success of innovative small organisations.

(a)   *Need orientation:* lacking resources, successful small entrepreneurs soon find that it pays to approach potential customers early, test their solutions in the user's hands, learn from their reactions and adapt their designs rapidly.

(b)   *Experts and fanatics:* commitment allows the entrepreneur to persevere despite the frustrations, ambiguities and setbacks that always accompany major innovations.

(c)   *Long time horizons:* time horizons for radical innovations make them essentially irrational from a present-value viewpoint – delays between invention and commercial success can range from three to 25 years.

(d)   *Low early costs:* innovators incur as few overheads as possible, their limited resources going directly into their projects. They borrow whatever they can and invent cheap equipment or processes, often improving on what is available in the marketplace.

(e)   *Multiple approaches:* committed entrepreneurs will tolerate the chaos of random advances in technology, adopting solutions where they can be found, unencumbered by formal plans that would limit the range of their imaginations.

(f)   *Flexibility and quickness:* undeterred by committees, the need for board approvals and other bureaucratic delays, inventor-entrepreneurs can experiment, recycle and try again, with little time lost. They quickly adjust their entry strategies to market feedback.

(g)   *Incentives:* tangible personal rewards are foreseen if success is achieved and the prospect of these rewards (which may not be principally of a monetary nature) is a powerful driver.

Within large *organisations* the following barriers to innovation and creativity may typically be encountered.

(a)   *Top management isolation:* financially-focused top managers are likely to perceive technological innovation as more problematic than, say, acquisitions or organic growth: although these options are just as risky, they may appear more familiar.

(b)   *Intolerance of fanatics:* big companies often view entrepreneurial fanatics as embarrassments or trouble makers.

(c)   *Short time horizons:* the perceived corporate need to report a continuous stream of upward-moving, quarterly profits conflicts with the long time-spans that major innovations normally require.

(d)   *Accounting practices:* a project in a big company can quickly become an exposed political target since its potential *net present value* may sink unacceptably.

(e)   *Excessive rationalism:* managers in large organisations often seek orderly advance through early market research studies or systematic project planning.

(f)   *Excessive bureaucracy:* bureaucratic structures require many approvals that cause delays; the interactive feedback that fosters innovation is lost, important time windows can be missed and real costs and risks rise for the corporation.

(g)   *Inappropriate incentives:* when control systems neither penalise opportunities missed nor reward risks taken, the results are predictable.

Successful large organisations, in the field of innovation and creativity, have developed techniques that emulate or improve on the approaches used in small, fleet-of-foot companies. The most important patterns are as follows.

(a)   *Atmosphere and vision.* Continuous innovation occurs largely because top managers appreciate innovation and support it. They project clear long-term vision for the organisation that goes beyond simple economic measures.

(b)   *Orientation to the market.* Within innovative organisations, managers focus primarily on seeking to anticipate and solve customers' emerging problems.

(c)   *Small, flat hierarchies.* Development teams in large organisations normally include only six to seven key people; operating divisions and total technical units are kept below 400 people.

(d)   *Multiple approaches.* Where possible, several prototype programmes are encouraged to proceed in parallel. Such redundancy helps the organisation to cope with uncertainties in development, motivates people through competition and improves the amount and quality of information available for making final choices on scale-ups or new-product/service introductions.

(e)   *Development shoot-outs.* The most difficult problem in the management of competing projects lies in re-integrating the members of the losing team. For the innovative system to work continuously, managers must create a climate that honours high-quality performance whether a project wins or loses, reinvolves people quickly in their technical specialities or in other projects and accepts rotation among tasks and groups.

(f)   *Skunkworks.* This is the name given the system in which small teams of engineers, technicians, designers and model makers are placed together with no intervening organisational or physical barriers, to develop a new product from idea to commercial prototype stage. This approach eliminates bureaucratic controls; allows fast, unfettered communications; permits rapid turnround times for experiments; and instils a high level of group identity and commitment.

(g)   *Interactive learning.* Recognising that the random, chaotic nature of technological change cuts across organisational and even institutional lines, the big company innovators tap into multiple sources of technology from outside as well as to their customers' capabilities.

2.1 Creativity and innovation

Creative ideas can come from anywhere and at any time, but if management wish to foster innovation they should try to provide an organisation structure in which innovative ideas are encouraged to emerge.

(a) Innovation requires creativity. Creativity may be encouraged in an individual or group by establishing a climate in which free expression of abilities is allowed. The role of the R&D department will be significant in many organisations.

(b) Creative ideas must then be rationally analysed to decide whether they provide a viable proposition.

(c) A system of organisation must exist whereby a viable creative idea is converted into action through effective control procedures.

The pressures of innovation

The *Financial Times* in June 1986 reported the ideas of *Rosabeth Moss Kanter* on leadership styles. She criticises excessively authoritarian and non-participative management on the ground that it stifles innovation and entrepreneurship. Her list of 'Rules for stifling innovation' is a critique of 'management by terror'.

1 Regard any new idea from below with suspicion.

2 Insist that people who need your approval first go through several other levels of management.

3 Get departments/individuals to challenge each other's proposals.

4 Express criticism freely, withhold praise, instil job insecurity.

5 Treat identification of problems as signs of failure.

6 Control everything carefully. Count everything in sight – frequently.

7 Make decisions in secret, and spring them on people.

8 Do not hand out information to managers freely.

9 Get lower-level managers to implement your threatening decisions.

10 Above all, never forget that you, the higher-ups, already know everything important about the business.

Activity 2   **(5 minutes)**

How far does your organisation exemplify any of the ten rules for stifling innovation listed by Rosabeth Moss Kanter?

How far, on the other hand, does your organisation exhibit any of the more positive features connected with innovation and creativity as listed above?

In *When Giants Learn to Dance*, Moss Kanter went on to describe some of the impossible or incompatible demands made in order to achieve improved performance and excellence through innovation, such as the following.

(d) *Accounting practices:* a project in a big company can quickly become an exposed political target since its potential *net present value* may sink unacceptably.

(e) *Excessive rationalism:* managers in large organisations often seek orderly advance through early market research studies or systematic project planning.

(f) *Excessive bureaucracy:* bureaucratic structures require many approvals that cause delays; the interactive feedback that fosters innovation is lost, important time windows can be missed and real costs and risks rise for the corporation.

(g) *Inappropriate incentives:* when control systems neither penalise opportunities missed nor reward risks taken, the results are predictable.

Successful large organisations, in the field of innovation and creativity, have developed techniques that emulate or improve on the approaches used in small, fleet-of-foot companies. The most important patterns are as follows.

(a) *Atmosphere and vision.* Continuous innovation occurs largely because top managers appreciate innovation and support it. They project clear long-term vision for the organisation that goes beyond simple economic measures.

(b) *Orientation to the market.* Within innovative organisations, managers focus primarily on seeking to anticipate and solve customers' emerging problems.

(c) *Small, flat hierarchies.* Development teams in large organisations normally include only six to seven key people; operating divisions and total technical units are kept below 400 people.

(d) *Multiple approaches.* Where possible, several prototype programmes are encouraged to proceed in parallel. Such redundancy helps the organisation to cope with uncertainties in development, motivates people through competition and improves the amount and quality of information available for making final choices on scale-ups or new-product/service introductions.

(e) *Development shoot-outs.* The most difficult problem in the management of competing projects lies in re-integrating the members of the losing team. For the innovative system to work continuously, managers must create a climate that honours high-quality performance whether a project wins or loses, reinvolves people quickly in their technical specialities or in other projects and accepts rotation among tasks and groups.

(f) *Skunkworks.* This is the name given the system in which small teams of engineers, technicians, designers and model makers are placed together with no intervening organisational or physical barriers, to develop a new product from idea to commercial prototype stage. This approach eliminates bureaucratic controls; allows fast, unfettered communications; permits rapid turnround times for experiments; and instils a high level of group identity and commitment.

(g) *Interactive learning.* Recognising that the random, chaotic nature of technological change cuts across organisational and even institutional lines, the big company innovators tap into multiple sources of technology from outside as well as to their customers' capabilities.

2.1 Creativity and innovation

Creative ideas can come from anywhere and at any time, but if management wish to foster innovation they should try to provide an organisation structure in which innovative ideas are encouraged to emerge.

(a) Innovation requires creativity. Creativity may be encouraged in an individual or group by establishing a climate in which free expression of abilities is allowed. The role of the R&D department will be significant in many organisations.

(b) Creative ideas must then be rationally analysed to decide whether they provide a viable proposition.

(c) A system of organisation must exist whereby a viable creative idea is converted into action through effective control procedures.

The pressures of innovation

The *Financial Times* in June 1986 reported the ideas of *Rosabeth Moss Kanter* on leadership styles. She criticises excessively authoritarian and non-participative management on the ground that it stifles innovation and entrepreneurship. Her list of 'Rules for stifling innovation' is a critique of 'management by terror'.

1 Regard any new idea from below with suspicion.

2 Insist that people who need your approval first go through several other levels of management.

3 Get departments/individuals to challenge each other's proposals.

4 Express criticism freely, withhold praise, instil job insecurity.

5 Treat identification of problems as signs of failure.

6 Control everything carefully. Count everything in sight – frequently.

7 Make decisions in secret, and spring them on people.

8 Do not hand out information to managers freely.

9 Get lower-level managers to implement your threatening decisions.

10 Above all, never forget that you, the higher-ups, already know everything important about the business.

Activity 2 **(5 minutes)**

How far does your organisation exemplify any of the ten rules for stifling innovation listed by Rosabeth Moss Kanter?

How far, on the other hand, does your organisation exhibit any of the more positive features connected with innovation and creativity as listed above?

In *When Giants Learn to Dance*, Moss Kanter went on to describe some of the impossible or incompatible demands made in order to achieve improved performance and excellence through innovation, such as the following.

Demands of managers		
Be entrepreneurial and risk taking	*but*	Don't lose money
Invest in the future	*but*	Keep profitable now
Do everything you're doing now but even better	*but*	Spend more time communicating, on teams and new projects
Lead and direct	*but*	Participate, listen, co-operate
Know everything about your business	*but*	Delegate more
Work all hours	*but*	Keep fit
Be single-minded in your commitment to ideas	*but*	Be flexible and responsive

Demands of organisations		
Be 'lean and mean'	*but*	Be a good employer
Be creative and innovative	*but*	'Stick to the knitting'
Decentralise to small, simple autonomous units	*but*	Centralise to be efficient and integrative
Have a sense of urgency	*but*	Deliberately plan for the future

2.2 Creativity and creative thinking

We have already looked at some of the conditions needed if innovation and creative thinking are to flourish. On a more personal (as opposed to organisational) level, these are the typical obstacles to creativity.

(a) *Experience and habit.* It is difficult to avoid ready-made solutions when the current problem appears similar to one dealt with successfully in the past. Yet past experience can be a poor guide to problem-solving today.

(b) *Over-motivation and over-exertion.* New ideas seldom occur when the individual is under too much pressure, since the brain develops something similar to a feedback effect, going round and round with nothing getting in.

(c) *The lack of a positive outlook.* A positive approach ('the problem *can* be solved') is more likely to produce an answer than a negative attitude ('It can't be done').

(d) *Premature evaluation of possible solutions.* This involves either the immediate dismissal of one's own ideas as they come to mind, on the grounds that all one's own ideas are automatically inadequate, or the failure to express an idea because of fear of criticism from others.

(e) *Excessive reliance on so-called 'expert' advice.* The dangers of listening to 'experts' too much are well illustrated by the case of the bumblebee. Aerodynamically it seems that the bumblebee should be unable to fly, but (fortunately for the bumblebee) it cannot read books on aerodynamics. Remember that experts once said that the Titanic was unsinkable.

(f) *A generalised resistance to new ideas.* This is expressed through such sentiments as 'It would never work', 'It's not practical', 'Why change something when it's working all right?'.

(g) *Whole-brain thinking.* The brain's neo-cortex is divided into two. Because the left hemisphere processes speech, it is often characterised as verbal, logical and step-by-step; the right hemisphere processes pictures and has therefore been thought to be more visual, more pattern manipulating, more intuitive and more creative. In practice the division between the two halves of the brain is more apparent than real, at least psychologically, and creative thinking is not associated with the abandonment of left-brain dominance: as Tudor Rickards puts it,

'At the moment of insight creativity may well be the result of both sides of the brain working together.'

(h) *Mind sets and perception patterns generating 'stuckness'.* Mind sets lead to 'stuckness' when things have changed but everything continues to look the same. We are then too ready to accept the similarities with the past, and carry on too long with our incorrect assumptions before discovering our error (eg pilots who fail to notice when dials show abnormal readings).

(i) *Intellectual backgrounds associated with analytical and systematic thinking.*

'Successful scientists and engineers are often their own worst enemies in a creativity setting. Their training and prior successes compel them to blot out things that seem silly, or that smack of irrational thinking and fanciful excursions. Yet these are the very practices that lead one down new alleys and passages that may culminate in creative new solutions.' (William E Souder and Robert W Ziegler, 'A review of creativity and problem-solving techniques', Research Management, 1977).

Activity 3   **(5 minutes)**

Given the above list of barriers or obstacles to innovation and creative thinking, what positive steps can you take in order to increase your own personal creative powers?

2.3 Post-excellence

What Moss Kanter identified in 1989 was a weariness with superheroes and an inability to fit the notion of 'excellence' into the 'mundane issues managers struggle with every day'. In the post-entrepreneurial revolution there is a backlash against the idea that managers should do more with less.

What she observed was that large companies are converging on a balance between bureaucracy (the old order) and entrepreneurship/innovation (the new order) based on synergies, alliances and 'newstreams'.

(a) *Synergy* occurs in a combination of businesses, internal services and organisation structures which means that the whole is worth more in value than the sum of the parts. People at all levels focus on doing what they do best.

(b) Organisations are also seeking to extend their reach without increasing their size by forming *alliances* (closer working relationships) with other organisations. This involves partnerships and joint ventures as well as contracting out services to outside suppliers. It results in improved access to information and technology, and quicker responses. However, alliances are vulnerable to management failures and so must be carefully selected; in addition they involve genuine moves away from bureaucracy and hierarchy.

(c) A flow of new business possibilities within the organisation is termed a *newstream* by Moss Kanter. But instead of relying on the lucky break of an innovation just happening, official channels are created to speed the flow of new ideas such as special funds, creativity centres and incentives. To ensure that newstream projects are successful the strategies must be implemented effectively and differently to mainstream projects by being sensitive, flexible, persistent and autonomous. Most importantly, an organisation should not get involved in a newstream activity unless it understands and expects the financial and organisational uncertainties which tend to surround them, as well as the effects they have on mainstreams: often, the latter regard themselves as the 'have nots' and the newstreams as the 'haves' who are allowed to prove new ideas.

Finally, Moss Kanter identifies certain human attributes required of the post-entrepreneurs.

(a) They must learn to operate without the support of a bureaucracy.

(b) They must be competitive in a way which enhances rather than undercuts co-operation.

(c) They must operate to the highest ethical standards.

(d) They must have a dose of humility (in order to effect alliances and facilitate synergies).

(e) They need to be aware that how things are done is as important as what is done.

(f) They must not be narrow-minded nor rigid.

(g) They must gain satisfaction from results.

2.4 Entrepreneurship and intrapreneurship

Koontz, O'Donnell and Weihrich list the 'entrepreneurial' aspects of managing.

- Profit maximisation
- Risk-taking
- Innovation

'We usually think of an entrepreneur as existing only in business – as a person who sees a business opportunity, obtains the needed capital, knows how to put together an operation successfully, and has the willingness to take a personal risk of success or failure. But in a real sense we see entrepreneurial ability also as an important input in most non-business operations.'   *Koontz et al*

Garfield (Peak performers: The New Heroes in Business) quotes the example of 3M.

'It is company policy to measure the results of innovation, and actually to require it. At least 25 percent of sales in every 3M division each year must come from products introduced within the last five years. Toward that end, employees can spend 15 percent of their office time on independent projects.'

Peters and Waterman define 'excellent' as 'continually innovative'. They, too, note that the promotion of exploration, experimentation, willingness to change, opportunism and internal competition create an entrepreneurial climate in organisations that keeps them adaptive to their environment and enables consistent success.

Business Basics: Organisational behaviour

Intrapreneurial groups

An intrapreneur pulls together diverse strengths within the organisation to promote innovation. In 1982 *Macrae* developed the idea that a company should consider several different ways of doing the same thing by creating separate intrapreneurial groups consisting of a small number of people, each group being in competition with the others. Together each group would seek the best way of doing something to maximise productivity.

Macrae used the example of a small typing pool as an intrapreneurial group within a large pool, each person being paid for what he or she produced rather than merely for turning up at work. Each group was autonomous in its organisation. He identified great differences in the groups' operations compared with classical structures.

Macrae's intrapreneurial groups		
	Role organisation	*Intrapreneurial organisation*
Emphasis	Bureaucracy	Enterprise
Control	Exercised by managers down	Internal within group by members
Size orientation	Single large unit	Many small units
Inter-unit relation	Co-ordination	Competition
Relationship to centre	Strictly controlled	Independent
Work flexibility	Low	High
Sphere of operation	Company	Company but can also take on outside work
Leadership	Appointed by management	Group's choice of leader accepted by management
Work design	Done by experts and managers	Done by group members themselves

3 KNOWLEDGE AND LEARNING

A criticism levelled at British universities and industries is that the UK has, historically, been good at creating ideas, but not so good at converting these into products and services. There is little point for an organisation to encourage creativity, unless this creativity can be exploited for the organisation's benefit.

EXAMPLE: ACCURATE CUTTING SERVICES LTD

The Guardian reported (23 March 1994) that a firm, Accurate Cutting Services Ltd, had been asked to cut through a meteorite 4,500 million years old, so that its component parts could be distributed to a number of museums. The firm's distinctive competence is in precision cutting, and this distinctive competence arises not only out of acquiring the right equipment, but the knowledge of what sort of blades should be used, where they can be obtained, and so on. Underpinning this distinctive competence therefore would be knowledge about materials (which have different cutting requirements) and knowledge about precision cutting.

Ikujiro Nonaka holds that the successful creation of *ideas*, as opposed to the mere processing of information, depends on a number of organisational factors.

(a) 'Creating new knowledge is not simply a matter of processing objective information. Rather it depends on tapping the highly subjective insights, intuitions, and hunches and making those insights available for testing and use by the company as a whole'. This has two aspects.

    (i) No one individual or group of individuals can, even in principle, be the source of all knowledge about a firm's activities

    (ii) There must be a way whereby all individuals can communicate their insights to other members of the organisation, so that these insights flow into a pool of knowledge from which the whole company can draw

(b) Furthermore, there is the idea that a company is a *living organism*. This means that it can learn.

Nonaka identifies two types of *knowledge*. These he derives from a small case history. A company wished to make a bread-making machine. After several trials and errors, one of its researchers suggested visiting a master baker to see how he kneaded and rolled his dough. These movements were eventually incorporated in a product specification.

(a) The product specifications for the machine are an example of *explicit knowledge*. This is formal, and systematised, and can easily be shared and communicated.

(b) The baker's skills and techniques are an example of *tacit knowledge*, which is personal and rooted in a specific context. Whilst the baker developed his technique through trial and error over many years, he may not have realised the scientific principles underlying his actions, and might not have been able to articulate accurately what he did.

Nonaka describes four basic patterns for creating knowledge.

(a) *From tacit to tacit*. The baker's skills might be transferred to an apprentice. However, the knowledge is not systematised, so is hard to analyse.

(b) *From explicit to explicit*. This is the standard way by which management information (eg monthly accounts) is created and synthesised.

(c) *From tacit to explicit (articulation)*. This is what occurred with the baker's tacit knowledge being transformed into the explicit knowledge of a product specification.

(d) *Explicit to tacit (internalisation)*. Individuals take in the knowledge, and it becomes part of their set of expertise (rather like learning to drive which becomes second nature).

Nonaka argues that Japanese companies have been better than American or European companies at type (c) and (d) knowledge interchanges, and it is these which generate new knowledge and information. This is contradicted, perhaps, by the record of innovation by US and European companies.

However, these interchanges of knowledge have to be managed, to ensure an interchange between individual tacit knowledge and shared explicit knowledge. Tacit knowledge has to be tapped and articulated. Nonaka suggests a number of techniques.

(a) In discussion, metaphors, analogies and models are ways of stimulating thought.

(b)   A 'conceptual umbrella' can encourage innovation (the slogan 'steady as she goes' would imply do not 'innovate at all'; the slogan 'let's gamble', as used by Honda in the late 1970s to motivate its designers, sends quite a different message).

These techniques are by no means unique to Japanese companies, although these were the bases of Nonaka's research.

Activity 4   **(5 minutes)**

Nonaka suggests that the use of metaphors and analogies can be a very useful way of stimulating new ideas and new perspectives. Test your own ability in this field by trying either of the following.

(a)   In how many ways is an idea like an iceberg?

(b)   In how many ways is working in an organisation like driving along a motorway?

Both technical and management skills are embodied in the ways people relate to each other in the organisation.

The learning organisation therefore does three things.

- It encourages continuous learning and knowledge generation at all levels.
- It has the processes to move knowledge around the organisation.
- It can transform knowledge into actual behaviour.

Senge argues that to create a learning organisation, individuals and groups should be encouraged to learn five disciplines.

(a)   *Systems thinking.* This is the ability to see particular problems as part of a wider whole, and to devise appropriate solutions to them.

(b)   *Personal learning and growth.* Individuals should be encouraged to acquire skills and knowledge.

(c)   *Mental models.* These are deeply ingrained assumptions which determine what individuals think. Mental models must be made explicit, challenged and developed until management teams share appropriate ideas.

(d)   There must be a *shared vision*, but not so forceful as to discourage organisational learning. It should not filter knowledge which undermines the vision.

(e)   *Team learning.* Some tasks can only be done in groups. Teams, however, must be trained to learn, as there are factors in group dynamics which impede learning.

Organisational learning would seem to turn some of the ideas about managing on their head, as it is about *group* communication and responsiveness. It also challenges some of the assumptions about creativity (eg that it resides only in the individual) that underpin one of the basic stereotypes of Western culture.

Finally, we need to note here two types of learning.

- Learning actual knowledge.
- Learning *how to learn*, in other words how to acquire new knowledge.

According to Peter Senge, there are seven sources of learning disability in organisations which prevent them from attaining their potential – which trap them into mediocrity when they could be achieving excellence.

(a) *'I am my position'*. When asked what they do for a living, most people describe the tasks they perform, not the *purposes* they fulfil; thus they tend to see their responsibilities as limited to the boundaries of their position. As a result, individuals within departments can be performing efficiently, yet when you put the efforts of several departments together, the result is more poor quality and performance than would have been the case had the various departments pooled their efforts.

(b) *'The enemy is out there'*. A by-product of 'I am my position', a result of over-identification with the job is the fact that if things go wrong it is all too easy to imagine that somebody else 'out there' was at fault.

(c) *The illusion of taking charge*. True learning should lead to proactivity, but too often proactiveness can mean that the individual decides to be more active in fighting the enemy out there, trying to destroy rather than to build. Senge states that if we believe the enemy to be 'out there' and we are 'in here', then proactiveness is really reactiveness in overdrive: true proactiveness comes from seeing how our own actions contribute to our problems.

(d) *The fixation on events*. Conversations in organisations are dominated by concern about events (last month's sales, who's just been promoted, the new product from our competitor), and this focus inevitably distracts us from seeing the longer-term patterns of change. At one time, concentrating on events was essential to man's survival (you had to worry about whether you had a sabre-toothed tiger over your left shoulder) but today, according to Senge, 'the primary threats to our survival, both of our organisations and of our societies, come not from sudden events but from slow, gradual processes'.

(e) *The parable of the boiled frog*. Maladaptation to gradually building threats to survival is so pervasive in systems studies of corporate failure that it has given rise to the parable of the boiled frog. If you place a frog in a pot of boiling water, it will immediately try to scramble out; but if you place the frog in room temperature water, he will stay put. If you heat the water gradually, the frog will do nothing until he boils: this is because 'the frog's internal apparatus for sensing threats to survival is geared to sudden changes in his environment, not to slow, gradual changes'.

(f) *The delusion of learning from experience*. We learn best from experience, but we never experience the results of our most important and significant decisions. Indeed, we never know what the outcomes would have been had we done something else.

(g) *The myth of the management team*. All too often, the management 'team' is not a team at all, but is a collection of individuals competing for power and resources, forming short-term alliances when it suits them, looking for someone to blame when things go wrong. *Chris Argyris* believes that

> *'Most management teams break down under pressure. The team may function quite well with routine issues. But when they confront complex issues that may be embarrassing or threatening, the 'teamness' seems to go to pot.'*

Activity 5   **(10 minutes)**

How far do Senge's seven learning disabilities apply to your own organisation, or to some other significant organisation with which you may be familiar?

---

4   CHARACTERISTICS OF THE LEARNING ORGANISATION

The chief executive of Shell stated at the start of the 1990s that

'The ability to learn faster than your competitors may be the only sustainable advantage for the nineties.'

But what is *learning?* Organisations must view their environment and forge a direction based on a meaningful product/service portfolio, a proactive approach to turbulence and a shared vision. It is the way and speed with which people learn within the organisation that will make the competitive difference. Effective delegation, coaching, facilitation and empowerment will make all the difference in the *application* of that learning. Amersham International has found that the forecasts it made about itself five or ten years ago bear little relationship to what it is actually doing today: as a result, it correctly places little reliance on today's projections into the future. How can Amersham International train and develop its people, then, if the future is largely unknown? The company's answer is that it wants employees to value learning almost for its own sake. To that end Amersham International encourages staff to learn more or less anything, whether obviously work-related or not, so that they will be more receptive to learning when it becomes essential in order to fulfil a new consultancy assignment. Amersham International comes close to being the paradigm for a *learning organisation*, therefore, by insisting that learning is a core feature of its strategic planning rather than simply a laudable option.

What do we mean by learning organisation, after all?

(a)   In their book *The Learning Company: A Strategy for Sustainable Development, Pedler, Burgoyne and Boydell* suggest the following might be a good description of a learning company:

       'A learning company is an organisation that facilitates the learning of all its members and continuously transforms itself.'

(b)   *David Galvin* ('*Building a Learning Organisation*' in the *Harvard Business Review* July-August 1993) suggests that:

       'a learning company is an organisation skilled at creating, acquiring, and transferring knowledge, and at modifying its behaviour to reflect new knowledge and insights.'

Pedler, Burgoyne and Boydell indicate that the idea of the learning organisation derived from several recent practices, including excellence programmes and organisation development, whose approach was to improve and shake up stultifying bureaucracies by a programme of planned change. (The trouble with one-off change programmes is that there are too many of them, and they might compete with each other.)

The characteristics of the learning company are listed below, and then we shall describe each of them in a little more detail.

- Learning approach to strategy
- Participative policy making
- Informating

- Formative accounting and control
- Internal exchange
- Reward flexibility
- Enabling structures
- Boundary workers as environmental scanners
- Intercompany learning
- A learning climate

4.1 The learning approach to strategy

The strategy process is designed as a learning process with experimentation and feedback loops built into a system. Pedler, Burgoyne and Boydell cite as an example Royal Dutch Shell, where a senior executive from another plant and/or country is invited to review the operation of a plant, to discover its hidden fundamentals and ways of doing business. As much information as possible is brought to bear on a problem.

4.2 Participative policy making

All members of a learning company have the chance to participate in the learning process. In practice it means that a variety of stakeholders' influences are accepted. There are three important assumptions.

- Various stakeholder groups are morally entitled to participate.
- Diversity, while complex and messy, generally leads to better solutions
- Long-term success requires delighting customers, not just satisfying them.

An example cited by Pedler, Burgoyne and Boydell is the *search conference*, as used by a hotel chain. People representing different stakeholder groups are sent away on a conference. Groups work on a variety of problems.

4.3 Informating

Informating is the use of information not as a control mechanism, but as a resource for the whole organisation to exploit in order to develop new insights.

4.4 Formative accounting and control

Accounting and budgeting systems should be structured for the benefit of all their internal users to assist learning. Such systems might encourage individuals to act as 'small businesses treating internal users as *customers*'.

EXAMPLE: MEXICAN WINDOWS

Pedler, Burgoyne and Boydell cite the example of Mexican Windows, whose finance department has set up a 'roadshow' to visit the organisation's branches, in order to explain the way the company uses money, the firm's attitudes to risk and the effective use of finance in marketing and operating decisions. These roadshows can be the beginning of further training.

4.5 Internal exchange

Internal exchange develops the idea of the *internal customer* which is being promoted by some marketing specialists. Each unit regards the other units as customers, whose needs must be identified and satisfied, in the context of the company as a whole.

4.6 Reward flexibility

In a learning company, there is a flexible approach to remuneration which questions why some people are paid more than others. The underlying principles of the salary remuneration system should be brought out into the open. Changing the reward system might result in a change in the distribution of power within the company. Rewards are not only financial but relate to the pleasure, enjoyment, and social life that people get out of work.

4.7 Enabling structures

The notion of enabling structures implies the features of the organic organisation with indeterminate roles which alter to allow for growth. Organisation structures are temporary arrangements that must respond to changed conditions and opportunities.

EXAMPLE: DIGITAL EQUIPMENT

Issues of enabling structures and organisation design can refer to the physical layout of the site, as well as organisation hierarchy. An example is Digital Equipment's use of IT in office design in its Stockholm office (*Guardian* 4 August 1993). People were asked to relinquish their desks; instead, staff 'wheel their mobile workstation with drawers to a position next to a fully networked terminal ... when the desks are not used, they are parked ... next door'. This has led to changed working practices and increased efficiency, and also made the company easier to deal with. 'While no-one at Digital would claim the innovations were the only reasons for the remarkable turnaround in the business, they were given star billing.' The changed office layout supported new working practices.

4.8 Boundary workers as environmental scanners

Earlier in this text we described organisations as open systems, situated in an environment. The organisation's boundary is where the interchanges take place. In a learning organisation, environmental monitoring is not restricted to specialists or managers. All employees dealing with the boundary should try and monitor the environment.

EXAMPLE: DAIICHI

Daiichi, a Japanese electronics appliance firm, offers three year warranties on its products. Before the warranty expires, it sends a repairman to service the customer's machine. Before he leaves, the repairman offers to check other appliances, whether or not the customer acquired them from Daiichi. This is a means of gathering product and market information. When the repairman returns to the office, he fills out a detailed report on the types of products in the home, their models and ages. This information is made available to Daiichi's sales force, who can offer the customer an appropriate mix of products.

4.9 Intercompany learning

Benchmarking is an example of intercompany learning, which we have already encountered. Pedler, Burgoyne and Boydell cite the example of *Rank Xerox*, which sent a team to learn from *Caterpillar*, as a benchmark for the delivery of heavy equipment.

4.10 Learning climate

A management function is the support, as opposed merely to the control, of operations. This recognises that, in order to maintain productive efficiency, the process of production must be unimpeded. Those who are directly involved on the production line (ie the operational workforce) are those who have the greatest knowledge of the process's inefficiencies and efficiencies. Supporting the workforce involves:

(a) soliciting their expertise and allowing them to take some operation decisions;

(b) supporting operations (eg backing them up and helping them become efficient);

(c) providing counselling and advice;

(d) bringing the organisation's resources to bear on problems identified by the workforce.

In short, this means that the worker is no longer the silent automaton responding to management instructions, but a speaking partner. This approach is used when the production workforce is divided into small multi-skilled teams.

Management has three functions in a learning organisation.

- To encourage continuous learning and knowledge around the organisation
- To create processes to move knowledge around the organisation
- To transform knowledge into actual behaviour, products and processes

4.11 Self development opportunities for all

A variety of training resources should be offered, initiating courses, seminars, counselling, work experience. Training and development has a high priority in a learning organisation, as it increases the flow of information and ideas, and develops the skills which can make use of them.

Activity 6   **(Over the next few days)**

As you can see, the learning organisation is not easy to define; so your task is to scan the newspapers for further glimpses into organisation learning.

---

5 BUILDING A LEARNING ORGANISATION

The learning organisation and concepts of continuous improvement are related. However, implementing the *culture* and *structure* of organisational learning is a different matter. How do you travel from your current situation towards the vision offered by organisational learning? Arguably Senge's prescriptions sound fine in principle, but they are hardly a programme of action.

Even firms which are successful at producing new knowledge have less success in applying it to their activities. To ensure that they do, some organisations 'actively manage the learning process'.

Learning organisations are *good* at some important activities.

- Systematic problem solving
- Experimenting with new approaches
- Learning from their own past experiences
- Learning from others' experiences
- Transferring knowledge quickly through the organisation

Systematic problem solving is based on TQM.

(a) A scientific approach (eg proposing, testing, then abandoning or refining hypotheses) is used to diagnose problems.

(b) Data, not intuition, is used as the basis of decision making.

(c) Simple statistical tools are used to highlight relationships.

The conventional wisdom has to be challenged. At *Xerox* in the US, the Leadership Through Quality initiative offered by senior managers ensures that *all* employees are trained in various problem solving tendencies.

Experimentation is a search for knowledge, but not so much a solution to past problems. For example, pharmaceuticals companies often experiment with new drug formulations. *Ongoing* programmes need two things.

(a) New ideas, from any source including competitors. Rover cars acquired expertise from Honda).

(b) Investment in specialised facilities to try out new equipment and management techniques.

Experimental knowledge moves from superficial acquaintance to deep understanding, or from tacit to explicit knowledge.

Learning from past experience. The knowledge gained from product failures and successes can be used to enhance new developments. *Boeing* used lessons from earlier model development to help give the 767 the most successful, error-free launch in its history. Case studies and post-project reviews, by managers or with the help of outsiders, can offer lessons and generate new insights.

Learning from others. This includes such practices as benchmarking, identified earlier, which is a search for best practice. Customers are also a good source of ideas. An American steel company sends members of the workforce to customers' factories to discuss their needs.

Knowledge transfer. 'Ideas carry maximum impact when they are shared broadly rather than held in a few hands.'

- Reports can highlight information.
- Specialised tours can show new techniques and/or achievement.

Translating tacit into explicit knowledge is more difficult. In practice, it might involve shifting personnel between divisions to carry over their expertise with them.

Education and training programmes need to be linked to implementation plans, so that there are structures to encourage workers to apply their training experiences. Training is thus not so much for individual development as for organisation enhancement.

5.1 Measurement

If learning is to be managed so that it is directed towards useful organisational outcomes, perhaps it should be *measured*.

(a) The learning curve effect is an early example of the value of experience. Learning curves are used to control production processes in the US aerospace industry.

(b) Half-life curves, developed by *Analog Devices*, a US manufacturer of semi-conductors, as a way of comparing internal improvement rates. A half-life curve is based on the time it takes to produce a 50% improvement in performance.

The problem with these measurements is that they are simply results-based, whereas organisational learning is a way of approaching the total situation of the company. The process, according to *David Garvin*, occurs in three steps.

- *Cognitive*. People change their way of thinking.
- *Behavioural*. People change their way of behaving.
- *Performance*. People actually start improving.

How do you measure each phase of the learning process? *Attitude surveys* are used to obtain information about the attitudes and motivation of employees. Management will wish to do this if it holds any of the beliefs listed below.

(a) Operational efficiency depends to some extent on employees' attitudes towards their work.

(b) When organisation changes are planned, attitudes towards the change should be monitored closely.

(c) Communications between employees and their managers might be inadequate, and there might be considerable frustration within the organisation.

(d) Finding out more about what employees want and think will help senior management to plan pay and reward schemes which are better suited to employees' interests.

Attitude surveys can be carried out by means of interview or questionnaire, and a scoring or marking system can be used to give quantitative values to attitudes, if these are thought useful. In the UK, attitude surveys are not nearly as widely used as they are in the USA.

There are various ways of monitoring *behavioural changes*. Some firms employ mystery shoppers to evaluate standards of service in retail outlets.

Ultimately, constructing a learning organisation can be a significant challenge.

(a) The environment must be conducive to learning: 'learning is difficult when employees are hurried or rushed; it tends to be driven out by the pressures of the moment'.

(b) Boundaries within the organisation and between the organisation and its customers must be opened up to facilitate the flow of new ideas.

NOTES

Chapter roundup

- Innovation can cover the organisation's products/services, the way it makes them, and its resources. It assists in coping with change.

- Innovation can be encouraged by management practices which suggest new ideas.

- Innovation depends on the use and dissemination of knowledge. Explicit knowledge is easily shared. Tacit knowledge is personal.

- A learning organisation is 'skilled at creating, acquiring and transferring knowledge, and at modifying its behaviour to reflect new knowledge and insights.'

- The idea of organisational learning is derived from practices such as excellence and continuous improvement.

- A learning organisation is characterised by: a learning approach to strategy; participation; 'informating'; reforming accounting and control systems; internal exchange; reward flexibility; enabling structure; boundary workers; inter-company learning; a learning climate; and self-development opportunities for all.

- Structures have to be in place to develop these characteristics.

Quick quiz

1 How can problems be categorised?

2 Are small organisations more innovative than large ones?

3 What did Rosabeth Moss Kanter mean by a *newstream?*

4 Which US corporation aims for 25% of turnover to come from product less than 5 years old?

5 What are the two types of knowledge identified by Nonaka?

6 What is systems thinking?

7 What are enabling structures?

8 What are the three processes involved in organisational learning, according to Gavin?

Answers to quick quiz

1 *Insight problems* have unexpected answers; solution to *wicked problems* can only be proved by trying them out; *vicious problems* are like wicked problems but involve people; *fuzzy problems* are ill defined and not susceptible to logical approaches.

2 No, it just looks that way.

3 A flow of new business possibilities within an organisation.

4 3M.

5 Explicit knowledge is systematised and easily shared. Implicit knowledge is personal and rooted in a specific context.

6 Thinking based on an appreciation of wider structures and implications.

7 Organisational features that allow for growth, innovation and flexibility of response.

8 Cognitive change; behavioural change; performance improvement.

Answers to activities

1 Clearly the answers to this activity will depend on the individual, but experiences could include the following.

    (a) Issues about career planning and development.
    (b) Choosing a partner for marriage or cohabitation.
    (c) Purchasing a house/flat or a car.

2 The response to activity 2 is conditioned by the characteristics of your organisation or, more accurately, your organisation's characteristics as you perceive them. Your view of organisational reality may not coincide with the perceptions of others. You should check your own assessment with the opinions advanced by colleagues, your boss, your staff, or people in the personnel department, for instance. If there is disagreement maybe it stems from some features of your psychological make-up rather than from, say, uncritical enthusiasm displayed by the personnel people. So you should try to be as objective and impartial as possible: if you can, contrast your own organisation's track record for innovation with that of its nearest competitors.

3 These are some of the steps which the textbooks advise individuals (and organisations) to take if they need to become more creative.

    (a) *Diversionary tactics.* Dominant left brain assumptions have to be put to one side in order to permit right brain contributions, so the left brain can be distracted by such diversionary tactics as physical exercise, meditation, fasting, dreaming, eating, reading about something else and so forth.

    (b) *Creating a climate for creativity in the organisation.* General organisational factors which can encourage or inhibit creativity among employees include work practices, pressures of work, management style and reward systems. A poor climate for creativity is one where people avoid risks, are over-critical (or contemptuous) about new ideas, and resist attempts to introduce change. Techniques for positive climate-setting stem from the simple idea that a good manager can reinforce behaviour by recognising and rewarding it; this means that the manager should seek to send out two messages whenever staff produce ideas:

        • it is always a good thing to come up with ideas; and
        • this particular idea may need working on, but don't give up.

    In practical terms, this means approaching any idea but appraising its strength first, and then by seeking ways round its weaknesses.

    (c) *Deferment of judgement.* The impulse to evaluate prematurely is a fundamental way of reducing creative input. The causes of such behaviour are unconscious, possibly a defence against the uncertainties of change, possibly a reflection of the 'rational' way in which people are supposed to behave. Fortunately, rejecting behaviours are learned rather than innate; they can therefore be un-learned.

    (d) *Goal orientation.* This implies the specification of a desired result ('I want to persuade my client to accept my proposal') and the obstacles ('What's stopping me from getting what I want'). Goal orientation is particularly appropriate for open-ended scenarios whose boundaries are unclear but where there are fairly well-defined needs and obstacles to overcome. Thus 'I want to persuade my client to accept my proposals' can be turned into goal statements like 'How to persuade my client', 'How to win his confidence' and 'How to reduce his fears of change' – expressed in such a fashion, the difficulties become easier to handle and resolve.

4   (a)   An idea is like an iceberg in these ways:

- It floats and moves

- It is slippery

- It grows bigger and is anchored at the bottom

- You'll know it when you see it

- It has a commanding presence

- It gets a chilly reception

- It doesn't show the work that's gone into it

- It is 90% submerged and to appreciate its magnitude you have to look below the surface

- It sometimes melts away

- It can be moved to other places

- It's a wonder of nature

- When conditions are right, many will be created

(b)   Working in an organisation is like driving on the motorway

- It's hard to do if you don't keep your eyes open

- You have to co-operate with other people

- Some people go faster than others

- Some people break the rules

- It can be noisy and dangerous at times

- It's confusing until you've done it for a while

- Sometimes passengers take a nap while you do the work

- You are in control of the journey: you can pull over, slow down or accelerate

- It's challenging and exciting sometimes, but very routine and boring at others

- Road signs can help you to stay on the right road

5   As with some other exercises, the response here depends on the organisation selected. Some at the bureaucratic end of the cultural spectrum are likely to be more resistant to change and to learning; it is the organic, market- or customer-responsive organisations which are more addicted to continuous learning, especially if they are in a highly competitive, aggressive marketplace where new entrants can easily begin operations.

Further question practice

Now try the following practice questions at the end of this text

Multiple choice questions: **82 to 88**

Exam style question: **12**

Chapter 13 :
STRATEGIES FOR CHANGE

Introduction

Making change happen requires five phases of managerial action.

- Analysing and planning the change.

- Communicating the change.

- Gaining acceptance for the required modifications in behaviour.

- Making the initial transition from the status quo to the new situation.

- Consolidating the new situation and continuing to follow up.

This chapter examines the comprehensive need for continuous change management in the organisations of today, shows how to introduce change systematically and explores some of the skills and techniques needed.

In this chapter you will learn about these things.

(a) The circumstances in which organisations typically have to introduce change or react to environmental turbulence

(b) Why organisations fail to accommodate themselves to the necessity for continuous change

(c) Systematic approaches to the planning and management of change

(d) Why people resist change and how such resistance is articulated through words and actions

(e) The management of change using a mixture of appropriate techniques

(f) Culture change in organisations

1 WHY CHANGE?

1.1 Introducing change

The ability to introduce change with minimum resistance is a key managerial skill, since change is a necessary way of life for all organisations. Even if a company intrinsically does not want to change, it must eventually respond to movements in the social and economic environment if it is to survive. Resistance to change is an endemic feature of behaviour, and makes the effective implementation of change one of the most intractable problems that managers can encounter. *Bertram Gross* writes:

'Lead them to water in an effort to make them drink and some, misunderstanding your message, may swim away. Others may give your message the 'file and forget' treatment. Those who are spurred to action may take a sip and then try to hold your head under. Those who comply obediently may respond with inertia or resistance on the next occasion. Some may be more interested in activating you than in being activated by you ... Although activation is the use of power, or influence, this is not a mere matter of turning on a switch.'

Essentially similar arguments are frequently found in the literature about organisational change and show the impracticality of continuing to accept that (in Greiner's phrase), 'organisation change is heavily dependent on a master blueprint designed and executed in one fell swoop by an omniscient consultant or top manager.' Even if precise procedures for the implementation of change are adopted, there are bound to be unplanned events as subordinates raise issues which top management had not anticipated.

Change is one of those situations in which conflict arises, unless steps are deliberately taken to dampen down the issues. Many employees apparently lack any internal commitment to a change and are therefore extremely reluctant to take any initiative necessary for the change to be successful.

One further issue is raised by the fact that change takes time to plan and operationalise. If the change is directed at the solution of a specific and defined problem, it is quite likely that the problem itself will have changed by the time the change process is complete.

The vital point about managing change successfully is that some degree of *participation* in the process nearly always helps to reduce levels of conflict, stress and tension. According to *A K Rice*,

Change, particularly organisational change, can seldom be achieved without giving rise to disappointment for some of those whose jobs and prospects are affected; what is important is to avoid, as far as possible, the resentment and bitterness that so often follow reorganisation.'

Even when participative methods are used, their effectiveness may be jeopardised if they are not presented properly at the initial stage, because first impressions are crucial in determining the individual's subsequent attitudes, not only to the proposed change, but also to the trustworthiness of management as the change introduction process unfolds.

1.2 The meaning of change

When we discuss change, we might be discussing an environmental change or a change within the organisation made in response to it.

One change can lead on to another and another and thence to another. *Buckley and Perkins*(1984) made a distinction between *change* and *transformation*.

(a) *Change* is gradual and small. The organisation may adapt. For example, *adaptive change* occurs when an organisation's environment changes slowly. Adaptive change mirrors this step-by-step: it is change in little stages, and thus has the advantage of minimising the resistance faced at any one time.

(b) *Transformation* is change on a significant scale.

    (i) *Organisational transformation* includes major changes in job definitions, reporting lines, departmentation and so on.

    (ii) *Transformation in the way the system operates* involves major changes in communication patterns and working relationships and processes.

    (iii) *Transformation in employee consciousness* involves major changes in the way things are viewed, involving shifts in attitudes, beliefs and myths.

1.3 The nature of change

Changes can be brought about in a variety of different ways, such as new technology, and so forth. Here are some examples of the different types of change.

(a) *New technology*

- Computerisation
- New products
- New working methods
- Better management information systems

(b) *Reorganisation*

    (i) A company is taken over, and so has to adopt the organisation policies of the new parent company.

    (ii) Growth causes reorganisation into divisions, or more specialist functional departments.

    (iii) Divestment of businesses.

    (iv) A drive to keep costs down leads to cost cutting measures.

(c) *Working conditions*

- New offices
- Shorter working week
- More varied work times
- Telecommuting
- Greater emphasis on occupational health

(d) *Personnel policies*

    (i) Changes in rules and procedures – eg about smoking at work

    (ii) Promotions, transfers, separation of employees, training and development, problems perhaps growing in complexity

(e) *Philosophy of management (relations between management and employees)*

    (i) New senior manager introduces new style of leadership

    (ii) Attitudes of managers and employees change over time

    (iii) Communications with employees becomes more open

    (iv) Greater collaboration between management and trade unions in labour relations

Peter Drucker suggests some kinds of change are especially relevant for organisations today.

- (a) The explosion of new technologies, producing new industries and service sectors, whilst simultaneously ensuring the collapse of others.

- (b) The move from a national to an international and ultimately to a global economy.

- (c) The emergence of new pluralistic institutions, to pose political, philosophical and spiritual challenges for the continuance of the status quo.

- (d) The new universe of knowledge based on mass education and its implications for work, leisure and leadership.

Activity 1   **(5 minutes)**

Which of the factors listed above are the key drivers for change in any organisation with which you are familiar?

To what extent, if at all, is the impetus for change in that organisation propelled by any factors not listed above?

---

2   CHANGE, ORGANISATIONAL DECLINE AND CRISIS

Stuart Slatter, from an analysis of UK companies during the severe recession of the early 1980s, identifies ten *symptoms* of corporate decline. Change is a necessary response.

- (a) Declining profitability

- (b) Decreasing sales volume (sales revenue adjusted for inflation)

- (c) An increase in gearing (debt as a proportion of equity)

- (d) A decrease in liquidity, as measured, conventionally, by accounting ratios (eg aged debtors, current ratio)

- (e) Restrictions on the dividend policy

- (f) Financial engineering (eg changes in accounting policies and periods, delays in publishing accounts, sudden changes in auditors)

- (g) 'Top management fear'

- (h) Frequent changes in senior executives

- (i) Falling market share

- (j) Evidence of a lack of planning

A slightly different set of warning signs about organisational decline was presented by *Lorange and Nelson* in a 1987 article for the *Sloan Management Review*.

- (a) *Excess personnel* often coupled with too many levels in the hierarchy and numbers of jobs whose titles begin with words like 'assistant' or 'deputy' (a clear indication that such jobs do not add value).

- (b) *Tolerance of incompetence*. Poorly performing individuals are shunted around the organisation or are given non-essential roles within an 'elephants' graveyard'.

(c) *Cumbersome administrative procedures* with excessive paperwork and slow approval systems before anything substantive can be done.

(d) *Disproportionate staff power* with departments like personnel having too much influence in the development of strategies.

(e) *Replacement of substance with form* so that formal adherence to procedures becomes more important than the achievement of performance outcomes.

(f) *A scarcity of goals and benchmarks.* Because of a lack of common vision, decision-making becomes a lengthy process with most of the time spent in sorting out the criteria for the decision.

(g) *Fear of embarrassment and conflict.* An emphasis on mistake-avoidance and consensus leads to groupthink and the suppression of dissent.

(h) *Loss of effective communication.* Essential information is withheld.

(i) *Outdated organisation structure,* especially with a strong emphasis on status, titles, differentials and centralised decision-making.

John Van Maurik (*Discovering the Leader in You*) reports that when he worked for *Ernst & Whinney*, the firm's insolvency function had devised a list of features that might indicate whether an organisation was likely to go bust, even before the figures had been examined.

- Recent achievement of the Queen's Award for Export.
- Rolls Royce in the car park.
- Flagpole outside head office.
- Fish tank in reception.
- CEO recently elected as president of the local chamber of commerce.

As is the case with much cynicism or humour, this list is meaningful because it contains more then a grain of truth, probably signifying the fact that the people running the organisation are no longer concentrating on the essentials.

These are all observable externally. Internally, however, there may be a severe *crisis*, whose severity for the long term depends on the behaviour of managers. *Slatter* identifies four stages in the crisis.

(a) *Crisis denial.* Managers are complacent, ignore warning signs or do not appreciate their significance. This may result from poor control systems and poor environmental monitoring. Managers might rest on their laurels.

(b) *Hidden crisis.* When the signs of crisis appear, managers explain them away, or say that there is nothing they can do. The problem is that if they admit something is wrong they will be blamed. If a radical change is required, it might adversely affect their position.

(c) *Disintegration.* Managers decide that things are amiss and act to do something about them, usually too little. Moreover, management becomes more autocratic, reducing alternative sources of information.

(d) *Collapse.* Slatter says that, in the end, action is impossible. An expectation of failure increases, the most able managers leave, and there are power struggles for the remaining spoils. Eventually, usually after the prompting of a bank, the receiver is called in.

Activity 2   **(5 minutes)**

To what extent is Slatter's four-phase crisis development process exemplified in any recent instance of organisational or corporate collapse with which you are familiar?

Slatter identifies the causes of decline and the strategies to deal with them as follows.

(a)   *Poor management.* This should be dealt with by the introduction of new management and perhaps organisation restructuring (this should only be embarked upon once the new executive knows how the firm *really* works, including its informal organisation).

(b)   *Poor financial controls.* This can be dealt with by new management, financial control systems which are tighter and more relevant, and, perhaps, decentralisation and delegation of responsibility to first line management of all aspects except finance.

(c)   *High cost structure.* Cost reduction is important in improving margins in the long term. New product-market strategies are adopted for the short term to boost profitability and cash-flow. Growth-orientated strategies are only suitable once survival is assured. A focus strategy (whether cost-focus or differentiation-focus) is perhaps the most appropriate.

(d)   *Poor marketing.* The firm's marketing activities can be redeployed. Slatter believes that the sales force of a crisis-ridden firm is likely to be particularly demotivated.

(e)   *Competitive weakness.* This is countered by cost reduction, improved marketing, asset reduction (eg disposing of subsidiaries, selling redundant fixed assets) and of course, a suitable product-market strategy.

(f)   *Big projects/acquisitions.* Acquisitions can go bad, or there can be a failure of a major project (eg Rolls Royce Aerospace once went into receivership because of the cost of developing the RB211 engine).

(g)   *Financial policy.* Firms might suffer because of high gearing. Arguably many of the firms subject to management buyouts financed by interest-bearing loans are acutely vulnerable. Converting debt to equity and selling assets are ways of dealing with this.

2.1   Crisis management

Ansoff argues in *Corporate Strategy* that

'there is an increasing likelihood that the firm will fail to perceive some rapidly developing and novel discontinuities until they forcefully impact upon the firm. When a change appears to imperil the firm's survival and places the firm under severe time pressures, the firm is confronted with a crisis.'

Crisis has the effect of inducing panic – which managers must do what they can to minimise – but it can also promote an immediate willingness to change.

If a group of managers see an impending crisis on the horizon, there are three options.

(a)   Convince the others of the crisis and prepare preventative measures.

(b)   Accept that the crisis will happen anyway and prepare to capitalise on it by acting as saviours.

(c)   Trigger an early artificial crisis:

'usually by inventing an 'external enemy' who threatens survival of the firm. This is an approach which has been used by political leaders throughout history.'

Artificial crises reduce resistance, and perhaps build up support for recovery.

3   STRUCTURAL REORGANISATION

If further growth or decline within the same organisation structure would create inefficiencies and ineffectiveness, there should be a structural reorganisation. The type of new organisation structure will depend on the circumstances in which the organisation operates (contingency theory). Changes in what an organisation does – eg the products and services it provides, the number of people it employs etc – could also lead to a need for a restructuring of the organisation, to maintain its efficiency in the face of change. The need for reorganisation might be caused by any of the following.

(a)   *Changes in the environment of the organisation.* For example, greater competition might create pressures for cost-cutting, and so staff cuts.

(b)   *Diversification into new product-market areas.* There is a need for better lateral and vertical integration as an organisation becomes more complex and differentiated. A possible role for special co-ordinators can be found. Another issue which might be addressed is when to switch from a functional to a divisional organisation structure.

(c)   *Growth.* Employing more people creates problems of extended management hierarchies and poor communication.

(d)   *New technology.*

(e)   *Changes in the capabilities of personnel employed.* These can include changes in education levels, the distribution of occupational skills or employee attitudes to work.

Initially, there is a problem of *identifying the need to reorganise*. The need for restructuring might become apparent in the following circumstances.

(a)   The existing organisation might be showing signs of weakness and strain.

- Management overload
- Poor integration and co-ordination
- Insufficient innovation
- Weakening control

These are common management problems, but made worse by deficiencies in the organisation structure.

(b)   It is anticipated that reorganisation will be beneficial: the structural changes can be planned in advance before the deficiencies have time to develop.

Restructuring is not always necessary every time that changes take place in an organisation's circumstances. When a problem arises with an organisational deficiency, management has to analyse and diagnose the fault.

(a)   What is the scope of the problem?

(b)   What is the source of the problem? (Or is relatively easy to spot personal problems, when a manager isn't doing his or her job properly, or there are personal rivalries and conflicts, but it is less easy to diagnose faults in organisational structure.)

(c)   Is the problem temporary or permanent, unique or recurrent?

(d)   At what level in the management hierarchy and organisation structure is the problem located? This is the point where restructuring will be needed.

4   PLANNING FOR CHANGE

A systematic approach should be established, for planning and implementing changes. A step-by-step model for change is shown below.

A MODEL FOR CHANGE

Step

1   Determine need or desire for change in a particular area.

2   Prepare a tentative plan.

- Brainstorming sessions a good idea, since alternatives for change should be considered (Lippitt 1981).

3   Analyse probable reactions to the change.

4   Make a final decision from the choice of alternative options.

- Decision taken either by group problem-solving (participative) or by manager on his own (coercive).

5   Establish a timetable for change.

- 'Coerced' changes can probably be implemented faster, without time for discussions.

- Speed of implementation that is achievable will depend on the likely reactions of the people affected (all in favour, half in favour, all against etc).

- Identify those in favour of the change, and perhaps set up a pilot programme involving them. Talk with the others who resist the change.

6   Communicate the plan for change.

- This is really a continuous process, beginning at Step 1 and going through to Step 7.

7   Implement the change. Review the change.

- Continuous evaluation and modifications.

Organisational changes need careful planning. This is true of all but the smallest changes, and it is especially true of major changes. It is also necessary to assess the impact of change on the political system of the organisation.

Kurt Lewin developed a simple technique of visualising the change process called *force field analysis*. This can be used to identify ways of dealing with an unsatisfactory situation. It is based on the idea that in any group or organisational situation there is an interplay of restraining and driving forces that keeps things as they are. Force field analysis maps the forces that are pushing toward the preferred state and the restraining forces, which are pushing back to the current state. They can then be presented in a chart.

Force field analysis is itself derived from the notion of *equilibrium* – the idea that people like to develop an established and familiar set of relationships with their environment. They learn acceptable ways of behaving towards each other, how to perform their jobs, how to accommodate themselves to group norms. They develop expectations about the actions of others which are reinforced by experience. When this state of personal equilibrium is reached, the individual no longer has to devote conscious effort to his or her own behaviour patterns because he or she has internalised satisfactory responses and modes of action.

Just as individuals seek a kind of self-sustaining equilibrium in their relationships with the outside world, so too do groups of individuals. Both individuals and groups create a series of mechanisms designed to restore the balance whenever their equilibrium is disturbed. These mechanisms are an application of the biological principle of *homeostasis*, the desire to establish a steady state of need fulfilment and the mobilisation of protective resources if this optimum adjustment is threatened.

The principles of *equilibrium* and *homeostasis* are easier to understand if we apply them to a practical situation. Let us imagine a group of workers who are producing 70% of the efficiency that might be expected on purely technical grounds. This being so, their output can be visualised as a balance between two opposing sets of forces, ie *driving forces* which are propelling their output upwards and *restraining forces* which are preventing it from going beyond the 70% level.

Note that these *driving forces* and *restraining forces* represent perceptions entertained by the workers themselves. They are not merely a list of impersonal advantages and disadvantages because, as is often the case with complex scenarios, an advantage for one person turns out to be a disadvantage from someone else's point of view. If the workers in question were to increase their output, that may prove beneficial for the organisation's management team, but the workers themselves would feel their job security to be threatened.

Activity 3   **(10 minutes)**

Before going on, can you think of some *restraining forces* which, in the eyes of the workers concerned, deter them from producing more than 70% of what is technically feasible? Equally, can you think of some *driving forces* – again, in the eyes of the workers involved – which ensure that output remains at the 70% level without falling to, say, 60%?

Remember that your driving and restraining forces have to be the kinds of arguments which would be meaningful for the workers themselves, so you have to try to put yourself in their place and visualise how you would feel: in other words, you must empathise with the kinds of feelings, attitudes, beliefs, emotions and goals likely to be uppermost in their minds.

The *restraining forces* could include the following.

(a)   Dislike of the work itself.

(b)   Fear that if they produce more, the organisation will then be unable to sustain sales at the higher level of output, so redundancies will ensue.

(c)   Fear that once higher output norms have been established, the organisation will expect such norms to be sustained permanently.

(d)   Dislike of the supervisor, the management and even the organisation as a whole, thereby making the workers unco-operative and resentful.

The *driving forces* could include the following.

(a) Fear of dismissal if output falls below a reasonably well-defined rate acceptable to or tolerated by the management.

(b) Financial incentives, without which output would be significantly lower than 70%.

(c) Fear of losing special privileges, such as concessionary prices for the organisation's products or services.

(d) Response to pressure from the management – and thus a desire to reduce that pressure to acceptable proportions.

In a force field diagram, the number of forces on each side of the equilibrium does not have to be identical. However, the cumulative impact of the forces on each side (with the stronger forces being represented by longer arrows) does have to be the same, as a necessary precondition for the existence of an equilibrium, or balance of forces.

Once the equilibrium has been established, the organisation may be perfectly content, provided that a 70% level of performance is viewed as reasonable. Alternatively, management may believe that the disruption 'costs' arising from any disturbance to the status quo may outweigh the potential 'benefits' involved.

On the other hand, if management wants to increase output levels to, say, 80%, then logically this can only be done by *either* of the following.

(a) *Overcoming resistance* through strengthening the driving forces, ie increasing management pressure, enhancing fears of dismissal and so forth; *or*

(b) *Reducing resistance* by weakening the forces that currently hold down output, for example through job redesign, adoption of a more people-centred management style etc.

Overcoming resistance tends to be the more popular strategy. As *Tom Lupton* puts it,

'Most significant organisational changes originate with higher management, and are 'pushed through' in one way or another.'

Overall, the approach appears to succeed because management works very hard, applies pressure and knocks a few heads together (eliminating some, if necessary), but it does create resisting forces which are costly to organisational flexibility and efficiency in the long run, as well as damaging people at all levels.

Chris Argyris, commenting on 32 major changes in large organisations, says that not one was fully completed and integrated even three years after the change had been announced.

'That is, after three years there were will many people fighting, ignoring, questioning, resisting, blaming the re-organisation without feeling a strong obligation personally to correct the situation.'

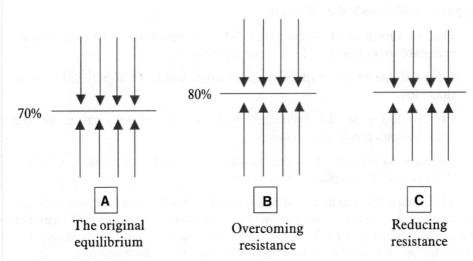

A	B	C
The original equilibrium	Overcoming resistance	Reducing resistance

The essential characteristic of *overcoming resistance* as a strategy for change (reflected in diagram B) is that increasing any of the upward 'push' factors will prompt an opposite reaction on the other side of the equilibrium: management gets what it ostensibly wants – an increase in production – but at the cost of more tension, conflict, suspicion and hostility. With *reducing resistance*, on the other hand, the same objective is accomplished as output rises, but the resultant balance of forces operates at a significantly lower level of tension.

The force field model therefore suggests two ways of dealing with change.

- Strengthening your own side
- Weakening the opposing forces

Once the driving and restraining forces have been identified, an action plan can be drawn up covering the following issues.

(a) People associated with the driving forces can be co-opted to educate opponents.

(b) Vested interests will have to be addressed directly.

How much coercion should be used?

(a) Some element of coercion may ultimately be necessary. However, it helps, for example if a supposedly neutral consultant can be persuaded to suggest measures supported by the proponents of the innovation.

(b) Involving people in diagnosing problem situations (eg in quality circles) wins over 'hearts and minds'.

5 RESISTANCE TO CHANGE

Change may affect individuals in several areas.

(a) There may be *physiological* changes in a person's life, both as the natural product of development, maturation and ageing, and as the result of external factors: a change in the pattern of shift-working, for example, may temporarily throw the individual's eating, waking and sleeping routine out of synch with the body's sense of time.

(b) *Circumstantial* changes – living in a new house, establishing new relationships, working to new routines – will involve letting go of things, perhaps 'unlearning' old knowledge, and learning new ways of doing things.

(c)   Above all, change affects individuals *psychologically*.

    (i)   It may create feelings of disorientation before new circumstances have been assimilated: you may have felt this on waking up in an unfamiliar room, or performing a familiar task in an unfamiliar setting at college or at work.

    (ii)   Uncertainty may lead to insecurity, especially acute in changes involving work, where there can be very great pressures for continuity and fast acclimatisation.

    (iii)   The secure basis of warm, accepting relationships may be up-rooted and the business of forging new relationships can be fraught with personal insecurity, risk of rejection, the feeling of being an outsider.

Change can affect the individual's self-concept quite radically.

(a)   A new psychological contract may result from the change, bringing with it new expectations, challenges and pressures, in the face of which the self-image may have to be revised – perhaps, initially, with an uncomfortable experience of dissonance.

(b)   A new set of models may have to be confronted, if the change involves a new role set and new relationships.

(c)   The individual's uncertainty of being able to cope with new circumstances can shake his or her sense of competence. Many people feel guilty and inadequate as beginners, even though they know, and are told, that it is perfectly natural and acceptable, that their performance will improve as they get used to it.

(d)   Change can be particularly threatening if it is perceived as an outside force or agent against which the individual is powerless. This may be a blow to the concept of self as the agent, the controller of its destiny.

Activity 4   **(3 minutes)**

Which of the following observations about change do you find to be the more accurate?

(a)   *Pareto's optimisation principle:* 'It is possible for change to leave some people better off and no people worse off.'

(b)   *Veblen's real-world principle:* 'Every change adversely affects some people and benefits others.'

5.1   Resistance to change at work

Resisting change means attempting to preserve the existing state of affairs against pressure to alter it. Despite the possibly traumatic effects of change *per se*, as discussed above, most people do *not* in fact resist it on these grounds alone. Many people long for change, and have a wealth of ideas about how it should be achieved.

Sources of resistance to change itself may include age and inflexibility, strong needs for security and emotional instability. Sources of resistance to particular proposed changes may include the following.

(a)   *Attitudes or beliefs*, perhaps arising from cultural, religious or class influences (for example resistance to changes in the law on Sunday trading).

(b) *Loyalty to a group and its norms*, perhaps with an accompanying rejection of other groups. Groups tend to close ranks if their independent identity is threatened.

(c) *Habit, or past norms.* This can be a strong source of clinging to old ways, whether out of security needs, respect for tradition, or the belief that 'you can't teach an old dog new tricks'.

(d) *Politics* – in the sense of resisting changes that might weaken the power base of the individual or group or strengthen a rival's position. Changes involving increased delegation may be strongly resisted by senior management, for example. In the same way the introduction of automation, or new methods, may be seen by the workforce as an attempt to devalue their skills and experience in the job market: they will be superfluous, or will be 'starting at the bottom again', and will have lost their position of strength as suppliers of labour in demand.

(e) The way in which any change is put forward and implemented.

Arthur Bedeian cites four common *causes* of resistance.

(a) *Self-interest:* if the status quo is perceived to be comfortable, or advantageous to the individual or the group.

(b) *Misunderstanding and distrust:* if the reasons for, or the nature and consequences of, the change have not been made clear. This aggravates uncertainty and suspicion about the perceived threat.

(c) *Contradictory assessments:* different individuals' evaluations of the likely costs and benefits of some change. Resistance arises from individuals' perceptions of the undesirability of change.

(d) *Low tolerance of change itself:* as a result of differences in tolerance of ambiguity, uncertainty, challenge to self-concept and so on.

Reactions to proposed change include the following.

(a) *Acceptance*, whether enthusiastic espousal, co-operation, grudging co-operation or resignation

(b) *Indifference*, where the change does not directly affect the individual

(c) *Passive resistance*, such as refusal to learn and working to rule

(d) *Active resistance*, such as go-slows, deliberate errors, sabotage, absenteeism or strikes

John Hunt highlights a number of responses that may not look like resistance on the face of things, but are behaviours aimed at reinforcing the status quo. There are a number of responses that the manager should learn to recognise.

(a) Pleas of ignorance: ('I need more information')

(b) Delayed judgement: ('let's wait and see ...'), perhaps stalling for time with comparisons ('there are other ways ...')

(c) Defensive stances: ('This isn't going to work', 'It'd be too expensive', 'It's the wrong time to ...')

(d) The display of various personal insecurities: ('I won't be able to cope', 'I won't see my team anymore', 'We won't have control over our planning any more', 'Why can't we just go on as we are?'); fear, anxiety, resentment at the manner of change, frustration at perceived losses

(e)   Withdrawal, or disowning of the change: ('Oh well. On their heads be it', 'I'm not interested in flexitime anyway')

EXAMPLE: MANAGEMENT AND UNION VIEWS

It is interesting to set side by side the comments of Sainsbury's director of personnel and a senior official of the shop worker's union Usdaw, as reported in *Personnel Management Plus* in February 1992. See if you can tell which is which!

(a)   'I have taken a close personal interest, and so have my colleagues, to ensure that in every branch the people who are working are those who volunteered. Not working on Sunday is not going to affect promotion prospects, it is not going to affect people's pay, and it is not going to affect our attitude to them.

'There are some who say "I will not work on Sunday because I feel it's not right to do so". There are others, and this includes managers, who say: "I am not going to work on Sunday because I want to play football" and we say: "That's a nuisance, isn't it" and we find a way round it.'

(b)   'Connor maintains some retailers have ways of making their staff work Sundays without resorting to blackmail. "Very clever retail employers work through the ranks. They take the weakest, the people who have less than two years' experience and who have no rights for unfair dismissal, then they pick the starry-eyed people who think they are going to be managing director, then they pick the people who work low hours and need a few bob. Then they come to the resolute minority and say: "You are out of step".'

5.2   Overcoming resistance to change

When thinking about how to deal with resistance to a planned change, managers should consider the pace, the manner and the scope of the proposed developments.

Changes ought generally to be introduced slowly. Apart from people problems, there may be a long planning process or financial risks to be considered: a range of alternatives will have to be considered, and information gathered. Change is, however, above all a people management process: relationships are changed, and must be reformed, old ways have to be unlearned and new ways learned.

The more gradual the change, the more time is available for questions to be asked, reassurances to be given and retraining (where necessary) embarked upon. People can get used to the new methods at each stage, with a consequent confidence in the likely success of the change programme, and in the individual's own ability to cope.

(a)   Presenting the individual concerned with a *fait accompli* may short-circuit resistance at the planning and immediate implementation stages. But it may cause a *withdrawal reaction*, if the change is radical and perceived as threatening, and is thus likely to surface later, as the change is consolidated, probably strengthened by resentment.

(b)   *Timing* will also be crucial: those responsible for change should be sensitive to incident and attitude that might indicate that 'now is not the time'.

The *manner* in which a change is put across is very important: the climate must be prepared, the need made clear, fears soothed, and if possible the individuals concerned positively motivated to embrace the changes as their own.

(a) Resistance should be welcomed and confronted, not swept under the carpet. Talking thorough areas of conflict may lead to useful insights and the adapting of the programme of change to advantage. Repressing resistance will only send it underground, into the realm of rumour and covert hostility.

(b) There should be free circulation of information about the reasons for the change, its expected results and likely consequences. That information should appear sensible, clear, consistent and realistic: there is no point issuing information which will be seen as a blatant misrepresentation of the situation.

(c) The change must be sold to the people: people must be convinced that their attitudes and behaviours *need* changing. Objections must be overcome, but it is also possible to get people *behind* the change in a positive way.

    (i) Pure *position power* (of individual managers or powerful groups or functions in the organisation) is often used to force people to accept changes: this makes the change *look* more unreasonable than it may really be, and resistance may increase. The same kind of power will constantly have to be applied to ensure continuing compliance.

    (ii) If those involved understand that there is a real problem, which poses a threat to the organisation *and* themselves, and that the solution is a sensible one and will solve that problem, there will be a firm rational basis, at least for implementing change. If the people can be positively committed to the change – for example by emphasising the threat which the problem poses, or the advantages of the solution, *to them* – so much the better. Changes in crisis often face less resistance than changes of a *routine* nature.

    (iii) The people should also be reassured that they have the learning capacity, the ability and the resources to implement the plan. It may even be possible to get them really *excited* about it by, again, 're-affirming the heroic element' (the challenge and opportunity) by injecting an element of competition perhaps (who can get their system running better, faster?) or simply offering rewards and incentives.

(d) Individuals must be helped to learn, that is, to change their attitudes and behaviours.

    (i) Few individuals will be able to see the big picture in a proposed programme of change. In order to put across the overall objective, the organisation should use visual aids to help conceptualise. Professional outside consultants, who specialise in conceptualising, may be useful.

    (ii) Learning programmes for any new skills or systems necessary will have to be designed according to the abilities and the previous learning experience of the individuals concerned.

(e) The effects of insecurity, perceived helplessness, and therefore resentment, may be lessened if the people can be involved in the planning and implementation of the change, ie if it is not perceived to have been imposed from above.

    (i) *Persuasion* will depend on the political forces in the organisation – the position of personal power of the change agent, the importance of his function in the organisation structure, any influential support he has been able to gain, the backing of experts. Encouragement and rewards at each stage of learning may help in the transitional period.

(ii)   The degree to which *consultation* or *participation* will be possible (or genuine) will depend on management's attitude towards the competence and trustworthiness of its workforce. Successful change will usually be initiated from the top (otherwise the politics are too complicated) but there could certainly be opportunity for those who are, after all, most immediately involved in the changing systems, processes or structures to assess and advise on the detail of the change programme.

The *scope* of change should also be carefully reviewed. Total transformation will create greater insecurity – but also greater excitement, if the organisation has the kind of innovative culture that can stand it – than moderate innovation. There may be hidden changes to take into account: a change in technology may necessitate changes in work methods, which may in turn result in the breaking up of work groups. Management should be aware of how many various aspects of their employees' lives they are proposing to alter – and therefore on how many fronts they are likely to encounter resistance.

The use of *pilot projects* can often be valuable in managing change. According to this technique, the initiators of a proposed change undertake to make specific (and agreed) alterations to the existing organisation on an experimental basis. After a given period of time, an attempt is then made to analyse the change in terms of 'before' and 'after' criteria on the implicit understanding that if the change has been unsuccessful, it will be withdrawn.

(a)   The principal advantages of the pilot project approach are as follows.

(i)   It helps to solve the practical difficulties of change not foreseen in the preliminary planning – on the argument that 'no plan ever survives contact with reality'.

(ii)   It helps to reassure the less confident members of the organisation that the proposed change is workable.

(iii)   Managers outside the experimental change need not become emotionally committed at an early stage, but can jump on or off the bandwagon once the outcome has been clarified.

(b)   On the other hand, there are disadvantages with pilot projects.

(i)   Experimental change only prolongs the inevitable period of tension and uncertainty surrounding any change.

(ii)   Pilot changes generally involve a period of close (or closer than normal) supervision, which can be disruptive if carried on for a long time.

(iii)   There is always the chance that employees will seek to influence the success or otherwise of the experimental change through boycotts, sabotage and so forth.

(iv)   Sometimes, changes observed in one part of the organisation will not be replicated if adopted on a large scale. This sometimes happens with market research where sales in a test area can generate what turns out to be an unwarranted level of optimism about sales in the country as a whole.

6 THE CHANGE PROCESS

In the words of John Hunt (Managing People at Work):

'Learning also involves re-learning – not merely learning something new but trying to unlearn what is already known.'

This is, in a nutshell, the thinking behind *Lewin and Schein's* three-stage approach to changing human behaviour.

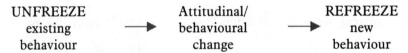

UNFREEZE	Attitudinal/	REFREEZE
existing	behavioural	new
behaviour	change	behaviour

Unfreeze is the most difficult (and in many cases neglected) stage of the process, concerned mainly with selling the change, that is, with giving individuals or groups a motive for changing their attitudes, values, behaviour, systems or structures.

(a) If the need for change is immediate, clear and perceived to be associated with the survival of the individual or group (for example change in reaction to an organisation crisis), the unfreeze stage will be greatly accelerated. Routine changes may be harder to sell than transformational ones, if they are perceived to be unimportant and not survival-based.

(b) Culture change is perhaps hardest of all, especially if it involves basic assumptions. Unfreezing processes need four things.

    (i) A trigger

    (ii) Someone to challenge and expose, in a visible way, the existing behaviour pattern

    (iii) The involvement of outsiders

    (iv) Alterations to power structure

Kurt Lewin's force field analysis discussed earlier can be used to indicate how *unfreeze* works.

Change is the second stage, mainly concerned with identifying what the new, desirable behaviour or norm should be, communicating it and encouraging individuals and groups to adopt the new attitude or behaviour. This might involve the adoption of a new culture. To be successful, the new ideas must be shown to work. Also, the support of junior managers can be enhanced if their status is improved.

Refreeze is the final stage, implying consolidation and reinforcement of the new behaviour. Positive reinforcement in the form of praise or reward, or negative reinforcement in the form of sanctions applied to those who deviate from the new behaviour may be used.

EXAMPLE: THE ABOLITION OF THE GLC

On 31 March 1986 the Greater London Council was abolished and the London Residuary Body (LRB) was established to wind up the GLC's affairs. In 1990 the LRB took on the additional responsibility of winding up the Inner London Education Authority (ILEA). The LRB thus increased its workforce from three people to 4,000 overnight, shed nearly 3,500 jobs over the next four years, only to go back up again to 2,700 overnight, and finally reduced its staff to 60 overnight.

An article in *Personnel Management* (February 1992) describes the extent of the changes and how the LRB coped.

'The degree of unavoidable change facing the LRB's staff was considerable. They had a new employer, County Hall (which was more than just their place of work) was to be sold, and many realised that more changes to their employer and their careers were not far away.

Furthermore, their new employer was not like their old one. Like many other local authority employers, GLC councillors had taken a close interest in staffing matters and seen themselves at the pinnacle of most employee relations procedures, but the LRB's approach was different. The small board (all appointed by the Secretary of State) sought an approach which was more akin to the private sector. A great deal was delegated to managers and there was to be no member involvement in procedures.

Equally significant was the change from an organisation that created, developed and maintained things to one which cleared things up, disposed of them or handed them on. This is a quite different culture and one in which some 'professionals' are not always comfortable.

It was necessary, therefore, to help staff understand the new culture without being unsettled by it. Communications and other measures played a large part in promoting staff understanding, but wherever feasible only essential changes were contemplated.

By and large, then, staff continued with their previous terms and conditions, and the basic negotiating groups were similar. The LRB also tried to continue many GLC practices and policies and granted facilities and limited financial assistance so the old GLC staff clubs and societies could continue.

Of course, changes needed to be discussed and negotiated with trade unions. The trade unions, however, while striving at all times to protect their member's interests, realised the special nature of the LRB. As a result it was possible to break new ground in settling long-running disputes and in introducing revised procedures and terms and conditions of employment.

Most importantly, the LRB observed one of the golden rules of change management – 'don't criticise those involved in what has gone before'. The board, and especially the chairman, Sir Godfrey Taylor, took every opportunity when communicating with employees to point out that the abolition of the GLC was in no way the staff's fault, and that the board had nothing but the highest regard for their professional competence and commitment.'

The article points out that the more successful the LRB's staff were at achieving their task the sooner they would be redundant! It goes on to describe how the remuneration

PUBLISHING

system was modified, attention was given to information provision and consultation, and how careful redundancy planning, selection procedures, counselling and active assistance in the form of finance and training were successfully implemented.

7 THE KEYS TO SUCCESSFUL CHANGE

Donald Kirkpatrick (*How to Manage Change Effectively*) identified three keys to successful change: *empathy*, *communication*, and *participation*.

7.1 Empathy

Empathy means understanding another person's emotions: it implies getting to know the people involved in and affected by changes. The manager should consider each person's (or group's) reaction to change accordingly. In other words: 'If I were in their shoes, what would I be thinking about this, and how would I be reacting?'

To show empathy, a manager has to get to know various matters about each individual. Kirkpatrick calls these *must know* factors, which include name and nickname, where the individual lives, whether he or she is married or single, the individual's work experience, formal education, outside hobbies, health, children, religion, politics, attitudes, problems, friends, financial situation, intelligence, personality, ambitions, date of employment, social background and continuing education.

7.2 Communication

Communication is not just telling subordinates what to do, but is the process of creating an understanding. The importance of communication and the barriers to proper communication were discussed in an earlier chapter of this text. However, the aspects of communication which might be particularly relevant to change are as follows.

(a) Who needs to know and who else will want to know? These people should be told.

(b) When should the information be given about planned changes?

- Bosses ought to be told before subordinates.
- Trade union officials ought to be told before workers.

(c) How should the information be given? Should it be given verbally, face-to-face? Or in writing? Or a mixture of both?

(i) If emotions are likely to run high, the communication ought to be verbal, and face-to-face. If individuals need persuading, the manager must give himself the opportunity to talk to them, and to try to persuade them.

(ii) If the changes are complex, and individuals need time to study them or to refer to them later (eg proposed changes to the company pension scheme) they should be set out in writing.

(iii) The information should be communicated directly, not via a go-between or middleman.

(d) *Feedback* from the people affected should be obtained. Employees should be encouraged to ask questions and voice any doubts or worries they might have.

7.3 Participation

Kirkpatrick argues that a participative approach is needed for innovation; otherwise new ideas will get stifled and discouraged. Here are three examples of participation.

- Quality circles
- Task forces
- Problem-solving groups

Two important aspects of participation determine the nature and extent of the participation.

- When should the manager start to involve staff?
- how should participation be made to work?

When to start participation	How participation is achieved in practice
(a) From the beginning, discuss ideas. Gradually, acceptable ideas will emerge.	The desire of the manager for participation must be genuine. It won't work if 'participation is something the top orders the middle to do from the bottom'. (*Kanter*)
(b) Make tentative plans for change, and then start to discuss them with subordinates.	1. Ask for input of ideas.
(c) Decide to make a change and then try to sell the idea to subordinates.	2. Seriously consider input and evaluate it objectively.
	3. Use good ideas.
Approaches (a) or (b) are preferred	4. Reject bad ideas.
	5. Give credit to providers of good ideas.
	6. Convince the providers of bad ideas that their ideas were bad.

There are practical difficulties with achieving participation in change.

(a) Managers might pay lip service to participation, but do not believe in it.

(b) Employees suspect that their good ideas will result in jobs losses.

(c) If there is no current culture of participation, it would be difficult to introduce suddenly. Participation would have to be introduced gradually, perhaps starting with one or two pilot groups.

(d) Participation is sometimes impossible.

7.4 Coercive change

Change is sometimes enforced without participation. Changes of culture and power structures are left to the end of the change process. There are problems with a coercive approach, of course.

- Underestimation of the forces of resistance
- Failure to muster forces in favour
- Failure to attack root causes of resistance
- Management shift their attention too quickly elsewhere
- Failure to ensure implementation

NOTES

This approach is necessary in situations of crisis where there simply is no time to consult, or where decisions need to be taken quickly. An example is a sudden 'environmental' shock.

Activity 6   **(12 minutes)**

You might like to try, as an exercise in empathy, to put yourself in the shoes of a 28-year old accountant, Sam Francisco, who works for a growing manufacturing company in its accounting department, as a junior manager. He has just qualified, but has so far had relatively little experience with computerised accounting systems. He is quite ambitious.

The chief executive of the company now announces that owing to the continuing growth of the company, new product divisions will be created, and the company will switch from a functional to a divisionalised organisation structure, each with its own production, marketing, personnel and accounting functions. Each division might be re-located in a different part of the country. The authority for most decision-making will be delegated to each division (although head office will exercise control) and, to improve the company's control system, there will be a new networked database system, which the accounting and marketing departments of the new divisions will set up. The changes will be explained in more detail by the new divisional managers, and will start to take effect immediately.

If you were in Sam Francisco's shoes, how would you react to these changes?

---

8 Acceptance of change

It takes time for changes to get accepted. *Conner and Patterson* (1981) identified three phases and eight stages in the process of accepting change by the people affected.

Phase 1:	**Preparation phase**	
Stage 1	Contact	First knowledge that a change is 'in the air'
Stage 2	Awareness	Knowledge that change will happen
Phase 2:	**Acceptance phase**	
Stage 3	Understanding	Gaining an understanding of the nature and purpose of the change
Stage 4	Positive perception	Developing a positive view towards the change, and accepting the need for it
Phase 3:	**Commitment phase**	
Stage 5	Installation	The change becomes operational
Stage 6	Adoption	The change has been in force for long enough and its value has become apparent
Stage 7	Institutionalisation	The change has been in for long enough to become 'routine' and the 'norm'
Stage 8	Internalisation	Individuals are highly committed to the change because it is now congruent with their personal interests, goals and value systems.

Conner and Patterson argued that *commitment to change* is necessary for its successful implementation.

(a) Getting commitment is expensive, and calls for an investment of time, effort and money. It involves providing information, involving subordinates in the planning and implementation process, rewarding them for their participation and so on.

(b) Strategies for commitment ought to be developed. For any change, management needs to decide how far through the eight stages the acceptance process needs to go. Some changes can stop at Stage 5; other must go to Stage 7 or Stage 8, otherwise the benefits of the change will be lost.

(c) Management must plan to win the commitment of employees, or prepare for the adverse consequences.

(d) Human reactions to change are a function of both intellect and emotion. Reactions can be either positive or negative, on both an intellectual and an emotional level.

9 CHANGES AND GROUP NORMS

Participation in decisions for making changes should recognise the strength of group attitudes and group norms.

Definition

A *norm* is 'any uniformity of attitude, opinion, feeling or action shared by two or more people. Groups are characterised by the norms their members share' (*Blake and Mouton*).

A group would not be a group if it lacked norms to co-ordinate and regulate the interactions between group members.

A manager can try to use power and authority to break up prevailing norms, in order to make changes easier to introduce. This might work successfully, but it is more likely to fail because of passive resistance from the group members. Blake and Mouton suggested that the most effective way of changing group norms is to involve the people affected in studying what the existing norms are and what would be better.

'Only after prevailing norms are understood can specific steps necessary for shifting from the old to the new be considered and implemented. The key factor is to involve those who are controlled by a norm to change the norm itself.'

(a) The group should be led by the manager who is responsible for the ultimate decisions.

(b) However, all *norm carriers* should actively participate, and be involved in the problem of deciding how to change.

   (i) The group should be allowed to study their situation objectively, and be given the information they need to carry out a full analysis. The reasons for the current problems should be identified after discussions and by common agreement.

(ii) Agreements for change should be reached, made explicit and introduced.

(iii) Changes in norms should be followed up (monitored and enforced), to prevent backsliding. New group norms are always weaker than old ones, until they become well-established.

It is worth adding the point that although Blake and Mouton favoured group participation in decisions to make changes, coerced changes will sometimes work better. *Hersey and Blanchard* suggested that coerced change is better for 'immature' groups and can be introduced comparatively quickly whereas participative change is better for 'mature' groups, to overcome the problem of resistance.

10 CORPORATE CULTURE CHANGE

10.1 Can a culture be changed?

Edwin Baker, in 1981, observed twelve corporations which developed *unhealthy corporate cultures*. He found a common pattern.

(a) The organisation flourished initially under its founder who created, usually without conscious effort, a cohesive group of employees who shared his beliefs and values.

(b) On the founder's retirement the organisation continued to flourish but many employees become rigid and insular in their thinking and behaviour.

(c) Concern for survival faded and, as a result, so did values regarding speed, flexibility, innovation and concern for the customer.

(d) Increased growth led to formalisation and the development of rules and procedures. Divisions occurred between employees and management because of specialisation. Communication and willingness to accept responsibility decreased.

(e) Employees identified with their departments, not with the organisation as a whole.

(f) Corrective action needed to challenge problems of mature products and markets met inertia. It was thwarted by the rigid culture.

In one case the rigidified culture led directly to bankruptcy. Baker warned that:

'*changing the distinctive culture of a large, old organisation is enormously difficult and may take years.*'

Ralph H Kilmann suggests the following steps for closing *culture gaps*.

- Find out about what norms of behaviour are currently present.
- Decide the ways in which norms need to be changed.
- Establish new norms.
- Identify culture gaps between the norms.
- Close culture gaps.

The sorts of norm which Kilmann is talking about relate to attitudes toward performance, excellence, teamwork, communication, leadership, profitability, staff relations, customer relations, honesty, security, training and innovation. Positive norms of behaviour arose where individuals identify their own goals with those of the organisation. Negative norms are insularity, slowness, complacency and hostility. The difficult task, obviously, is to establish new and positive norms of behaviour. The elements listed below will be essential.

(a)   Top management commitment

(b)   Modelling behaviour: management should be seen to be acting on the new norms themselves, not merely mouthing empty words about change

(c)   Support for positive behaviour and confrontation of negative behaviour

(d)   Consistency between the evaluation and reward system and positive behaviour, including linking pay to acting on positive norms

(e)   Communication of desired norms

(f)   Recruitment and selection of the right people

(g)   Induction programmes for new employees on the desired norms of behaviour

(h)   Training and skills development

Most research has shown that, in a large organisation, shifting the value system can take between three and eight years.

Why might it take so long? One of the disadvantages of strong cultures is that, as we have seen, they discourage the questioning of their basic assumptions.

Furthermore, culture is reflected in an organisation's recruitment policies. These might be changed.

(a)   Recruitment is a means of perpetuating the old order. People are recruited who conform to the corporate culture irrespective of their technical or other qualifications. Also people promote others with similar values to themselves.

(b)   In other cases, however, recruitment is a means of developing a new corporate culture from scratch. In the UK Civil Service, outsiders are being brought in at senior levels to bring a different perspective and approach to management.

EXAMPLE: BRITISH AIRWAYS

On 3rd July 1993, British Airways opened a new aircraft maintenance hangar in Bristol, on the principles of Japanese-style management (as reported by the Financial Times). 'BA was careful in who it chose to work at the plant. It was wary of mechanics accustomed to sloppy work in local car repair garages and wanted people who already had a flexible approach to their work. Half the 340 staff recruited so far have never worked on aircraft and only 31 came from elsewhere in BA.'

The management ideas included flexible working, identical uniforms for workers and a single canteen.

Changes in culture can also have a significant impact on the effectiveness of mergers and takeovers.

(a)   In the 1990s, UK high street banks took over broking and jobbing firms in the City of London, as well as merchant banks. There were newspaper reports of conflicts arising from the merger of the different cultures.

(b)   In October 1993, two UK building societies, the Leeds Permanent and the National & Provincial called off a planned merger. The chairmen of both companies indicated that they thought 'it would be too difficult to combine the different cultures, on top of the efforts needed to bring together two complex businesses' (*Financial Times* 29 October 1993). It was said that the Leeds tended towards a more hierarchical role-based culture, whereas the N&P adopted more of a task-based culture.

Activity 7   **(3 minutes)**

You are consultant to a large airline. As you walk through its offices, you notice that people's job titles are on their office doors, not their names. Late one evening as you leave you encounter one of the senior directors overlooking the airport. 'They're all here', he says, 'The whole fleet, apart from one which is due back from Switzerland in half an hour.' 'What if you wish to fly to Switzerland tonight?' you ask. 'Go by Helvetic Airways. None of this lot are leaving until tomorrow morning', he says.

What does the above tell you about the culture of the airline?

10.2 Challenging cultural norms

How do you go about changing culture?

'Changing a culture to increase a corporation's effectiveness is a hazardous undertaking '
(Charles Hampden-Turner)

Hampden-Turner recommends a number of steps that senior managers, perhaps with the advice of management consultants, should take.

Senior managers, if they wish to change a culture, have to know about it in detail. Hampden-Turner suggests *six modes of intervention:* these produce a knowledge about how the culture works.

(a)   *Find the dangers ('Locate the black sheep').* In other words, the best way to find out about how a culture works is to violate it, by doing something culturally shocking.

'Violation .... makes the 'invisible' nature of the culture visible. So long as everybody complies, culture may not be articulated.'

If you break the unwritten rule, then the force of the culture will be mobilised against you. Change managers need to find out about previous cultural rebels, so they can plan their attacks more circumspectly. In short, cultural taboos are elicited.

(b)   *Bring conflicts into the open.* Interviewing and observation are the principal tools of cultural investigation. Interviews identify what people believe as *individuals,* as opposed to what they affirm as *employees.*

'Many corporate cultures greatly reduce the permissible variety of individual expression. The interviewees may be trying to use the interviewer as a messenger.'

The danger is that consultants can unwittingly become involved in an orchestrated strategy to get rid of an unpopular boss. The interviewer should uncover dilemmas (eg safety versus performance). An example quoted was British Airways:

> '*The demeanour of cabin and ground staff .... towards customers .... could make or break the airline .... [but] such staff were largely without the power to initiate improvements or control events.*'

Sometimes the dilemmas are embroiled in social conflicts.

(c) *Play out corporate dramas.* The manager or consultant then discusses the culture with its members.

  (i)   'A repressive culture may simply deny that remarks qualifying or criticising it were ever made.'

  (ii) 'A narrow or low context culture may agree that such remarks were made, but treat them as the utterances of private persons, irrelevant to the common task.'

This can result in heated, but constructive argument.

(d) *Reinterpret the corporate myths.* Corporate stories passed round to recruits indicate something about competing value systems. Sometimes these corporate myths have to change. Hampden-Turner cites the experiences of *Volvo* in France. The French sales force considered the cars they were selling to be boring; after a long trip to Sweden, when they were shown around the factories, they changed their views.

(e) *Look at symbols, images, rituals.* An example quoted by Hampden-Turner is PepsiCo, where every month there is a formal meeting comparing Pepsi's sales with Coca-Cola's.

> '*Juniors entered first, sitting near the walls, then more senior executives, then the Nielsen team [the marketing researchers who had produced the statistics], and then the president, to whom a waiter brought a Pepsi poured in a Tiffany glass. The monthly figures were presented, the president growled or beamed and signalled the end of the proceedings by leaving.*'

This symbolises deference, hierarchy and the firm's competitive context. Rituals are used to celebrate achievement, or to mark changes (eg in a merger): 'changing a corporate culture can mean that new symbols, rituals and approaches are devised.'

(f) *Create a new learning system.* Cultures filter and exclude information. They need to be modified to accept new types of data.

Any programme of cultural change involves three processes.

- Identifying and exposing the hidden assumptions of the new culture
- Trying to identify the conflicts hidden in the culture
- Identifying cultural mechanisms for change

Culture is part of a process of organisation restructuring. The commitment of senior management is important if it is not to be viewed cynically.

NOTES

Chapter roundup

- Change occurs in the environment, goods/services, technology, management organisation structure or culture.

- Even if an organisation prefers stability, it still has to innovate and it may be faced by discontinuous environmental change.

- Organisations grow for many reasons. Similarly they may decline. Both processes have effects on organisation structure.

- Corporate decline is caused by poor management, poor financial controls, high cost, poor marketing, a variety of competitive weaknesses, a failure of big projects, and financial policy. Turning the situation or acquisition round can mean addressing these issues independently of preconceptions.

- Change involves structural and behavioural factors. Resistance to change results from individual uncertainties, distrust of management. Some of this may arise from poor information. Some resistance may result from uncertainty about the nature of the change itself, or from poor information.

- Corporate culture is often the hardest matter to change, because it is often unwritten, and resistance can be powerful. Change agents need to expose the hidden assumptions of the corporate culture and offer alternatives.

Quick quiz

1 Give examples of different types of change.

2 How does change differ from transformation?

3 State four stages in corporate collapse.

4 What is force field analysis?

5 In what ways does change affect people?

6 What is meant by 'refreezing'?

Answers to quick quiz

1 New technology, reorganisation, altered working conditions, revised personnel policies, developments in style of philosophy of management.

2 Change is gradual and takes place in small increments. Transformation is rapid and wide-ranging.

3 Crisis denial; hidden crisis; disintegration; collapse.

4 Kurt Lewins' technique for visualising the interplay of restraining and driving forces that promotes equilibrium.

5 Change can lead to physiological, psychological and circumstantial effects.

6 Consolidation and reinforcement of new attitudes and behaviour after change has taken place.

Answers to activities

1   The answers to this activity will depend very strongly on the nature of your own organisation. However, if you want to add to the list of factors prompting change in organisations, you may care to consider the following.

    (a)   *Competitive behaviour* from existing competitors or from the arrival of new entrants, perhaps from overseas.

    (b)   *Governmental regulations and control* not only within the UK, but also prompted by the European Union and other international agencies.

    (c)   *Changing social conditions* such as greater concern for the environment and/or animal welfare.

2   Relevant organisational or corporate disasters could include the rescue operation mounted for the derivatives investment firm Global Financial Management, whose collapse it was feared would undermine the international financial system; and the Millennium Dome, which at the time of writing appears to be at stage 3, at least, with stage 4 imminent.

3   The answers to this activity appear in subsequent paragraphs of the text, though it would be possible for you to generate your own responses. Always bear in mind, however, that you are supposed to be looking at the situation *from the perspective of the workers concerned*, and their viewpoint is likely to be founded on self-interest rather than on an altruistic loyalty to their employing organisation.

4   We think that Pareto (an Italian economist) was optimistic. If a change leaves some people better off, then other people may not be worse off in absolute terms, but they will certainly *feel* themselves to be worse off. Giving a pay rise to some parts of the organisation does not mean that other employees have had their pay reduced, but it will certainly feel like that to them.

    Veblen's feet seem to be more firmly planted on the ground. What he seems to say is that there is a price for everything and it has to be paid by someone. This is surely plausible. Can you think of any change which does not furnish supporting evidence for Veblen's real-world principle?

6   Sam will probably be worried by quite a few things. First of all, where does he fit into the new structure? Which division will he be working for? Will he be separated from his colleagues, who might go to work in different divisions? Where might he be working, and is the threat of relocation to a different area a serious one? Does he like the idea of living somewhere else? He hasn't had much experience with computer systems, and so is he worried about the prospect of having to work with a new database system? Will he get any training? He is ambitious, and so how does the reorganisation affect his career prospects? Does the divisional management structure make it more difficult for a specialised functional manager (eg. an accountant) to reach a general management position, or easier?

    The company's management should have thought about the fears and doubts of its employees before it announced any changes, and done something pro-active to overcome them.

7   This is not so much a commercial airline, but a military airforce. Hence, the concentration on rank, and emphasis on control. A corporate culture which delighted in, or was relieved by, assets not used and more

importantly, potential customers not served, is hardly a business operation at all. (*Note*. This activity was drawn from a case history described by Charles Hampden-Turner.)

Further question practice

Now try the following practice questions at the end of this text

Multiple choice questions: **89 to 95**

Exam style question: **13**

Chapter 14 :
ETHICS AND SOCIAL RESPONSIBILTY

Introduction

The issue of ethics and social responsibility is complex because what constitutes ethical or non-ethical behaviour is seldom clear cut; it is important because society increasingly expects organisations to behave in an ethically acceptable manner. If an organisation fails to behave ethically, it may lose business, sometimes irrevocably and disastrously. At the same time, acting ethically can constrain the organisation's achievement of its goals.

In this chapter you will learn about these things.

    (a)   The importance and complexity of the issues surrounding ethics and social responsibility for organisations and their various stakeholders

    (b)   Ethical and unethical actions undertaken by employees acting individually or employees as representatives of their organisations

    (c)   The difficulties associated with applying broad concepts of ethics and social responsibilities into the everyday operational actions of employees within organisations

1   SOCIAL RESPONSIBILITY AND THE ORGANISATION

Throughout the course of this book we have repeatedly considered the impact of the environment on the activities of organisations. In this chapter we will consider the issues of business ethics and social responsibility, and consider how organisations can and should interact with the environment in which they operate. *Koontz, O'Donnell and Weihrich* suggest

'A society, awakened and vocal with respect to the urgency of social problems, is asking the managers of all kinds of organisations, particularly those at the top, what they are doing to discharge their social responsibilities and why they are not doing more.'

Increasingly organisations of all types - businesses, governments, universities, charities – are expected to behave in a socially responsible way. In doing so the decision makers in these organisations must balance a variety of different objectives.

(a)   Local government is expected to provide services to the local community, and to preserve or improve the character of that community, but at an acceptable cost to the ratepayers.

(b)   Businesses are expected to provide goods and services, which reflect the needs of users and society as a whole. These needs may not be in harmony – arguably, the development of the Concorde aeroplane and supersonic passenger travel did not contribute to the public interest, and caused considerable inconvenience to residents near airports who suffer from excessive aircraft noise. A business should also be expected to anticipate the future needs of society; examples of socially useful products might be energy-saving devices and alternative sources of power.

Pollution control is a particularly important example of social responsibility; some progress has been made in the development of commercial processes for recycling waste material. British Coal attempts to restore the environment by planting on old slag heaps.

(c)   Universities and schools are expected to produce students whose abilities and qualifications will prove beneficial to society. A currently popular view of education is that greater emphasis should be placed on vocational training for students.

(d)   In some cases, legislation may be required to enforce social need, for example to regulate the materials used to make crash helmets for motor cyclists, or to regulate safety standards in motor cars and furniture. Ideally, however, organisations should avoid the need for legislation by taking earlier self-regulating action.

1.1   Social responsibility and businesses

Institutions like hospitals and schools exist because health care and education are seen to be desirable social objectives. However, how far is it reasonable for businesses to pursue similar social objectives by giving to charities, voluntarily imposing strict environmental objectives on themselves and so forth?

We can begin to answer this question by considering what social responsibility really means. Johnson and Scholes *(Exploring Corporate Strategy)* suggest that we analyse this using a three level model.

(a)   The *macro* level is concerned with the behaviour, power, and influence of business at a national and global level. An example is the lobbying process through which business interests may seek to influence government decision making.

(b) The *corporate* level is concerned with the ethical issues encountered by individual organisations pursuing their mission and goals. For example, should an organisation use the cheapest source of raw materials regardless of the impact of that source on the natural environment?

(c) The *individual* level concerns the behaviour of individual employees in a given organisation, for example, non-discrimination against minority groups within the labour force and ethical use of power.

1.2 Macro level

The growth and concentration of business has had a major impact on power and influence throughout the world. In his article '*Limits to the Social Responsibility of Business*', *David C Korten* suggests that corporate institutions have overtaken national government and become the most powerful institutions in the world. The power of big business is demonstrated by his claim that the 500 largest corporations in the world control 25% of the world's economic output and yet only employ 0.05 of 1% of the world's population, and that the top 300 transnationals, excluding financial institutions, own some 25% of the world's productive assets. Korten also points to an article from The Economist which suggested that in the consumer durables, automotive, airline aerospace, electronic components, electrical and electronics and steel industries, the top five firms control more than 50% of the global market.

The relationship between organisational influence and government decision making is subject to considerable scrutiny. In the UK the Conservative party has traditionally been seen by many as the political ally of business, the Labour party has been considered as the ally of the labour movement and trade unions (a belief Labour sought to minimise in the 1997 election campaign).

At an international level much comment has been made of the ways in which multinationals have often used their financial power to gain concessions from the governments of developing countries – some commentators argue that such concessions have been at the expense of local people, whilst others claim that the presence of big business will increase the rate of development in such countries.

A key concern is to what extent business can be relied on to avoid an abuse of power and to what extent other institutions such as governments can and should provide checks and balances? Your answer to this question will depend very much on your beliefs about the role of business in society: this is an issue we will consider in the next section.

1.3 Corporate level

It is obvious that organisations exist in a variety of environments and therefore experience a range of ethical considerations in their decision making. Underpinning the decisions taken are inevitable assumptions about the role of business in society. Johnson and Scholes suggest four categories into which organisations may fit.

The first category are those organisations which accept *Milton Friedman's* claim that 'the business of business is business' and that 'the only responsibility of business is to increase its profit'. These organisations limit their behaviour only to the extent that they comply with legislation. However as we have already suggested organisations may well seek to influence legislation. Some organisations in this category would even raise doubts about the need for legislation arguing that the most appropriate control mechanism is the free market. According to subscribers to this approach the interests of society as a whole are best served by allowing organisations a free rein.

Secondly, there are those organisations which, despite tending towards the beliefs of the first group, also acknowledge the growing social pressure for business to recognise and meet its social responsibilities. These organisations recognise that there are commercial benefits from investing in and maintaining positive relationships with all their stakeholders – including the general public at large. Examples of activities typical of such groups would be community education programmes. Profit remains the ultimate measure of performance.

The third group are termed 'progressive' organisations and are characterised by a belief that performance should be judged by more complex criteria than profit alone. These organisations are prepared to accept lower profits as a result of ensuring that their behaviour is in line with the common good. Johnson and Scholes suggest that firms with Quaker origins typify this approach, and examples are Clark's Shoes and Cadbury.

Finally, there are organisations which have core objectives of meeting particular social needs; in this case making a profit is at best secondary to meeting need. Financial considerations are more likely to be seen as a constraint limiting the achievement of the core objectives. A good example of this type of organisation is Shelter, a charity which promotes the interests of homeless people. Despite the fact that the organisation undertakes fund raising and has retail interests the money earned is a means to an end. Despite the non-profit motive such organisations have equal (and arguably greater) responsibilities to society.

It is worth noting that this final category has traditionally included public services such as hospitals which, in the UK, have faced increasing pressures from central government to become more commercially focused.

Activity 1 **(Over the next few days)**

Identify two additional organisations in each of the above categories. Provide evidence to support your reasoning.

1.4 Individual level

As we have developed our ideas about organisations in this book we have continually emphasised the need to remember that organisations are ultimately made up of individual human beings all of whom will have their own agenda and behavioural patterns. Similar consideration needs to be given to the impact of employee behaviour on corporate ethics and social responsibility. Formal statements about these issues will be meaningless if individuals do not pursue them in practice.

A clear issue is the *exercise of power* within the organisation. Managers, for example, have the opportunity to make decisions about corporate behaviour and, through their control of information flow, to influence the expectations of others. Associated with this however is a need for high levels of personal integrity.

Managers may also experience a sense of conflict over whose interests should be served when deciding on issues of corporate responsibility; this is an issue requiring perspective and balance.

A dilemma facing many managers is how to deal with strategy or activity within their organisation which they believe to be socially irresponsible. Should they draw attention to what is going on or should they simply leave the organisation? Where does the responsibility for social responsibility ultimately lie? This dilemma is to a large degree likely to be influenced by culture and the organisational strength of the commitment to socially responsible behaviour within the organisation: this commitment must be reflected in internal policies and mechanisms. For example, it is pointless expecting employees to make decisions based on a range of criteria in addition to bottom line profit if the reward system does not define results in an appropriate way.

1.5 Arguments for social responsibility

Friedman argues that the only responsibilities of business are to obey the law and to maximise the economic interests of the stakeholders. However, there are other views.

(a) Businesses possess increasing levels of *power and influence* at both national and global levels. This concentration of power opens up the possibility of misuse.

(b) Large corporations can *manipulate markets*. Social responsibility, forced or voluntary, is a way of recognising this.

(c) Businesses receive a lot of *government support*. The public pays for roads, infrastructure, education and health, all of which benefits businesses. Although businesses pay tax, the public ultimately pays, perhaps through higher prices.

(d) Strategic decisions by businesses always have *wider social consequences*. In other words, says *Mintzberg*, the firm produces two outputs.

- Its goods and services
- The social consequences of its activities

If it is accepted that businesses do not bear the total social cost of their activities, then the exercise of social responsibility is a way of compensating for this.

An example is given by the environment. Industrial pollution is injurious to health: if someone is made ill by industrial pollution, then arguably the polluter should pay the sick person, as damages or in compensation, in the same way as if the business's builders had accidentally bulldozed somebody's house.

In practice, of course, while it is relatively easy to identify statistical relationships between pollution levels and certain illnesses, mapping out the chain of cause and effect from an individual's wheezing cough to the dust particles emitted by Factory X, as opposed to Factory Y, is quite a different matter.

EXAMPLE: ASBESTOS

In April 1994, BBC2 showed a programme which explored the dangers of asbestos and the cynicism of big business. By the year 2025, it is estimated that more than 50,000 people will have died of mesothelioma, an asbestos-related, incurable cancer of the chest; it is already, according to Professor Julian Peto (Institute of Cancer Research), 'by far and away the most important occupational cancer'.

Against this background, BBC2 investigated the history of T&N, the British multinational once known as Turner & Newall. In the 1950s and 1960s, T&N was the largest asbestos company in the UK: it fireproofed the QE2 and its asbestos-blasting system, Limpet, was used to fireproof the steel walls of the Chase Manhattan Bank on Wall Street.

Newall's insulation factory at Washington, Tyne & Wear, closed down in 1980. As far back as 1958, the factory was regularly provided with evidence of the links between asbestos and mesothelioma, but had chosen to ignore (or suppress) the situation.

Pressure from the widows and widowers of T&N's workers had failed to achieve very much, the company claiming that it had no material relating to its early history (including Newall's workforce at Washington).

However, Chase Manhattan Bank has sued T&N for several million dollars for the cost of stripping asbestos from its 60-floor building – and its New York lawyers have unearthed more than a million documents from the T&N headquarters in Manchester.

This is just one instance of the damage which can be done when an organisation (to put it at its most charitable) makes mistakes, but then refuses to admit that it has done so and, of course, does not acknowledge liability. The consequential damage to the organisation's reputation is made worse if it appears, as in the T&N scenario, that there could have been deliberate suppression of information which, had it been available, might have caused employees to behave in different ways.

It does not seem unreasonable for society to expect organisations to behave responsibly within a mutually acceptable and demonstrable code of ethics.

There are reasons why it may well prove to be *in an organisation's interest* to act in a socially responsible manner and to exercise what we might term *enlightened self interest*. This may go beyond solely taking responsibility for the activities associated with their core business.

(a) If the stakeholder concept of a business is held, then the public is the stakeholder in the business. A business only succeeds because it is part of a wider society. Giving to charity is one way of encouraging a relationship.

(b) Charitable donations and artistic sponsorship are a useful medium of public relations and can reflect well on the business. It can be regarded, then, as another form of promotion, which like advertising, serves to enhance consumer awareness of the business, while not encouraging the sale of a particular brand.

(c) Social responsibility may pre-empt legislation which could ultimately prove more restrictive.

This is not to suggest that socially responsible behaviour is without cost – there may in some cases be pressures for a firm to behave less than responsibly in pursuit of short-term profit. However in the longer term the costs of behaving irresponsibly may prove greater than those associated with responsible behaviour.

Activity 2   **(10 minutes)**

The Heritage Carpet Company is a London-based retailer which imports carpets from Turkey, Iran and India. The company was founded by two Europeans who travelled independently through these countries in the 1970s. The company is the sole customer for carpets made in a number of villages in each of the source countries. The carpets are hand woven. Indeed, they are so finely woven that the process supposedly requires that children be used to do the weaving, thanks to their small fingers. The company believes that it is preserving a 'craft', and the directors believe that this is a justifiable social objective. Recently a UK television company has reported unfavourably on child exploitation in the carpet weaving industry. There were reports of children working twelve-hour shifts in poorly lit sheds and cramped conditions, with consequent deterioration in eyesight, muscular disorders and a complete absence of education. The examples cited bear no relation to the Heritage Carpet Company's suppliers. There has been a spate of media attention. The regions in which the Heritage Carpet Company's supplier villages are found are soon expected to enjoy rapid economic growth.

What boundary management issues are raised for the Heritage Carpet Company?

---

2 SOCIAL RESPONSIBILITY IN PRACTICE

Irrespective of the categories we considered above, the general trend within society has been to expect organisations to behave in a socially responsible way towards all their stakeholders. Stakeholder is a much broader category than shareholder or employee; it is probably best thought of as all those who are directly or indirectly affected by an organisation's activities. All organisations will have a wide range of stakeholders. Examples of these groups, together with the possible responsibilities towards them are listed below:

Employees – safe, pleasant working conditions, job security, good wages and fringe benefits, interesting work design, avoidance of discrimination

Shareholders – profits, growth and return on their investment

Consumers – reliable, safe products, honest and responsible sales and marketing techniques, availability, value

Suppliers – fair purchase price, regular orders, prompt payment

Community – safe products and manufacturing methods, contribution to community projects, contribution to the performance of the national economy

Environment – use of sustainable sources of raw materials, minimisation of pollution, energy efficiency

Competitors – fair competitive practices (which will ultimately also benefit the consumer in terms of factors such as choice and price)

Activity 3   **(15 minutes)**

Consider the specific social responsibilities of an organisation of your choice in relation to each of the above categories.

In practice many organisations have recognised that there is considerable commercial potential associated with a high profile social responsibility. Many will even incorporate such concerns within their mission statement. Good examples of organisations which have been highly visible and successful in this way are:

The Body Shop promotes cruelty-free products, recyclable containers, fair trade with producers in developing countries, anti-cruelty campaigns and support the *Big Issue* initiative for the homeless.

Such organisations must endeavour to ensure that the claims made are fulfilled in practice – media claims and evidence to the contrary can be extremely harmful.

Similarly there are numerous examples of organisations who have experienced the impact of being seen as irresponsible.

McDonald's is a good example of an organisation that has experienced considerable criticism and accusation of corporate irresponsibility, particularly from environmentalists. McDonald's have sought to address this image through providing customers with easily accessible in-store information on the sources of their raw materials and on the environmental friendliness of their packaging materials.

Another frequently quoted example is the supply of formula baby milk to nursing mothers in the developing world, ignoring the hygiene and health problems that may be associated with this approach to feeding.

2.1 Social responsibility in the global market place

In the same way as organisations around the world exist and operate in different political and legal frameworks, they must also accommodate differing social and ethical environments:

(a) The *social environment* consists of the customs, attitudes, beliefs and education of society as a whole, or of different groups in society.

(b) The *ethical environment* consists of a set (or sets) of well-established rules of personal and organisational behaviour.

Importantly these environments will be associated with behavioural norms which will in turn influence the expectation and behaviour of stakeholders associated with the organisation in the given environment. Acceptable behaviour in one culture, such as patronage and rewards for help given would be seen as unacceptable discrimination and bribes in another.

This may prove particularly difficult for multinational and transnational organisations which, in addition to accommodating local differences, also seek to avoid creating inconsistencies in the overall corporate image.

Evidence of this problem can be seen in a 1987 survey of 300 US and European companies (*Defining Corporate Ethics* by *Ronald E Berenbeim*), which shows how ambiguous ethical considerations can become once they are extended beyond narrow social boundaries.

Most of the respondents agreed that sexual harassment, inappropriate corporate gifts and environmental protection were ethical issues and therefore the exercise of power to prevent them or encourage them (as appropriate) could itself be ethically justified. Much more contentious were topics like workplace safety, product safety standards, disinvestment, advertising content, whistle-blowing and the techniques used to win (government) contracts.

Activity 4   **(20 minutes)**

In his 1993 book, Riding the Waves of Culture, *Fons Trompenaars* uses some case study scenarios to illustrate how people in different societies address ethical dilemmas. Here are two examples. Produce your own response to each one, and then compare your 'solution' to the ideas advanced by managers from various countries.

Situation 1

You are riding in a car driven by a close friend. He hits a pedestrian. You know he was going at least 35 miles per hour in an area of the city where the maximum allowed speed is 20 miles per hour. There are no witnesses. His lawyer says that if you testify under oath that he was only driving 20 miles per hour it may save him from serious consequences.

What right has your friend to expect you to protect him?

(a)   My friend has a definite right as a friend to expect me to testify to the lower figure.

(b)   He has some right as a friend to expect me to testify to the lower figure.

(c)   He has no right as a friend to expect me to testify to the lower figure.

What do you think you would do in view of the obligations of a sworn witness and the obligation to your friend?

(a)   Testify that he was going 20 miles per hour.
(b)   Not testify that he was going 20 miles per hour.

Situation 2

You have just come from a secret meeting of the board of directors of a company. You have a close friend who will be ruined unless she can get out of the market before the board's decision becomes known. You happen to be having dinner at the friend's home this evening.

What right does your friend have to expect you to tip her off?

(a)   She has a definite right as a friend to expect me to tip her off.
(b)   She has some right as a friend to expect me to tip her off.
(c)   She has no right as a friend to expect me to tip her off.

Would you tip her off in view of your obligations to the company and your obligation to your friend?

(a)   Yes
(b)   No

---

3   ETHICS AND POWER

In our discussion we have frequently referred to the issue of power. An important part of socially responsible behaviour for both organisations and the individual is the ethical use of power. How can the extent to which power is being used in a unethical way be determined? Here are two simple rules.

    (a)   *Power should be wielded on behalf of the organisation* rather than purely to further the self interest of a single individual or small cabal

(b)   *Power should be used in conformity with Argenti's 'no harm' principle*, to further the positive goals of the organisation rather than solely or principally to damage others.

Given these rules, the exercise of organisational power becomes unethical if either is broken.

(a)   If self interest takes precedence over corporate advantage

(b)   if deliberate action or inaction results in intentional damage to others, either inside or outside the organisation

Unfortunately, the apparent straightforwardness of this framework runs into immediate problems. The first is whether the attempt to discriminate between the ethical and non-ethical use of power is actually self-defeating. *Morgan McCall* has pointed out that creative leaders (and thus effective leaders) are often inconsistent, devious and two-faced. His implication – that directing organisations has little to do with social morality – is shared by *F G Bailey* in the introduction to his book, *Humbuggery and Manipulation: The Art of Leadership* (1988). After considering the role of leaders in society, Bailey concludes:

'Leaders are often villains and ... it is very difficult to be an effective leader and at the same time a good person ... one does better to look dispassionately at the institution [of leadership] itself and admit that it has no place for those who practise nothing but the right and the good.'

The borderline between what constitutes the ethical and the unethical use of power is often little more than a hair's breadth – and successful outcomes will excuse unsavoury methods. The acceptable face of power varies from one society and one organisation to another, making it difficult to regulate through any universal code of ethics. Frank Field, replying to Sir Geoffrey Chandler, would like to see ethics as an extension of Christian (ie transcendental) doctrine:

'No industrial society seeking agreed means of regulating all forms of human behaviour can operate ... unless some basic beliefs are not only agreed but regularly affirmed.'

Power is often used in and by organisations for undesirable purposes.

- To gain more than a fair share of whatever benefits are available
- To block other people's legitimate and worthwhile work plans
- To set people against one another
- To seek more and more power for the sake of it
- To pursue personal advancement at the expense of the organisation
- To generate personal immunity from criticism
- To pursue personal vendettas
- To exert power merely for display purposes

Equally, dubious tactics may be used when exercising power for dubious reasons.

- Withholding information from people who need it
- Distorting information
- Circulating slanderous gossip
- Claiming credit for the ideas of others
- Inventing new rules simply to restrict other people
- Empire-building
- Forming defensive cliques and in-groups
- Blackmail

- Sabotage

This list is not exhaustive.

3.1 Ethical purity and the pursuit of profit

Corporate social responsibility should not be seen as a catch-all, and it is naive to assume that there is no conflict between ethical behaviour and profit. Some business ethicists have, according to *Andrew Stark ('What's the matter with Business Ethics?' Harvard Business Review* May-June 1993), taken issue with the *enlightened self interest approach* to ethics.

(a) They argue that ethical behaviour is *not* always in a company's best interest. For example, large proportions of the shareholding in many companies are held by pension funds – these shareholders may put considerable emphasis and pressure for prioritising profits. Also, despite our arguments that consumers will seek out socially responsible producers, the public is not always prepared to pay the additional cost associated with this type of production and may purchase the cheaper, less socially responsible alternative; a good example of this is the meat industry.

(b) They then argue that because enlightened self interest is not *altruistic*, it cannot by definition be ethical. Altruism involves always putting other people first. This is a philosophical point about definitions with which many would disagree. There is surely no good reason why acting ethically should necessarily involve sacrifice.

Furthermore, some business ethicists take fairly absolutist views: 'if in some instance it turns out that what is ethical leads to a company's demise, so be it', says *Richard DeGeorge*. But, to take issue with this, we must remember that a company is more than just a vehicle for investors: it provides work and security. The demise of a company, and all the attendant suffering caused by redundancy, is surely not something that an ethicist can contemplate with equanimity.

It is true to say, however, that ethics and interests may conflict, and managers have to deal with a variety of conflicting interests where there is no clear course of action. Some approaches to business ethics can help bring this abstract moral theorising down to earth.

(a) To be of use to practising managers, business ethics cannot concern itself with the moral standing of the capitalist system itself, and must accept the fact that people work in and for profit-orientated organisations, just as medical ethics takes for granted the doctor-patient relationship.

(b) Business ethicists should also accept that people have mixed motives. *Robert Solomon* suggests that *Aristotle's* approach to ethics, whereby a vice is an excess or a deficiency of a virtue (a golden mean), can be applied to businesses: for example, to what extent is toughness in a manager a virtue ('decisiveness')? When does it become a vice ('dictatorial inflexibility')? What is the golden mean?

(c) Finally, some business ethicists argue that it is not reasonable to act with regard to somebody *else's* interest if that regard is not reciprocated. Ethics has to be grounded in mutual trust. Furthermore, it could be argued that if businesses have responsibility to stakeholders, *then stakeholders owe obligations to businesses*. Pressure groups who pressure companies to produce expensive ethical products should at least try and change public attitudes too.

4 ETHICS WITHIN ORGANISATIONS

Definition

> *Ethics* is a code of moral principles that people follow with respect to what is right or wrong.

Ethical principles are not necessarily enforced by law, although the law incorporates moral judgements (murder is wrong ethically, and is also punishable legally).

Companies have to follow legal standards, or else they will be subject to fines and their officers might face similar charges. Ethics in organisations has two aspects.

(a) Issues of social responsibility as discussed in the previous sections

(b) Issues of business practices, between organisations, and between the individuals in the organisation

People who work for organisations bring their own values into work with them. Organisations contain a variety of ethical systems.

- Personal, deriving from upbringing, political opinions and personality.
- Professional (eg medical ethics).
- Organisation cultures (eg 'customer first').
- Organisation systems

EXAMPLE: SEARS, ROEBUCK

Organisation systems and targets do have ethical implications. The *Harvard Business Review* reported that the US retailer, Sears, Roebuck was deluged with complaints that customers of its car service centre were being charged for unnecessary work: apparently this was because mechanics had been given targets of the number of car spare parts they should sell.

Lynne Paine (Harvard Business Review, March-April 1994) suggests that ethical decisions are becoming more important as penalties become tougher, in the US at least, for companies that break the law. This might be contrasted with UK, where a fraudster whose deception ran into millions received a sentence of 180 hours of community service. Paine suggests that there are two approaches to the *management of ethics* in organisations.

- A compliance-based approach.
- An integrity-based approach.

These two approaches are now briefly described.

4.1 Compliance-based programmes

A *compliance-based approach* is primarily designed to ensure that the company acts within the letter of the law, and that violations are prevented, detected and punished. Some organisations, faced with the legal consequences of unethical behaviour employ lawyers to install appropriate measures.

    (a)   Compliance procedures

    (b)   Audits of contracts

    (c)   Systems for employees to inform superiors about criminal misconduct without fear of retribution

    (d)   Disciplinary procedures

Corporate compliance is limited in that it refers only to the law, but legal compliance is 'not an adequate means for addressing the full range of ethical issues that arise every day'. This is especially the case in the UK, where voluntary codes of conduct and self-regulating institutes, are perhaps more prevalent than the US.

An example of the difference between the legality and ethics of a practice is the sale in some countries of defective products without appropriate warnings.

> 'Companies engaged in international business often discover that conduct that infringes on recognised standards of human rights and decency is legally permissible in some jurisdictions.' (Paine)

The compliance approach also overemphasises the threat of detection and punishment in order to channel appropriate behaviour. Arguably, some employers view compliance programmes as an insurance policy for senior management, who can cover the tracks of their arbitrary management practices. After all, some performance targets are impossible to achieve without cutting corners: managers can escape responsibility by blaming the employee for not following the compliance programme, when to do so would have meant a failure to reach target.

Furthermore, mere compliance with the law is no guide to *exemplary* behaviour.

4.2 Integrity-based programmes

'An integrity-based approach combines a concern for the law with an emphasis on managerial responsibility for ethical behaviour. Though integrity strategies may vary in design and scope, all strive to define companies' guiding values, aspirations and patterns of thought and conduct. When integrated into the day-to-day operations of an organisation, such strategies can help prevent damaging ethical lapses, while tapping into powerful human impulses for moral thought and action. Thus an ethical framework becomes no longer a burdensome constraint within which companies must operate, but the governing ethos of an organisation.' *(Paine)*

It should be clear from this quotation that an integrity-based approach to ethics treats ethics as an issue of *organisation culture*. Ethics management has three tasks.

- To articulate and give life to an organisation's defining values
- To create an environment that supports ethically sound behaviour
- To instil a sense of shared accountability amongst employees

The table below indicates some of the differences between the two approaches.

	Compliance	Integrity
Ethos	Obey legal rules	Choose ethical standards
Objective	Keep to the law	Enable legal and responsible conduct
Originators	Lawyers	Management, with lawyers, HR specialists and other advisors
Methods(both includes education, and audits, controls, penalties)	Reduced employee discretion	Leadership, organisation systems
Behavioural assumptions	People are solitary self- interested beings	People are social beings with values
Standards(including law)	The law	Company values, aspirations
Staffing	Lawyers	Managers and lawyers
Education	The law, compliance system	Values, the law, compliance systems
Activities	Develop standards, train and communicate, handle reports of misconduct, investigate, enforce, oversee compliance	Integrate values into company systems, provide guidance and consultation, identify and resolve problems, oversee compliance

In other words, an integrity-based approach incorporates issues of ethics in corporate culture and systems.

In an effort to cope with these issues, many organisations have developed corporate codes of conduct for themselves, their employees and (sometimes) their suppliers. The initial tendency with such codes is to construct a negative or prohibitive system which forbids every imaginable inappropriate or undesirable act. Yet negative codes, containing a great number of restrictions, pose several problems.

(a) A focus on prohibitions, often imposed from the top of the organisation, inspires little support or respect.

(b) The negative code presents interpretative difficulties.

(c) Completely prohibitive codes either involve overkill or encourage the creation of loopholes.

Codes founded on affirmative or positive principles, on the other hand, are more inspirational, goal-directed and persuasive. *Robert Austin* of Harvard University has proposed guidelines for an affirmative code as follows.

(a) The manager and employee assert that they will place the organisation's interests first.

(b) They affirm that they will place their duty to society above their duty to the organisation.

(c) They accept an affirmative duty to reveal to those in authority in the organisation the entire facts of any situation where their private interests conflict with those of the organisation, or where the interests of the organisation conflict with those of society.

While a purely affirmative code, which expresses a desired course in positive goals, offers a lucid and concise statement of general concepts, and also addresses conflicts of interest through disclosure (not merely penalty), such a code has its deficiencies as well. An affirmative code often assumes that the organisation's employees possess a reservoir of legal and business knowledge which enables them to translate the code's general provisions into specific standards of conduct.

All this suggests that a combination of prohibitive and affirmative principles represents the optimal mix. Thus most professional bodies will have a code of professional ethics (comprising the affirmative guidelines) plus some detailed rules of conduct to spell out the minimal levels of expected behaviour as well as a set of prohibitions and sanctions.

EXAMPLE: WESTERN OIL

Charles Hampden-Turner (in his book *Corporate Culture*) notes that attitudes to safety can be part of a corporate *culture*. He quotes the example of a firm called (for reasons of confidentiality) Western Oil.

(a) Western Oil had a bad safety record. 'Initially, safety was totally at odds with the main cultural values of productivity (management's interests) and maintenance of a macho image (the worker's culture) ... Western Oil had a culture which put safety in conflict with other corporate values.' In particular, the problem was with its long-distance truck drivers (which in the US have a culture of solitary independence and self reliance) who drove sometimes recklessly with loads large enough to inundate a small town. The company instituted *Operation Integrity* to improve safety, in a lasting way, changing the policies and drawing on the existing features of the culture but using them in a different way.

(b) The culture had five dilemmas.

(i) *Safety-first vs macho-individualism.* Truckers see themselves as 'fearless pioneers of the unconventional lifestyle ... "Be careful boys!" is hardly a plea likely to go down well with this particular group'. Instead of trying to control the drivers, the firm recommended that they become *road safety consultants* (or design consultants). Their advice was sought on improving the system. This had the advantage that 'by making drivers critics of the system their roles as outsiders were preserved and promoted'. It tried to tap their heroism as promoters of public safety.

(ii) *Safety everywhere vs safety specialists.* Western Oil could have hired more specialist staff. However, instead, the company promoted cross-functional safety teams from existing parts of the business, for example, to help in designing depots and thinking of ways to reduce hazards.

(iii) *Safety as cost vs productivity as benefit.* 'If the drivers raced from station to station to win their bonus, accidents were bound to occur ... . The safety engineers rarely spoke to the line manager in charge of the delivery schedules. The unreconciled dilemma between safety and productivity had been evaded at management level and passed down the hierarchy until drivers were subjected to two incompatible

injunctions, work fast and work safely'. To deal with this problem, safety would be built into the reward system.

(iv) *Long-term safety vs short-term steering.* The device of recording 'unsafe' acts in operations enabled them to be monitored by cross-functional teams, so that the causes of accidents could be identified and be reduced.

(v) *Personal responsibility vs collective protection.* It was felt that if 'safety' was seen as a form of management policing it would never be accepted. The habit of management 'blaming the victim' had to stop. Instead, if an employee reported another to the safety teams, the person who was reported would be free of official sanction. Peer presence was seen to be a better enforcer of safety than the management hierarchy.

It has also been suggested that the following institutions can be arranged.

(a) An *ethics committee* is a group of executives (perhaps including non-executive directors) appointed to oversee company ethics. It rules on misconduct. It may seek advice from specialists in business ethics.

(b) An *ethics ombudsperson* is a manager who acts as the corporate conscience.

Members of some professions can also appeal to their professional body for ethical guidance.

Definition

> *Whistle-blowing* is the disclosure by an employee of illegal, immoral or illegitimate practices on the part of the organisation.

In theory, the public ought to welcome this action, which should contribute to public trust. However, whistle-blowing frequently involves *financial loss* for the whistle-blower.

(a) The whistle-blower may lose his or her job.

(b) If the whistle-blower is a member of a professional body, he or she *cannot*, sadly, *rely* on that body to take a significant interest, or even offer a sympathetic ear.

(i) Some professional bodies have narrow interpretations of what is meant by ethical conduct. For many the duties of *commercial confidentiality* are felt to be more important.

(ii) The whistle-blower might have higher ethical values than most of his fellow-professionals, who might object to people rocking the boat.

Activity 5 [10 minutes]

Why do you think that whistle-blowers often suffer as a result of their activities – and may even suffer more than the people committing the offences for which the whistle is blown?

4.3 Corporate governance

An issue that is closely linked to power and its use within the organisation is that of corporate governance. This debate has been particularly active in the UK since the late 1980s and examines the legal cultural and institutional arrangements that determine the direction and performance of corporations – in other words who is really making the decisions and in whose interest. This is a question that becomes increasingly significant for those organisations where there is separation of ownership and control.

This is a huge debate beyond the scope of this text, but a brief overview of the key issues and concerns does provide a good illustration of power issues within an organisation.

Mark Wasilweski and Paul Chavasse ('Making shareholders active and "fat cats" answerable') suggest that the framework for establishing effective corporate governance should be built around four key elements:

- The structure and role of the board
- The role of auditors
- The reporting and accountability of the parties
- Reward and incentive mechanisms

The framework is based on four key principles.

(a) Balance of power (ensuring discussion of power and responsibility between individuals, for example the separation of the roles of chief executive and chairman)

(b) Independence,

(c) Accountability (generally directors are subject to re-election processes after a given period of time)

(d) Appropriate rewards (incentives that are tied to performance levels).

In the light of considerable media attention and criticism, many companies (and their investors) are paying increasing attention to these issues and to the contents and recommendations of two influential reports, the *Cadbury report* (on corporate governance) and the *Greenbury report* (on top people's pay)

5 SOME SPECIFIC ETHICAL PROBLEMS FACING MANAGERS

Managers have a duty in most enterprises to aim for profit. At the same time, modern ethical standards impose a duty to guard, preserve and enhance the value of the enterprise for the good of all touched by it, including the general public. Large organisations tend to be more often held to account over this than small ones.

The types of ethical problem a manager may meet with in practice are numerous. A few of them are suggested in the following paragraphs.

In the area of *products and production*, managers have responsibility to ensure that the public and their own employees are protected from danger. Attempts to increase profitability by cutting costs may lead to dangerous working conditions or to inadequate safety standards in products. In the United States, product liability litigation is so common that this legal threat may be a more effective deterrent than general ethical standards. The Consumer Protection Act 1987 and EU legislation generally is beginning to ensure that ethical standards are similarly enforced in the UK.

This problem is particularly acute in the pharmaceutical industry. On the one hand, managers may be influenced by a genuine desire to benefit the community by developing new drugs which at the same time will lead to profits; on the other hand, they must not skimp their research on possible side-effects by rushing to launch the new product. In the UK, the Consumer Protection Act 1987 attempts to recognise this dilemma. Drugs companies are not held liable for side-effects which could not have been foreseen by scientific knowledge as it existed at the time the drug was developed – the 'development risk' defence.

Ethical issues also arise in the area of corporate governance and finance. An example is provided by the various Maxwell scandals and some accusations that companies use creative accounting techniques.

Another ethical problem concerns *payments by companies to officials* (particularly officials in foreign countries) who have power to help or hinder the payers' operations. In *The ethics of corporate conduct*, Clarence Walton describes the fine distinctions which exist in this area.

(a) *Extortion*. Foreign officials have been known to threaten companies with the complete closure of their local operations unless suitable payments are made.

(b) *Bribery*. This refers to payments for services to which a company is not legally entitled. There are some fine distinctions to be drawn; for example, some managers regard political contributions as bribery.

(c) *Grease money*. Multinational companies are sometimes unable to obtain services to which they are legally entitled because of deliberate stalling by local officials. Cash payments to the right people may then be enough to oil the machinery of bureaucracy.

(d) *Gifts*. In some cultures (such as Japan) gifts are regarded as an essential part of civilised negotiation, even in circumstances where to Western eyes they might appear ethically dubious. Managers operating in such a culture may feel at liberty to adopt the local customs.

Business ethics are also relevant to competitive behaviour. This is because a market can only be *free* if competition is, in some basic respects, *fair*. There is a distinction between competing aggressively and competing unethically. The dispute between British Airways and Virgin was concerned with issues of business ethics, and involved accusations of unethical conduct.

(a) The theft of information

(b) The planting of inaccurate and derogatory stories in the press

(c) The refusal of normal aircraft service to Virgin (when it was offered to other airlines)

(d) An unethical price war

6 APPLYING PRINCIPLES OF ETHICS

Ethical issues concern the sort of obligations people have to each other, and testing these moral beliefs in practice. For example, killing another person is regarded as morally wrong – but does this apply to killing in self defence?

It might be useful to mention some of the approaches that maybe taken in pursuit of an ethical enquiry.

(a) *Cognitivism vs non-cognitivism*. Ethical judgements are not like scientific ones. Some say, for a variety of reasons, that this lack of a scientific basis invalidates ethical debate.

(i) *Cognitivism* suggests there are objective moral truths which can be known, with the certainty that the Earth goes round the sun. An action is either good or bad: stealing is always wrong.

(ii) *Non-cognitivism* holds that there is no truth or falsity to be discovered. Ethical thinking is merely a cultural preference, like table manners. In practice, though, few people are prepared to take relativism to extremes: instead people suggest a variety of sources of ethical truth.

(b) *Consequentialism vs non-consequentialism* Consequentialism holds that the goodness or badness of an action results from its consequences. An action that gives rise to a social benefit is good. One which does not is bad, or neutral.

(i) A consequentialist would argue that employees who pilfer from stores act badly *because* of the effect on profits and the harm done.

(ii) A non-consequentialist would argue that theft is always wrong, whatever the consequences.

A consequentialist would argue that a fraud of £1m is perhaps worse, all other things being equal, than the theft of £1 from a petty cash tin. The danger in this approach is the idea that computer frauds, or false insurance claims, are victimless crimes. However the public pays through higher fees. Perhaps, also, such ideas act against the public interest in reducing respect for law. Such an ethical viewpoint includes *utilitarianism*, and variants of it. The yardstick of such ethics is *the greatest good to the greatest number:* in other words, utilitarians believe that what is morally right is that which adds most to the general welfare. The simplicity of this rather bland statement is deceptive, however: what constitutes the general welfare? How do you calculate how much 'happiness' is available?

(c) *Duty. Immanuel Kant* said that to act morally, you must act in such a way that you could want everyone else to be bound to follow your example, regardless of individual circumstances or consequences. That is, your example would become a universal law. Kant called his view that we should act in this way the categorical imperative. The guide to what we should accept as a universal law is that people should always be treated as ends and not as means. Kant said that we have a duty to act morally (in the way he set out), whether or not it suits us to do so.

(d) *Rights*. It is often asserted that there is an objective moral law, over and above human legislation. An example is the belief that all people have a bag full of 'human rights' which can be thwarted by malign governments or organisations. Some people ascribe similar rights to animals.

In applying ethical theories to business situations, we can use the following checklist adapted from *Chrissides and Kaler (Introduction to Business Ethics)*. This we can apply to business situations and practices.

(a) *Welfare*

(i) To what extent does an action promote or harm happiness?

(ii) To what extent does an action maintain rules generally held to be of social benefit?

(iii) To what extent is there a just distribution of benefits and harm?

(b) *Duties*

(i) What was the person's motivation for doing something?

(ii)   Is a person actually acting out of self-interest, under the guise of altruism?

(c)   *Rights*

    (i)   Are people's fundamental rights being respected?

    (ii)   In the case of conflict, are the most fundamental rights given priority?

As a general rule of thumb, consider the following.

(a)   Who is or are affected by the course of action, other than the person instigating the action?

(b)   What rights do they have?

(c)   How far have those rights been considered in the decision-making process?

(d)   Have these other parties been dealt with honestly?

(e)   Has appropriate compensation been offered?

Sadly, this is easier said than done.

According to *Archie Carroll* (*'Principles of business ethics – their role in decision-making and an initial consensus'*, *Management Decision*, 1990) there are eleven different ethical criteria which managers sometimes use to judge issues of ethics, conflicts of interest and other problems.

(a)   *The categorical imperative*. Do not adopt principles of action unless they can, without inconsistency, be adopted by everyone else.

(b)   *The conventionalist ethic*. You should act to further your own self interest, so long as you do not violate the law.

(c)   *The golden rule*. Do unto others as you would have them do unto you.

(d)   *The hedonistic ethic*. If it feels good, do it.

(e)   *The disclosure rule*. If you are comfortable with an action or decision, after asking yourself whether you would mind at all if your associates, friends or family were aware of it, then you should act or decide accordingly.

(f)   *The intuition ethic*. You should do whatever your instinct tells you to do.

(g)   *The means-end ethic*. If the end justifies the means, you should act.

(h)   *Might-equals-right ethic*. You should take whatever advantage you are strong enough and powerful enough to take, without respect for ordinary social conventions and laws.

(i)   *The organisation ethic*. Your loyalty to your organisation should take precedence over everything else.

(j)   *Professional ethic*. You should do only that which can be explained before a committee of your professional peers.

(k)   *The utilitarian principle*. You should pursue the greatest good for the greatest number.

Activity 6 **(5 minutes)**

Carroll asked a representative sample of managers to rank these eleven guidelines in terms of the usefulness of each. Before we give you the responses generated by these managers, answer the following two questions in relation to yourself.

(a) Which of the eleven ethical guidelines coincides most closely with the way in which you personally behave in an organisational context?

(b) Which of the eleven guidelines is the one which you would most like the members of your organisation to comply with, so far as their behaviour towards you is concerned?

We can now discuss a practical issue, drawing on an article by *Tom Sorrell* ('*Business Ethics Two Introductory Questions*', in *Readings in Strategic Management*): how quickly should a firm pay its debts?

Payment periods

Payment periods have been the subject of some comment. Small businesses, especially, accuse larger firms of delaying payment. This has the effect of squeezing the creditor's cash flow, and forcing the creditor to rely on overdraft finance. Some have claimed to have been put out of business because of delayed payments from customers.

From a financial management point of view, the advantage of delaying payment is that it means that the debtor can smooth over fluctuations in cash flow and save on overdraft charges. There are thus clear incentives to delay payment.

Sorrell argues that ethical theories offer several reasons why delaying settlement is morally wrong. Most invoices are sent with payment terms even though these might be in small type at the bottom. Certainly there is an understanding that the invoice will be paid. Ethicists would argue that breaching this agreement is wrong, as the creditor has already offered the debtor a benefit. There are several reasons *why* this might be wrong.

(a) *Utilitarianism* would say that breaking one agreement implies a tendency to break more. Trust between contracting parties would be weakened, and so the costs of enforcing contracts would rise: this would be a real social cost.

(b) Aristotle might argue that breaking such an agreement was a character defect.

There are other examples. Sorrell believes that because there are so many reasons to *adhere to contracts*, that this is a good argument in itself for condemning late payment.

Therefore, late payment is wrong because it is a type of breach of an agreement. (We can also add that it is wrong if it does harm to the creditor, but this is a different argument.) However, there are further considerations.

(a) To what extent are terms and conditions added to invoices, not as a formal expectation, but as a fail-safe, so that the creditor can sue if necessary?

(b) What if the creditor itself pursues a similar policy towards its own suppliers?

Furthermore, what if the debtor is undergoing a cash flow crisis? Theories suggest that the moral wrong of non-payment is mitigated if three conditions apply.

(a) The creditor is *able* to withstand the delay.

(b)   The creditor is *willing* to withstand the delay (although under no obligation).

(c)   The creditor informs the debtor of (a) and (b).

Even if the creditor is able and willing to accept a delay, the debtor is still according to Sorrell, acting unethically if the delay is caused by poor management.

Many firms, especially in times of recession, have to juggle with their cash. Sorrell argues that while it is wrong to break an agreement with one creditor, there might be occasions when choices have to be made between two wrongs.

(a)   Creditor A is a large powerful company, with masses of cash. Creditor A is a significant supplier of a vital component.

(b)   Creditor B is a small cash-hungry company, currently teetering on the verge of bankruptcy. The debtor does not need any more of Creditor B's supplies.

The debtor owes each firm £10,000, but has only £10,000 to spend.

In practice, the debtor would pay Creditor A, as it is powerful, and the debtor depends on future supplies from it. Ignoring other considerations, however, paying Creditor B may be the ethically right option as not to pay would drive Creditor B to bankruptcy which is an *additional* wrong to the initial wrong of late payment.

Sorrell also argues that the survival of the debtor company is a factor to be taken into account. If Creditor A threatens to withhold future supplies, thus imperilling the debtor company, Creditor B should still be paid, even if it means bankruptcy. Creditor B, according to Sorrell, should still be paid, on the grounds that the fact that a condemned man can escape execution by implicating an innocent person, does not make this a moral action. (In other words, it is tough on the debtor firm.)

A basic problem, however, is that while a firm is a legal person, in practice a firm has many employees, and is a network of relationships. The analogy between the condemned man does not apply, because it is an individual manager's decision to pay Creditor B rather than Creditor A, and the manager's action affects investors in the firm, employees and others who may not be party to the decision.

However, many or most delayed payment decisions are not life and death issues for either the debtor or the creditor. As a basic principle, Sorrell argues, 'the needier the creditor, the better the reason for paying promptly'.

7   CONCLUSION

Sir Adrian Cadbury's Harvard Business Review article ('Ethical managers make their own rules', 1987) offers some salient observations on the desirability of alignment between individual value-systems and corporate ethics, coupled with the difficulties involved in achieving that objective. Most of Cadbury's significant points and conclusions are listed below.

Ethical and commercial considerations have always been in conflict. Sir Adrian's grandfather had been commissioned by Queen Victoria in 1900 to provide bars of chocolate for soldiers serving in South Africa. Deeply opposed to the Boer War, but intent on building a successful business, he resolved this issue by accepting the order, but carrying it out at cost. Using examples like this, Cadbury argues that ethical signposts glibly presented by single-minded commentators, do not always point in the same direction.

The Milton Friedman doctrine – 'the business of business is business' – is too simplistic. Whether we like it or not, business is part of the social system. The economic elements of major decisions (like the closure of coal mines) cannot be isolated from their social consequences. The UK defence forces may want Chinook helicopters, but these are made in the USA, so a decision to purchase Chinooks may result in high unemployment for Westland Helicopters in Yeovil, itself a marginal Labour parliamentary constituency – and so the decision-making parameters and issues are blurred.

Actions speak louder than words. Ethics are 'the guidelines or rules of conduct by which we aim to live'. It is the actual conduct of the people in the organisation which, collectively, determines the organisation's standards: in other words, it isn't what the organisation *says*, it's what the organisation *does*. While setting down statements of intent is a proper and useful activity, the important test is the actual behaviour of managers when faced with judgements to be made on ethical-or-commercial criteria.

Black-and-white alternatives are a regrettable sign of the times. Organised interest groups possess an inherent debating advantage because they are single-minded and, because of their single-issue fanaticism, do not have to take account of the interests of other parties (or stakeholders). They then display what Cadbury calls the 'ethical superiority of the uninvolved'.

Actions are not ethical if they won't stand scrutiny. It may be culturally acceptable to promote by merit in one country, or by seniority in another. Paying bribes to customs officers may be acceptable in some cultures, but taboo in another. Cadbury suggests two rules.

(a)   Is the payment on the face of an invoice?

(b)   Would it embarrass the recipient (or the donor) to have the incident mentioned in the company newspaper?

Shelving hard decisions is the least ethical course. Faced with tough decisions, managers can put off making them. This comes to the fore when the need for increased efficiency calls for headcount reductions. To put off the evil day, argues Cadbury, is unethical in that, inevitably, it will result in more serious and more widespread adverse consequences later.

Make the satisfaction of your customers, profitably, the primary purpose of your organisation. This should be the overriding moral imperative: if this is done, then the creation of jobs cannot be the aim of the organisation as well. Not to place customers first means that they will be denied the benefits of progress, shareholders will be short-changed – and in the long run, jobs will be lost anyway.

Chapter roundup

- There are differing views about the extent to which external environmental constraints modify (or should modify) business objectives and form boundaries to the exercise of managerial discretion.

- Organisations operate in a social environment and an ethical environment – both these environments have an impact on the behaviour displayed by the organisation and its employees.

- Some believe that a business has only one social responsibility, which is to maximise wealth for its shareholders; however, this is a simplistic view which takes no account of other 'stakeholders' (for example, the government, the environment, customers, employees, suppliers and so forth).

- Ethical considerations in the behaviour of managers are becoming increasingly significant, with organisations adopting either 'compliance-based' or 'integrity-based' approaches in their expectations about managerial (and employee) action.

- Some types of behaviour are acceptable in certain cultural contexts, frowned on in others, or prohibited in a few.

- Organisational employees should develop an ethical stance with which they feel comfortable and which is consistent with the expectations of the organisation.

Quick quiz

1   What is Milton Friedman's view of corporate ethical responsibility?

2   Give two considerations relevant to a wider concept of corporate ethics?

3   How can enlightened self interest help a company?

4   Give two ethical rules for the exercise of power.

5   What two approaches to business ethics did Lynne Paine identify?

6   What is whistle-blowing?

7   What categories of payments to officials did Clarence Walton identify?

8   What is the yardstick of utilitarian ethics?

9   What is Kant's categorical imperative?

10 What principal considerations did Crissides and Kaler suggest for judging business conduct.

Answers to quick quiz

1   'The business of business is business' and 'the only responsibility of business is to increase its profit'. Compliance with the law is the only constraint.

2   The power and influence of business; the ability of large businesses to manipulate markets; the amount of public money flowing into businesses; the wider social consequences of business activity.

3   Business success may be enhanced by a positive image. Self-regulation may pre-empt more restrictive regulation.

4   Power must be used to benefit the organisation rather than the individual possessing it. Power must not be used to harm others.

5   Compliance-based and integrity based.

6   The disclosure by an employee of illegal, immoral or illegitimate practices on the part of the organisation.

7   Extortion, bribery, grease money, gifts.

8   The greatest good to the greatest number

9   Act in accordance with principles that you believe everyone should follow.

10 Welfare, duties, rights.

Answers to activities

1   The answer to this situation will be individual to each respondent, the aim is to think about additional examples to those provided in the text.

2   *Many*. This is a case partly about boundary management and partly about enlightened self-interest and business ethics. The adverse publicity, although not about the Heritage Carpet Company's own suppliers, could rebound badly. Potential customers might be put off. Economic growth in the area may also mean that parents will prefer to send their children to school. The Heritage Carpet Company as well as promoting itself as preserving a craft could reinvest some of its profits in the villages (eg by funding a school), or by enforcing limits on the hours children worked. It could also pay a decent wage. It could advertise this in a 'code of ethics' so that customers are reassured that the children are not simply being exploited. Alternatively, it could not import child-made carpets at all. (This policy, however, would be unlikely to help communities in which child labour is perceived as an economic necessity.)

3   Once again responses will be individual – it may be useful to your overall understanding to play a 'devil's advocate' role here, raising counter-arguments from perspectives based on the Johnson and Scholes model.

4   With *situation 1*, North Americans and most north Europeans emerge as almost totally 'universalistic' in their approach, ie they think that the friend has no right or only some right to expect you to testify falsely. The proportion falls to under 70% for the French and Japanese, while in Venezuela two-thirds of respondents would lie to the police to protect their friend – according to the figures generated by Trompenaars in *Riding the Waves of Culture*. The 'universalists' seem to be saying that 'the law is broken and the serious condition of the pedestrian underlines the importance of upholding the law'. Particularist cultures, however, are more likely to support their friend as the pedestrian's injuries increase, their argument being, in effect, 'my friend needs my help more than ever now that he is in serious trouble with the law.'

For *situation 2*, however, Trompenaars reports some interesting differences. The Japanese in particular jump from the situational ethics (ie the 'particularist' position) they showed previously to a strongly 'universalistic' stance on corporate confidentiality. Quite possibly this occurs because the situation is broader than a particular friend: at stake here is loyalty to a group or corporation versus loyalty to an individual outside that group.

Both case study scenarios show that ethical perspectives differ significantly between societies.

5   Whistle-blowers often suffer, we suggest, because senior people in organisations suspect their motives. Whistle-blowers may seem to be acting dispassionately on behalf of the organisation, but more often they are individuals with strong moral views which could, one day, be displayed to the organisation's disadvantage.

Whistle-blowing to the external world, moreover, is almost always damaging to the organisation. Whistle-blowers may act because their attempts to change the organisation internally have failed or been rebuffed: this is why it is important for organisations to supply legitimised conduits for the articulation of ethical doubts, so that the need for external revelations is reduced or even removed altogether.

6   In the Carroll study, the golden rule was ranked highest. The key to this principle is impartiality and reciprocation: if we want to be treated fairly, then we should treat others fairly. This moral rule is part of the teachings of the world's great religions; it is straightforward and easy to understand; motives for endorsing it may appear to be altruistic but are actually a reflection of precautionary, defensive self interest.

The *disclosure rule* also attracts strong support as it moves the focus on to how others, whose opinions you respect, would regard your decisions, actions or behaviour. Ethically, you are on a sound footing if you are still comfortable with your decision after your family and friends have examined it.

The classification of the eleven different ethical principles immediately clarifies some of the circumstances in which the principles of individual employees may conflict with those espoused by the organisation as a whole. For some, adherence to a *professional ethic* takes precedence over the *organisational ethic;* there may be those who subscribe to the *means-end ethic*, like those British Airways employees who actively pursued some dubious strategies and tactics in the competitive struggle with Virgin.

As an individual, you may choose an ethical stance which is different from that you would like others to display towards you. Think carefully about the implications of this contrast, if it applies to you. There are dangers in behaving 'unethically' towards others, especially if they detect what you are doing, since they may decide to retaliate.

Further question practice

Now try the following practice questions at the end of this text

Multiple choice questions: **96 to 102**

Exam style question: **14**

GLOSSARY

Beliefs What we feel to be the case on the basis of objective and subjective information.

Belief systems 'All the beliefs, sets, expectancies, or hypotheses, conscious or unconscious, that a person at a given time accepts as true, and which in the ordinary course of events he does not question.' (Rokeach)

Business process re-engineering (BRP) The introduction of radical changes in business processes to achieve breakthrough results in terms of major gains in levels of performance plus reductions in costs. Also known as process innovation and core process redesign.

Charities Organisations which exist for a variety of socially useful purposes, for example, to promote the welfare of the elderly, in particular those who are poor, sick and vulnerable.

Closed loop control system A system where part of the output is fed back, so that the output can initiate control action to change either the activities of the system or the system's input. A feedback system or a feedback loop carries output back to be compared with the input.

Co-operatives Businesses owned by the workers who share their profits.

Corporate objectives Those objectives which are concerned with the firm as a whole. Such objectives should be explicit, quantifiable and capable of being achieved.

Counter cultures Groups of people within society whose values and norms are hostile to those held in the wider society.

Culture The beliefs, knowledge, attitudes of mind and customs to which people are exposed in their social conditioning.

Customs Modes of behaviour which represent culturally accepted ways of behaving in response to given situations.

Decision support systems (DSS) Computer systems which are designed to produce information in such a way as to help managers to make better decisions.

Demography The study of human populations, using statistics relating to births, deaths and social matters such as class and ethnicity.

Employers' associations Organisations formed to represent employers, to promote and protect their business interests.

Ethics A code of moral principles that people follow with respect to what is right or wrong.

Executive information system (EIS) An information system which gives the executive easy access to key internal and external data.

Feedback Modification or control of a process or system by its results or effects, by measuring differences between desired and actual results. Feedback is an element in a feedback system and forms the link between planning and control.

Fiscal policy Involves policies on taxation and other sources of income, government spending, borrowing whenever spending exceeds income and repaying debt when income exceeds expenditure.

Flexible manufacturing system (FMS) A highly automated manufacturing system, which is computer-controlled and capable of producing a broad 'family' of parts in a flexible manner. It is characterised by small batch production, the ability to change quickly from one job to another and very fast response times, so that output can be produced quickly in response to specific orders that come in.

Goals 'The intentions behind decisions or actions, the states of mind that drive individuals or collectives of individuals called organisations to do what they do.' (Mintzberg)

Group Any collection of people who perceive themselves to be a group.

Half-life curve The time it takes to produce a 50% improvement in performance.

Informating The use of information as a resource for the whole organisation to exploit in order to develop new insights.

Just-in-time (JIT) Refers to methods of purchasing and production. Items are not bought or manufactured until needed, eliminating the need to hold stocks.

Limited company status The business's debts and the personal debts of the business's owners (shareholders) are legally separate. The shareholders cannot be sued for the debts of the business unless they have given some personal guarantee. Businesses with 'plc' or 'Ltd' after their names are limited companies. They are owned by the shareholders; shares can be traded. They are run by the directors.

Management by objectives (MBO) A comprehensive approach to managing people by setting objectives, targets and plans. MBO is a scheme of planning and control which provides co-ordination in three areas.

(a)   Short-term plans with longer-term plans and goals
(b)   The plans (and commitment) of junior with senior management
(c)   The efforts of different departments

Management information system (MIS) A system which collects and presents management information to a business in order to facilitate its control.

Mission The organisation's basic function in society, in terms of the products and services it produces for its clients. (Mintzberg)

Mission statement A written statement that can incorporate some, but not all, of an organisation's mission.

Monetary policy Policy that attempts to influence economic activity through interest rates, exchange rates, control of the money supply and controls over bank lending and credit.

Negative feedback Information which indicates that the system is deviating from its planned or prescribed course, and that some re-adjustment is necessary to bring it back on course. This feedback is called 'negative' because control action would seek to reverse the direction or movement of the system back towards its planned course.

Norm An attitude, opinion, feeling or action shared by two or more people.

Open loop control system A system where control is exercised regardless of the output produced by the system.

Organisation A social arrangement for the controlled performance of collective goals.

Partnerships Arrangements between individuals to carry on a business in common with a view to profit. Partnerships are governed by a partnership agreement.

Personality The total pattern of characteristic ways of thinking, feeling and behaving that constitute the individual's distinctive method of relating to the environment.

Positive feedback Information which results in control action that causes actual results to maintain (or increase) their path.

Professional associations Organisations that exist for people doing a similar job. Examples are the main accountancy institutes.

Quality The features and characteristics of a product or service connected to its ability to meet stated or implied needs.

Reference groups Groups with which an individual closely identifies. They have a major influence on the individual's behaviour, by offering models and norms for appropriate conduct. The individual need not be a member of the group itself: any group to which the individual aspires to belong to is also a reference group.

Risky-shift The tendency of individuals in groups to take greater risks than their individual, pre-discussion preferences would imply.

Socialisation The process by which individuals learn the social expectations, goals, beliefs, values and attitudes that enable them to exist in society. Socialisation is the process by which we acquire sufficient knowledge of a society and its ways to be able to function and participate in it.

Sole tradership A business owned and run by one individual who may employ one or two assistants and who controls their work. Although the individual will keep separate business and personal accounts, this has no significance other than for convenience. The individual's business and personal affairs are, for legal and tax purposes, identical.

Stakeholders Different groups or individuals whose interests are directly affected by the activities of a firm.

Strategic intent Involves (a) the desire to attain a particular leadership position (b) communicating the value of the target as the main motivating factor to employees (c) a guide to resource allocation. (Hamel and Prahalad)

Sub-cultures Cultures which exist within cultures.

Total Quality Management (TQM) A culture aimed at continually improving performance in meeting the requirements in all functions of a company. The basic principle of TQM is that the cost of preventing mistakes is less than the cost of correcting them once they occur.

Trade unions Organised associations of working people in a trade, occupation or industry (or several trades or industries), formed for protection and promotion of their common interests, mainly the regulation and negotiation of pay and conditions. They receive subscriptions from their members.

Values Beliefs which are (i) relatively enduring (ii) relatively general (not tied to specific objects) (iii) fairly widely accepted as a guide to culturally appropriate behaviour – and therefore as a standard of desirable and undesirable beliefs, attitudes and behaviour.

Whistle-blowing The disclosure by an employee of illegal, immoral or illegitimate practices on the part of the organisation.

World class manufacturing (WCM) A term coined in the mid 1980s to describe the fundamental changes taking place in manufacturing companies. It has four key elements: 1) a new approach to product quality, 2) Just-in-time manufacturing (JIT), 3) utilising the skills and abilities of the workforce to the full, 4) a flexible approach to customer requirements. WCM policy is to develop close relationships with customers.

MULTIPLE CHOICE QUESTIONS

Chapter 1

Data for questions 1 and 2

BZ Ness Ltd is an organisation with a strongly traditional outlook. It is structured and managed according to classical principles: specialisation, the scalar chain of command, unity of command and direction. Personnel tend to focus on their own distinct tasks, which are strictly defined and directed. Communication is vertical, rather than lateral. Discipline is much prized and enshrined in the rule book of the company.

1   From this scenario, one may assume that BZ Ness Ltd is *not*

     A   a bureaucratic organisation
     B   a mechanistic organisation
     C   an organismic organisation
     D   a role-culture organisation

2   From the information given, we can infer that the management of BZ Ness Ltd models itself on the theories of

     A   Charles Handy
     B   Henry Fayol
     C   Abraham Maslow
     D   Elton Mayo

3   Which of the following commonly recognised features of bureaucracy could most clearly be identified as a disadvantage of the system?

     A   Insensitivity to the environment
     B   Rigidity of behaviour
     C   Delegation of authority
     D   Rules

4   Which of the following writers is not a member of the school of thought to which the others belong?

     A   Fayol
     B   McGregor
     C   Maslow
     D   Herzberg

5   Joan Woodward conducted a survey of firms in Essex, and observed that: 'It appeared that .... was the most important factor in determining organisational structure and in setting the tone of human relationships inside the firm'

The missing words are:

     A   employee needs
     B   control requirements
     C   technical methods
     D   leadership styles

6   Which of the following writers is not a member of the school of thought to which the others belong?

    A   Joan Woodward
    B   Eric Trist
    C   Frederick Taylor
    D   Lawrence and Lorsch

7   Which of the following statements is true?

    A   Limited company status means that a company is only allowed to trade up to a predetermined turnover level in any one year

    B   The benefit of being a sole trader is that you have no personal liability for the debts of your business

    C   For organisations that have limited company status, ownership and control are legally separate

    D   Partnerships offer the same benefits as limited companies but are usually formed by professionals such as doctors and solicitors

Chapter 2

8   Which of the following are generally considered as elements of mission?

    (i)   Purpose
    (ii)   Values
    (iii)   Policies and standards of behaviour
    (iv)   Strategic vision

    A   (i), (ii) and (iv)
    B   (ii), (iii) and (iv)
    C   (iv) and (iii)
    D   All of the above

9   Which of the following statements is true?

    A   Strong values will inevitably improve corporate performance

    B   Strong values will make organisational decision making ineffective

    C   Strong values are useful because they ensure that there is no disagreement throughout the organisation

    D   Strongly held values may be dangerous if they filter out 'uncomfortable' environmental information

10   In Selling the Dream Guy Kawasaki claims that good mission statements:

    A   are prepared by senior managers with no consultation with junior staff
    B   are brief, flexible and distinctive
    C   are prepared by external management consultants
    D   are prepared by senior managers in consultation with shareholders

11   Which of the following groups may be considered to be stakeholders in the activities of a nuclear power station?

(i)   The government
(ii)   Friends of the Earth
(iii)   Employees
(iv)   Local residents

A   All of the above
B   (I), (iii) and (iv)
C   (iii) only
D   (iii) and (iv)

12   Which of the following may impact on the development of corporate objectives and strategy?

(i)   Economic requirements
(ii)   Organisational mission
(iii)   Influence of stakeholder groups
(iv)   Social responsibilities

A   All of the above
B   (i), (ii), (iii)
C   (ii), (iii), (iv)
D   None of the above

Chapter 3

13   According to Greiner's Life Cycle model each phase of growth is characterised by:

A   A distinctive factor which directs organisational growth, and a crisis which it must pass through before reaching the next phase

B   A period of reflection and readjustment

C   A change in structure and outlook

D   None of the above

14   The Sigmoid Curve is used to illustrate:

A   Changes in organisational income and expenditure throughout the organisation's lifecycle

B   Changes in organisational and individual effectiveness over time

C   The reduction of organisational effectiveness over time

D   The increase of organisational effectiveness over time

15   Quinn's Logical Incrementalism means that:

A   Businesses make continuous small adjustments based on their situation and changes in the environment

B   All decisions about organisational change should be based on quantifiable logic

C   Organisations grow rapidly during the initial stages of their life cycle, but this growth slows dramatically as they reach maturity

D   Any attempt at a logical approach to organisational decision making is doomed to failure

16   Which of the following is not a characteristic of bureaucracy?

A   Hierarchy
B   Stability
C   Specialisation
D   Flexibility

17   The best explanation of the 'organisational multiplier' is:

A   One additional member in a given division will trigger the need for additional resources throughout the organisation

B   As organisations mature they tend to increase the range of products they produce

C   As organisations grow their profitability increases because resources are more fully utilised and the costs are therefore distributed more thinly

D   As an innovative organisation enjoys success in a new market the number of competitors in that market will rapidly multiply

18   Which of the following writers is most closely linked to the concept of bureaucracy:

A   Crozier
B   Weber
C   Wilson   A B C D
D   Quinn

19   The stages of growth shown on the Sigmoid Curve are:

A   Growth, Maturity, Decline
B   Birth, Growth, Maturity
C   Birth, Growth, Maturity, Decline
D   Birth, Growth, Maturity, Decline, Dissolution

Chapter 4

20   Which of the following is not an element of fiscal policy?

A   Government spending
B   Government borrowing
C   Exchange rates
D   Taxation

21   Which of the following is not an element of monetary policy?

A   Government spending targets
B   Borrowing to cover the shortfall between income and expenditure
C   Changing taxation levels on an annual basis
D   All of the above

22   PEST is:

A   An approach to management based on dismissing troublesome staff

B   An acronym used to describe the four key elements of an organisation's environment

C   A process theory of motivation

D   None of the above

23   Which of the following is untrue?

A   Growing populations often require fast economic growth to maintain living standards

B   Falling populations exhibit changing consumption patterns

C   Increasing populations do not exhibit changing consumption patterns

D   Growing populations often lead to enhanced labour mobility

24   Which of the following is not a characteristic of culture?

A   Learned
B   Dynamic
C   Unchanging
D   Shared

25   Demographic studies are:

A   A study of the impact of educational change on regional unemployment

B   An analysis of statistics on birth and death rates, age structures of people and ethnic groups within a community.

C   A study of employment and motivation

D   A study of the impact of government policy on organisational decision making

26   Culture embraces the following aspects of social life:

(i)   Customs
(ii)   Beliefs and values
(iii) Symbols

A   (ii) and (iii)
B   (i) only
C   All of the above
D   (i) and (iii)

Chapter 5

27   Span of control is:

    A   the number of employees subordinate in the hierarchy to a given manager

    B   the number of levels in the hierarchy 'below' a given manager's

    C   the length of time between a manager's decision and the evaluation of it by his superior

    D   the number of employees directly responsible to a manager.

28   An organisational chart is not able to:

    A   show how power is distributed in the organisation
    B   describe the formal structure of the organisation
    C   show formal communication channels of the organisation
    D   indicate problems in the structure of the organisation

29   Which of the following statements is true?

    (i)   An informal organisation exists with every formal organisation

    (ii)   The objectives of the informal organisation are the same as those of the formal organisation

    (iii)   A strong, close-knit informal organisation is desirable within the formal organisation

    A   Statement (i) only
    B   Statements (I) and (iii)
    C   Statements (ii) and (iii)
    D   Statement (iii) only

30   In the Hughes Bossere chart below the authority of the Training Manager would be defined as:

    A   line only
    B   staff only
    C   functional and staff
    D   line and staff

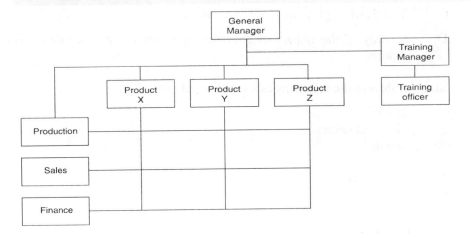

31   If the chain of command in an organisation is short, problems will most likely arise with:

    A   none of the following
    B   management development
    C   crisis management
    D   communication

32   The lower the proportion of non-supervisory (but routine) work in a manager's work load:

    A   the wider the span of control may be
    B   the narrower the span of control will be
    C   the greater his delegation of authority should be
    D   the less his delegation of authority should be

33   Which of the following statements about Tall Organisations is correct?

    A   Keep spans of control narrow and minimise management overhead costs

    B   Keep spans of control narrow and ensure effective communications

    C   Ensure wide spans of control but cause communication problems

    D   Keep spans of control narrow and result in more expensive management overhead costs

34   Nysslit Lerner plc, an organisation of some 400 employees, has an average span of control of three, throughout its management. From this, one might infer that:

    A   the work is systematic and routine
    B   job satisfaction is high
    C   the level of complexity in the work is high
    D   the organisation structure is flat

Chapter 6

35   A mechanistic organisation is associated with:

    A   conditions of rapid change
    B   automated processes
    C   task culture
    D   bureaucracy

36   From the information given for questions 1 and 2, BZ Ness's structure is likely to offer advantages for:

    A   innovation
    B   motivation
    C   communication
    D   control

BPP
PUBLISHING

37   Which of the following terms is not used by Mintzberg in his description of organisational structure:

    A   Strategic apex
    B   Strategic base
    C   Technostructure
    D   Operating core

38   The organisational technostructure:

    A   Describes the range of technology needed for effective organisational performance

    B   Is made up of analysts such as accountants and workplanners whose objective is to effect certain forms of standardisation on the organisation

    C   Consists of shopfloor workers and their supervisors

    D   Is the central strategy setting element within the organisation

39   Which of the following statements is true:

    A   The tendency of the strategic apex is to centralise decision making

    B   The tendency of the strategic apex is to decentralise decision making

    C   The tendency of the operating core is to centralise decision making

    D   The tendency of the operating core is to withhold strategic information form the apex

40   The term product organisation is used to describe:

    A   The situation where organisational activities are grouped together on the basis of products or product lines

    B   A manufacturing as opposed to a service sector industry

    C   The situation where individuals are grouped into departments based on their functional expertise

    D   An organisation where the main focus is on exploiting current product strengths rather than investing in innovation

41   Which rule of classical management is challenged by matrix management:

    A   Structuring the organisation on functional lines
    B   Structuring the organisation on geographical lines
    C   Unity of command
    D   Decentralisation of decision making

Chapter 7

42   Closed loop control makes no use of:

    A   Environment input
    B   Feedback
    C   Feedforward
    D   Double loop control action

43   Double loop control is concerned with:

    A   Forecast results
    B   Modifying the plan
    C   Open loop control
    D   Modifying feedback

44   Feedforward control compares planned results with:

    A   historical results
    B   actual results
    C   anticipated results
    D   ideal results

45   Which of the following does Child argue to be possible control strategies in an organisation:

    (i)   Personal control
    (ii)   Bureaucratic control
    (iii)   Cultural control
    (iv)   Output control

    A   All of the above
    B   (ii), (ii) and (iv)
    C   (iii) only
    D   (i), (ii) and (iii)

46   In Handy's equation illustrating the trust-control dilemma, $T + C = Y$.

    A   T represents the mutual trust of managers and their subordinates
    B   T represents the extent to which managers trust each other
    C   T represents the extent to which subordinates trust their managers
    D   T represents the extent to which managers trust their subordinates

47   Which of the following is generally accepted as an advantage of having an effective MBO system?

    (i)   Helps ensure the alliance of individual motivation with corporate goals

    (ii)   Facilitates qualitative and quantitative assessment of management performance

    (iii)   Provides periodic feedback for managers

    A   None of the above
    B   (ii) and (iii)
    C   (i) and (iii)
    D   All of the above

48   MIS stands for:

    A   Management Improvement Strategy
    B   Management Initiation Strategy
    C   Management Information System
    D   Motivating Individuals Strategically

Chapter 8

49   Which of the following is a 'primary working group'?

    A   A small work team
    B   A large department
    C   A trade union
    D   A business

50   The four stages of group formation, in order of occurrence are:

    A   storming, norming, forming, performing
    B   storming, forming, storming, performing
    C   forming, storming, norming, performing
    D   storming, forming, norming, performing

51   At the Soli-Darretty Bros factory a project team has been put together by management to solve a problem with workflow in the factory floor. As we see this team, they are engaged in debating how they are going to approach the task, and who is going to do what; some of their first ideas have obviously not worked out. At the same time, they are starting to put forward some really innovative ideas: they get quite excited in brain storming sessions, and are uninhibited in putting forward their views and suggestions. Factions are emerging, not only around different ideas, but around two individuals who seem to dominate the discussion and always seem to disagree.

This team, is at the stage of:

    A   forming
    B   storming
    C   norming
    D   Performing

52   Conforming with group norms without real commitment, is called:

    A   compliance
    B   internalisation
    C   counter-conformity
    D   identification

53   Which of the following features of a cohesive work group will invariably be advantageous for the organisation?

Features
(i)   Conformity to group norms
(ii)   Solidarity or mutual support in the face of threat
(iii)   Satisfaction of social and affiliation needs
(iv)   Increased confidence and willingness to take risks

A   None of these features
B   Features (i) and (iii) only
C   Features (ii) and (iv) only
D   Features (ii), (iii) and (iv) only

54   'Groupthink', will be encouraged rather than prevented by:

A   actively encouraging self-criticism
B   paying more attention to group maintenance
C   welcoming outside ideas and criticisms
D   responding positively to conflicting evidence

55   Egon Krezy, at the Paris office, needs to get an important message to his boss, who is in the London office for the day. He telephones, only to find that refurbishment is in progress in the London office, and his boss can't hear him clearly over the hammering and drilling. Giving up, Egon sends a fax instead – but five minutes later gets a return fax saying:' Can't read your handwriting. Please phone.' Egon phones his boss, who has found a quiet office somewhere. By this time Egon is exasperated, and soothes his nerves by telling his boss about it. He then relays the message.

Which types of 'noise' has Egon fallen foul of?

A   Physical noise and psychological noise only
B   Technical noise and psychological noise only
C   Technical noise, physical noise and social noise only
D   Physical noise, technical noise and psychological noise only

56   If a supervisor in the Sales department requests the help of the Personnel Director in a complex disciplinary matter, communication flow is said to be:

A   vertical
B   horizontal
C   lateral
D   diagonal

Chapter 9

57   Phil T Luker & Son offers its employees a reward package which includes salary and company car. Its factory is safe and clean and rather smart. The work is technically challenging and employees are encouraged to produce innovative solutions to problems. The company is offering intrinsic rewards in the shape of:

A   the salary
B   the car
C   the factory
D   the work

58   Maslow's need categorisation does not include:

A   'physiological needs'
B   'freedom of inquiry and expression needs'
C   'need for affiliation'
D   'safety needs'

59   Of the following criticisms levelled at Maslow's hierarchy of needs theory, which is not a valid objection?

    A   Progression up the hierarchy does not always work in practice
    B   A need once satisfied doesn't always become less powerful
    C   Needs can be satisfied by aspects of a person's life outside work
    D   The hierarchy is only relevant to Western English-speaking cultures

60   Keepham (Hungary) Ltd offers its employees:

    (i)   sensible company policies
    (ii)   good salaries and bonuses
    (iii)   considerate supervision
    (iv)   training programmes

    Employees will, according to Herzberg, derive satisfaction from and be motivated to superior effort by:

    A   (i) only
    B   (iv) only
    C   (ii) and (iv) only
    D   (iii) and (iv) only

61   Willy Dewitt-Ornott is an employee in Sales. There is always a competition in the firm in January to try and boost post-Christmas sales. Everybody knows that the winner has for the last three years been made a team leader. Willy's quite certain that he will be able to win: all his mates think so too. Willy knows that as team leader he will have more responsibility – which he would like. But he would also have to work much longer hours, and he has just promised his wife he would take two weeks holiday to help her organise Christmas: it is very import to both of them. If an expectancy equation were used to assess Willy's motivation to work hard at January sales, based on the information given:

    A   valence would be high, expectancy high, motivation high
    B   valence would be high, expectancy low, motivation high
    C   valence would be around 0, expectancy high, motivation low
    D   valence would be around 0, expectancy high, motivation high

62   Handy's 'E factors' would *not* include:

    A   expectancy
    B   effort
    C   energy
    D   enthusiam

63   Which of the following would Herzberg call hygiene factors?

    (i)   salary
    (ii)   job security
    (iii)   gaining recognition
    (iv)   challenging work

    A   (ii) and (iv)
    B   (i) only
    C   All of the above
    D   (i) and (ii)

64   Which of the following is not a type of psychological contract?

A   Cognitive
B   Cooperative
C   Coercive
D   Calculative

Chapter 10

65   Otto Kratt is a team manager. He wants to change the working day to a flexi-time system. He knows this is an important change for the members of the team, so he calls a team meeting, and asks them what they think. Few group members want to go over to flexi-time, because the group will be working at less than full strength during the flexible times. Otto explains that this won't be critical, because the core period will be as normal, and it will cover most of the day. He tells them about the personal convenience flexi-time offers. He invites further objections – and is able to counter most of them. 'I'll take your views into account' he says. Flexi-time is in operation a month later.

Otto's style may best be described as:

Λ   'tells'
B   'sells'
C   'consults'
D   'joins'

66   Research has demonstrated that the consultative styles of management is the most:

A   popular among subordinates
B   popular among leaders
C   productivity-inducing
D   hostility-provoking in groups

67   On the Ohio State managerial grid, a 1.9 management style is called:

A   impoverished
B   task management
C   country club
D   dampened pendulum

68

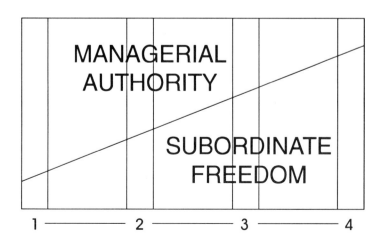

Points 1, 2, 3 and 4 represent management styles

Point 4 represents:

- A   joins
- B   consults
- C   sells
- D   delegates

69   Betty Willnot is a team leader in the R&D department of an electronics firm. She would really like to be a democratic leader. She's got every confidence in her subordinates – and so have they: they're all highly skilled, and enjoy a challenge. However, complex problem solving is required, and research projects have long time-horizons. The department manager responds to this by exercising an autocratic style of management: 'That's how we do things here', he says.

Betty has read Handy's 'best fit' theory, and is trying to decide whether her situation is 'tight' or 'flexible'. Which factor(s) will be on the 'tight' rather than 'flexible' end of the continuum?

- A   Subordinates and task only
- B   Task and leader only
- C   Subordinates, task and leader
- D   None of the above.

70   The purpose of leadership theories may be:

Purpose

- (i)   Aiding management assessment
- (ii)   aiding management training and development
- (iii)   making managers into leaders
- (iv)   changing management styles

For which of the above purposes will such theories be effective?

- A   Purposes (i) and (ii) only
- B   Purposes (ii) and (iii) only
- C   Purposes (ii) and (iv) only
- D   Purposes (i), (ii), (iii) and (iv)

71   According to Hofstede:

- A   a masculine culture exists where people tend to behave in a domineering and aggressive manner

- B   a masculine culture exists where there are high levels of discrimination against women in senior jobs

- C   a key characteristic of masculine cultures is marked sex-based differentials

- D   a key characteristic of feminine cultures is marked sex-based differentials

72   Which of the following is not used by Hofstede to describe a key dimension of culture?

    A   Power-distance
    B   Acquisitive-generous
    C   Individualism/collectivism
    D   Uncertainty-avoidance

Chapter 11

73   The 'Happy Family' view of organisations is that:

    A   they are co-operative, harmonious structures where conflict is exceptional

    B   they are most effective when they are small family run firms

    C   small organisations are harmonious but ineffective decision makers

    D   small organisations are best because they avoid the communication problems associated with larger organisations

74   Which of the following is not a model for examining conflict within organisations?

    A   'Happy Family'
    B   Conflict
    C   Evolution
    D   Parent – Child

75   According to Alan Fox a unitary ideology:

    A   believes that solidarity within different groups (eg management, the workforce) but conflict between these groups

    B   believes that conflict is inevitable both between and within groups

    C   believes that despite their different roles all organisational members have common objectives

    D   believes that the responses of the workforce to management will be conflictual and disruptive

76   The Marxist view of capitalist organisations is most closely linked to:

    A   Radical ideology
    B   Pluralist ideology
    C   Unitary ideology
    D   Inspirational ideology

77   Which of the following statements is most representative of modern organisations?

    A   Conflict is inevitably present and destructive
    B   Conflict is generally absent because of goal consensus
    C   Conflict is present but contrary to popular belief is constructive
    D   Conflict is generally present but may be constructive or destructive

78   Sherif and Sherif are associated with:

    A   research into Marxist interpretations of organisational behaviour
    B   studies of group behaviour at a boys' camp
    C   management/Union conflict negotiation
    D   none of the above

79   'Risky Shift' is best defined as:

    A   A high risk move to a completely new range of organisational activities

    B   An attempt by managers to coerce workers into accepting change, eg through the threat of redundancy

    C   A tendency for individuals in groups to take greater risks than their individual, pre-discussion preferences would suggest

    D   A high risk change to corporate strategy

80   Rosenmann and Friedman are best known for:

    A   Research into the effect of personality type on individual experience of stress

    B   Research into the impact of management style on motivation levels

    C   Research into the dynamics of individual versus group decision making

    D   Offering practical solutions to the problem of groupthink

81   Role underload is:

    A   Caused by individuals finding themselves with too little to do

    B   Caused by individuals finding themselves in a set of roles which they perceive as below their abilities; this results in burn-out

    C   Caused by individuals finding themselves in a set of roles which they perceive as below their abilities; this results in rust-out

    D   Is a description applied to a department or functional area working below full capacity

Chapter 12

82   Of the following four terms, the term which invariably means doing something completely new, which hasn't been done before, is:

    A   change
    B   transformation
    C   growth
    D   innovation

83   Which of the following statements is generally true?

    A   A turbulent environment requires a more innovative response than a stable one

    B   A stable environment requires a more innovative response than a turbulent one

    C   The nature of the environment has no impact on desirable levels of innovation

    D   Innovation is dangerous in a turbulent environment because it exposes the organisation to greater levels of risk

84   Organisational innovation is likely to come from:

    A   Management
    B   External consultants
    C   Caste of innovators
    D   Anyone

85   A 'Wicked' problem is

    A   A problem where the supposed solution cannot be proved until it has actually been implemented

    B   A problem which turns out to have a totally unexpected solution

    C   A problem concerning a situation with unclear boundaries which makes it difficult to resolve by logical or analytical approaches

    D   A really exciting, stimulating and complex problem

86   The term used to describe the situation where the whole is worth more than the sum of the parts is:

    A   Synchrony
    B   Simultaneous alliance
    C   Synergy
    D   Organic

87   Which of the following do Pedler, Burgoyne and Boydell claim to be characteristics of the learning organisation?

    (i)   Mechanistic structure

    (ii)   Committed senior management decision making

    (iii)   Clearly defined and formalised payment structures with annual increments for all staff

    A   All of the above
    B   None of the above
    C   (i) and (ii)
    D   (ii) and (iii)

88   According to David Garvin organisation learning:

A   occurs in three steps: cognitive, behavioural and performance improvement

B   can be most effectively measured through the use of attitude surveys

C   is a major contributor to the growth of management labour disputes

D   is given greater attention and commitment in Japan than in the UK or USA

Chapter 13

89   A change which does not directly affect an individual is likely to rouse in him:

A   acceptance
B   indifference
C   passive resistance
D   active resistance

90   *Changes*   *Sources of resistance*

1   Repeal restrictions on Sunday trading   (i)   Fear of the unknown

2   Relocation so that two previously   (ii)   Attitudes or beliefs
     distinct teams share office

3   Introduction of word processing to   (iii) Organisational politics
     the typing pool

4   Formation of a personnel department   (iv)   Loyalty to a group identity
     with functional authority throughout
     the organisation

Matching up the proposed changes (1-4) with the most likely source of resistance to them ((i)-(iv)) you get:

A   1(i)   2(iii)   3(iv)   4(ii)
B   1(iii)   2(iv)   3(i)   4(ii)
C   1(ii)   2(i)   3(iii)   4(iv)
D   1(ii)   2(iv)   3(i)   4(iii)

91   Ché Njova is a person who doesn't mind risk and uncertainty, and who feels passionately that organisations must adapt to environmental changes in order to survive. Given a choice of organisations, he will want to work in:

A   an organic system
B   a mechanistic system
C   a bureaucracy
D   a role culture

92   Which of the following represents Lewin's/Schein's approach to changing human behaviour?

   A   Discuss, Advise, Decide
   B   Consider, Inform, Implement
   C   Consult, Debate, Resolve
   D   Unfreeze, Change, Refreeze

93   Which of the following does Donald Kirkpatrick identify as keys to successful change?

   (i)   Empathy
   (ii)   Reward Power
   (iii) Communication
   (iv)   Participation

   A   All of the above
   B   None of the above
   C   (i), (ii) and (iii)
   D   (i), (iii) and (iv)

94   According to Blake and Mouton, a group norm is:

   A   Any uniformity of attitude, opinion, feeling or action shared by two or more people

   B   The average group output level calculated over a monthly period

   C   The general tendency for groups to hold opinions in conflict with those held by other groups within the organisation

   D   A description used to describe a group of the optimum size of 6 members

95   What do Blake and Mouton suggest to be the most effective way to change established group norms?

   A   Management providing clear decisive instruction on the changes to be made

   B   Offering rewards to those individuals who comply with the desired new norms

   C   Identifying one individual within each group and appointing them as agent of change

   D   Involving the people affected in studying what the existing norms are and what would be better

Chapter 14

96   Who is associated with the claim that 'the only responsibility of business is business'

   A   Max Weber
   B   Andrew Stark
   C   Milton Friedman
   D   Fons Trompenaars

97   The term 'stakeholder' can embrace:

(i)   The investors who own shares in the organisation
(ii)   Managers
(iii)   Consumers
(iv)   Competitors

A   (i), (ii), (iv)
B   All of the above
C   (i) only
D   (i),(ii), (iii)

98   Trompenaars is best known for his work in the area of:

A   Ethics
B   Corporate governance
C   Social responsibility
D   Culture

99   Lyne Paine describes an approach to ethics which 'combines a concern for the law with an emphasis on managerial responsibility' as a:

A   Socially responsive approach
B   Combined approach
C   Integrity-based approach
D   Compliance-based approach

100   The disclosure by an employee of illegal, immoral or illegitimate practices on the part of the organisation is often known as:

A   Whistle-blowing
B   Organisational accountability
C   Corporate conscience
D   Synergy

101   Which of the following is true?

(i)   Social responsibility guarantees increased profit levels

(ii)   Social responsibility adds cost to organisational activities and reduces profit levels

(iii)   Social responsibility may have commercial benefits

(iv)   Social responsibility is a concern confined to business organisations

A   All of the above
B   (i) and (iii)
C   (ii) and (iv)
D   (iii)

EXAM STYLE QUESTIONS

Chapter 1

1   CONTINGENCY THEORY

Introductory note to students:

This question is based on schools of management theory that are discussed in chapter 1. Information to expand your answer can also be found in chapters 6, 8 and 9.

'The contingency approach to organisational design evolved as a direct reaction against the "one-best-way" panaceas of classical theory and the human relations school'. Outline the major features of the contingency approach and show how it can be distinguished from the other two theories mentioned in the quotation.

Chapter 2

2   IMPORTANCE OF STAKEHOLDERS

Define what is meant by a stakeholder in an organisation.

Explain the importance of stakeholders to an organisation with which you are familiar.

Draw a stakeholder diagram to illustrate your answer.

Chapter 3

3   ORGANISATIONAL LIFE CYCLES

Identify a well known model used to explain organisational life cycles. To what extent is this model of use to the practising manager?

Chapter 4

4   ENVIRONMENTAL INFLUENCES

Various areas of the environment are said to influence policies of both business and non-business organisations. One classification identifies these environmental influences as being economic, technical, social and political. Describe how they influence the policy making of such organisations.

Guidance note

Don't forget that the PEST model is only a model. Real life issues do not easily fall into these categories.

Chapter 5

5   INFORMAL ORGANISATIONS

What, in terms of management theory, is the distinction between a formal and an informal organisation? What are the advantages and disadvantages of informal groups from a managerial point of view? What can managers do to overcome the disadvantages?

Chapter 6

6 ORGANIGRAMS

(a) Describe the principles underlying Mintzberg's theory of structural configurations.

(b) Describe two of the structural configurations arising from the influences exerted by different parts of the organisation.

Chapter 7

7 TQM AND BPR

(a) Explain the differences and similarities between Total Quality Management and Business Process Re-engineering, choosing up to four points for discussion.

(b) Summarise the effect that either theory has had on an organisation of your choice.

Chapter 8

8 PERSONALITY AND SELECTION

What is meant by the term personality? Why do people have different personalities? To what extent is it appropriate for an organisation's recruitment and selection practices to take into account the personality of any given job applicant?

Chapter 9

9 PERFORMANCE MOTIVATION

Explain and discuss at least three theories on performance motivation in the workplace.

Comment on the usefulness of these theories.

Chapter 10

10 WHAT IS LEADERSHIP?

Defining what makes an effective leader is not an easy task. Explain your understanding of leadership with reference to some of the leading theorists on the subject.

Chapter 11

11 STRESS

Discuss the range of factors that may influence the stress levels of individuals in modern organisations. How can an understanding of these factors help the practising manager?

Chapter 12

12   INNOVATION

If constant innovation is the key to ongoing success, why do so many organisations find it hard to achieve once they become large established players in the marketplace?

Chapter 13

13   MANAGEMENT OF CHANGE

Imagine that you are a senior manager anxious to introduce a significant change in your organisation: either the geographical move of your corporate headquarters to a new location about 300 miles away, or the implementation of a performance-related pay and appraisal scheme for your entire workforce. Taking one of these two examples, answer the following specific questions.

(a)   What, in general, are the attitudes of your employees to your proposals likely to be?

(b)   What guidance would you derive from the literature on the management of change which might help you in considering how to gain acceptance for your ideas?

Chapter 14

14   SOCIAL RESPONSIBILITY

Social responsibility may be defined as the obligations which an organisation has towards society and the broad environment in which the organisation operates. Management, therefore, should concern itself with the way in which the organisation interacts with its environment.

Explain how and to what extent should management recognise social responsibility extending beyond the boundaries of the organisation.

SOLUTIONS TO MULTIPLE CHOICE QUESTIONS

Chapter 1		Chapter 5		Chapter 9		Chapter 12	
1	C	27	D	57	D	82	D
2	B	28	A	58	C	83	A
3	A	29	A	59	C	84	D
4	A	30	D	60	B	85	A
5	C	31	B	61	C	86	C
6	C	32	A	62	A	87	B
7	C	33	D	63	D	88	A
		34	C	64	A		

Chapter 2		Chapter 6		Chapter 10		Chapter 13	
8	D					89	B
9	D	35	D	65	B	90	D
10	B	36	D	66	A	91	A
11	A	37	B	67	C	92	D
12	A	38	B	68	A	93	D
		39	A	69	D	94	A
		40	A	70	D	95	D
Chapter 3		41	C	71	C		
13	A			72	B	Chapter 14	
14	B	Chapter 7				96	C
15	A	42	A	Chapter 11		97	B
16	D	43	A	73	A	98	D
17	A	44	C	74	D	99	C
18	B	45	A	75	C	100	A
19	C	46	A	76	A	101	D
		47	D	77	D		
Chapter 4		48	C	78	B		
20	C			79	C		
21	D			80	A		
22	B	Chapter 8		81	C		
23	C	49	A				
24	C	50	C				
25	B	51	B				
26	C	52	A				
		53	A				
		54	B				
		55	D				
		56	D				

SOLUTIONS TO EXAM STYLE QUESTIONS

Chapter 1

1 CONTINGENCY THEORY

> *Tutorial note.* One of the disadvantages of contingency theory, from your point of view, is that it refers to both management style and organisation design.

Following the emergence of the open systems approach and its recognition of environmental influences on the organisation, an essentially pragmatic view was developed which argued that no single theory can guarantee the organisation's effectiveness. Essentially, 'it all depends'.

This contingency approach aims to suggest the most appropriate organisational design and management style in a given set of circumstances. It rejects the universal, one-best-way approach, in favour of analysis of the internal factors and external environment of each organisation, and the design of organisation and management as a best fit between the tasks, people and environment in the particular situation. As Buchanan and Huczynski put it: 'With the coming of contingency theory, organisational design ceased to be 'off-the-shelf', but became tailored to the particular specific needs of an organisation.'

The contingency approach grew from the results of a number of research studies which showed the importance of different factors on the structure and performance of an organisation, and indicated that there is in fact no inevitable correlation between the structures and cultures prescribed by previous theories and organisational effectiveness. Joan Woodward, for example, demonstrated that 'different technologies imposed different kinds of demands on individuals and organisations and that these demands have to be met through an appropriate form of organisation'. Lawrence and Lorsch, and Burns and Stalker, found that different types of environment, with a different pace of change and degree of uncertainty, suited different organisation structures and cultures: Burns and Stalker's mechanistic and organismic systems, for example.

Two main factors distinguish this approach from the preceding schools of classical management and human relations. Firstly, it no longer assumes that it is possible to prescribe a set of principles which, if correctly applied, would inevitably result in an efficient and effective organisation.

The other main difference is in orientation. Classical management theory was essentially an organisational theory, while human relations was a management theory. Each concentrated on a particular aspect of the work situation, seen as most important at the time: in a sense, human relations emerged as a 'corrective' approach, from a critical perception of classical theory. In the same way, contingency theory evolved from a critical perspective on both.

The classical approach to management was primarily concerned with the structure and activities of the formal organisation. Effective organisation was seen to be mainly dependent on factors such as the division of work, the establishment of a rational hierarchy of authority, span of control and unity of command.

The practical application of Taylor's scientific management approach was the use of work study techniques to break work down into its smallest and simplest component parts, and the selection and training of workers to perform a single task in the most efficient way.

The classical school contributed techniques for studying the nature of work and solving problems of how it could be organised more efficiently.

The origins of human relations thought are generally attributed to Elton Mayo, whose ideas suggest that the effectiveness of classical management principles is inevitably limited because the focus fails to recognise the impact of social dynamics on organisational behaviour.

Mayo's ideas were based on his interpretation of the major early social research project known as the Hawthorne Studies, from which emerged the approach emphasising the importance of human attitudes, values and relationships for the effectiveness of organisations. It concentrated mainly on relationships and the concept of social man, with an emphasis on how employees' social or belonging needs could be satisfied at work. This was called the human relations movement.

These ideas were followed up by social psychologists such as Maslow, McGregor, Herzberg and Likert – but with a change of emphasis. People were still considered to be the crucial factor in determining organisational effectiveness, but were recognised to have more than merely physical and social needs. Attention shifted towards higher psychological needs for growth and self-fulfilment. This was labelled the neo-human relations school.

Contingency theory was founded on research evidence showing that the principles advanced by the two previous schools did not necessarily correlate with organisational effectiveness. The need for organisation structures to be adaptive (Lawrence and Lorsch, Burns and Stalker) rather than universal, on classical principles, became clear. Mayo's human relations ideas, applied at the Western Electric Company following the Hawthorne Studies, failed to make an impact. Contingency thinkers moved away from particular aspects and into consideration of the whole organisational system and its environment.

Another difference between the schools was the viewpoint of those behind them. The classical theorists were mainly early practising managers – such as Henri Fayol and F W Taylor. They analysed their own experience in management to produce a set of what they saw as principles applicable in a wide variety of situations. The human relations approach, however, was pioneered mainly by social scientists – rather than practising managers – and was based on research into human behaviour, with the intention of describing and thereafter predicting behaviour in organisations. Contingency theory, as befits its flexible nature, has been championed by a wide variety of researchers, writers and managers in a number of disciplines.

Practical value to managers

From the perspective of a practising manager this is far more than a purely theoretical debate. The contingency approach suggests that, far from simply being able to apply one best style of management or type of structure, managers will have to actively evaluate their options on the basis of factors such as size, competitive environment and technology. Moreover they must recognise the need to adapt their choice of options as these factors change. Awareness of the contingency approach can therefore be argued to be of value in the following ways.

(a) Managers are encouraged to identify and define the particular circumstances of the situation they need to manage, and to devise appropriate ways of handling them. A belief in universal principles and prescriptive theories can hinder problem solving and decision making by obscuring some of the available alternatives. It can also dull the ability to evaluate and choose between alternatives that are clearly open, by preventing the manager from developing relevant criteria for judgement.

(b) This approach encourages responsiveness and flexibility to changes in environmental factors through organisational structure and culture. Task performance and individual/group satisfaction are more important design criteria than permanence and unity of design type. Within a single organisation, there may be bureaucratic units side by side with task-centred matrix units (for example in the research and development function) which can respond to particular pressures and environmental volatility.

Some writers have raised doubts about the contingency approach. John Child writes: 'One major limitation of the contemporary contingency approach lies in the lack of conclusive evidence to demonstrate that matching organisational designs to prevailing contingencies contributes importantly to performance'.

In a world where the rate of change is rapid, a model which encourages managers to evaluate the compatibility of their choices with the environment in which those choices are to be applied, seems to have undoubted value.

Chapter 2

2 IMPORTANCE OF STAKEHOLDERS

Tutorial note. The question asked you to identify an organisation with which you are familiar. We have not done so here, to avoid closing off your options. Relevant considerations, however, are these:

- non profit organisations have a different set of stakeholders, including their ultimate beneficiaries, from profit orientated organisations

- government organisations pursue many different goals

- In a business, the goal of maximising shareholder wealth is important, but shareholders often maintain their distance from management

A stakeholdr can be defined as a person, group or organisation with an interest in the workings of the organisation.

The *stakeholder* view of company objectives is that many groups of people have a stake in what the company does. Shareholders own the business, but there are also suppliers, managers, workers and customers. A business depends on appropriate relationships with these groups, otherwise it will find it hard to function. Each of these groups has its own objectives, so that a compromise or balance is required. Management must balance the profit objective with the pressures from the non-shareholder groups in deciding the strategic targets of the business.

There are three broad types of stakeholder in an organisation such as a company.

- internal stakeholders – employees, management
- connected stakeholders – shareholders, customers, suppliers, financiers
- external stakeholders – the community, government, pressure groups.

These types are indicated in the diagram below.

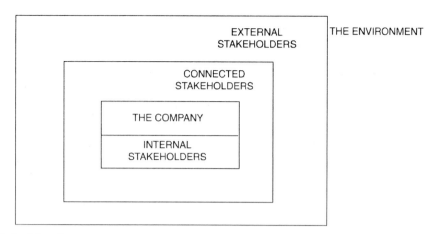

Stakeholders in a company

Internal stakeholders

These include employees and management. As they are so intimately connected with the company, their objectives are likely to have a strong and immediate influence on how it is run. The goals of employees and managers include those given below.

(a)   Money, for which the organisation must survive and prosper

(b)   Careers (hence leading to growth, which reduces the organisation's vulnerability to the environment)

(c)   Efficiency

(d)   Control (over the environment)

Other goals relate to both hygiene and motivator factors in the workplace, and the overall well being of employees.

(a)   Interesting work

(b)   Training

(c)   Healthy and safe environment

Connected stakeholders

The objective of *shareholders* – which is generally that of making a profit – is often taken as the prime objective which the company's management seeks to fulfil. But clearly financiers such as banks have similar objectives which must be met (usually the payment of loan interest is a contractual obligation whilst the payment of dividends is not), whilst the customer's objectives, in a market-led company, must also be fulfilled if the company is to be successful. Other stakeholders directly connected with the company are suppliers and distributors.

(a)   *Bankers*. Businesses generally need a bank account for all their monetary transactions. The bank is often an important stakeholder of a business. A bank, unlike shareholders, employees and management, does not have an *overriding* interest in the growth, or even the survival, of the business, but is primarily interested in minimising *risk*. Managing relationships with bankers involves the following.

    (i)   The firm should monitor and forecast its cash flow: this is good business practice, but it is especially relevant to dealing with banks.

    (ii)   The firm should keep its bankers regularly informed of its activities, not only when, as a new business, it presents a business plan.

(iii) The firm should consider forms of financing which minimise any drain on cash flow.

(b) *Customers*. Customers, as stakeholders, are interested in the business because of the service a business provides. Without customers, no business would exist. Just how strong the position of customers will be depends on a number of factors.

(i) Whether the customer's purchases represent a substantial proportion of total sales by the producer. If yes, the customer will be in a strong position relative to the producer.

(ii) Whether the customer's purchases from the industry represent a large or a small proportion of the customer's total purchases. If most of a customer's supplies come from a single industry, the customer will be in a weaker bargaining position than if only a small proportion do so.

(iii) Whether switching costs are high or low. In other words, would the customer suffer in terms of money or inconvenience by changing suppliers.

(iv) Whether the products supplied by the industry are standard items and undifferentiated. A supermarket chain may feel obliged to stock leading brands of a product because its own customers might expect to find these brands in any supermarket.

(v) A customer who makes low profits will be forced to insist on low prices from suppliers.

(vi) The threat that customers might take over sources of supply, if suppliers charge too much.

(vii) The skills of the customer purchasing staff, or the price-awareness of consumers.

(viii) When *product quality* is important to the customer, the customer is less likely to be price-sensitive, and so the industry might be more profitable as a consequence. For example, although the Ministry of Defence may wish to keep control over defence spending, it is likely as a customer to be more concerned that the products it purchases perform satisfactorily than with getting the lowest price possible for everything it buys.

(c) *Suppliers and distributors*. Suppliers have an interest in a business because the business is a customer. Suppliers can have quite a powerful influence over a business in some cases. Suppliers influence an industry's profitability by exerting pressure for higher prices. The ability of suppliers to get higher prices depends on the following factors.

(i) Whether there are just one or two dominant suppliers to the industry, able to charge monopoly prices.

(ii) Whether the suppliers are threatened by new entrants to the market, or by substitute products.

(iii) Whether the suppliers have other customers outside the industry, and do not rely on the industry for the majority of their sales.

(iv) The importance of the supplier's product to the buyer's business.

(v) Whether the supplier has a differentiated product which buyers need to obtain.

(vi)   Whether switching costs for buyers would be high.

External stakeholders

External stakeholders include anybody else with an interest in the organisation.

(a)   The government has an interest as firms provide employment, generate taxes and contribute to the economic prosperity of society as a whole. Government and EU institutions are important for three purposes.

- The overall conduct of economic policy
- Providing financial aid
- Passing laws which affect the activities of business

(b)   *Interest and pressure groups.* Interest and pressure groups have obvious concerns with how organisations are run. Trade Unions represent their members. Other groups might be interested in the effect of the firm's activities on the environment.

(c)   *The public as a whole.* Under this heading comes the general concern with social responsibility, although such practices are largely in response to pressure group and government activity. There is a debate as to the extent businesses should be socially responsible, given the requirements of wealth maximisation, and the redistribution of wealth through the tax system.

Chapter 3

3   ORGANISATIONAL LIFE CYCLES

This essay will begin with a discussion of the organisational life cycle model proposed by Greiner. The second half of the essay will provide an evaluation of the practical value of this theory.

A number of writers have suggested that organisations progress through a life-cycle.

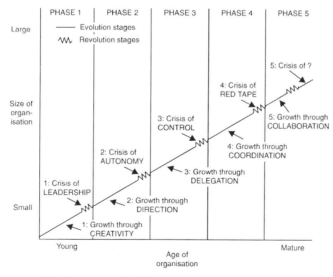

Greiner's argument is that organisations pass through a number of distinct stages as shown in the diagram above, and each stage has its own characteristics. However there are two important features of each stage.

(a)   A distinctive factor that directs the organisation's growth

(b)   A crisis, through which the organisation must pass before achieving the next phase

The phases can be described as follows.

Phase 1

A small recently founded organisation with direct personal management from the founders. However, there will eventually be a need for distinct management skills relating less to product and marketing issues and more to co-ordination of activities – in other words there will be a crisis of leadership.

Phase 2

Management is professionalised, and additional employees join the organisation. This results in a loss of autonomy and increased hierarchy. This leads to employee resentment and there is a crisis of autonomy.

Phase 3

In response to the problems of phase 2, considerable delegation is introduced. However, associated with this are new problems of co-ordination and control. Eventually there is a crisis of control.

Phase 4

In an attempt to improve internal control the organisation adopts new systems and procedures – this leads to a crisis of red tape.

Phase 5

Information collaboration develops as a means of overcoming red tape – there is an increased sense of teamwork. While this may be satisfying in the short term Greiner argues that this will result in a psychological saturation as a result of excessive teamwork.

Greiner continues to suggest that the organisation will then move into a sixth phase he terms dual organisation – this combines a habit structure for daily work routines and a reflective structure for stimulating new perspectives and personal enrichment.

The important question for a practising manager is, of course, the practical value of these ideas. In these terms there are a number of criticisms that can be made, some examples of which are summarised below.

(a) How representative of actual organisational behaviour is the model – do organisations really pass through such distinct stages, in practice? Other writers such as Quinn suggest that they may go through a process of continual, gradual adaptation.

(b) Not all organisations originate in the way suggested. They may for example be formed by mergers, joint ventures, or division of existing organisations (in which case there will be established norms and systems from the outset).

(c) Businesses grow and develop in many different ways – for example niche markets may expand their range of outlets but not their range of products.

(d) The model is too complex, it tries to combine too many factors (eg culture, structure, management style) and it is hard to identify what is cause and what is effect.

(e) It is hard to verify or quantify the model. For example, even if it is accepted that an organisation is passing through the stages identified, where does each individual stage start and end?

Despite these criticisms, however, the model does retain some value: it serves as a means of focusing manager's minds on the fact that organisations do evolve and change – and that as they do so, all aspects of management and organisational behaviour need re-evaluation and possibly adaptation.

Chapter 4

4   ENVIRONMENTAL INFLUENCES

> *Tutorial note*. The acronym PEST (Political-legal, Economic, Social-cultural, Technological) is a useful framework for this topic: do learn it. If our solution below looks rather longer than you could achieve in the exam, don't worry: we've given you a wide range of examples, from which your own may be drawn.

(a)   *Political-legal factors*

    (i)   Political factors can take the form of direct legislation or controls. An example is the Broadcasting Act which put up for auction the franchise for independent television companies. Other political activities are regulation and control.

    (ii)   Other political factors

        (1)   Wars

        (2)   Alliances between states (eg 'tied' aid)

        (3)   Political parties' ideological preferences (eg in favour of privatisation)

    (iii)   The government can aid business by providing a more stable operating environment and by direct financial assistance. Examples of such assistance include the following.

        (1)   Setting or targeting appropriate interest and exchange rates.

        (2)   Providing education and training relevant to business either directly through the state educational institutions or via grants to firms and local technical and educational councils.

        (3)   Protection of intellectual and physical property through making the laws (eg patents, theft) and enforcing them.

        (4)   Economic planning of key industrial areas, for example information technology.

        (5)   Acting as a customer to the private sector, for example when purchasing from the aerospace and defence industries.

        (6)   Giving incentives for capacity expansion, for example capital allowances and investment grants.

        (7)   Giving support to emerging business, for example the Business Expansion Scheme.

        (8)   Creating entry barriers by restricting the activities of foreign businesses in the country, or by imposing import tariffs.

        Conversely, the government can act as an impediment to business. Governments may be the source of instability and lead to costs, in addition to tax, being incurred by organisations. There is an argument that the commercial logic which drives competitors and markets can be learned by an adaptive organisation and hence allowed for. The government can be less easily anticipated. Examples of the government acting as an impediment to business include the following.

(1)   Creation of legal regulations which are costly to comply with.

(2)   Distortion of markets by the use of indirect taxation and discretionary production licenses.

(3)   Uncertainty and volatility in financial markets occur when governments change their policies in response to political pressure.

(4)   Imposition of restrictions such as monopolies and mergers controls and equal opportunities legislation may limit business activities.

(5)   Putting short-term political advantages before long-term national benefit.

(6)   Acting solely on behalf of sectional interests.

(b)   *Economic factors*

These factors are manifested through markets, customers, investors, suppliers, labour, competition, price levels and, indirectly, legislation and government policy.

(i)   Markets are continually changing. Old markets can decline and new ones emerge. An organisation sells its produce to markets, therefore changes must influence the organisation's decisions about what products to sell and where to sell them.

(ii)   The availability of capital and investors willing to put money into an organisation will influence the spending decisions of the organisation. An organisation will not raise money to invest if the profits from the investment are insufficient to pay sufficient interest or dividends on the money raised.

(iii)   The supply and cost of raw materials or energy can influence an organisation. If raw materials are in scarce supply, it might be necessary to switch to a substitute material. If the raw material is a commodity with large fluctuations in price, it might be prudent to buy forward to remove uncertainties in a future buying price. High energy costs might persuade an organisation to close down factories.

(iv)   The availability of labour, its skills and cost, are an aspect of the economic environment. An organisation may site its operations in areas where labour is either cheap or well-paid, skilled and productive.

(v)   An organisation with competitors must always be aware of their activities, so as not to be out-manoeuvred in the market.

(vi)   Government legislation and policy are clearly influential. Fiscal policies will determine rates of taxation and government grants, as well as government spending as a customer. Monetary policies will affect the cost of borrowing. Membership of the EU has influenced the choice of markets for many British companies, because of lower tariffs.

(vii) Inflation inevitably influences an organisation's decisions with respect to buying, rewarding labour and investors, setting prices and so on.

(c) *Social-cultural factors*

    (i) Health and safety of products and their impact. The last twenty years have seen increased pressure against cigarette smoking in Europe and the United States. In consequence of this tobacco companies have been forced to diversify either away from tobacco into packaging and insurance or to find different markets for tobacco products.

    (ii) Careful handling of the product. The nuclear industry has to handle waste carefully. The chemical industry has to avoid the risk of leakages.

    (iii) Pollution of the environment. This can be audible, visual or toxic. Airlines must control noise of operations and fly aircraft that comply with noise levels. Oil refineries must be screened for view and emissions from chimneys and waste outlets controlled.

    (iv) Trade relations

    (v) Treatment of employees

    (vi) Avoidance of sharp practice. Companies must behave acceptably towards customers, creditors and employees.

    (vii) Fashion changes. In the West there is a new strong lobby against the use of sealskins, and other animal skins for fashion garments.

    (viii) The needs and expectations of customers in relation to the organisation's products will influence the organisation. Customers may expect an organisation to offer low price goods or alternatively quality goods for a high price (for example Rolls Royce); they might expect certain standards of service from a nationalised industry. Organisations should try to fulfil their customers' expectations.

(d) *Technological factors* concern the way in which an organisation does its work and also the products it offers.

    (i) New technology might affect methods of production (the development of robots), storage (containerisation), sales and distribution (some years ago, the development of supertankers).

    (ii) Computerisation has transformed information systems in organisations, the nature of office working, and the techniques available for management decision making.

    (iii) New technologies may alter an organisation's requirements for staff (numbers, education and skills). In Britain, the long-term decline in manual working seems more obvious.

    (iv) New types of product become available for selling to customers. Consumer products which have emerged in recent years are home computers, video recorders and digital watches.

    (v) Technology also affects the availability and price of energy.

    (vi) Various researchers (such as Woodward) have suggested that an organisation's structure is determined by the technology it uses.

(vii) Researchers at the Tavistock Institute (for example Trist) suggested that the behaviour of employees at work is influenced by their technological surroundings.

Chapter 5

5   INFORMAL ORGANISATIONS

> *Tutorial note.* This question highlights informal groups of employees, but managers can use the formal organisation, too.

Formal and informal organisations

Formal organisation refers to the way an organisation is structured to carry out its tasks and achieve its objectives. The primary task and decisions on how to achieve these objectives will directly affect the form of the organisation and impose constraints on the place, time and nature of the work done and the resources used to perform it. Formal organisation reflects the needs of the organisation itself and views on how these might be efficiently achieved. This will include the four things.

- Definition of the tasks to be performed
- Chains of command
- Levels of authority and responsibility
- Channels of communication

In summary, formal organisation defines the way an organisation is designed to work. Earlier writers such as F W Taylor and H Fayol considered this to be the most important aspect of organisational effectiveness. The studies by E Mayo demonstrated the existence and importance of the informal organisation.

The informal organisation develops spontaneously as a complex system of its own with a pattern of personal and group relationships, with its own communication channels (grapevine) which differs from the formal organisation from which it was derived. The Hawthorne Studies showed how such groups had a powerful effect on their members. The effect was often quite the opposite to the economic man assumptions of the earlier writers, which were that social needs for 'belonging' will regulate the individual's economic behaviour in relation to output and attitudes to management. The studies also showed the existence of informal leaders who often act as opinion leaders in group reactions to particular situations.

In summary, informal organisation rises out of the social relationships necessary in any formal organisation. Such informal groupings or cliques will affect substantially the performance and behaviour of their members quite independently of any formal organisation.

The advantages of informal groups are as follows.

(a) Individuals satisfy their need for social relationships. It is argued that this will make them work more efficiently, as they will not experience stress and isolation.

(b) Through the group, individuals gain a sense of identity and status which they find difficult to gain on their own in a large organisation. Again, this may have a motivating effect.

(c)   They may develop their own performance targets, which may be better for motivation, and more consistently adhered to, than goals imposed from above.

(d)   Communications may be improved because of the existence of the 'grapevine'.

(e)   The activities of different individuals and departments will be better co-ordinated.

(f)   Problems will be shared and ideas generated through the interaction of different opinions and backgrounds.

The disadvantages of informal groups are as follows.

(a)   Group norms for performance may be below the required level, but the members of the group may feel bound by them.

(b)   Loyalty to the group may be more absorbing than, or even conflict with, loyalty to the organisation.

(c)   Creativity and innovation may be sacrificed because of the need to conform.

(d)   Groups may indulge in counter-productive competition with each other, rather than co-operating.

(e)   The grapevine invariably carries inaccurate and often subversive information.

(f)   The group may be resistant to necessary change because it is happy with the way things are.

(g)   The informal organisation may not fit into the formal structure.

(h)   Counter- or sub-cultures may emerge in opposition to the mainstream system of values that management wishes to promote.

Managerial control of the informal organisation

It is important that managers understand that the organisation is unlikely to work in precisely the way it was designed to work. The existence of informal groupings is inevitable even within a small branch, and are likely to regulate the work patterns and work output.

The manager must attempt to understand the value system of cliques or groupings since they may determine the reaction to his orders or instructions. The group attitude can either help or hinder his task in managing. It will undoubtedly create the environment or climate of the organisation. Whilst he may not be able to directly alter the nature of the group or its values he can help by ensuring that adequate official communications exist, instead of allowing rumour and the grapevine to fill the gaps. He can also help by using democratic and participative leadership styles and generally creating an 'openness' between the formal and informal organisations.

Further ways of overcoming these problems are:

(a)   ensuring that the formal organisation is flexible enough to accommodate the change and to incorporate the various informal groupings;

(b)   making clear what is expected of individuals and groups before collective norms develop;

(c)   encouraging individuals to suggest new ideas and procedures;

(d)   displaying positive leadership qualities so that the informal group does not become a law unto itself.

Chapter 6

6   ORGANIGRAMS

(a)   *Principles underlying Mintzberg's theory of structural configuration*

Henry Mintzberg's theories begin with the necessity to co-ordinate work activities. Work activities can be co-ordinated in five different ways: mutual adjustment, direct supervision, standardisation of skills, work processes or outputs.

Mintzberg's theory of organisational configuration is a way of expressing the main features by which both formal structure and power relationships are expressed in organisations. Organisations exist to co-ordinate work, and have five component parts.

(i)   The operating core encompasses those members who perform work directly related to the production of goods and services.

(ii)   The strategic apex has to ensure that the organisation serves its mission. The apex is responsible to the organisation's owners.

(iii) The middle line connects the strategic apex to the operating core, in a formal hierarchy.

(iv)   The technostructure contains analysts (eg accountants, work planners) who aim to effect 'certain forms of standardisation in the organisation'.

(v)   Support staff provide support outside the normal workflow. They have no standardising function or control over the work of the operating core.

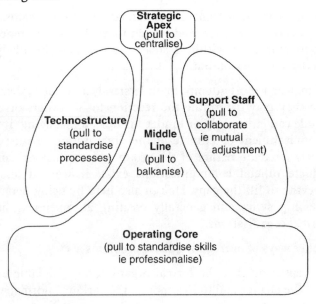

(b)   Mintzberg has written that there are five ideal types of organisation, each of which configures the five components above in a significantly different way. Why should this be so?

(i)   The strategic apex wishes to retain control over decision-making. An example is a manager's refusal to delegate. A more direct example in the decision-making structure is a dictatorship, where power is closely controlled at the centre. It achieves this when the co-ordinating mechanism is *direct supervision*.

(ii)   The technostructure's reason for existence is the design of procedures and standards. For example, the preparation of accounts has become more highly regulated. Technicians spend hours designing management information systems, when, according to Mintzberg, many managers rarely use them.

(iii)   The members of the operating core seek to minimise the control of administrators over what they do. They prefer to work autonomously, achieving what other co-ordination is necessary by mutual adjustment. As professionals, they rely on outside training (such as medical training) to standardise skills.

(iv)   The managers of the middle line seek to increase their autonomy from the strategic apex, and to increase their control over the operating core, so that they can concentrate on their own segment of the market or with their own products.

(v)   Support staff only gain influence when their expertise is vital. Mutual adjustment is the co-ordinating mechanism.

The simple (or entrepreneurial) structure

The *strategic apex* wishes to retain control over decision making, and so exercises what Mintzberg describes as a *pull to centralise*. Mintzberg believes that this leads to a *simple structure*, thus:

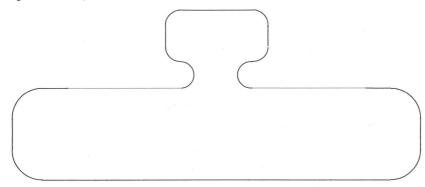

(i)   *Note:*

    (1)   the wide control span;

    (2)   the lack of a middle line, implying minimal hierarchy;

    (3)   the lack of technostructure, implying little formalisation or standardisation of behaviour.

(ii)   Co-ordination is achieved by *direct* supervision with few formal devices. It is thus flexible.

(iii)   The environment for such a configuration should be relatively simple but fast moving, therefore standardisation cannot be used to co-ordinate activities.

(iv) Mintzberg believes the simple structure is characteristic of small, young organisations.

(v) Centralisation is advantageous as it reflects management's full knowledge of the operating core and its processes.

(vi) It is risky as it depends on the expertise of one person.

The *technostructure* exerts a pull for standardisation of procedures and processes. It thus creates a machine bureaucracy.

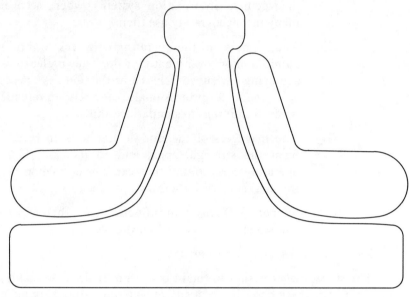

(i) This is the classic bureaucracy, working on a sophisticated and well-tuned set of rules and procedures.

(ii) The operating core is highly standardised. Direct supervision by the strategic apex is limited, as work standardisation ensures co-ordination.

(iii) The technostructure is the key part. Power rests with analysts who standardise other people's work.

(iv) Formal communication is most important. Authority is hierarchical.

(v) There is a strong emphasis on the division of labour, and in particular on control. Uncertainty has to be eliminated.

(vi) Conflict is rife between different departments, between line and staff, and between operating core and management.

(vii) The environment is simple and stable. Machine bureaucracies are associated with routine technical systems.

(viii) The machine bureaucracy is the most efficient structure for integrating sets of simple and repetitive tasks.

(ix) Machine bureaucracies cannot adapt: they are designed for specialised purposes. They are driven by performance, not problem solving.

The *operating core* has a pull for standardisation, not of work processes but of individual skills. (For example, a machine bureaucracy would denote exactly how financial transactions should be posted, whether people understood them or not.) The operating core seeks to minimise the influence of all administrators (mainly the middle line and technostructure) over work. The resulting configuration is called the professional bureaucracy. Examples are hospitals and accountancy firms.

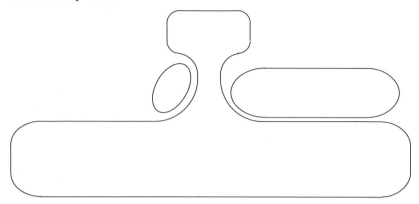

(i)   It hires trained specialists who are all socialised in the skills and values of the profession. A school is an example. Teachers' work in the classroom is not directly supervised.

(ii)   Co-ordination is achieved by common standards, which originate outside its structure. (A hospital's procedures of doing simple operations may not be developed in house, but imported.)

(iii)   Power is based on expertise, not formal position.

(iv)   Work processes are too complex to be standardised by a technostructure.

(v)   The operating core is the key part. There is an elaborate support staff to service it. A technostructure might exist for budgeting but not for designing work processes.

(vi)   Work is decentralised. Professionals control their own work, and seek collective control over the administrative decisions which affect them.

(vii)   There might be two organisation hierarchies.

    (1)   Bottom-up for the operating core doing the work.
    (2)   Top-down for the support staff.

    An example is a barristers' chambers. Barristers are co-ordinated by the clerk, but they retain collective authority over the clerk. The clerk, on the other hand, will exercise direct control over secretarial services.

(viii) Professional administrators also manage much of the organisation's boundary.

(ix)   It can be democratic.

(x)   The professional bureaucracy cannot always cope with any variations of standards, as control is exercised through training.

The divisional (or diversified) form

The middle line seeks as much autonomy for itself as possible. It exerts a pull to balkanise (ie to split into small self-managed units). The result is the divisional form, by which autonomy is given to managers lower down the line. Sometimes divisionalisation is referred to as federal decentralisation. The prime co-ordinating mechanism is standardisation of outputs.

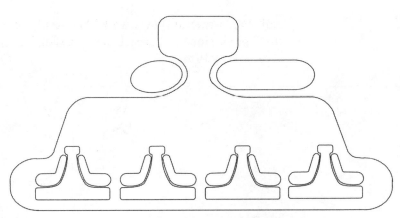

(i)   Divisionalisation is a very widely used configuration. It is the division of a business into autonomous regions or product businesses, each with its own revenues, expenditures and profits.

(ii)   A machine bureaucracy is the configuration of each division. This is because each division is monitored by its objective performance towards a single integrated set of goals. In other words, divisions have to reach performance targets set by the strategic apex.

(iii)   There is a division of labour between the divisions and the head office. Communication between divisions and head office is restricted, formal and related to performance standards. Influence is maintained by headquarters' power to hire and fire the managers who are supposed to run each division.

The adhocracy

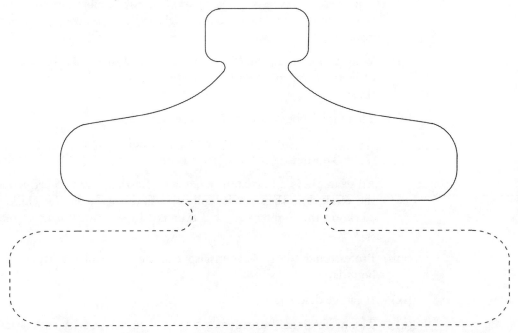

The *support staff* exert a pull of their own, towards *collaboration*. The *adhocracy* does not rely on standardisation to co-ordinate its activities, yet it is much more complex than the simple structure.

(i)   The adhocracy is complex and disorderly.

    (1)   There is little formalisation of behaviour.

(2)   Specialists are deployed in market-based project teams which group together and disperse as and when a project arises and ends.

(3)   Co-ordination is informal.

(ii)   The adhocracy relies on the expertise of its members, but not through standardised skills. Instead the mix of skills is important. For example, a film is made by a director, actors, camera people, set designers and so on.

(iii)   A matrix structure might exist, but there are a large number of management roles eg project managers. Managers do not plan or supervise, but co-ordinate.

(iv)   Decision-making power depends on the type of decision and the situation in which it is made, rather than level in hierarchy. 'No-one ... monopolises the power to innovate'.

Chapter 7

7   TQM AND BPR

Tutorial note. BPR is slightly more recent than TQM, but both have been bandied around in recent years as the elixir of success: both have in part disappointed wilder expectations of firms who see them as the latest quick fix. In part (b) of the question, remember that while both techniques contain vital insights, management failings can neutralise their benefits.

(a)   Total quality management (TQM) is an approach to running a business which involves both the application of particular techniques and way of management. Although TQM in Europe and the US has developed in response to Japanese competition, many of its tenets originated from American theorists. Deming identified a number of points, which are relevant to the way in which TQM is being conducted.

1	Create constancy of purpose for the improvement of product and service.
2	Adopt the new philosophy, ie strive to eliminate every kind of waste.
3	Cease dependence on mass inspection to achieve quality.
4	End the practice of awarding business on the basis of price alone.
5	Improve constantly and forever the system of production and service.
6	Institute training.
7	Adopt and institute leadership.
8	Drive out fear.
9	Break down barriers between staff areas.
10	Eliminate slogans, exhortations, and targets for the workforce.
11	Eliminate numerical quotas for the workforce and numerical goals for people in management.
12	Remove barriers that rob people of pride of workmanship.
13	Encourage education and self improvement for everyone.
14	Take action to accomplish the transformation.

(i)   Item 3 represents some of the techniques described above. Item 4 also represents quality assurance.

(ii)   However to introduce the techniques requires changes in management style.

Quality means fitness for use of the finished product. In the past, inspection departments had to reject substandard output, but the purpose of TQM is to ensure that substandard output is not made in the first place (ie the goal of *zero defects*). Although TQM employs statistical techniques to reduce variations, it is also a *culture of continuous improvement* to work practices and all operations. An important component is the need for team work and the involvement of the production workforce. Attention to detail, in order to eliminate waste and defective production, is at its heart. Specific targets for customer satisfaction can be built into the design of products.

As part of the requirement to eliminate waste of all kinds, TQM often goes hand in hand with *just in time* purchasing and production, which means that items are not bought or manufactured until needed, thus eliminating the need to hold stocks. The disciplines this requires go further back along the supply chain.

Business process re-engineering (BPR) has both a broader and a narrower focus than TQM. Re-engineering, according to Mike Hammer, involves: 'the fundamental rethinking and radical redesign of business process to achieve dramatic improvements in critical, contemporary measures of performance such as cost, quality, performance and speed'.

Whereas TQM is methodical approach to continuous improvement by judicious tinkering supported by a culture, BPR is more radical.

(i)   The process involves a root and branch review of how a business goes about satisfying its customers. In theory, nothing is considered out of bounds.

(ii)   BPR also exploits IT, not necessarily at the heart of TQM, not to automate or improve existing procedures, but to design new ones, in order to cut out unnecessary procedures.

(iii)   Once the processes have been redesigned, other aspects of organisation design, such as span of control, job design and performance measurement fall, in a sort of domino effect. Of course, TQM can have a similar radical effect, for example by the creation of multiskilled teams.

(iv)   Arguably, because BPR involves not only a new way of working but a severe challenge to vested interests, it is more likely to be imposed from the top down. TQM, on the other hand, requires the commitment of everybody in the company, over the long term. BPR has echoes of scientific management, in that planning the process is divorced from implementing it, but the attention to the detail of the work process is also characteristic of TQM.

BPR cannot be planned and implemented in small steps. It is an all or nothing proposition. As with any systems change, where possible it should be preceded by piloting.

(b)

> *Tutorial note.* This part of the question indicates that you need to keep your eyes peeled for articles in the business press about these developments.

Ford has re-engineered its whole accounts payable process, covering the separate functions of purchasing, material control and accounts, with the result that they have introduced a system of invoiceless processing and have reduced their accounts payable staff headcount by 75%. Union Carbide eliminated $400 million of fixed costs in just three years; Mutual Benefit Life reduced its turnround of customer applications from 5-25 days to 2-5 days and jettisoned 100 field office positions; IBM Credit cut their time for preparing quotes from 7 days to one; and Bell Atlantic reduced its delivery times from 15 days to just one.

TQM has been adopted by many companies: an example is Bosch at its plant in Cardiff. According to an article in *People Management* in 1992, Bosch's approach to quality has been base upon continuous improvement, teamworking and synergy, internal customers, and measurement and feedback. All of these support each other.

Chapter 8

8 PERSONALITY AND SELECTION

> *Tutorial note.* You should have defined personality, examined the influences on it, mentioned personality tests, and tried to relate these to corporate culture or the work situation. Avoid platitude.

Personality in the context of organisational behaviour can be defined as the 'total pattern of characteristic ways of thinking, feeling and behaving that constitute the individual's distinctive method of relating to the environment'. The concept of personality integrates most behaviour patterns of learning, motivation and so forth. It focuses on consistent stable properties or characteristics (the expression 'to act out of character' means to act in a way that is inconsistent with your normal behaviour). The concept of personality is also used to distinguish one person from another.

The source of personality, or even whether the very concept is too general and all-embracing to defy analysis, has exercised thinkers and psychologists for many decades. It is, however, possible to identify certain factors.

(a)   *Nature* – some theorists argue that personality is partially inherited, part of an individual's genetic makeup. Other theorists argue that it is the environment that has the greater influence. This is sometimes known as the nature/nurture debate.

(b)   *Childhood*. Childhood is the period where an individual is, it is believed, most able or capable of learning (eg it is easy for children to learn how to speak a language). This learning is given by the family, and by peer groups. Here the child will learn the behaviour acceptable within the family or culture (eg some families encourage demonstrations of emotion, some do not), although these two do not necessarily coincide. The child will also learn certain things about himself or herself which may affect self-image and confidence in later life. The influence of toilet-training is cited as an example of the effect of childhood on later life. Childhood is therefore the stage when children become socialised, and develop a sense of 'self'.

(c)   *Education and culture.* The type of educational institution attended can affect a person's behaviour in certain ways as a result both of the influence of peer groups and of the social values the institution supports.

(d)   *Age.* A person's character develops over time, and is shaped by experience.

Argyris points out a number of common trends that develop and impact upon personality as individuals mature:

- An increasing tendency to activity rather than passivity
- Increasing complexity and diversity in behaviour patterns and responses
- A tendency from dependence to independence
- Acceptance of equal or superior relationships with others
- Lengthening time perspectives
- Deepening and more stable interests
- Increasing self-awareness

Many people spend a considerable amount of their lives in some sort of work environment, where they are paid to produce goods or services for consumption by others, or to be involved in the administration of that production. For this reason alone, it is possible that personality factors can be important in recruitment and selection, although there are other influences too.

Personality is relevant to recruitment and selection in three areas.

- The task or job
- The roles a person is expected to play in a team
- The culture of the work environment

For example, a person who was naturally gregarious might be appropriate for a job involving a lot of social contact and interaction, whereas someone with a methodical, academic mind might be more suited to a job where intellectual skills are employed. What would be irksome to the social butterfly would be bearable to the scholar.

Some jobs are undertaken by teams. While it is a truism to say that some people are better at co-operating in teams than others, and this is in part a cultural factor (the Japanese culture is supposed to favour group activity more than others), the different roles in group situations (eg shaper, completer and so forth) may require people of different talents and personalities.

The culture of the work environment is also an influence. By this is meant the official culture of the organisation and the individuals within it. Some companies have very strong corporate cultures. In the early days of microcomputing, the management styles of IBM and Apple were very different. Corporate culture may be promoted as a conscious choice on the part of management (especially involved in change), or it may result simply from managers recruiting people like themselves. There may be occasions, then, when a person might have the right sort of abilities and aptitudes for the job, but may not fit in with the corporate culture.

Employer assessment of personality

An important question is the extent to which it is possible to comprehensively and accurately assess an individual's personality. The most commonly used selection technique is the interview, but the effectiveness of this process in assessing ability and personality is questionable – people may respond and behave very differently in this scenario than they would in the everyday work environment. Similar comments can be made of application forms.

Some firms, believing that the methods above cannot predict performance or even say a great deal about personality, use other methods to assess and measure personality. Graphology is an example, although its use is controversial. Other ways include personality tests and psychometric tests which are supposed to give more accurate responses than just a chat.

However, to what extent should personality be included in the selection process at all? There may be cases where it is inappropriate.

(a)   Where there are skill shortages, getting the right personality might be a luxury which will have to be forgone. The organisation might have to make an effort to accommodate the personality, rather than the other way round.

(b)   Assuming that only a certain class or type of personality can do a job can lead to false stereotyping of personalities, or a false assessment of what the job really entails. To take an extreme example, some actors, who you would expect to be flamboyant extroverts, are personally quite shy when not acting.

(c)   The corporate culture might be dysfunctional to the well being of the organisation as a whole, and might need to be changed. It is often possible to change corporate cultures without changing personnel. People are often able to adapt their personalities to the demands of the work environment. Therefore, any new recruit can adapt his or her personality through socialisation.

(d)   How a person gets on at work, or how someone's personality fits in, often depends on the relationships already existing in the workplace.

(e)   Different types of personality play different roles. It may be that recruiters confuse roles with personalities.

To conclude then, personality can be an important factor in recruitment when the corporate culture is an issue, or where the job or team situation demands it. However, it is easy to fall into the trap of stereotyping, and it may be that it is the organisation culture that needs changing. Moreover, the personality types that are pleasant to meet socially may not be those who are the best workers at the task. Recruiting on the basis of personality perhaps underestimates the extent to which people can adapt themselves.

Chapter 9

9   PERFORMANCE MOTIVATION

Tutorial note. Part (a) was not too tricky, but you had to think a bit for part (b): usefulness to whom? The question also asks you to discuss at least three theories.

(a)   *Theories of motivation*

(i)   *Maslow's hierarchy of needs*

Maslow's hierarchy of needs describes what motivates people to do anything, and is not restricted to the work situation. In principle, it suggests that each individual has a set of needs, arranged in a hierarchy of relative prepotency. These needs are, in ascending order:

physiological, safety, social, esteem, self-actualisation (the fulfilment of personal potential).

A need which has been satisfied no longer has the power to motivate, so the next need up in the hierarchy takes over. Only then can the next need begin to motivate. The need for self-actualisation can never be satisfied.

However, beyond a basic common sense approach (eg assuaging thirst and hunger may be necessary for survival and more urgent than self-actualisation) the theory has a number of problems.

(1)   It is hard to verify, and research does not bear out the proposition that needs become less powerful when satisfied.

(2)   It massively oversimplifies human behaviour (for example esteem might be bound up with someone's self-image).

(3)   The hierarchy cannot be used to predict the behaviour of any individual.

(ii)   Another needs-based theory is *Herzberg's two factor theory*. People are motivated by a need to avoid unpleasantness and a need for personal growth

The avoidance of unpleasantness is achieved by attention to *hygiene factors*,

sometimes referred to as *context* or *maintenance factors*, which can include company policy, supervisory style, working conditions and job security. If deficient in some way, these can demotivate; but they cannot motivate a person positively.

Motivator factors satisfy a need for personal growth, and include such matters as status, recognition, interesting work and responsibility. In other words, the job itself, rather than the conditions surrounding it provide motivation. Herzberg suggested practical techniques of job enlargement, job rotation and job enrichment (the ancestor, perhaps, of empowerment).

(iii)   *Expectancy theory*

Expectancy theory (Vroom) narrows the focus still further, and based, not so much on needs which must be dealt with, but on the processes by which people are motivated. In its simplest form:

The force of motivation $=$ Valence $\times$ Expectancy

where Valence is the value of an outcome to an individual, and Expectancy is the individual's expectation that the desired outcome will occur. Expectancy theory accepts, therefore, that people might have a variety of needs giving rise to Valence. A distinction is also made between the individual and the organisation.

(b)   Usefulness of motivation theories

A motivation theory is only useful if managers are able to apply it successfully. Any attempt at evaluating the usefulness must begin by asking the question 'Usefulness for whom?' In the context of this answer:

The workers. What are the implications of each of the theories for them? To what extent would application of the theories ensure that their needs were met in the workplace?

The managers. To what extent do the theories offer practical guidance for their management style? Also, to what extent will using the theories help managers achieve their objectives?

The organisation. Following on from the above two categories, to what extent will understanding and application of the theories benefit the organisation as a whole?

Of the needs-based theories, some of the problems with Maslow's have already been mentioned. People's needs differ over time, and it is too vague to identify precisely what to do. Jobs satisfy many needs: pay, a social life, status, even self-actualisation. Furthermore, the organisation itself has needs for discipline and standardisation which may prevent employees doing their own thing. Herzberg's theory is work-based and useful in broadening management horizons as to the factors managers can consider in getting the best out of people.

The benefits of these theories can therefore be summarised as drawing managers' attention to the fact that motivation is a complex issue and that each individual may be motivated by a range of factors. Overly simplistic motivation strategies, for example those that rely solely on money as a motivator and ignore other aspects of the total experience of work, are therefore likely to be ineffective.

A serious limitation of these theories however, is the failure to explain why the same reward may result in different levels of motivation in different individuals.

Expectancy theory provides valuable insights into individual responses to motivators. Managers' attention is drawn to the fact that a 'reward' will only be motivating if it is something that the individual values. The theory's emphasis on the influence of the extent to which the individual believes a given pattern of behaviour will result in a particular outcome is also important. This draws attention to the importance of management delivering promised rewards.

From the point of view of workers within the organisation, a sound management understanding of motivation has the potential to create benefits both in terms of the work itself (eg job design) and the benefits they gain from doing it (promotion, salary, comradeship and so on).

Finally the organisation as a whole will also benefit. A motivated workforce is likely to exhibit lower levels of absenteeism, lower labour turnover rates and greater commitment to their work (which in turn may reflect in quality and productivity levels).

Chapter 10

10   WHAT IS LEADERSHIP?

> *Tutorial note.* An old chestnut of a question, this, and liable to be interpreted in different ways. Be clear in your mind what you consider to be the marks of effectiveness in a leader. There are a number of leadership theories you could have considered. We have quoted three of them.

According to John Kotter, leadership involves interacting with people, rather than things, and the leadership task involves the following.

(a)   Creating a sense of direction, usually borne out of dissatisfaction with the status quo. Out of this challenge, a vision for something different is created.

(b)   Communicating the vision, which must meet the realised or unconscious needs of other people, to give it credibility.

(c)   Energising, inspiring and motivating, to stimulate others to translate the vision into achievement:

(i)   subordinates
(ii)   other people in the organisation
(iii) people with power to support or hinder the leader's effort.

Of course, these factors are more relevant in some leadership situations than others. We can expand on this notion of effectiveness to include the following.

(a)   Successful leadership requires not only the consent, but the active support of followers, in a group, a company or whatever.

(b)   According to the contingency approach an effective leader must have the flexibility to adjust his or her leadership style.

(c)   Implied in Kotter's list above is an ability to communicate and manage the need for change.

A number of theories cam be cited which suggest how leaders can be effective. Most of them suggest that leaders are rarely born with a set of characteristic traits. The ability to lead depends on a hidden understanding with followers.

(a)   The *Ashridge model* identifies four different styles of leadership: tells, sells, consults and joins, each of which has its own strengths and weaknesses. The tells style involves a leader taking an autocratic, dictatorial role; subordinates are not expected to contribute and must do what they are told. *Sells* is still basically autocratic, but the leader prefers to win hearts and minds by convincing them that the choice is good one. *Consults* implies that subordinates do have something to contribute, although the leader still has the final say. Joins implies that decisions are, effectively, taken by consensus.

Subordinates prefer the consults style, and leadership style did affect employee's motivation. Most preferred consistency above all.

Leadership is an interpersonal skill, but it also involves setting direction. The Ashridge model highlights the difficulty in reconciling the needs of the task, the group and the individual. On occasions, the leader will have to be autocratic. The tells style is necessary perhaps in a crisis, where speed is needed, but, on the other hand, if all decisions are taken by a leader, this failure to delegate and empower might mean that employees are demotivated. Another problem with tells and sells is that the leader is assumed to be all-knowing, whereas this is less likely than before to be the case. Finally, leadership involves communicating a vision not only to subordinates but to colleagues and other audiences (eg shareholders). This does not feature in the Ashridge model.

(b)   *Blake and Mouton*

Blake and Mouton identified how managers can be effective leaders by identifying the leader's concerns for the task and for people. Such concerns are not incompatible, in contrast to what might be expected from the Theory X/Y continuum. They concluded that the best leaders showed high concern for both, which is what you would expect from a definition of leadership effectiveness as being related to having a vision, and motivating people to fulfil it.

Handy also suggests a contingency approach in which there are four important variables which contribute to the effectiveness of a leader, which are:

(a)   the leader (personality and preferred style of operating)
(b)   the subordinate (personalities and preferred leadership style)
(c)   the task (objectives of the job, technology, methods of working)
(d)   the environment

He argues that the first three factors can each be illustrated on a spectrum ranging from 'tight' (autocratic leader with low estimation of subordinate capability; subordinates like routine, prefer directive leadership, and regard work as trivial; task is routine and repetitive) to 'flexible' (democratic leader with confidence in subordinates; subordinates who accept uncertainty, seek out challenge, have confidence in their own abilities and favour independence; complex, longer-term, important tasks).

Leadership will be most effective when all three elements are at the same level on the spectrum. If the elements are out of line then the manager must make a decision on which elements to change in order to bring them back into line.

A final influence on leadership effectiveness is the environment. Factors included by Handy in this category include the leader's personal power and organisational norms and values.

A basic problem is that the leadership role is very varied. Leadership skills may be required as much by a project manager seeking to motivate a small team to meet a punishing deadline as by the chief executive of a large company seeking to arrest the company's decline and to introduce a major programme of organisational change. The models described above appear to be on the small scale; but even the chief executive needs the right interpersonal skills to inspire his or her managers with the vision.

Chapter 11

11   STRESS

This answer will begin with a discussion of what is meant by stress. Then it will move to a consideration of the range of individual characteristics and organisational factors that combine to create an individual's own unique experience of stress. Finally there will be discussion of how stress awareness can help to maximise organisational effectiveness.

Stress is a term which is frequently used – often fairly loosely – to describe demands on an individual's physical and mental energies. Up to a certain level these demands may have a motivating effect; beyond this point stress begins to have a detrimental effect both on performance and health. These negative effects may show up in a variety of ways.

(a)   Mood changes – anxiety, depression, feeling unable to cope

(b)   Cognitive changes – problems in concentrating, difficulty in making decisions

(c)   Behavioural changes – making errors, reliance on painkillers, alcohol

(d)   Physical symptoms – headaches, chest pain, ulcers

Clearly these effects will affect the individual in all aspects of their lives, including their performance in the workplace.

There are a number of factors that may contribute to an individual's level of stress. Some of these are external to the individual, but it should also be noted that individual characteristics, most notably personality type, will also play an important role.

A major investigation into personality types was carried out by Drs Rosenman and Friedman (1968). They argue that there are two distinctive personality types, which they call type A and type B.

Type A personalities are competitive, dynamic, impatient, restless and easily agitated. Type B personalities are the opposite. Type A people are generally the self starters and innovators – thus they may actively place themselves in more stressful situations, and moreover they may add to this stress by trying to overcome it.

Other important individual characteristics which may influence stress levels include:

(a)   *sensitivity* – emotionally sensitive individuals may feel more pressured by conflict and doubt which less sensitive people may shrug off;

(b)   *flexibility* – individuals who are seen to give in to pressure tend to invite further pressure from those who seek to influence them; more stubborn individuals may suffer less from this, although, when they are subject to pressure, they tend to snap rather than bend, as there is more dissonance involved in their giving way.

(c)   *interpersonal competence* – the effects of stress may be handled better by individuals with strong supporting relationships with others. Good personal skills may also help to prevent stressful situations from arising or enable individuals to deal with such situations more effectively;

(d)   *sense of responsibility* – individuals vary in their sense of accountability to others and the associated sense of pressure if they fail to meet their 'obligations'.

In addition to these personal variables there are many external potential stress-increasing factors which will impact on different individuals at varying times in their lives and careers. These include factors outside the workplace, for example a death in the family or financial problems, and a range of factors within the workplace.

Specific jobs within an organisation each have their own associated stressors. Until recently it was often claimed that executives were the greatest victims of stress; however, more recent research has suggested that blue collar workers are more likely to suffer from stress related illness, due to a variety of actors such as boredom, lack of control over their work and unclear work roles. In practice all jobs will have some stress associated with them. An awareness of the following categories of organisational stress may help in making a meaningful comparison (once again some factors are related to the job itself and others to the context in which the job is performed).

In terms of the job itself there are a number of issues concerning an individual's role which may give rise to stress. These include: role ambiguity (uncertainty about one's role), role compatibility (differences in expectation of a given role), role conflict (holding multiple roles which are incompatible in some ways), role overload/underload (having too many/few roles to cope with). All are possible causes of stress.

In terms of the environment in which the role is performed, an important factor is management style. In an article in the Administrator (January 1987), Sarah Rookledge describes the finding of an American report entitled 'Working Well: Managing for Health and High Performance'. This report was based on factors identified by a number of workshop participants as being responsible for stress and health problems. These include factors such as unpredictability, destruction of workers' self esteem, turning work relationships into a battle for control and providing too much (or too little) stimulation.

The article also discusses the findings of similar research in the UK where primary criticisms were: not giving credit where it is due, poor communication and lack of staff involvement in decision making, supervising too closely, and not defining duties clearly enough.

From the point of view of a manager, an understanding of the issues associated with stress is important for two key reasons. Firstly, at a personal level it may help them to recognise symptoms in themselves, to understand the factors that are causing them stress and why; these are important steps in being able to deal with stress more effectively. Secondly, it will enable them to recognise causes and signs of stress in others, and encourage them to seek mechanisms for addressing and resolving the stressors.

As stress is known to cause both illness (potentially resulting in absenteeism) and behavioural changes (potentially resulting in decreased performance levels, increased numbers of mistakes and accidents) it clearly represents a very real cost to organisations and as such managers should do everything to reduce it both for themselves and others.

Chapter 12

12   INNOVATION

This answer will consider a number of issues. Firstly, what is innovation and how can it contribute to organisational success? Secondly, if innovation is accepted as a key success factor why then do 'successful' organisations experience difficulty in being innovative? The answer will conclude with a discussion of the steps that such organisations could take to facilitate innovation.

Innovation is best defined as something completely new. Increasingly it is attracting the attention of management theorists, many of whom are arguing that the ability to innovate is the key to competitive advantage in the increasingly changing and turbulent market environment of the late twentieth century.

The Japanese management theorist Ikujiro Nonaka argues:

> 'In an economy where the only certainty is uncertainty, the one sure source of lasting competitive advantage is knowledge. When markets shift, technologies proliferate, competitors multiply, and products become almost obsolete overnight, successful companies are those that consistently create new knowledge, disseminate it widely throughout the organisation, and quickly embody it in new technologies and products. These activities define the 'knowledge creating' company whose sole business is innovation'

> (*Harvard Business Review*, November-December 1991)

BPP
PUBLISHING

Innovation can take place in all areas of an organisation – it is not a process that is simply about coming up with new product ideas. The following list provides some examples of areas of potential innovation within an organisation.

(a) New product technology, eg digital camera technology

(b) New features on existing technology, eg driver airbags in cars

(c) New production/manufacturing techniques, eg JIT

(d) New services, eg telephone banking

(e) New internal processes, eg the computerisation of stock control and automated ordering in supermarkets

(f) New marketing strategies or target segments, eg introduction of a mail order service by Next

(g) Organisational structure, eg decentralising decision making in an historically bureaucratic organisation.

If this claim that innovation is the key to success is accepted, then how is it that organisations which are prominent and profitable in the marketplace (and therefore 'successful') achieve success and tend to find innovation hard to achieve?

In practice it may be that such organisations were at one time highly innovative and that this was the basis for their success. It may also be that the organisation became established during a period where the market place was less turbulent, where there was less technological change, fewer competitors and less discerning customers. To some extent such organisations may now be living on reserves built up in the good years. It is, however, unlikely that they will continue to prosper if they fail to innovate. The problem is that as organisations grow and mature a number of barriers to innovation become established.

(a) *Top management isolation:* financially focused managers are likely to perceive technological innovation as riskier than, say, a policy of acquisition. In addition they tend to be distanced from the shopfloor where much of the knowledge that could facilitate innovation often lies. Creative ideas may come from anywhere within an organisation and at any time – in order for these ideas to become reality they must be able to reach the decision makers.

(b) *Intolerance of fanatics:* entrepreneurs are not afraid to challenge and break with convention; this is often seen as disruptive within the organisation. Recruitment policies often seek out those whose background and outlook fits with the existing culture – this protects the status quo but does little to promote new ways of thinking and behaving.

(c) *Short-time horizons and the need for profitability:* the need to perform profitably now encourages a short-term focus on activities with a 'guaranteed' return and discourages investment in longer-term and riskier projects.

(d) *Excessive rationalism:* managers in large organisations often seek orderly advance through early market research studies or systematic project planning.

(e) *Excessive bureaucracy:* bureaucratic structures require ideas to obtain many levels of approval which creates delay. Formal vertical communication prevents interaction and cross fertilisation of ideas: interactive feedback that fosters innovation is lost, delays and associated costs and missed opportunities are inevitable.

(f)   *Inappropriate incentives, motivation and reward mechanisms:* if the internal control systems do not reward and encourage innovative behaviour (and indeed often penalise it), then there is little to encourage employees to become entrepreneurs.

Many of these difficulties can be avoided by small organisations and individual entrepreneurs who are committed to the ideas, and persevere despite setbacks and possibly long time-spans between invention and commercial success. Limited cash reserves encourage such organisations to be highly responsive to their customers and environments – their survival is likely to depend upon it. Their size means that they do not have complicated structures and processes to hamper this responsiveness and flexibility. The possibility of considerable personal reward from those ideas which are developed into commercial reality, serves to reinforce appropriate behaviour and acts as an important motivator.

This is not to say that all small organisations and entrepreneurs are successful. There are obviously a number of other factors which will contribute to their success or failure, including the ability to rationally analyse ideas (and the willingness to drop ideas which do not stand up to this), and to translate ideas into practice (many 'ideas people' are not good completer-finishers). In the same way not all large organisations are poor innovators. Those organisations that wish to improve their innovation record should:

(a)   create vision and innovative culture – senior management support is vital;

(b)   focus outward on the market – anticipate and find product solutions that solve customer problems;

(c)   develop small, flat hierarchies, and small development teams of six or seven people;

(d)   encourage multiple approaches to solving problems, 'competing teams' working on the same problem often results in improved amounts and quality of research and ideas – however care must be taken to avoid excessive duplication and ensure that healthy competition does not degenerate into divisive antagonism;

(e)   interact with the external environment – not just consumers but also consider partnership with other individuals and organisations with specialist knowledge;

(f)   ensure that internal policies and procedures (eg reward systems and recruitment strategies) reinforce the above points.

As has been illustrated, many organisations may achieve their success as a result of innovation. Growth and maturity, however, tend to act as inhibitors to innovation for a number of reasons. Unfortunately it may be success itself which results in the long term decline of the organisation. To avoid this organisations need to rethink their structure, management style and policies.

Chapter 13

13   MANAGEMENT OF CHANGE

> *Tutorial note.* Good answers to this question will show an awareness of the general concepts and demonstrate an ability to understand how those concepts may apply in a given scenario.

PUBLISHING

(a) *Employee attitudes to proposals*

There are a number of possible reactions to change, spanning a spectrum of acceptance, indifference, passive resistance and active resistance.

Individuals will exhibit different responses to different proposals for change. The level of this resistance will be a product of:

(i) individual personality and characteristics such as age, self-confidence, emotional stability, and level of need for security. For example, a young, well qualified and self-confident single person may be less likely to resist change than a more mature, less skilled person with a dependent family;

(ii) factors relating to the specific change such as:

attitudes and beliefs – does the proposed change undermine a strongly held belief? For example, a practising Jewish worker may resist a move towards Saturday working;

group identity and loyalty – does the proposed change threaten existing group composition and norms? For example, does the introduction of a new lunch rota system mean that Friday lunch time drinks are no longer possible?

habit or tradition – based on the notion that 'It's always worked OK till now so why change?' (This may be closely linked to self-confidence.)

organisational politics and self-interest – how does the proposed change affect the power base of the individual or the group to which they belong? For example, combining two departments under the leadership of one manager may pose a considerable threat to the position of the existing heads of department.

misunderstanding or poor communication – resistance to change is often based on rumour and assumptions rather than 'reality'.

With regard to specific scenarios identified in the question the following comments would be valid:

(i) *The circumstantial disruption.* Particularly where employees are older and more rooted in the present location of home and office, there is likely to be resistance not only to the sheer effort and inconvenience of moving, but more fundamentally to the insecurity of giving up established patterns of life, familiar surroundings – perhaps a community lived in for generations. The alternative – redundancy – is equally threatening to employees' psychological and financial security.

Some individuals are more risk-averse than others. Background and age may attach certain people to the old area more than others. Much will depend on the type of area the firm is relocating to, and whether it offers an incentive or disincentive to move. Nevertheless, generally speaking the attitude of employees is likely to be one of clinging to the status quo, the stable equilibrium.

(ii) *Social disruption.* The secure basis of established relationships may be up-rooted by the change of community and the loss of workmates who choose not to relocate. The forging of new work and non-work relationships can be fraught with personal insecurity, and the risk of not fitting in.

(iii) The *perception that change is being forced on employees* in the form of an ultimatum: 'Move with the company, or it will move without you'. This is a blow to the self image of the individual apart from anything else, since it robs him or her of the sense of personal control over his or her own destiny. It will be particularly resented by employees who have given long service to the firm and feel that the harsh realities of the relocation represent a rejection and an ingratitude (particularly since relocations are frequently planned in order to save costs, and it will not be possible for the firm to be universally open-handed with financial help and incentives to employees reluctant or unable to move).

Some individuals may, however, welcome the change: if the move is to a desirable area, if they have not put down roots in the present area, if they are of secure and extrovert personality, or even if they anticipate promotion as a result of superiors' failure to relocate. Appropriate financial incentives to move may also be a consideration for some. In some cultures, moreover, geographical mobility may not be a radical and threatening form of change. In some large and sparsely populated countries, for example, 300 miles may not be perceived as an insuperably large distance for commuting and therefore minimising circumstantial disruption.

The implementation of performance-related pay and appraisal for the entire workforce is likely to generate resistance for the following reasons.

(i) It may be perceived as a threat to the individual's financial security. Particularly in types of work which are not self-contained, but rely on other people and groups, it may be felt that the individual is not in control of his earnings. Holidays, sickness and absence will be seen to put employees under pressure in such a system.

(ii) The performance measurement and appraisal which form part of such systems may themselves be perceived as threatening to the psychological and political position of the employee. It may be felt that management is trying to find fault, to catch out workers and cut rates, to weaken the employees' position. The process of 'being watched' can also seem unattractive, as a perceived symptom of lack of trust and doubt of workers' competence.

(iii) There are complex political implications to a company-wide scheme. Workers may feel they are being manipulated into greater production. On the other hand, performance-related systems are associated with higher-level employees who may feel that their position is being eroded: this will be more acute if differentials are in fact seen to be squeezed, where lower-level employees earn significant performance-related bonuses.

(iv) There may be uncertainty and suspicion about the basis on which performance is measured and awards calculated.

However, much will depend on the political history and culture of the organisation and the type of work done. In entrepreneurial cultures, where employees are encouraged to be individualistic and risk-taking, performance-related pay may be felt to be highly desirable. (Burns and Stalker, for example, suggested that organismic structures require and foster roles and personalities who thrive on freedom of manoeuvre, insecurity and uncertainty.) Individuals with high need for achievement may welcome the tangible proof of success that performance-related pay and appraisal offers.

(b) *Guidance on gaining acceptance of change ideas*

The following ideas taken from the literature on the management of change provide important insights into how best to gain acceptance of change.

There are three important steps:

(i) Identify and understand the spectrum of possible responses to proposed change. These may range from enthusiastic approval to active resistance. Each of these are associated with particular behaviours, for example active resistance may manifest in the form of sabotage or strikes. Recognising behaviour patterns, and more importantly changes in behaviour patterns, will provide important clues to the underlying attitude to the changes.

Effective managers recognise that resistance may not be overt. Hunt argues that there are a variety of behaviours which may not appear to be resistance, but which in practice undermine or delay change. Examples include:

Pleas of ignorance – 'I need more information' (a delaying tactic)

Defensive stances – using counter-information to develop the opinion that the proposed change is doomed to failure anyway

(ii) Understand the possible causes of resistance. These were discussed in section (a), and are important because it is only by understanding the root cause that they can be tackled effectively.

(iii) Manage the process of change. There are a number of key factors and guiding principles:

(1) The timing and pace of change – allowing time for issues to surface and a new balance to be achieved. Introducing change gradually and in stages is useful because it provides the opportunity to ask questions and to acclimatise to change over a period of time – this is likely to be less disruptive and unsettling than sudden dramatic change.

(2) Define the scope of the change – total transformation may seem initially appealing but is it really necessary or attainable? Clearly defined scope will lessen uncertainty and anxiety.

(3) Sell the change – two way communication is vital to the change process – explaining the need and mechanisms for the proposed changes and identifying expected consequences.

(4) Participation – allowing groups and individuals to take part in the decision-making process and to express their doubts and fears is equally important. Management needs to address these issues in as honest and convincing a manner as possible – unrealistic responses will simply magnify fears. Aim to persuade rather than force. This may also add value to the process by showing up information that is clear to the workforce but which has not been previously considered by management.

(5)   Support – provide training and counselling for those affected by the change.

(6)   Reward and motivation – ensure that company reward and motivation strategies actively reinforce desired behaviour.

Above all managers should remember that they are attempting to change behaviour and to do this individuals will need to go through a learning process. The issues involved are neatly expressed by John Hunt (*Managing People at Work*) who says:

'Learning also involves re-learning – not merely learning something new but trying to unlearn what is already known.'

The overall challenge facing managers of change is effectively illustrated by Lewin and Schein's three-stage approach to changing human behaviour.

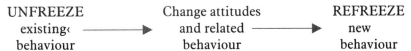

UNFREEZE	Change attitudes	REFREEZE
existing	and related	new
behaviour	behaviour	behaviour

Chapter 14

14   SOCIAL RESPONSIBILITY

Social responsibility is a term which embraces a wide range of definitions and models. It is also a topic which attracts considerable attention from the media and the general public. No organisation would wish to attract the reputation for being commercially irresponsible and many organisations make considerable efforts and investment in order to be seen as being socially responsible.

This essay will examine the range of viewpoints which attempt to define the scope of organisational social responsibility, and consider what this means for practising managers.

There are a number of factors which contribute towards the argument that organisations have an obligation to behave responsibly, and these include:

(a)   The degree of power and influence exercised by organisations at national and international levels

(b)   The ability of large organisations to manipulate markets, eg through limiting availability of a product

(c)   The subsidies that organisations receive from government in the forms of benefits such as transport infrastructure and education for which the organisations do not incur direct charges

(d)   The indirect costs of organisational activity on society as a whole such as the use of natural resources, pollution etc.

Organisations are open systems, which means that an organisation can influence and is influenced by the environment. Within the environment there are a range of groups or stakeholders who are affected by the organisation's behaviour. Examples of these groups and their concerns include:

(a)   *Investors* – who are affected by organisational profitability

(b)   *Consumers* – who expect well priced, well designed and safe products

(c)   *General public* – who will be affected by factors such as pollution resulting from an organisation's activities

(d)   *Employees* – conditions of employment and job security

In practice of course these concerns are not mutually exclusive. If an organisation gains bad publicity for polluting the environment, consumers may boycott its products and the value of shareholders' investments will fall, and redundancies may follow.

There are many different interpretations of the limits of an organisation's social responsibilities. A useful framework for discussing this is provided by Johnson and Scholes who argue that organisations fall into one of three broad categories:

(a)   Firstly, there are those who follow the opinion that 'The only responsibility of business is to increase its profit' – a claim associated with Milton Friedman. This is based on the noting that allowing organisations a free rein in the market place will ultimately result in progress and benefits for society as a whole through a 'trickle down' effect.

(b)   Secondly, there is the group who recognise that the growing social pressure for socially responsible behaviour means that there are real commercial benefits to be derived from investing in and maintaining positive relationships with all stakeholders. Within this model profit remains the ultimate measure of corporate performance.

(c)   Finally, there is a view that organisations should be judged by criteria that go beyond a simple measure of profitability – to some extent at least lower profit levels would be seen as a fair trade-off against activity that promotes the common good.

So the extent to which managers should concern themselves with issues of social responsibility will be dependent on the model that their organisation adopts. Social responsibility is therefore a very real management concern, and as with most business decisions will involve a cost-benefit analysis.

The current trend is for many organisations to fit within the middle category, good examples being Marks and Spencer (with a policy of 'Buy British'), and the Body Shop (recyclable packaging, fair trade schemes, opposition to animal testing). Managers have become increasingly sensitive to the fact that being seen as commercially irresponsible may have significant effects on overall profit levels – in other words the costs associated with behaving responsibly may be nothing to the costs linked to a reputation for irresponsibility. An example of this is the producers of baby milk who have encountered negative publicity for their policies of supplying free initial samples to new mothers in developing countries; this has resulted in negative public feeling towards these organisations from consumers in industrialised countries.

In practice managers should do five things

(a)   Remain sensitive to change in social trends, values and expectations and ensure that organisational policy and behaviour reflects such change; this may prove particularly difficult for managers operating in multi-national organisations where expectations may vary from culture to culture.

(b)   Remain sensitive to the standards set within their given sector.

(c)   Ensure that their organisation's responsible behaviour is visible and acknowledged, avoid situations that will cause bad publicity and carry out effective damage limitation if negative situations do arise.

(d)   Ensure that when strategy is formulated and decisions are made that social responsibility issues are a consideration.

(e)   Consider involvement in projects that are beyond the commercial activities of the organisation but may have a positive impact on overall corporate image, for example charitable giving, education programs.

In conclusion, organisations are not islands. The effects of the decisions and activities within them have a real effect on wider society, and as such each organisation has a huge number of stakeholders. The trend within society is to expect organisations to recognise and accommodate the associated responsibilities, and failure to do so is likely to have serious commercial effects.

INDEX

Business Basics: Accounting

Death rate, 75
Decision support systems, 172
Defenders, 244
Delayered structures, 25
Delayering, 225
Delegation, 225
Deutsch, 278
Development, 55
Development shoot-outs, 295
Dilemma of Apollo, 241
Dionysus, 240
Direct supervision, 107
Disintegration, 318
Distortion, 209
Divisional form, 132
Donald Kirkpatrick, 332
Double loop feedback, 162
Dr Clive Morton, 180
Driving forces, 322
Drs Rosenman and Friedman, 283
Drucker, 16

E J Hay, 91
Edward Thorndike, 192
Elton Mayo, 17
Embourgeoisement, 231
Empowerment, 25, 225
Enabling structures, 306
Entrepreneurial structure, 129
Environmental audit, 42
Environmental scanners, 306
Equilibrium, 322
Ernst & Whinney, 318
Ethics, 353
EU, 69
Executive agencies, 7
Existential culture, 240
Expert power, 259
Experts, 240
Explicit knowledge, 301
External failure costs, 175
External locus of control, 285

F G Bailey, 352
Fayol, 11, 112
Feedback control loop., 162
Financial Times, 87
Finisher, 204
First direct, 68
Flexible manufacturing systems, 89
Folkways, 78
Force field analysis, 321
Formal goals, 53

Formal groups, 198
Forming, 199
Fortune 500, 290
Frank Field, 352
Frederick Herzberg, 219
Frederick W Taylor, 15
Functional authority, 115
Fuzzy problem, 106

Gareth Morgan, 9
Garfield, 299
Geert Hofstede, 246
General Sir Ian Hamilton, 112
Globalisation, 96
Goal articulation, 260
Goals, 40
Goffman, 11
Golden mean, 353
Goldthorpe, 231
Graicunas, 112
Graves, 60
Greater London Council, 331
Greiner, 56
Groupthink, 202
Growth, 55
Guy Kawasaki, 35

Habitat, 262
Halo effect, 192
Hammer, 23
Hammer and Champy, 23
Handy, 158
Harry Braverman, 229
Hawthorne studies, 17
Henri Fayol, 11
Henry Ford, 85
Henry Mintzberg, 9
Herzberg, 17
Hicks, 60
Hidden crisis, 318
Hierarchy of needs, 222
Hitachi, 23
Hofstede, 246
Holmes, 180
Homeostasis, 322
Honda, 85
Hostiles, 286
Human Relations School, 121
Humanistic belief system, 82
Humble, 158
Hygiene factors, 224

BPP
PUBLISHING

BPP
PUBLISHING

450

ORDER FORM

Any books from our Business Basics range can be ordered in one of the following ways:

- Telephone us on **020 8740 2211**
- Send this page to our **Freepost** address
- Fax this page on **020 8740 1184**
- Email us at **publishing@bpp.com**
- Go to our website: **www.bpp.com**

We aim to deliver to all UK addresses inside 5 working days. Orders to all EU addresses should be delivered within 6 working days. All other orders to overseas addresses should be delivered within 8 working days.

BPP Publishing Ltd
Aldine House
Aldine Place
London W12 8AW
Tel: 020 8740 2211
Fax: 020 8740 1184
Email: publishing@bpp.com

Full name: _____

Day-time delivery address: _____

_____

_____ Postcode _____

Day-time telephone (for queries only): _____

Please send me the following quantities of books:

	No. of copies	Price	Total
Accounting		£13.95	
Law		£13.95	
Quantitative Methods		£13.95	
Information Technology		£13.95	
Economics		£13.95	
Marketing		£13.95	
Human Resource Management		£13.95	
Organisational Behaviour		£13.95	

Sub Total	£	

Postage & Packaging

UK : £3.00 for first plus £2.00 for each extra	£
Europe : (inc. ROI) £5.00 for first plus £4.00 for each extra	£
Rest of the world : £20.00 for first plus £10.00 for each extra	£

Grand Total	£

I enclose a cheque for £_____ (cheque to BPP Publishing Ltd) or charge to Access/VISA/Switch

Card number: ⬚⬚⬚⬚⬚⬚⬚⬚⬚⬚⬚⬚⬚⬚⬚⬚⬚⬚⬚⬚

Issues number (Switch only): _____

Start date: _____ Expiry date: _____

Signature _____

REVIEW FORM & FREE PRIZE DRAW

We are constantly reviewing, updating and improving our publications. We would be grateful for any comments or thoughts you have on this book. Cut out and send this page to our Freepost address and you will be automatically entered in a £50 prize draw.

Jed Cope
Business Basics Range Manager
BPP Publishing Ltd, FREEPOST, London W12 8BR

Full name: _____

Address: _____

_____

_____ Postcode _____

Where are you studying?

Where did you find out about BPP books?

Why did you decide to buy this book?

Have you used our texts any other BPP books in your studies?

What thoughts do you have on our:

- Introductory pages

- Topic coverage

- Summary diagrams, icons, chapter roundups and quick quizzes

- Activities, case studies and questions

The other side of this form is left blank for any further comments you wish to make.

Please give any further comments and suggestions (with page number if necessary) below.

FREE PRIZE DRAW RULES

1. Closing date for 31 January 2001 draw is 31 December 2000. Closing date for 31 July 2001 draw is 30 June 2001.

2. Restricted to entries with UK and Eire addresses only. BPP employees, their families and business associates are excluded.

3. No purchase necessary. Entry forms are available upon request from BPP Publishing. No more than one entry per title, per person. Draw restricted to persons aged 16 and over.

4. Winners will be notified by post and receive their cheques not later than 6 weeks after the relevant draw date.

5. The decision of the promoter in all matters is final and binding. No correspondence will be entered into.